A Case for

AMILLENNIALISM

EXPANDED EDITION

A Case for

AMILLENNIALISM

UNDERSTANDING THE END TIMES

KIM RIDDLEBARGER

BakerBooks

a division of Baker Publishing Group
Grand Rapids, Michigan

© 2003, 2013 by Kim Riddlebarger

Published by Baker Books
a division of Baker Publishing Group
P.O. Box 6287, Grand Rapids, MI 49516-6287
www.bakerbooks.com

Printed in the United States of America

Library of Congress Cataloging-in-Publication Data
Riddlebarger, Kim, 1954–
    A case for amillennialism : understanding the end times / Dr. Kim Riddlebarger.—
Expanded Edition.
        pages cm
    Includes bibliographical references and index.
    ISBN 978-0-8010-1550-2 (pbk.)
    1. Millennialism. I. Title.
BT892.R53 2013
236′.9—dc23   2013009356

13   14   15   16   17   18   19   7   6   5   4   3   2   1

In memory of my ancestors who died in Christ:

Christian Riddlespurger	(1715–1790)
John Riddelsperger	(1743–1828)
Jacob Riddlesberger	(1785–1828)
Daniel Riddlesberger	(1814–1878)
David Riddlesbarger	(1838–1909)
Albert Riddlesbarger	(1867–1931)
Glenn Riddlebarger	(1894–1964)
Clayton Riddlebarger	(1918–1969)

They have come to life and are reigning with Christ for a thousand years.

Contents

Acknowledgments

Thanks to the consistory of Christ Reformed Church for the sabbatical leave and support needed to do the research associated with this project. Thanks also to the members of our congregation for all your prayers and support, especially those of you who ask the hard questions during the Wednesday night Bible study. But a special word of appreciation goes to the *White Horse Inn* crew—Michael Horton, Ken Jones, Rod Rosenbladt, and our producer, Shane Rosenthal—for much encouragement and fruitful conversation throughout the years. Thanks also to Dr. Lee Irons and Dr. Brett Provance for your helpful suggestions with the manuscript. And as always, thanks to my wife, Micki, and sons, David and Mark, for being so patient.

Foreword

"Christ has died; Christ is risen; Christ will come again." Part of the communion liturgy from ancient times, this sentence is the gospel *in nuce*. For two millennia, Christians who disagree over a host of other important points have confessed this faith together. They have recognized that, according to Scripture, the promise of Christ's future return is inseparable from his crucifixion and resurrection in the past. So we fix our eyes on Christ, the author and finisher of our faith (Heb. 12:2).

Before taking up areas of controversy, it is important that we recognize that remarkable consensus. As we confess in the Nicene Creed, Christ "will come again, with glory, to judge the living and the dead, whose kingdom will have no end." Therefore, the issues raised in *A Case for Amillennialism* are part of an ongoing conversation—even debate—among Christians who do not question the integrity of each other's profession of faith.

In that case, what's the point? Why invest the time in reading a book like this, when the issues are not life and death and there seem to be so many fine Christians holding significantly different views? Let me offer a few reasons in favor of engaging these issues.

First, all of Scripture is inspired by God and therefore profitable (2 Tim. 3:16). In the Great Commission itself, Jesus commanded his disciples to teach their disciples *everything* he had delivered to them. Kim Riddlebarger and I share a similar church background, where commitment to the dispensational system (premillennial-pretribulational rapture) was expected. In fact, statements of faith often gave more space to this point than to the Trinity or the person and work of Christ. Bible conferences could spark lively debate, sometimes leading to serious dissension, over the identity of the Antichrist or the precise sequence of end-times events. In reaction, many who were raised in a similar background profess agnosticism regarding eschatology, beyond the simple formula, "Christ will come again." These brothers and sisters are correct to see this formula as the primary eschatological affirmation that binds all Christians, but if Scripture reveals more than this, then we are all obligated to learn more than this.

Second, all of Scripture is unified around the person and work of Jesus Christ. There is one unfolding plot from Genesis to Revelation. Although there are distinctive subplots, they too feed ultimately into the drama that begins with the promise of a Satan-crushing Redeemer in Genesis 3:15 and ends with the "Hallelujah Chorus" in the book of Revelation. From an amillennial perspective, dispensationalism tends to undermine this narrative unity that centers on promise and fulfillment in Christ with one plan of redemption for one people of God drawn from every nation. Dispensationalists respond with the charge that amillenarians have a "spiritualizing" way of interpreting Scripture that negates its literal sense. What this means is that our differences are not merely over what we believe Scripture teaches about the end times but how we interpret Scripture from beginning to end. Both sides in the controversy will agree that these differences are no small matter.

Third, although eschatology means "last things," it has enormous bearing on the way we understand the past and the present. We are created as inherently prospective beings, with a goal. That goal to a large extent determines our identity and way of living in the present. Postmillennialism has tended to generate optimistic programs for ushering in the kingdom of God, while premillennialism (especially in its dispensational form) is by comparison more pessimistic. For amillenarians, though, things are not getting better and better or worse and worse. Rather, the whole period between Christ's two advents is marked, paradoxically, by miraculous growth of Christ's kingdom by his Word and Spirit alongside the obdurate opposition of the world to the Messiah and his coheirs. The kingdom is already and not yet: present here and now in the form of weakness yet in the power of Christ's resurrection, to be revealed at Christ's coming as the kingdom of glory. Only then will the kingdoms of this age become the kingdom of our God and of his Christ forever. Obviously, this has tremendous implications for the identity of the church and its mission—as well as its relation to the nations and empires of this age—and the hope for the future that drives us in the present.

For these and many other reasons, the topics covered in this book are of enormous importance for us. And this particular book is exactly what we have needed. While helpful defenses of the amillennial view are available, Kim Riddlebarger's is unique. First, he once held the views he critiques. It is easier to be dismissive or to unintentionally mischaracterize the views of others from afar. However, I've been impressed over the years with how informed and sympathetic Kim is in his engagement with alternative eschatologies. He does not lump postmillennialism with theocratic movements or premillennialism with popular end-times novels. Nor does he overlook the important differences between classic and progressive dispensationalism.

Second, Kim is a model scholar-pastor. He has studied under great biblical scholars as well as historical and systematic theologians at the graduate and postgraduate level. As a pastor, he brings these resources to bear on every sermon and lecture without burying his flock in footnotes. For nearly two decades, he has been the pastor of the same church and has brought God's Word to bear on the daily lives of Christ's people. Both of these key aspects of his calling are evident throughout *A Case for Amillennialism*.

I had the privilege of hearing this material as lectures, then reading it as a book. And now I have the pleasure of commending it in a foreword to a new and updated edition. Whether you are a seasoned scholar or a new Christian, whether you accept all of its arguments or demur, I am confident that you will find this book to be a rich and rewarding banquet on your way to "the city with foundations, whose architect and builder is God" (Heb. 11:10).

Michael Horton

Preface to the Expanded Edition

No one is more surprised than I that *A Case for Amillennialism* (published in 2003) is still in print and now available in an updated edition. I am very grateful for the positive feedback I have received throughout the years. I am also thankful for those who have disagreed with my particular brand of Reformed amillennialism but who have found my efforts worthy of constructive engagement. Iron sharpens iron. I, for one, have found the engagement helpful in many ways.

This edition of *A Case for Amillennialism* includes two new chapters and a foreword from my friend and colleague Dr. Michael Horton. The two new chapters are "The Antichrist" and "Signs of the End." The latter seeks to answer the question, How do we interpret the signs of the end? while the former is a summation of the material in my book *The Man of Sin: Uncovering the Truth about the Antichrist* (Grand Rapids: Baker, 2006). Since it may be said (facetiously) that a sound eschatology must be supported by good eschatology charts, I have also included a series of outstanding charts prepared by Mark Vander Pol. The reader should note that in the two new chapters I utilize the ESV, which was not available when the first edition was published in 2003.

Since Dr. Horton was very instrumental in encouraging me to submit *A Case for Amillennialism* for publication, as well as helping me to get it published, I am thrilled at his willingness to contribute a foreword to this edition. A hearty thanks must also go to the people at Baker who listened to Michael's recommendation and gave my manuscript consideration, and especially to Chad Allen, my editor, who has since advanced through the ranks at Baker and encouraged me to consider preparing this edition.

Since the publication of the first edition of *A Case for Amillennialism*, two important eschatological controversies have arisen that readers may expect me to address in this edition. The first of these controversies is the case of date-setter Harold Camping, whose stubborn unwillingness to grasp the meaning of Matthew 24:36 ("No one knows about that day or hour, not even the angels in heaven, nor the Son, but only the Father") brought repeated embarrassment to himself and his followers. It was Camping's contorted end-times calculations, and his misuse of the biblical signs of the end, that, in part, prompted the inclusion in this volume of a new chapter dealing with the signs of the end and the way in which we should seek to interpret them.

The other controversy that merits discussion is that raised by John MacArthur's lecture "Why Every Self-Respecting Calvinist Is a Premillennialist," given at the Shepherd's Conference at Grace Community Church on March 7, 2007. In his lecture, MacArthur made the startling claim that dispensational premillennialism is the only eschatological position consistent with five-point Calvinism. Such a claim came as a surprise to many, since the framers and the current signatories of the Canons of the Synod of Dort (from which the five points come) are overwhelmingly amillennial. Although I chose not to include my response to MacArthur's lecture in this revised volume, interested readers can find it in its entirety by consulting the notes.[1]

Several matters, however, should be addressed in this preface. Several dispensational writers have seized upon my admission that two leading pre–World War II Reformed theologians (Herman Bavinck and Louis Berkhof) dismissed dispensationalism on a number of grounds, one of which was the dispensational insistence that Israel would become a nation yet again (see chap. 18). That Bavinck and Berkhof got this wrong was all too evident in 1948, when Israel became a nation just as dispensationalists had expected.

This fact is taken by some as evidence of the inability of Reformed amillenarians to properly explain the role of Israel in biblical eschatology. MacArthur takes my admission as an illustration of the need for "those of a Reformed mindset to reconsider their eschatology in light of their commitment to literal hermeneutics and the doctrine of sovereign election."[2] The fact that a number of Reformed theologians do indeed believe there will be a future conversion of Israel (e.g., Beza, Vos, Holwerda, Venema, Horton) is taken by dispensationalists as confirmation of the inconsistency supposedly inherent in amillennialism because of a conflict between a literal interpretation of passages about Israel and the spiritualizing and allegorical hermeneutic that amillennial Christians allegedly utilize elsewhere when interpreting prophecy.

There are several things to say in response to this charge. First, I ask the reader to carefully consider the interpretation of Romans 9–11 set forth in chapter 15 of this volume and then ask whether or not this is a faithful and plausible interpretation of Paul's discussion of Israel's future role in redemptive history. While Reformed Christians disagree about the meaning of "all Israel" (in Rom. 11:26), all Reformed amillenarians do agree that in Romans 9–11—the one passage in which Paul does speak directly to the future of Israel—he fails to mention a single event that dispensationalists claim will come to pass for Israel based on their so-called literal hermeneutic. Paul makes no mention of Israel returning to the land. There is no mention of a rapture of Gentile Christians before the appearance of the Antichrist at the dawn of a seven-year tribulation. There is no mention of an earthly millennial kingdom. You would think that if these things were predicted for Israel throughout the Old Testament, the apostle Paul might think it important to mention them when he addresses Israel's future (vis-à-vis the role of the Gentiles). He does not. While it is important to be willing to reconsider one's viewpoint in light of new evidence to the contrary, I humbly ask that others be willing to do the same.

Second, all Christians interested in eschatology should learn the lesson Bavinck and Berkhof unwittingly teach us. Everyone who writes in the field of Bible prophecy and eschatology needs to ask themselves how someone reading our works a generation or two from now (barring the Lord's return, of course) will react to our conclusions, expectations, and predictions. While the Bible does not err, none of us is infallible, and none of us knows the future. A certain amount of restraint and a willingness to admit error come with the eschatological turf. Even though Bavinck and Berkhof were wrong about Israel, their eschatological opinions have largely withstood the test of time. This assertion is supported by the fact that even their contemporary critics find it noteworthy that they were wrong about Israel, and this comes as a matter of some surprise! Of all the different schools of interpretation associated with Bible prophecy, dispensationalists should be especially careful not to make too much of Bavinck's and Berkhof's comments regarding Israel, given the well-known propensity of many popular dispensationalist writers to make eschatological predictions that do not come to pass.

As for tying the dispensational view of Israel's role in redemptive history to the doctrine of election, it should be made clear that MacArthur distances himself from the way the Reformed tradition has historically framed the doctrine of election when he treats the election of national Israel in isolation from those covenants of works and grace that serve as the means through which God sends Jesus Christ to save his elect. At this point, we see the inseparable connection between Reformed varieties of amillennialism and covenant theology—an important connection for readers of this volume to make.[3]

To summarize briefly, the Reformed doctrine of election holds that God chooses those individuals whom he intends to save based on his own good pleasure and purpose and not because of anything good God foresees in the sinner. In his incarnation, Jesus came to earth to accomplish those things necessary to save those whom God has chosen (to die for their sins and fulfill the righteous requirements of the law). The Holy Spirit calls those whom God has chosen and for whom Jesus has accomplished his redemptive work. Those called by the Spirit through the preaching of the gospel exercise faith in Jesus Christ, are justified, and begin the lifelong process of sanctification. Presumably, MacArthur would agree with all of these points.

God has also chosen the nation of Israel to fulfill specific redemptive purposes—to bring forth the Word of God and the Messiah. But God also deals with his people (including Israel) through a series of covenants.[4] In the covenant of works, God created Adam to be the biological and federal head of the entire human race. The basis for acceptance before God under the terms of this covenant was perfect obedience (in thought, word, and deed) to all the commandments of God. When Adam fell into sin, the entire human race sinned in and with Adam and came under the curse (death). This is why no one can save themselves (because we are dead in sin), and this is why God must graciously choose to save particular individuals—those chosen amount to a multitude that cannot be counted—if any are to be saved.

God has promised to redeem all those whom he has chosen to save through a gracious covenant. Under the terms of the covenant of grace, the covenant mediator (Jesus Christ) will fulfill all the terms of the covenant of works and then impute his own obedience, as well as turn aside the wrath of God from those whom God has chosen but who cannot save themselves because they stand condemned under a covenant of works. This gracious covenant was promised to Adam, was formally ratified with Abraham, and was then renewed with David. According to the prophets (e.g., Jeremiah), this covenant pointed ahead to a new covenant (the final fulfillment of God's gracious promises) fulfilled in Jesus Christ. The new covenant, then, is this same gracious covenant promised to Adam now fulfilled in Jesus Christ.

In the case of Israel, God established his covenant with the nation at Mount Sinai. While this covenant was based on the works principle established under the original covenant of works (blessing promised for perfect obedience and curse threatened for any disobedience), this covenant was administered to Israel as part of the covenant of grace. This can be seen in the fact that God gave to Israel a priesthood, animal sacrifices, and a tabernacle (and then a temple) to relieve their guilt of sin and to instruct them about the coming Messiah and the nature of his saving work. This explains the typology present through the Sinai covenant and its temple, priesthood, etc.

When the nation of Israel comes under God's covenant curses because of their repeated disobedience and lack of repentance, and the nation is first cast from the land during the Babylonian captivity and then again after the events of AD 70, this has no bearing whatsoever on the fact that God has his elect believers among the Israelites (and who are, under the terms of the covenant of grace, saved by grace through faith in the promised Messiah), even though the nation of which they were citizens (Israel) came under God's covenant curse threatened in the covenant sanctions established at Sinai. Israel's possession of the land of promise, therefore, was part of a national covenant and was conditioned upon national obedience. The New Testament writers are clear (much to the dispensationalist's dismay) that the everlasting land promise God made to Abraham is now fulfilled in Jesus Christ, who is the true Israel. This becomes clear when Paul universalizes the Abrahamic promise of a land in Palestine now extending to the ends of the earth (Rom. 4:13). Abraham is now depicted as heir of the world.

Therefore, to tie God's choice of Israel to serve a critical role in redemptive history (as recipients of the Sinai covenant) to God's choice of those particular individuals whom he chooses to save ("sovereign election," to use MacArthur's phrase) is to overlook a very important distinction made throughout the whole of the Bible. One might be part of the visible people of God yet not be a true believer, nor numbered among God's elect. This is the classical distinction between the visible and the invisible church. To paraphrase Paul in Romans 9:6, "Not all Israel is Israel." Yet, says Paul, within national Israel (which receives and possesses the land based on obedience—Josh. 21:43), there is an elect remnant according to grace (Rom. 11:5–6) whom God will indeed save through the merits of Jesus Christ received through faith alone.

So to argue as MacArthur and other dispensationalists do—that the Reformed view of the election of Israel to be God's covenant nation is directly tied to God's decree of those particular individuals whom he will save through faith in Jesus—does not reflect the historic Reformed position. The basis for MacArthur's claim is the unfortunate conflation of Israel's divinely ordained role in redemptive history with God's sovereign choice of those individuals whom he intends to save. This reflects the dispensationalist's rejection of covenant theology as expressed throughout the Reformed tradition and confessions and illustrates an unfortunate willingness to discuss sovereign election in the abstract—apart from the biblical means and redemptive-historical context in which God saves his elect sinners (i.e., the covenants of works and grace) as these covenants unfold in biblical history.

Unless and until these hermeneutical differences between covenant theologians and dispensationalists are resolved, Reformed amillenarians and dispensationalists are not going to agree about Israel's role in redemptive history, nor will we agree about the way in which the New Testament reinterprets the Old in the light of the coming of Jesus Christ and the dawn of the messianic age.

This is why I hope the debate will continue and why I ask you, the reader, to weigh these matters with both an open mind and a well-worn Bible. It is my prayer that this expanded edition of *A Case for Amillennialism* will help you do exactly that.

Introduction

From my earliest youth, I was taught that a secret rapture of Christian believers was a cardinal doctrine of the Christian faith. I recall our family gathering in front of the television to watch Howard C. Estep of the World Prophetic Ministry explain how the Arab-Israeli conflict was setting the stage for the coming of the Antichrist. This man, Estep told us, would dazzle the world with his solution to the problems of the Middle East, guaranteeing peace for Israel. In the panic caused by the sudden removal of Christians from the earth after the rapture, the entire world would embrace this demonic leader, who would preside over a ten-nation confederacy and a revived Roman Empire of sorts. Shortly thereafter, Israel would be betrayed, and seven years of horrible tribulation would pass before Jesus Christ would return to earth to put an end to the Antichrist and the devil, who empowered him. The subject of Bible prophecy has interested me ever since.

As a teenager, I read with utter fascination Hal Lindsey's *The Late Great Planet Earth*. Lindsey gave biblical answers to the tumult and uncertainty that characterized the sixties. I wasn't the only one fascinated by Lindsey's book. *The Late Great Planet Earth* became the bestselling book of the 1970s, ensuring that dispensational premillennialism—a term for his book's view of the end times—would remain a major influence on American evangelicalism for a generation to come.

Many of us thought that the coming and going of Y2K and the beginning of a new millennium would cause people to question dispensational assumptions and preoccupation with signs of the end. However, the success of the Left Behind series of end-times novels, authored by Tim LaHaye and Jerry B. Jenkins, proves the influence and staying power of dispensational teaching. LaHaye and Jenkins have equaled if not surpassed Lindsey's amazing publishing success.

Because dispensationalism is so popular, the question is rarely asked, Do these books and the dispensational theology they represent reflect what the Scriptures actually teach about the return of Christ and the millennial age? As one born and bred a dispensationalist, I know these authors and the people who read their books to be sincere and committed Christians. But after a difficult journey from dispensationalism to the theology of the Protestant Reformation, I have come to believe that these books and the particular interpretation of biblical prophecy they present seriously default at many points. My goal in writing this book is to humbly attempt to point out these errors and provide what I think is a more biblical way to understand the Bible's teaching on the coming of the Lord and the millennial age.

It is difficult to write a readable book on a complicated subject. Eschatology—the study of future things—is by all accounts a complicated subject. Christians are deeply divided about these matters, and discussions of future events naturally tend toward sensationalism and undue speculation. Sadly, this is what we have seen in many recent books about this subject. Therefore, a brief word of explanation about the nature and scope of this book is in order.

My purpose is to set forth the historic Protestant understanding of the millennial age. This position is commonly known as *amillennialism* and is centered in the present reign of Jesus Christ. Amillennialism is grounded in *redemptive history*, the historical acts of God as they unfold in the Bible to provide for the salvation of his people.

Although it is commonly argued that amillenarians do not believe in any millennial age (the term itself, *a*millennial, could imply as much), this is not the case. Amillenarians believe that the millennium is a present reality (Christ's heavenly reign), not a future hope (Christ's rule on earth after his return).

Although amillennialism has fallen into disfavor among prophecy devotees, I believe this position makes the best sense of the biblical passages that address the subject. So I write from a Reformed perspective and make no pretense of being neutral on the millennial question. However, *A Case for Amillennialism* is not intended to be a comprehensive treatment of eschatology. That has already been done.[1] The scope of this effort is limited to an evaluation of the three prominent millennial views held by Christians: amillennialism, postmillennialism, and premillennialism.

Because this is a controversial subject, a number of biblical, theological, and historical matters are developed in some detail. Recent discussions of this subject, while interesting and informative, have suffered due to space limitations and editorial constraints.[2] To make my case for amillennialism in an effective manner, I have divided the discussion into four parts, each of which treats one particular aspect of this topic.

Part 1 includes definitions of key theological terms associated with the millennial question, including an overview of millennial viewpoints. This is followed by a discussion of hermeneutics—the science of biblical interpretation—which grapples with the question, How do our theological presuppositions affect our understanding of the millennial age?

Part 2 develops a number of biblical and theological matters, which will enable us to correctly understand the biblical data regarding the millennium. This section also discusses the Old Testament expectation of the last days and the development of this theme throughout the New.

I will offer a survey of the New Testament writers' use of the terms *this age* and *the age to come* as well as the related terms *already* and *not yet*. This so-called two-age model serves as the interpretive grid through which amillenarians should understand the biblical concept of future history. Such a model enables us to make sense of eschatological language in the New Testament, specifically as it relates to the future and the millennial age. I will also discuss the kingdom of God, Christ's resurrection, the new creation, the New Testament's identification of the church as the Israel of God, and the biblical teaching regarding the Antichrist. Part 2 concludes with a discussion of the heart of New Testament eschatology: our Lord's second advent.

Part 3 discusses key biblical passages that have bearing on the millennial age. The exposition of Daniel 9:24–27 calls attention to the context of messianic prophecy and answers the specific question, Does Daniel teach a future seven-year tribulation period? The exposition of the Olivet Discourse (Matt. 24; Mark 13) discusses Jesus's teaching about the signs of the end and the future course of redemptive history. The exposition of Romans 11 wrestles with the question, Is there a distinct future for ethnic Israel in God's redemptive purposes? Concluding part 3 is an exposition of the critical millennial text, Revelation 20:1–10, and such matters as John's use of symbolism, the binding of Satan, the first resurrection, the revolt of the nations, and the second coming of Jesus Christ.

Part 4 evaluates the signs of the end and how to interpret them before concluding with a discussion of the main problems associated with each of the millennial positions. What are the biblical and theological questions facing pre-, post-, and amillenarians? What about the presence of evil during the millennial age? Does the Bible teach that a golden age lies ahead for the church? Does the Bible teach that the millennium is characterized by a return to Old Testament "types and shadows" as claimed by dispensationalists? Does the Bible teach that Christ's coming occurred in AD 70 when God's judgment fell upon Israel, Jerusalem, and its temple as claimed by preterists? What about the charge that amillenarians do not interpret the Bible literally? What about the future of the nation of Israel? There are consequences for our millennial views, and we need to be aware of them.

One final note is in order. Sadly, when it comes to eschatology, a great deal of ad hominem argumentation goes on. For example, dispensationalists accuse amillenarians of being anti-Semitic, liberal, or of spiritualizing the Bible by not taking the Bible literally. Amillenarians accuse dispensationalists of being literalists who are prone to sensationalism. While we may have to agree to disagree, we should always strive to conduct this debate with charity and respect.

FIRST
THINGS
FIRST

1

Defining Our Terms

Whenever discussing theological topics about which so many Christians disagree, it is helpful to define important terms that will be used throughout the discussion. Theologians have developed an extensive vocabulary regarding this subject, and rather than avoiding the use of technical terms, I think it better to use them and thereby gain clarity from the precision of language. What follows is a discussion of the primary theological terms associated with this area of study.

Eschatology

Eschatology is a combination of two Greek words, *eschatos*, "last," and *logos*, "the word," meaning "the doctrine of last things." Most often eschatology is understood as referring to events that are still future, in relation to both the individual Christian and the course of world history. With regard to the individual, eschatology is concerned with physical death, immortality, and the intermediate state—the state of a person between death and when all people will be resurrected at the end of the age. In terms of world history, eschatology deals with the return of Christ, the bodily resurrection at the end of the age, the final judgment, and the eternal state.[1]

In much of contemporary evangelicalism, the study of eschatology is often devoted to the timing of the rapture, the role that Israel plays in Bible prophecy, and the period of time popularly known as the tribulation. Many Christians understand the tribulation to be a future seven-year period of unsurpassed political and spiritual turmoil in which those who remain on earth suffer at the hands of the Antichrist. Those left behind also endure the frightening images of God's judgment that appear throughout the book of Revelation (e.g., the seal, trumpet, and bowl judgments).

In much of popular literature about Bible prophecy, eschatological matters are read through the lens of current events, with Bible-prophecy experts correlating biblical texts to current geopolitical crises. This not only gives the Bible great relevance, we are told, but also ensures a never-ending stream of prophecy books designed to show how the Bible explains that a particular current event was foretold by the Hebrew prophets.

Historically, however, Christian theologians wrestled with the biblical text by itself, doing the more challenging but less sensational work of comparing Scripture with Scripture. The historic Protestant understanding of eschatology has a number of emphases that are different from what many evangelicals are accustomed to discussing under the heading of Bible prophecy. This study will not attempt to find biblical texts that explain current events in the Middle East. I will not evaluate potential Antichrist candidates. Nor will I discuss how rapidly developing technology is preparing the way for a totalitarian world government. Rather, this book's focus will be on biblical teaching about things future, and it will explore different biblical themes to develop a full understanding of the millennial age as taught by biblical writers.

With this in mind, we consider the following reminder that a study of eschatology concerns not only the future but also the present:

> We must insist that the message of biblical eschatology will be seriously impoverished if we do not include in it the present state of the believer and the present phase of the kingdom of God. In other words, full-orbed biblical eschatology must include both what we might call "inaugurated" [present or realized] and "future" eschatology.[2]

This is why theologians often remind us that God's revelation of himself in the Scriptures and his mighty acts in redemptive history are necessarily connected. There is no proper way to discuss what God will do in the future unless we have our feet firmly planted in biblical teaching about what God has done in the past. Looking back at the history of redemption, we see what God has done for his people to rescue them from the guilt and power of sin. This in turn helps us to understand how God's promises regarding the future will come to fruition.

It will become clear that a truly biblical expectation for the future is centered in the Christian hope of Christ's second coming. This means the Christian faith is thoroughly eschatological, and the subject of a millennial age must be considered from the perspective of the past, present, and future.[3] Until Jesus Christ returns to raise the dead, judge the world, and make all things new, Christians will always be concerned with the future and the unfolding course of history. Our redemption draws near as the days tick away before our crucified, risen, and ascended Savior returns. But the second coming makes sense only in light of what God has already done on Calvary and in the garden tomb. Therefore, developing these biblical and theological themes is critical to evaluating millennial views.

The Millennium

Another key term used throughout this study is *millennium*, which is derived from the Latin words *mille*, meaning "thousand," and *annus*, meaning "year." The term refers to a thousand-year period.[4]

Revelation 20:1–10 discusses this period of time, and it is characterized by the following: (1) it includes the binding of Satan (vv. 1–3) and (2) the testimony of the witnesses, the beheaded souls who have not worshiped the beast (vv. 4–5); (3) those who participate in the first resurrection reign with Christ because the second death has no power over them (vv. 4–6); (4) those who do not participate in the first resurrection do not live until after the millennium (v. 5); (5) Satan will be loosed for a brief period at the end of the millennium only to be thrown into the lake of fire (vv. 7–10); and (6) the thousand years ends with a great apostasy and the rebellion of nations led by Gog and Magog (v. 7).

The three major viewpoints regarding the millennium are *premillennialism*, which claims that the return of Christ precedes the millennium; *postmillennialism*, which holds that Christ returns after the millennium; and *amillennialism*, which holds that the millennium is not limited to a thousand years but includes the entire period of time between the first and second coming of Christ.

A related term is *chiliasm*, which comes from the Greek term *chilia*, literally meaning "thousand years." Historically, Protestants used this term to deride those who believed in a literal earthly millennium. As Richard Muller has pointed out:

> The Protestant orthodox, both Lutheran and Reformed, denied the notion of an earthly millennium to dawn in the future and viewed the text [Rev. 20] as a reference to the reign of grace between the first and second coming of Christ, the age of *ecclesia militans* [church militant]. The orthodox did distinguish

between the *chiliasmus crassus* [gross millennialism], as taught by the fanatics, and *chiliasmus subtilis* [subtle millennialism], as found among the pietists.[5]

The Protestant orthodox also used the more polemical term *chiliasmus crassissimus*, "the grossest millennialism," regarding those who stressed the earthly and Jewish elements of the millennial age, much like contemporary dispensationalists.[6] Most Protestants regard chiliasm as incompatible with Reformation orthodoxy. This may come as a surprise to many American evangelicals who assume that Bible-believing Christians throughout the centuries have held to premillennialism.

The Rapture

Another important term is *rapture*. "Though the word 'rapture' does not occur in our English translations of the Bible, it is derived from the [Latin] Vulgate rendering of the verb 'caught up' (*harpagesometha*) in 1 Thessalonians 4:17, *rapiemur*."[7] The rapture conveys the idea of the transporting of believers from earth to heaven at Christ's second coming. When used by dispensational writers, the term refers to Christ's secret coming when all believers are suddenly removed from the earth before the great tribulation.

Those who believe this sudden, secret event takes place seven years before Christ's bodily return to earth hold to a *premillennial, pretribulational* view of the rapture. This is the position taken by dispensationalists.

Many Protestants have historically seen this event as one aspect of the general resurrection at the end of the age (1 Cor. 15:50–55; 1 Thess. 4:13–5:11). The rapture, therefore, refers to the catching away of believers who are living at the time of Christ's bodily return to earth. When they are caught away in the resurrection, they join those who have died in Christ. While these two resurrection passages are often used by dispensationalists as biblical proof texts for a sudden and secret rapture, historically, Protestants have believed that both texts speak instead of the resurrection of believers from the state of life or death to glorification at the return of our Lord.

Those who place this event at the visible return of Christ to the earth hold to a *postribulational* view of the rapture. Historic premillennialism, amillennialism, and postmillennialism are all committed to this view. Christ returns at the end of the tribulation period, which is understood to be the entire church age (amillennialism) or the time of great apostasy that occurs immediately before the return of Christ, marking the end of the millennial age on the earth (postmillennialism).

Preterism and Futurism

In addition to the pre-, post-, and amillennial terminology, several other important terms relate to how one interprets the book of Revelation. Though these terms most often refer to events in the first century or future events, they have a much broader application as well.

The *preterist* understanding of biblical prophecy sees Christ's predictions in the Olivet Discourse (Matt. 24; Mark 13) as referring to the Roman army's destruction of Jerusalem and the temple in AD 70. Preterists also argue that the apostle John wrote the book of Revelation before AD 70 and that it describes Nero Caesar's persecution of the church.[8] The references to judgment on Babylon refer to Israel, not Rome. This means that virtually all the Bible's teaching about future things was fulfilled within the lifetimes of Christ's disciples. "Full" preterists contend that Christ's parousia (the second coming) occurred in AD 70, along with the resurrection and final judgment.[9] Moderate or partial preterists argue that the events of AD 70 fulfill the prophecies of the Olivet Discourse and the book of Revelation, but the general resurrection and the final judgment have not yet occurred.[10]

The opposite of preterism is *futurism*. A futurist is "one who centers his theological beliefs around national Israel, and believes that most prophecies concerning Israel are to have a literal fulfillment *in the future*, after the Christian church has been taken out of the world."[11] As with preterism, there are two types of futurism, a moderate approach and a more radical one. According to George Ladd:

> The futurist view has taken two forms which we may call the moderate and the extreme futurist views. The latter is also known as Dispensationalism. . . . A moderate futurist view differs from the extreme futurist view at several points. It finds no reason, as does the latter, to distinguish sharply between Israel and the church.[12]

According to this definition, dispensationalists are thoroughgoing futurists, while historic premillennialists and progressive dispensationalists tend to be moderate futurists. The next chapter discusses these views in more detail.

There are approaches to the book of Revelation other than preterism or futurism, however. One approach is the so-called *historicist* school, the traditional Protestant interpretation that stresses the identification of Babylon the Great with the city of Rome.

> This perspective views Revelation as a symbolic prophecy of the entire history of the church down to the return of Christ and the end of the age. The numerous

symbols of the book designate various historical movements and events in the western world and the Christian church. . . . One of the prevailing features of this interpretation has been the view that the beast is the Roman papacy and the false prophet the Roman Church. This view was so widely held that for a long time it was called the Protestant view.[13]

Few contemporary commentators hold this position, since, if true, it would mean that the apostle John was not speaking to his first-century audience but to Christians living centuries later.

A number of amillennial interpreters of Revelation (e.g., William Hendriksen) are idealists, contending that the book of Revelation is structured along the lines of *progressive parallelism*. Recently, however, amillennial interpreters such as G. K. Beale and Dennis Johnson have set forth highly refined and improved versions of the approach taken by Hendriksen. Progressive parallelism is the idea that the series of visions in Revelation describe the course of history between the first and second coming of Christ, each from a different prophetic perspective, although these visions intensify before the time of the end. As such, Revelation contains both prophetic and apocalyptic material. John's visions are revealed against the backdrop of Roman persecution of the church, and the image of the satanic beast clearly draws upon the historical image of Nero Caesar as a reference to a series of anti-Christian empires and their leaders throughout the age.

According to this view, Revelation is more likely to have been written after AD 70. John does not intend for his reader to see Babylon as referring to apostate Israel but to an evil secular empire that persecutes God's people. Given the nature of apocalyptic literature, those holding this view contend that Revelation cannot be reduced to strict preterist or futurist interpretations. According to the idealist interpretation, the Roman Empire may be a figure of continual persecution of God's people throughout the church period. This means that Revelation is a combination of historicist, preterist, and futurist elements. To insist that the book be read through one particular lens to the exclusion of the others, says this view, is to miss an important aspect of the genre of apocalyptic literature, namely, its complexity.[14]

2

A Survey of Eschatological Views

Keeping the definitions of the previous chapter in mind, we are now ready to look at the various eschatological positions.

Dispensationalism

Dispensationalism is a system of biblical interpretation that distinguishes among seven distinct periods or "dispensations" in biblical history: (1) innocence (before the fall); (2) conscience (from the fall to Noah); (3) human government (from Noah to Abraham); (4) promise (from Abraham to Moses); (5) law (from Moses to Christ); (6) grace (the church age); and (7) the kingdom (the millennium). Dispensationalism is much more than one view regarding the end times and the rapture, though it does encompass such under the heading *dispensational premillennialism*. Rather, dispensationalism is a comprehensive theological system with a distinct hermeneutic that colors how one reads any biblical text.[1]

Dispensationalists argue for literal interpretation of all prophetic portions of Scripture.[2] This means that all of the covenantal promises made to David and Abraham in the Old Testament are to be fulfilled literally in a future millennial age. Israel will regain the land promised by God, a prophecy that dispensationalists believe was fulfilled when the modern nation of Israel was born in 1948. The literal fulfillment of these two covenants (the Abrahamic and the Davidic) figures prominently in the dispensational system.

Dispensationalists insist that God's redemptive plan focuses on national Israel, with provision made for Gentiles during the church age (see chart on page 42). The church age is the period of time between Jesus's offer of a messianic kingdom to Israel and the beginning of the great tribulation, which commences with the rapture, when the Gentile church is removed from the earth. This distinction between God's purposes for Israel and his purposes for the church is another important feature of the dispensational framework. According to former Dallas Theological Seminary president John Walvoord, "Pretribulationism distinguishes clearly between Israel and the church and their respective programs."[3] This distinction characterizes dispensationalism with its pretribulation view of the rapture.

Since Israel has become a nation, in fulfillment of God's promise to the descendants of Abraham, the next event to occur on the prophetic time line, according to dispensationalists, is the rapture of Christian believers. This occurs when Jesus Christ secretly returns to earth at the beginning of the seven-year tribulation period, the so-called seventieth week of Daniel, which dispensationalists do not see as a fulfilled messianic prophecy but as a future event (cf. Dan. 9:24–27). According to dispensationalists, this period of tribulation refers to unbelieving Israel, not the church, which will have already been raptured from the earth. Therefore, the sixth dispensation, the so-called church age or age of grace, is that period of time when God is dealing with Gentiles prior to refocusing his redemptive plan on national Israel during the millennial age, which commences with Christ's second coming. Though the tribulation period commences with the secret rapture, the bodily return of Christ occurs after the great tribulation. This means that those who are converted to Christ during the tribulation, including Jews (the 144,000), go on into the millennium to repopulate the earth. During the millennium, the kingdom of God is fully manifested on earth. Glorified believers will rule with Christ during his reign over all the nations.

The dispensationalist hermeneutic colors how dispensationalists understand the Gospels as well. This is especially true of the parables of the kingdom found in Matthew 13.[4] According to dispensationalists, Jesus came to earth, bringing an offer of God's long-anticipated theocratic kingdom to the Jews, who tragically rejected their own Messiah. God then turned to dealing with the Gentiles, making the church age a parenthesis of sorts. Signs of the end of the age include the birth of the nation of Israel, the revival of the Roman Empire predicted in Daniel as seen in the emergence of the European economic community, and the impending Russian-Arab invasion of Israel. All of these point to the immediacy of the secret return of Christ for his church. The Antichrist is presently awaiting the removal of the church so he can be revealed and begin his reign of terror on Israel and those who accept Christ during the tribulation period.

According to dispensationalists, the millennium is marked by a return to Old Testament temple worship and animal sacrifices to commemorate the redemptive work of Christ.[5] At the end of the millennium, the nations revolt against Christ, resulting in the great white throne judgment, after which Satan and all unbelievers are cast into the lake of fire. At this point, the eternal state begins, when the promises God made to his people are at long last realized in the creation of a new heaven and earth.[6]

Dispensationalism is associated with J. N. Darby (1800–1882) and his followers. It was largely popularized through the notes of the *Scofield Reference Bible*, but a more current form of dispensationalism is represented in the notes of the *Ryrie Study Bible*. Hal Lindsey's hugely successful book, *The Late Great Planet Earth*, served to keep the movement in the mainstream of evangelicalism in the late 1960s and early 1970s.[7] The movement experienced a revival through the immensely successful Left Behind series of novels written by Tim LaHaye and Jerry B. Jenkins, which sold over sixty-five million product units (books, videos, comics, etc.).[8] Leading dispensational theologians include John Walvoord, Charles Ryrie, J. Dwight Pentecost, Norman Geisler, and Charles Feinberg. In addition to LaHaye and Jenkins, popular dispensational pastors and writers include Dave Hunt, Jack Van Impe, and John Hagee.

Several important social and cultural factors made dispensationalism popular among American evangelicals, who had been overwhelmingly postmillennial just a generation earlier. The horrors of World War I, the Great Depression, World War II, the Cold War, and the tense Middle East situation can all be explained by the dispensational system.[9] When people are uncertain about the future and afraid of what might come to pass, dispensationalists assure them that when things go from bad to worse, the church will be raptured from the earth and Christians will not be around to experience the great tribulation or the wrath of the Antichrist. In this way, dispensationalists offer comforting answers to painful questions.

The majority of those involved in the early charismatic movement were dispensational in their views on Bible prophecy, even though most dispensationalists emphasized that the *charismata* ceased with the completion of the New Testament. As the charismatic movement has matured and become more consistent in its own theology, it has jettisoned dispensationalism for the most part. Dispensationalism is clearly on the wane in academic circles.

Progressive Dispensationalism

Beginning in the late 1980s, a reforming movement known as *progressive dispensationalism* arose within traditional dispensational circles.[10] Progressive

dispensationalists are concerned about the distinction their traditional counter-
parts make between earthly theocratic promises made to national Israel fulfilled
in the millennial age and spiritual promises made to Christians ultimately
realized in heaven. Progressive dispensationalists seek to resolve this tension by
developing God's redemptive program to avoid an earthly-heavenly dualism.[11]

Progressive dispensationalism understands the distinction between national
Israel and the church "not as different arrangements between God and the
human race, as traditional dispensationalism does, but as successive arrangements in the progressive revelation and accomplishment of redemption."[12]

Progressive dispensationalists, therefore, see God's covenant promises to
Abraham fulfilled in the church and the Davidic covenant fulfilled in Christ,
not in a future millennial Davidic kingship. They make no artificial distinction
between the kingdom of God and the kingdom of heaven but move closer to
traditional forms of covenant theology and historic premillennialism.

Mediating between classical dispensationalism and covenant theology,
progressive dispensationalism will probably not satisfy traditional dispensationalists, who regard the system as a betrayal of the sine qua non of classical
dispensationalism.[13] Nor will it fully satisfy advocates of traditional covenant
theology, even though they regard progressive dispensationalism as a step in
the right direction. In their minds, it does not go far enough toward a fully
developed covenant theology typical of Reformed orthodoxy.[14] The success
of progressive dispensationalism remains an open question.

Historic Premillennialism

Historic premillennialism is often thought to be identical to dispensational
premillennialism but with a different timing of the rapture. In fact, historic
premillennialism is a completely different eschatological system that rejects
the dispensational understanding of redemptive history.[15]

The basic features of historic premillennialism are as follows (see chart on
page 43). The coming of Jesus Christ marks the beginning of a new age and
is the fulfillment of Old Testament prophetic expectations. When Jesus begins
his public ministry, the kingdom of God is manifest through his preaching,
teaching, and miracles, though that kingdom is not yet consummated. Upon
Jesus's ascension into heaven and the outpouring of the Spirit at Pentecost, the
kingdom remains present through the Spirit and advances until the end of the
age, which is marked by the return of Christ to the earth in judgment. Great
apostasy and tribulation occur immediately preceding the return of Christ.
After his return, a period of a thousand years (the millennium) separates the

first resurrection from the second resurrection. Satan is bound, and the kingdom is consummated. At the end of the millennial period, Satan is loosed, and a massive rebellion led by the mysterious Gog and Magog immediately precedes the second resurrection or final judgment. After this one-thousand-year earthly millennium, God creates a new heaven and earth.[16]

Historic premillennialism draws its name from the fact that many of the early church fathers (e.g., Irenaeus [140–203], who was a disciple of Polycarp, who in turn was a disciple of the apostle John; Justin Martyr [100–165]; and Papias [80–155]) believed and taught that there would be a visible kingdom of God on earth after the return of Christ.[17]

The most articulate and influential historic premillennialist on the American scene during the twentieth century was George Eldon Ladd of Fuller Theological Seminary. Through the work of Ladd, historic premillennialism gained scholarly respect and popularity among evangelical and Reformed theologians. Other historic premillenarians include John W. Montgomery,[18] J. Barton Payne, and R. Laird Harris of Covenant Theological Seminary, as well as Henry Alford (a noted Greek scholar), Theodore Zahn (a German New Testament specialist), and James Boice of the Alliance of Confessing Evangelicals and longtime pastor of Tenth Presbyterian Church in Philadelphia.

Postmillennialism

Although there are different varieties of postmillennialism—the classical/Puritan variety and the more recent "theonomic" position—postmillenarians affirm that the millennium is a period of universal peace and righteousness yet to come. This glorious age, foretold by Old Testament prophets, has five essential characteristics: (1) through the preaching of the gospel and the outpouring of the Holy Spirit, Christianity will experience a tremendous expansion not only in terms of numerical growth and missionary success but also in terms of spiritual vitality; (2) during this lengthy period of time known as the millennium, Christian influences will spawn increasing peace and economic well-being; (3) large numbers of ethnic Jews will come to faith in Jesus Christ; (4) at the end of this millennial age, a short period of apostasy will occur; (5) then Christ will return, an event followed by the resurrection and the final judgment.[19] According to J. Marcellus Kik, the postmillenarian "looks for a fulfillment of the Old Testament prophecies of a glorious age of the church upon the earth through the preaching of the gospel under the power of the Holy Spirit. He looks forward to all nations becoming Christian and living in peace with one another."[20]

The term *postmillennialism* is derived from the belief that Jesus Christ returns to earth *after* the millennium to judge the world, raise the dead, and make all things new. Postmillennialists are divided as to whether the period of time is a literal one thousand years and whether the millennial age begins abruptly or gradually.[21] Some understand the millennial age to be entirely future, while most argue that it will begin sometime during this present age. Postmillennialists also disagree as to the events that mark the beginning of the millennial age, such as the conversion of Israel (Rom. 9–11), the binding of Satan (Rev. 20), and the defeat of the Antichrist.[22]

Some argue that postmillennialism was the historic position of the church from the days of St. Augustine.[23] Since amillennial Christians are also technically postmillennial in their understanding of the millennium, theologians have often contrasted pre- and postmillennialism without distinguishing between a- and postmillennialism.[24] The difference of opinion between amillennial and postmillennial Christians centers on the starting point, character, and length of the millennial age.

Most contemporary postmillennialists see the millennial age beginning at some point during the present age (see chart on page 44). The kingdom of God triumphs over the kingdoms of this world, resulting in great economic, political, and cultural prosperity. Amillennial Christians, on the other hand, see the millennial age as occupying the entire period of time between the first and second coming of Christ. This period is one of both the triumph of the spiritual kingdom of God and the corresponding rise of evil in opposition to Christ and his kingdom.

The majority of Reformed Christians are amillennial, though there has always been a significant postmillennial minority. In Reformed circles, eschatological debate has centered around a different set of issues than one commonly finds in evangelicalism. The first has to do with the nature of the millennial age. Some postmillennial writers describe this matter as a debate between optimistic postmillenarians and pessimistic amillenarians,[25] while most amillennial writers locate the difference of opinion in the postmillenarian's confusion about the *already*—the present blessings of the kingdom of God—and the *not yet*—the eternal blessings of the consummation.[26]

A second point of contention among postmillennialists has to do with preterism. Most preterists are postmillennial, though not all postmillenarians are preterists. Preterists believe the Olivet Discourse and the book of Revelation describe the fall of Jerusalem in AD 70, while some postmillenarians think certain aspects of these prophecies may be yet future.[27]

Postmillennialism was a widely accepted eschatological position among American evangelicals in the period of unprecedented technological growth between 1870 and 1915.[28] But with the coming of the "war to end all wars"

(World War I), the Great Depression, and the horrors of Auschwitz and Hiroshima, optimism gave way to pessimism. Dispensationalism largely supplanted postmillennialism as an eschatological option for evangelicals.

It is also important to note that American postmillennialism took two distinct forms. One form—the subject of this study—is thoroughly supernatural. Future eschatological victory comes solely because of the power of the gospel to bring men and women to faith in Christ. Many Reformed theologians of the prewar period belong to this camp, including the "Old Princetonians": Charles Hodge, A. A. Hodge, and B. B. Warfield.[29] A second form of postmillennialism, a secularized version, dominated those circles influenced by rationalism in which antisupernatural, higher-critical scholarship eroded confidence in the supernatural elements of Christianity.

Both classical/Puritan and theonomic forms of postmillennialism have seen a resurgence, due in part to the rise of Christian reconstructionism (a philosophy aimed at bringing all institutions under subjection to God). In the theonomic version of postmillennialism, the millennial vision focuses on those things traditional postmillenarians hold dear, but, in addition, theonomic postmillenarians look for a Christian theocracy to be restored on earth. They emphasize the continuity of the civil law as applied to Israel under the old covenant and to all nations under the new covenant. Once established, this victorious kingdom will bind Satan, Christianize the nations, and largely subdue evil throughout the world. God exercises dominion through his church and establishes his law as the law of the land. Both individual Christians and civil magistrates are bound to this moral law. Noted theologians in the postmillennial theonomic movement are R. J. Rushdoony, Greg Bahnsen, and Gary North.[30] Popular writers include Gary DeMarr and Kenneth Gentry.

On the other hand, classical/Puritan postmillennialism is ably set forth in John Jefferson Davis's book *The Victory of Christ's Kingdom*.[31] This version of postmillennialism as taught by Reformed theologians such as the Hodges and Warfield differs markedly from the more recent theonomic variety of postmillennialism. While theonomic postmillennialism emphasizes the rise of a theocracy, classical postmillennialism emphasizes an optimistic view of the future of redemptive history, when people will convert to Christianity and society at large will prosper.

Amillennialism

Amillennialism was not recognized as a distinct position until around the turn of the twentieth century. Until then, amillenarians called themselves postmillennial because they believed Christ would come back after the millennial age, but they were different from traditional postmillenarians in that they did not believe in an earthly millennial age yet to dawn. Dutch statesman and theologian Abraham Kuyper (1837–1920) may have been the first to use the term *amillennial.*

In point of fact, it is the *amillennial* position that has been the predominant eschatological view of Christianity since the days of St. Augustine. It is the position held by the vast majority of Reformed and Lutheran theologians and set forth in all the Reformed and Lutheran confessions.

My own position is Reformed amillennialism, which can also be called "present" or "realized" millennialism. Reformed eschatology argues for a present millennial age manifest in the present reign of Jesus Christ in heaven.[32] I stand in the Dutch Reformed school and redemptive-historical trajectory of Geerhardus Vos, Herman Ridderbos, Anthony Hoekema, Cornelis Venema, and Meredith Kline.

Amillenarians hold that the promises made to Israel, David, and Abraham in the Old Testament are fulfilled by Jesus Christ and his church during this present age (see chart on page 45). The millennium is the period of time between the two advents of our Lord, with the thousand years of Revelation 20 being symbolic of the entire interadvental age. At the first advent of Jesus Christ, Satan was bound by Christ's victory over him at Calvary and the empty tomb. The effects of this victory continued because of the presence of the kingdom of God via the preaching of the gospel and were evidenced by Jesus's miracles. Because of the spread of the gospel, Satan is no longer free to deceive the nations. Christ is presently reigning in heaven and will reign during the entire period between his first and second coming. At the end of the millennial age, Satan is released, a great apostasy breaks out, the general resurrection occurs, Jesus Christ returns in final judgment for all people, and he establishes a new heaven and earth.

Even its critics have acknowledged that amillennialism has been the majority position of the Christian family.[33] Walvoord admits:

> Because amillennialism was adopted by the Reformers, it achieved a quality of orthodoxy to which its modern adherents can point with pride. They can rightly claim many worthy scholars in the succession from the Reformation to modern times such as Calvin, Luther, Melanchthon, and in modern times, Warfield, Vos, Kuyper, Machen, and Berkhof. If one follows traditional Reformed theology in many other aspects, it is natural to accept its amillennialism. The weight of organized Christianity has largely been on the side of amillennialism.[34]

First given systematic expression by St. Augustine in his famous *City of God,* amillennialism developed a distinctive Reformed emphasis in the work of

Geerhardus Vos through the "biblical-theological" approach. Because amillennialism has its roots deep in historic Christianity, when it comes to comparing amillennialism with dispensationalism, clearly the burden of proof lies with dispensationalists to prove their case. Evangelicals often assume the opposite. It should also be noted that all major thinkers in Christian history have held something akin to the amillennial position (e.g., Augustine, Aquinas, Luther, and Calvin). This does not mean that amillennialism is true simply because it has historical support within Catholic Christianity and historic Protestantism. Nevertheless, this is an impressive point, which is often not considered.

As the dispensational movement captured the hearts and minds of conservative American evangelicals with its stress on a literal interpretation of biblical prophecy, amillennialism was often equated with Protestant liberalism or Roman Catholicism. Many believers have rejected amillennialism because they presume it involves interpreting prophecy "spiritually" or "nonliterally." As with postmillennialism, amillennialism has suffered greatly from the failure of Reformed and Lutheran writers to defend the position against the barbs of popular prophecy writers such as Dave Hunt, Chuck Missler, and Hal Lindsey. Lindsey labeled the amillennialism position "demonic and heretical" and the root of modern anti-Semitism.[35] My purpose in this present study is to rectify this lamentable situation.

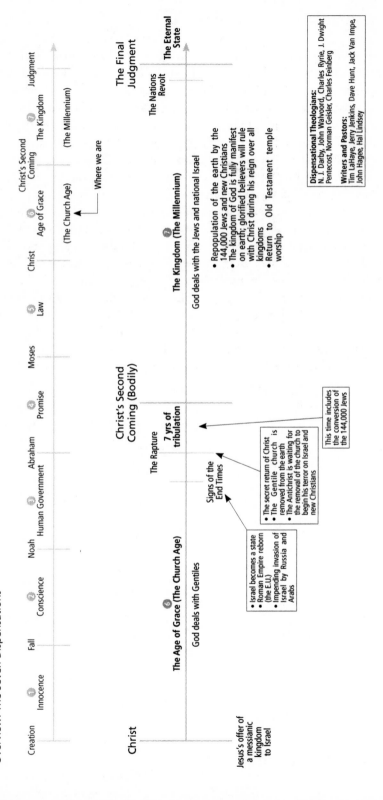

Historic Premillennialism

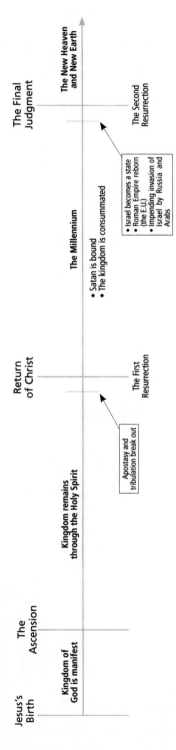

Jesus's Birth

The Ascension

Kingdom of God is manifest

Kingdom remains through the Holy Spirit

Apostasy and tribulation break out

Return of Christ

The First Resurrection

The Millennium

- Satan is bound
- The kingdom is consummated

- Israel becomes a state
- Roman Empire reborn (the E.U.)
- Impending invasion of Israel by Russia and Arabs

The Final Judgment

The New Heaven and New Earth

The Second Resurrection

Historic Premillennial Theologians:
George Eldon Ladd, John W. Montgomery, J. Barton Payne, R. Laird Harris, Henry Alford, Theodore Zahn, James Boice

Postmillennialism

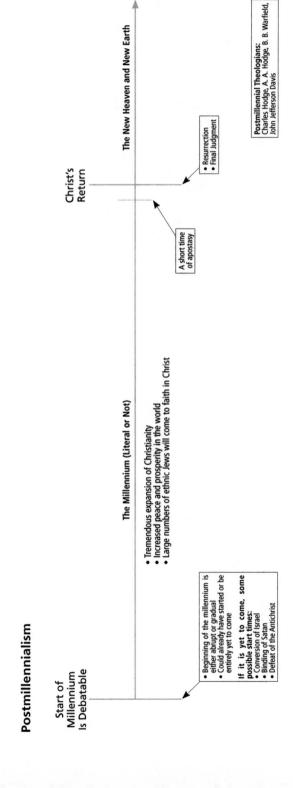

Start of Millennium Is Debatable

The Millennium (Literal or Not)

- Tremendous expansion of Christianity
- Increased peace and prosperity in the world
- Large numbers of ethnic Jews will come to faith in Christ

- Beginning of the millennium is either abrupt or gradual
- Could already have started or be entirely yet to come

If it is yet to come, some possible start times:
- Conversion of Israel
- Binding of Satan
- Defeat of the Antichrist

Christ's Return

A short time of apostasy

- Resurrection
- Final Judgment

The New Heaven and New Earth

Postmillennial Theologians:
Charles Hodge, A. A. Hodge, B. B. Warfield, John Jefferson Davis

Amillennialism

Christ's Birth

Christ's Second Coming

Christ's Resurrection and Ascension

The New Heaven and New Earth

The Millennium (This Present Age)

- Christ is presently reigning in heaven
- Triumph of the spiritual kingdom of God in the midst of the rise of evil in opposition to Christ and his kingdom
- Promises made to Abraham, Israel, and David are fulfilled by Christ or his church

First Advent

Satan Bound

Evident by the spread of the gospel and Satan is no longer able to deceive the nations

Satan is released and apostasy breaks out

Second Advent

- Resurrection
- Final Judgment

Amillennial Theologians:
Geerhardus Vos, Herman Ridderbos, Anthony Hoekema, Cornelis Venema, Meredith G. Kline

Close to Amillennial Theologians:
Augustine, Thomas Aquinas, Martin Luther, John Calvin

3

How Do We Interpret Bible Prophecy?

Everyone has presuppositions that color how they read the Scriptures. The assumption that any one of these millennial views is the result of a straightforward, unbiased reading of Scripture is overly simplistic. To understand why Christians reach such diverse opinions, we must identify and carefully evaluate the presuppositions they hold before they come to the biblical text. It is vital to know what these presuppositions are and to determine how they affect a reading of prophetic sections of the Bible if we are to get past trading proof texts with opposing viewpoints. Presuppositions are especially problematic if they go unstated and even more so if people don't believe they have any.

Historically, Protestants have been committed to *sola Scriptura* ("Scripture alone"). God has revealed in the Scriptures everything we need to know to be delivered from the guilt of sin and to gain eternal life. In addition, Protestants throughout history have believed that the Scriptures cannot err, since they are God-breathed. If we assume these two points to be true, and if we acknowledge that the three major millennial views contradict one another, we must conclude that at least two of the millennial views and possibly all three are in error. While all of them may be wrong, not all of them can be right.

The best way to choose the correct eschatological position from among the differing systems is to identify and evaluate the underlying hermeneutics involved. By examining the hermeneutical methods of each system, we can then decide which interpretation makes the most sense of the biblical data.

The Dispensational Hermeneutic

Two basic presuppositions underlie the dispensational system of biblical interpretation. These are (1) the "literal" interpretation of prophetic sections of the Bible and (2) the recognition of a distinction between the church and Israel.

As leading dispensational writers point out, dispensationalism is founded on a "literal" interpretation of the Scriptures. According to Charles Ryrie:

> Dispensationalists claim that their principle of hermeneutics is that of literal interpretation. . . . The prophecies in the Old Testament concerning the first coming of Christ—His birth, His rearing, His ministry, His death, His resurrection—were all fulfilled literally. There is no non-literal fulfillment of these prophecies in the New Testament. . . . The dispensationalist claims to use the normal principle of interpretation consistently in all his study of the Bible.[1]

At the same time, Ryrie stated, "It is this very consistency—the strength of dispensationalism—that irks the nondispensationalist and becomes the object of his ridicule."[2] Former Dallas Theological Seminary president John Walvoord adds:

> The Premillennial position is that the Bible should be interpreted in its ordinary grammatical and historical meaning in all areas of theology unless contextual or theological reasons make it clear that this was not intended by the writer. . . . The literal method [is] sustained by literal fulfillment. The literal method of interpreting prophecy has been justified by the history of its fulfillment. The most unlikely prophecies surrounding the birth of Christ, His person, His life and ministry, His death and resurrection have all been literally fulfilled. . . . Prophecies are therefore to be taken literally, the exact interpretation following the pattern of the law of fulfillment established by prophecies already fulfilled and in keeping with the entire doctrine.[3]

Since all the Old Testament prophecies regarding the life of Christ are literally fulfilled in the New Testament, dispensationalists contend that prophecies regarding other eschatological themes must also be literally fulfilled. These include the restoration of the nation of Israel, the revival of the Roman Empire, a reign of Christ on earth after his return, and the land promises of the Abrahamic covenant.

One thing is also clear. Dispensationalists do not like the historic Protestant hermeneutic's use of the "analogy of faith" and a supposed nonliteral interpretation. Ryrie argues:

> The nondispensationalist position is simply that the literal principle is sufficient except for the interpretation of prophecy. In this area, the spiritualizing

of prophecy must be introduced. The amillennialist uses it in the entire area of prophetic truth: the covenant premillennialist uses it only partially. This is why the dispensationalist claims he is the only one who uses literalism consistently.[4]

Walvoord expresses similar concerns.

It is quite apparent that the amillennial method of interpretation of Scripture which involves spiritualization has achieved a considerable popularity. It is not too difficult to account for the widespread approval of the spiritualizing method adopted by many conservative theologians as well as liberal and Roman Catholic expositors. Fundamentally, its charm lies in its flexibility. The interpreter can change the literal and grammatical sense of Scripture to make it coincide with his own system of interpretation.[5]

Buried within Ryrie's and Walvoord's comments are several criticisms worth noting. They argue that nondispensational writers do not consistently use a literal method of interpreting Scripture. The result, they say, is a spiritualizing of prophetical texts without reference to the passage's literal meaning. Implied in Walvoord's criticism is the assertion that the amillennial interpretation allows the interpreter to spiritualize the Scriptures to make them fit into an interpretive grid however he or she sees fit. This nonliteral hermeneutic supposedly provides no external controls other than one's own theological system, thereby undercutting Scripture's normative authority.

Notice too the not-so-subtle use of ad hominem arguments, which link amillennialism with Protestant liberalism or even Roman Catholicism. This approach, common with popular dispensational writers, reaches its low point in the writings of Hal Lindsey, who labels amillennialism "demonic and heretical":

Amillennialism . . . became a philosophical basis for anti-Semitism. Amillennialism teaches that the Church has been given the promises made to the Israelites because they crowned a history of unbelief by rejecting the Messiah. Therefore, since in this view the Israelites have no future in God's plan, and since they believe that "the Jews engineered the execution of Jesus," a subtle justification for the persecution of the Jews resulted. . . . This kind of teaching is demonic and heretical. I am thankful to say that no person who believes in the premillennial view can be anti-Semitic.[6]

The use of this nonliteral hermeneutic, according to dispensationalists, leads to a failure to distinguish properly between the church and Israel—a pillar of the dispensational hermeneutic. Ryrie is quite specific in his application of this distinction. Regarding the interpretation of the promise made to Abraham, he writes, "The dispensationalist understands the promises made to Abraham to require two seeds, a physical and a spiritual seed for Abraham."[7] This becomes the basis for the dispensationalist's notion that God has two mutually exclusive peoples—national Israel and the Gentile church—each with its own redemptive purposes and programs. This underlying hermeneutic leads Ryrie to the following conclusion:

> The dispensationalist recognizes two purposes of God and insists in maintaining the distinction between Israel and the Church. And all of this is built on an inductive study of the use of two words, not a scheme superimposed on the Bible. . . . It is not a matter of superimposing a dual purpose of God on the Scriptures, but it is a matter of recognizing that in the New Testament the word *Israel* does not mean the Church and vice versa. . . . In other words, consistent literalism is the basis for dispensationalism, and since consistent literalism is the logical and obvious principle of interpretation, dispensationalism is more than justified.[8]

Ryrie has expressed a noble goal. The question remains, however, whether dispensationalists are successful in living up to their own goals.

The Historic Protestant Hermeneutic

Three major presuppositions underlie the historic Protestant system.[9] The first is that the New Testament should explain the Old. This is one of the most basic principles of Bible study. The New Testament must be seen as the final authority and interpreter of the Old Testament. As Richard Gaffin asks in this regard:

> Is the New Testament to be allowed to interpret the Old as the best, most reliable interpretive tradition in the history of the church (and certainly the Reformed tradition) has always insisted? Does the New Testament as a *whole*—as the God-breathed record of the end point of the history of special revelation—provide the *controlling* vantage point for properly understanding the entire Old Testament, including its prophecies? Or alternatively, will the Old Testament . . . become the hermeneutical fulcrum?[10]

The answers to Gaffin's rhetorical questions seem self-evident, but this is not always the case and certainly not with dispensationalists.

Historically, Protestant interpreters have argued that the New Testament provides the controlling interpretation of the Old Testament. The goal of the interpreter of eschatology is to determine how prophecies made in the

Old Testament are treated and applied by writers of the New. If the New Testament writers spiritualize Old Testament prophecies by applying them in a nonliteral sense, then the Old Testament passage must be seen in light of that New Testament interpretation, not vice versa. Moreover, a major step toward finding an answer to the millennial question is to develop a contextual framework of interpretation from the New Testament itself.

Second, the Old Testament prophets and writers spoke of the glories of the coming messianic age in terms of their own premessianic age. They referred to the nation of Israel, the temple, the Davidic throne, and so on.[11] These all reflect the language, history, and experience of the people to whom these prophecies were originally given. But eschatological themes are reinterpreted in the New Testament, where we are told these Old Testament images are types and shadows of the glorious realities that are fulfilled in Jesus Christ. According to amillenarians, this means that Jesus Christ is the true Israel. Jesus Christ is the true temple. Jesus Christ is the heir to David's throne, and so on. A number of specific instances of this will be addressed in part 2.

A third critical factor is the *analogia fidei* or the "analogy of faith." This refers to the importance of interpreting an unclear biblical text in light of clear passages that speak to the same subject rather than taking the literal sense in isolation from the rest of Scripture.[12] Texts that speak of last things must, therefore, be interpreted by other biblical passages. This is especially the case when New Testament writers show how an Old Testament passage pointed to Christ and was fulfilled in him. As one writer notes in this regard:

> If we reject the literal method of interpretation as the universal rule for the interpretation of all prophecies, how are we to interpret them? Well, of course, there are many passages in prophecy that were meant to be taken literally. In fact a good working rule to follow is that the literal interpretation of the prophecy is to be accepted (a) unless the passages contain obviously figurative language, or (b) unless the New Testament gives authority for interpreting them in other than a literal sense, or (c) unless a literal interpretation would produce a contradiction with truths, principles, or factual statements contained in non-symbolic books of the New Testament. Another obvious rule to be followed is that the clearest New Testament passages in non-symbolic books are to be the norm for the interpretation of prophecy, rather than obscure or partial revelations contained in the Old Testament. In other words we should accept the clear and plain parts of Scripture as a basis for getting the true meaning of the more difficult parts of Scripture.[13]

The historic Protestant (or the amillennial) position holds that the New Testament is the final arbiter of the Old Testament. We must interpret all

Old Testament prophecy as do the writers of the New. We should place such prophecy in its redemptive-historical context if we are to interpret it correctly. The historic Protestant hermeneutic sees eschatology as more closely linked to the ebb and flow of redemption than do many popular dispensational writers.

A Literal or Literalistic Interpretation

The differences between the two millennial viewpoints are, therefore, largely due to the hermeneutical presuppositions that their adherents bring to the study of the data. Because of their commitment to a literal interpretation of the Bible, dispensationalists see Old Testament prophecy as the determinative category through which New Testament prophetic data is interpreted. For example, the book of Revelation must be interpreted by the book of Daniel, according to the dispensationalist hermeneutic.[14] The amillenarians, on the other hand, see the New Testament data as the determinative category by which Old Testament and future eschatology are to be interpreted. Therefore, amillenarians see the book of Revelation as the God-given interpretation of Daniel.

This leaves dispensationalists frequently stuck in the awkward position of insisting on an Old Testament interpretation of a prophetic theme that has been reinterpreted in the New Testament in the light of the messianic age, which dawned in Jesus Christ. Although dispensationalists claim to interpret Scripture literally, in actuality, they often read a passage literalistically, meaning they downplay or ignore how Old Testament passages are interpreted by the authors of the New. A specific example of what I mean might help to clarify the issue.

In Acts 15, the church in Antioch appointed Paul and Barnabas to report to the Jerusalem council regarding the salvation of the Gentiles and to seek help in resolving the question that had been troubling the church as a result. Should Gentile converts be circumcised in order to be saved? Once in the city, Paul and Barnabas reported to the elders and apostles on all the things God was doing among the Gentiles (v. 4). When certain converted Pharisees declared that Gentiles must be circumcised and obey the law of Moses (v. 5), Peter refuted their arguments by pointing out that it was God who had given these Gentiles the Holy Spirit: "We believe it is through the grace of our Lord Jesus that we are saved, just as they are" (v. 11).

Then James, the leader of the church, spoke (vv. 13ff.): "God at first showed his concern by taking from the Gentiles a people for himself. The words of the prophets are in agreement with this, as it is written," and James cited a passage from Amos 9:11–12: "'After this I will return and rebuild David's fallen tent. Its ruins I will rebuild, and I will restore it, that the remnant of men may seek the Lord, and all the Gentiles who bear my name, says the Lord, who does these things' that have been known for ages." James saw the prophecy as fulfilled in Christ's resurrection and exaltation and in the reconstitution of his disciples as the new Israel. The presence of both Jew and Gentile in the church was proof that the prophecy of Amos had been fulfilled.[15] David's fallen tent had been rebuilt by Christ.

In Amos's prophecy, "after this" indicated that the prophecy referred to what God would do for Israel after the exile. When James applied this prophecy to the church, was he spiritualizing an Old Testament text? Or was James reading the Old Testament through a Christ-centered lens typical of the greater light of the messianic age? This question lies at the heart of the debate between amillenarians and dispensationalists.

The famous notes of the *Scofield Reference Bible* (1909) say that from a dispensational perspective James's speech is the most important in the New Testament. According to Scofield, James is describing what will happen after the church age concludes ("after this"), i.e., in the millennium, when God will reestablish a Davidic rule over Israel. If this is true, when Paul and Barnabas sought guidance for a concern that was immediate to them (Should Gentile converts be circumcised?), James responded by pointing to a future millennium thousands of years distant.[16] Here is one instance in which dispensational presuppositions get in the way of the plain sense of the text. Scofield interprets the text literalistically, not literally.

Dispensationalists are often forced to reinterpret any New Testament data that does not fit in their Old Testament–derived prophetic scheme. Dispensational presuppositions will not fit with much of the interpretation supplied to Old Testament data by New Testament authors. A thorough survey of both Old Testament and New Testament eschatological categories will demonstrate the dispensational hermeneutic to be untenable. More importantly, such a survey gives us the proper framework and external controls to interpret prophetic sections of Scripture correctly.

The irony is that dispensationalists' practice of interpreting all prophetic texts in a literalistic fashion amounts to a repudiation of the historic Protestant hermeneutic and the principle of the analogy of faith. If amillenarians adopt the New Testament writers' interpretation of the Old Testament, are they not following the literal sense of Scripture, even if the New Testament writers universalize something that was limited to Israel in the Old Testament? The dispensationalists' literalistic reading of prophetic passages must not be confused with a literal reading. A literal reading—a reading that gets at the plain sense of the text—will allow the New Testament to interpret the Old. It is amillenarians, not dispensationalists, who interpret prophecy literally in that they follow the literal sense of how the writers of the New Testament interpret Old Testament prophecy.

Part 2

BIBLICAL AND THEOLOGICAL CONCERNS

4

The Covenantal Context
of Old Testament Eschatology

Christians believe that God is an infinite spiritual being and remains hidden
and unknowable unless he reveals himself. This he does both in nature and in
the Scriptures. But it is the mode and manner of God's revelation of himself
in the Scriptures that bring us to the subject of eschatology.

In contrast to the general revelation of God in nature, the Scriptures are the
self-revelation of God in human history, unfolding through a series of historical
events in which God speaks and acts to redeem sinful men and women.[1] The
redemptive-historical horizon includes the past, the present, and the future,
entailing a panoramic vision that extends from the creation of the world in
the first two chapters of Genesis to our final redemption in Revelation 22.
Because Christianity has focused on the history of redemption from the very
beginning, we can accurately say that Christianity is in its essence eschatological. As Jürgen Moltmann reminds us:

> From first to last, and not merely in the epilogue, Christianity is eschatology, is
> hope, forward looking and forward moving, and therefore also revolutionizing
> and transforming the present. . . . Hence eschatology cannot really be only a
> part of Christian doctrine. Rather the eschatological outlook is characteristic of
> all Christian proclamation, and of every Christian existence and of the whole
> Church.[2]

The entire Bible is eschatological in its outlook. This is especially true throughout the Old Testament, which anticipates the coming of Christ, the Redeemer of Israel and the Mediator of God's covenant. The prophets continually looked ahead to the "day of the Lord." The Redeemer came, and his promise to return a second time guarantees that even though the New Testament is grounded in the fulfillment of Old Testament promises, all is not yet accomplished. A final chapter in the story will yet play out in the theater of redemption.

Systematic theologians place eschatology at the end of their systems because of matters of logical organization. Biblical theologians remind us, however, that in many ways eschatology is the warp and woof of Scripture. As redemptive history unfolds in Holy Scripture, biblical writers continually point us to events that lie in the future. But these future events can be understood only in light of what God has already done in the past. When we speak of eschatology, we should keep the whole of redemptive history in view.

Many Christians, however, are under the mistaken impression that only limited sections of the Scriptures contain any reference to future things. This limits eschatology to the rapture, events in the Middle East, and Christ's millennial reign on earth. This produces the ironic situation in which those who speak about eschatology the most have the least to say. By limiting eschatology to the rapture and the millennium and by tying Old Testament prophecies to literal future fulfillments, the proper place of eschatology is eclipsed.

Eschatology is equally concerned with the past, the present, and the future. Redemptive history serves as the basis for much of our Christian faith because our salvation is grounded in God's historical acts. But history is also racing ahead toward its final goal. This panoramic perspective of eschatology explains why Reformed Christians have often spoken of redemption decreed, accomplished, and applied (i.e., the pattern spelled out by Paul in Eph. 1:3–14).[3] All these matters are colored by the knowledge of a certain and future judgment. What happens in the future grows out of God's saving work in the past.

Before we take up the various facets of Christian eschatology, we need to step back from the details and look at the entire panorama of redemption. The story begins with creation. God created all things and pronounced them good. Next we consider the fall of the human race into sin as the backdrop for redemptive history. Then we look ahead to the final goal. But the end is not merely paradise regained; it is paradise glorified. As William Dumbrell reminds us, "In very broad terms, the biblical sweep is from creation to the new creation by way of redemption, which is, in effect, the renewing of creation."[4] This sweeping vision is set out in the opening chapters of Genesis 1 and 2, which speak of creation and paradise, while Genesis 3 speaks of the fall into sin and paradise lost. From the moment paradise was lost and the curse declared on the human race, God promised final redemption (Gen. 3:15). We need not wait until the end of the story to learn that God's mercy and justice will triumph over human sin and its horrible consequences. When all is said and done, no trace of sin or the curse will remain.

Eschatology and the Covenants

To understand the eschatology of the Old Testament, we must consider the various covenants found throughout it. Covenants between kings (suzerains) and their vassals (servants) formed the basis of daily life in the ancient Near Eastern world. This was certainly true for ancient Israel. From a biblical perspective, covenants took on even greater importance, since Israel's king (suzerain) was the great King, and the nation was his chosen vassal.

In the Old Testament, a covenant was "a relationship under sanctions."[5] In each of the Old Testament covenants, two parties were involved: God and his people or their divinely chosen representative, such as Abraham or Moses. In these covenants, the two parties related to each other in terms of blessings and curses, the outcome depending on faithfulness to the terms set forth by the covenants. When the terms of the covenant were fulfilled, God's people received the blessings promised by him. But if the obligations of the covenant were not met, God imposed the covenant curses.

The major covenants in the Old Testament took two basic forms, covenants of promise and covenants of law. In covenants of promise, God himself swore the oath to fulfill all the terms and conditions. In covenants of works or law, the people of God swore the oath of ratification.[6]

The most prominent case of the former was God's covenant with Abram, recorded in Genesis 15. God swore on oath to him, "Do not be afraid, Abram. I am your shield, your very great reward" (v. 1). As Abram fell into a deep sleep, he saw a vision of a smoking firepot passing through butchered halves of various animals—a goat, a ram, a dove, and a pigeon. The implication of the vision was clear to Abram, who was steeped in ancient covenants and their rituals of ratification. If YHWH failed to be Abram's reward and shield, the covenant curse, graphically pictured by the severed animals, would fall on YHWH himself.

When the dream ended, "on that day the LORD made a covenant with Abram" (v. 18). Notice that in this particular covenant, God, who swore the oath of ratification, made this a covenant of promise. As is typical in such ancient covenants, the Lord also defined the geographic boundaries within which the terms of the covenant applied. This explains why the account of the ratification of this covenant included the list of peoples who resided between the two great rivers, the Nile and the Euphrates. This promise of a land was fulfilled when Joshua led the people of Israel back into Canaan (Josh. 1:2–9). As Joshua himself later put it, "So the LORD gave Israel all the land he had sworn to give their forefathers, and they took possession of it and settled there" (Josh. 21:43; cf. also 1 Kings 4:20–21).[7]

The clearest illustration of the second type of covenant (a covenant of law) is found in Exodus 24, when the people of God, not YHWH, swore the covenant oath of ratification. YHWH called Moses, Aaron, Nadab, and Abihu, along with seventy elders, up to Mount Sinai, where the group worshiped him at a distance. But Moses—the covenant mediator, anticipating the true covenant Mediator, Jesus Christ—approached God alone. "When Moses went and told the people all the LORD's words and laws, they responded with one voice. 'Everything the LORD has said we will do.' Moses then wrote down everything the LORD had said" (vv. 3–4). Unlike with the covenant of promise that God made with Abram, in this covenant of law, God did not swear the oath of ratification. Rather, the people of Israel did so. By swearing their obedience on oath, they would receive the promised blessings of the Mosaic covenant if they obeyed or the covenant curses if they disobeyed. The particular blessings and curses associated with this covenant were spelled out in Deuteronomy 27–30.[8]

The Covenant of Works and the Covenant of Grace

Keeping in mind the distinction between these two kinds of covenants—promise and law—we can now turn to the two overarching covenants, the covenant of works and the covenant of grace, under which all these individual covenants of law and promise fall. This is important to keep in mind because the covenant of works and the covenant of grace progressively unfold throughout the Old Testament, and the way they do says much about the eschatology of both testaments.

These two overarching covenants enable us to see the continuity that existed between the covenants in the Old Testament. The covenants God made with Abraham, Isaac, Jacob, and Israel were not isolated covenants with no connection with what went before or after. Rather, the particular covenants God made with his people were repeated ratifications of the one covenant of grace that God first promised in Eden after the fall, then later ratified with Abraham, the father of all who believe.

Seeing the essential continuity between these covenants is important at a number of levels. It prevents us from mistakenly seeing the Old Testament as essentially law and the New Testament as essentially gospel. Law and gospel are in both testaments. This covenantal structure also safeguarded the New Testament teaching of one gospel (Gal. 3:8), one plan of salvation (Eph. 1:4–6), and one common faith (Eph. 4:4–6). This explains why Old Testament covenants were often framed in terms of promise, while New Testament covenants were framed in terms of fulfillment. The individual covenants with Abraham, Moses, and David foreshadowed as part of a larger covenantal structure the new covenant ratified by Christ's blood (Heb. 10:11–18). The great redemptive events found throughout the Old Testament are unintelligible apart from this covenantal structure and an emphasis on God's promise of a coming Redeemer, who is also the covenant Mediator.[9]

As redemptive history unfolded, the first Adam—the biological and federal representative of all humanity—failed to do as God commanded under the terms of the covenant of works. The Lord God said to Adam, "You must not eat from the tree of the knowledge of good and evil, for when you eat of it you will surely die" (Gen. 2:17). This covenant of works or, as some Reformed writers speak of it, the "covenant of creation" lies at the heart of redemptive history.[10] Under its terms, God demanded perfect obedience of Adam, who would either obey the terms of the covenant and receive God's blessing—eternal life in a glorified Eden—or fail to keep the covenant and bring its sanctions down upon himself and all humanity. Adam's willful act of rebellion did, in fact, bring the curse of death on the entire human race. This covenant of works is never subsequently abrogated in the Scriptures, a point empirically verified whenever death strikes. This covenant also undergirds the biblical teaching that for any of Adam's fallen children to be saved, someone must fulfill all the terms of the covenant without a single infraction in thought, word, or deed (Matt. 5:48; 1 Pet. 1:16).

Some argue that there was no such covenant between God and Adam because the phrase "covenant of works" does not appear in the biblical text. Not only are all the elements of a covenant present, but later biblical writers referred to the Eden account in precisely those terms.[11] The prophet Hosea told us that Israel would come under God's judgment because, "like Adam, they have broken the covenant" (Hosea 6:7).[12] In Romans 5:12–21, Paul spelled out the perfect obedience required by this covenant when he wrote that sinners are declared righteous on the condition of Christ's obedience on their behalf. The critical question is simply this: Obedient to what? Paul's answer was that Jesus Christ was perfectly obedient to the same covenant that the first Adam disobeyed.[13] The resurrection is proof that Christ fulfilled the terms of this covenant, because after laying down his life for our sins, God raised him up as Lord of life (Rom. 4:25).

Because Adam acted as the federal head or representative of all those people who came after him, once he disobeyed the covenant of works, he plunged the entire human race into the guilt and consequences of sin. Though the curse subjects all humanity and creation to the bondage of sin, God decreed to redeem his people and his world. From the outset, the drama of redemption began unfolding when God rescued men and women from the guilt of Adam's sin as well as its consequences.

When Adam failed to live according to the covenant of creation, Adam and his family were cast from Eden and never allowed to return. This recurring theme of God making a covenant, the subsequent disobedience of his people, and the consequences of the covenant curse resulting in his people being cast from the land of promise repeatedly resurfaces throughout the drama of redemption. At Mount Sinai, God placed Israel under the law, epitomized by the Ten Commandments, in which were codified all of the requirements of the covenant of works. The commandments were written on human hearts because all of Adam's children bear God's divine image—a point that also implies a covenant of works in Eden.[14] But Israel too failed to keep God's commandments, which brought on them the curse of being removed from the land.[15]

Although God repeatedly sent his prophets to call Israel to repentance, the nation showed contempt for God by increasing her sins and killing his messengers. Like Adam, the nation came under God's covenant judgment and was cast from Canaan, the very land God had promised to Abraham. Adam had failed. Now Israel had failed. A redeemer was still needed who would fulfill the covenant of works. "For what the law was powerless to do . . . God did by sending his own Son in the likeness of sinful man" (Rom. 8:3).

The fact that God demands perfect obedience from his creatures necessitated the coming of a second Adam who became obedient unto death (Phil. 2:8) and who became "sin for us, so that in him we might become the righteousness of God" (2 Cor. 5:21). The fall necessitated the coming of a Redeemer who fulfilled the terms of the original covenant of works, which Adam had failed to keep. In addition, the Redeemer himself would have to establish a covenant of grace whereby God would deliver Adam's fallen children. Yet he had to do so without sacrificing his justice. This is why the Redeemer had to die on a cross, something beyond the realm of imagination for Old Testament believers looking for a coming deliverer.

The history of redemption is the progressive unfolding of a covenant of works and a covenant of grace throughout the whole of Scripture. These two covenants—the very essence of covenant theology—will continue to resurface as we speak of the eschatology of both testaments. In the progressive development of these two covenants, Jesus Christ—the only Mediator between God and man and the Redeemer promised throughout the whole Old Testament—was revealed.

This helps to explain, in part, why the coming Redeemer was revealed as the second Adam. He was not only the covenant Mediator but also the new representative of God's people and Lord of all creation. The second Adam ushered in a new creation when he rose from the dead that first Easter morning. Therefore, it was in the person and work of Jesus Christ that the seemingly diverse themes of covenant and new creation joined perfectly together. When the second Adam justified people through his own perfect obedience, he did so in terms of the new and better covenant in which God declared sinners righteous because of Christ's merits. Thus, God fulfilled all the promises he made to Abraham. As the apostle Paul put it, to participate in Christ's reconciling work is to participate in the new creation (2 Cor. 5:17). This new creation, which is nothing less than a paradise glorified, is also the New Jerusalem, which John described as follows: "No longer will there be any curse. The throne of God and of the Lamb will be in the city, and his servants will serve him. They will see his face" (Rev. 22:3–4). Once again, God and humanity will dwell together just as they did in Eden, only this time "for ever and ever" (v. 5).

The connection between the new creation and the covenant of grace is important to keep in mind. The one who makes all things new, Jesus Christ, is also the Mediator of the covenant of grace. Therefore, new creation and the covenant of grace are forever joined together in the person and work of Jesus Christ.

This reminds us that the basic panorama of eschatology is creation, fall, and re-creation. These play themselves out as God deals with his creatures in the covenantal structure of redemptive history. This is the picture we get by looking at the box top before we assemble the pieces of the redemptive puzzle.

5

These Things Were Foretold

We now move on to develop individual facets of redemptive history. The first thing we should note about Old Testament eschatology is that from the moment the human race fell into sin and came under God's curse, there was an expectation that God would send his promised Redeemer. He also promised to put an end to sin—its guilt, power, and presence. In fact, the first prophecy recorded in the Bible is found in Genesis 3:15. God told the serpent, "I will put enmity between you and the woman, and between your offspring and hers; he will crush your head, and you will strike his heel." "This passage, often called the 'mother promise,' now sets the tone for the entire Old Testament."[1] This promise stands at that critical juncture when the covenant of works had been broken and the curse of death hung menacingly over the human race.

God, who is rich in mercy, would deliver his people from the curse through a covenant of grace, under the terms of which he would meet all the demands he required of us under the covenant of works. What God demanded of us under the law, he freely gave us in the gospel. What God demanded of humanity under the covenant of works, he gave us in Jesus Christ, the Mediator of the covenant of grace.

From the beginning, we get a glimpse of the end of the story. Immediately after humanity's fall into sin, God pronounced a curse on the serpent, who had acted as Satan's agent. Thus, redemptive history began with the promise of coming judgment and will culminate with the destruction of the devil at the end of the thousand years (see Rev. 20:7–10).

The progress of redemptive history reflects the unfolding of God's plan of salvation throughout the pages of Scripture under the framework of two covenants: the covenant of works and the covenant of grace.[2] This preserves the unity of the gospel and the plan of redemption and sets before us the goal of redemption, which is the final consummation. This is a different expectation than that held by millenarians—pre- and post-—who see the earthly millennium as a halfway step before the final consummation.

This covenantal structure of redemptive history is contrary to the dispensationalist's notion of seven distinct redemptive-historical economies in which people repeatedly frustrate God's plan of redemption and which culminate in an earthly millennium before the final re-creation. This is one reason why dispensational premillenarians and amillenarians disagree. Each camp has vastly different eschatological presuppositions as well as expectations.

The amazing prophecy of Genesis 3:15 is known as the "protoevangel," and it briefly sketched the subsequent course of redemptive history. It also promised that the Redeemer would come from the seed of the woman. This Redeemer would be bruised, but in the process of bringing redemption to humankind, he would crush the head of the serpent. From this point forward, the whole of Old Testament redemptive history anticipated this coming Redeemer and set the stage for his appearance in human history when the fullness of time had finally come (Gal. 4:4).

The pattern of promise and fulfillment runs throughout the pages of Holy Scripture. Jesus Christ and his humble entrance into human history lie at the center of biblical eschatology, the last things, and the millennial age. This explains in part why Reformed theologians see the Old Testament in terms of promises about the Redeemer and the New Testament in terms of their fulfillment. This view preserves the redemptive-historical unity between the testaments. The Bible does not have two divergent testaments bound under one cover. Rather, the Bible is one book with one ultimate author and one central character who appears in two testaments, the Old of promise and the New of fulfillment.

The central character of the story, even in the Old Testament, was the Redeemer, Jesus Christ, the only mediator between God and sinful humans (1 Tim. 2:5). He lay hidden in Old Testament shadows but was revealed in the New. Seeing the flow of redemptive history in this light helps explain why those in the Reformed tradition are concerned about the dispensational tendency to interpret the New Testament in light of the Old and why they believe eschatology must be Christ centered. Our eschatological expectation should not be epoch centered[3] or even centered in an earthly golden age as in postmillennialism. Nor should eschatology be a correlation of current events and certain verses that supposedly explain them. The story of redemption is nothing less than the story of Jesus Christ and his kingdom, which is manifest in the covenant of works, the covenant of grace,[4] and finally the new creation. God's kingdom is the consummate manifestation of his covenant with his elect, originally made with Jesus Christ before the foundation of the world.

The Coming Prophet, Priest, and King

An important line of redemptive-historical themes comes into view in the form of promises made in the Old Testament about the coming one to whom Israel's prophets, priests, and kings all pointed.

The establishment of a monarchy in Israel played an important role in preparation for the coming Redeemer. "The Old Testament people recognized three special offices: those of prophet, priest, and king. The coming redeemer was expected to be the culmination and fulfillment of all three of these special offices."[5] This so-called *munus triplex* ("threefold office") became a major organizing principle in the development of Reformed Christology. Though the *munus triplex* did not become a focus of organization until John Calvin, the New Testament writers undoubtedly understood much of Christ's person and work in light of his fulfillment of these Old Testament offices.

As the story of redemption unfolded in the Old Testament, the offices of prophet, priest, and king repeatedly came into view. Moses prophesied that "the LORD your God will raise up for you a prophet like me from among your own brothers. You must listen to him" (Deut. 18:15). These words meant that the coming Redeemer would be a great prophet—in fact, he would be *the* Prophet, the Word of God incarnate. Throughout the Gospels, Jesus is presented as the new Moses, not the lawgiver but the consummate covenant Mediator who leads the people of God in a new exodus toward the final promised land, the heavenly city.[6] As God in human flesh, it was in his capacity as God's prophet par excellence that Jesus was the image of the invisible God (Col. 1:15). As Jesus told Philip, "Anyone who has seen me has seen the Father" (John 14:9). In Jesus Christ, God is fully revealed.

In addition to being the final prophet, the coming Redeemer was also the consummate high priest. We read in the Psalter, "The LORD has sworn and will not change his mind: 'You are a priest forever, in the order of Melchizedek'" (Ps. 110:4). As we look back from the perspective of New Testament fulfillment, we can see that the Epistle to the Hebrews was written to demonstrate that Israel's priesthood was a provisional institution that prepared the way for the true High Priest, the one who was both sacrificing priest and sacrificial victim.

Then there is the role played by Israel's kings throughout the nation's history. When viewed from the perspective of redemptive history, this kingly office is much more than a post of national leadership. The office itself was a type of redemption and will figure prominently in this study. Throughout the testimony of Israel's prophets, the coming Messiah was also to be a great king. Zechariah wrote, "Rejoice greatly, O Daughter of Zion! Shout, Daughter of Jerusalem! See, your king comes to you" (9:9). Nathan and Isaiah prophesied that the Redeemer would sit on the throne of David and establish an everlasting kingdom (see 2 Sam. 7:12–13; Isa. 9:7). Christians celebrate these events on Palm Sunday, when these prophecies were fulfilled as Jesus entered Jerusalem one week before his passion.

The threefold office of Christ is connected to Jesus's divinity. Indeed, the coming prophet, priest, and king was given titles connecting him directly to the person of YHWH. He would be called Immanuel ("God with us") and "Mighty God" (Isa. 9:6). But because the famous "Shema" (Deut. 6:4) was a national and covenantal profession of one true God, passages that connected the coming Redeemer to YHWH remained mysteries to premessianic Old Testament saints. It was not until Jesus was born of a virgin that the connection between YHWH and the coming one was made plain.

A New and Better Covenant

As we watch the history of redemption continue to unfold, we come to Jeremiah's prophecy of a new covenant yet to come that will fulfill in part the covenant God made with Moses and Israel at Mount Sinai (Jer. 31:31–34). In his prophetic capacity, Jeremiah functioned as a kind of Moses, serving as the messenger of the "new era." Jeremiah served as "a minister of God's word in a crisis situation."[7] Once again, context is important. As Anthony Hoekema points out, "In the days of Jeremiah . . . the people of Judah had broken God's covenant with them by their idolatries and transgressions. Though the main burden of Jeremiah's prophecies is one of doom, yet he does predict that God will make a new covenant with His people."[8]

The part of Jeremiah's prophecy that is particularly germane to our topic is found in 31:31–33, which reads, "'The time is coming,' declares the LORD, 'when I will make a new covenant with the house of Israel and with the house of Judah. . . . I will put my law in their minds and write it on their hearts. I will be their God, and they will be my people.'" Through these words, God reaffirmed his covenant oath and spoke of Judah and Israel as recipients of this new covenant.

How was this prophecy interpreted in the New Testament? According to dispensationalists, this prophecy will not be fulfilled until the millennial reign of Christ in the age of the new covenant.[9] But the author of Hebrews pointed out that this new covenant is a present and glorious reality for all who are in Christ. In chapters 8 and 10 of Hebrews, the author made the point that since the Mosaic covenant was a type and shadow of the reality in Christ and since the new covenant had come, God "made the first one obsolete" (Heb. 8:13). It is through Christ's priestly work (Heb. 10:12–14) that believers have been made perfect forever. As William Lane observes, "Because his one sacrifice has decisively purged the conscience of worshipers, Christ has consecrated the people of the new covenant to God in the qualitatively new relationship of heart-obedience proclaimed in this prophecy. Christ's death was the effective sin offering that removed every obstacle to the service of God."[10]

Who are these new covenant people? According to the author of Hebrews, they are the members of Christ's church. Couched in the premessianic context of Jeremiah's prophecy, the houses of Israel and Judah are typological of the church. This is another clear-cut case of an Old Testament prophecy that is fulfilled in the church, the members of which are the spiritual seed of Abraham through faith in Jesus Christ (cf. Gal. 3:6–14).

The Restoration of Israel

Another significant eschatological theme in the Old Testament is the promise that the nation of Israel will be gloriously restored in the distant future. Leading dispensationalists believe that these prophecies refer to national Israel even though the authors of the New Testament apply them to the church. Significant passages in this regard are Jeremiah 23:3, where the Lord declared he would gather the remnant of his flock, and Isaiah 11:11, where the Lord promised to gather a remnant out of Egypt a second time, harkening the reader back to the exodus as well as to Ezekiel 36:24–28 and Isaiah 24–27. As George Ladd notes:

> [The Old Testament prophets] foresee a restoration, but only of a people which has been purified and made righteous. Their message both of woe and weal is addressed to Israel that the people may be warned of their sinfulness and turn to God. . . . Perhaps the most significant result of the ethical concern of the prophets is their conviction that it will not be Israel as such that enters into the eschatological Kingdom of God but only a believing, purified remnant.[11]

According to Reformed theologians, the promised restoration of Israel pointed ahead to the church. This is because the New Testament explicitly represented this promise as being fulfilled in the church, which Paul called "the Israel of God" (Gal. 6:16). On several occasions, the New Testament writers spoke of the church in terms that the Old Testament could only apply to national Israel. In 1 Peter 2:9, we read, "But you are a chosen people, a royal priesthood, a holy nation, a people belonging to God, that you may declare the praises of him who called you out of darkness into his wonderful light."[12] In Galatians 3:28–29, the apostle Paul put it this way: "There is neither Jew nor Greek, slave nor free, male nor female, for you are all one in Christ Jesus. If you belong to Christ, then you are Abraham's seed, and heirs according to the promise."[13] In Hebrews 12:22–24, we read, "But you have come to Mount Zion, to the heavenly Jerusalem, the city of the living God. You have come to thousands upon thousands of angels in joyful assembly, to the church of the firstborn, whose names are written in heaven. You have come to God, the judge of all men, to the spirits of righteous men made perfect, to Jesus the mediator of a new covenant, and to the sprinkled blood that speaks a better word than the blood of Abel."[14]

The prophets predicted a glorious and redeemed Israel, which the New Testament writers contended was fulfilled in the church, the mystical body of Jesus Christ. To have a prophetic foretelling of the church in more literal terms would have been unintelligible to Old Testament believers.

6

According to the Prophets

Prophetic Perspective

The interpretation of Old Testament prophecy can be tricky business.[1] There are specific instances in the Scriptures when a prophet foretold what appears to be a single future event, but as history unfolded it became clear that the original prophecy referred to multiple events. Certain prophecies may have double or multiple fulfillments.

A simple analogy may be useful. As I stand in the greater Los Angeles basin and look toward the mountains to the northeast, I see a single mountainous ridge on the horizon. Yet, if I were to drive directly toward the mountains, I would soon realize that what appeared to be a single ridge was actually a series of hills, valleys, and mountains separated by many miles. So it is with some Old Testament prophecies.

One example of this type of fulfillment takes place with the prophecy of a future outpouring of God's Spirit (Joel 2:28–32; cf. Ezek. 36:24–28). The prophet Joel declared that "afterward, I will pour out my Spirit on all people. Your sons and daughters will prophesy, your old men will dream dreams, your young men will see visions. Even on my servants, both men and women, I will pour out my Spirit in those days" (vv. 28–29). Peter contended that this prophecy was fulfilled at Pentecost (cf. Acts 2:16).[2] Yet cosmic elements were also associated with this prophecy: "I will show wonders in the heavens and on the earth, blood and fire and billows of smoke. The sun will be turned to darkness and the moon to blood before the coming of the great and dreadful day of the LORD" (vv. 30–31). And Jesus spoke of similar cosmic signs that will accompany his return (Matt. 24:29–31). Was Joel's prophecy fulfilled at Pentecost? Or was it fulfilled when Jesus died on the cross and the afternoon sun became as dark as night? Will it yet be fulfilled at Christ's second advent? Or is it fulfilled multiple times? As Anthony Hoekema points out:

> This outpouring of the Spirit, therefore, was another of the eschatological events on the horizon of the future for which the Old Testament believer of that time looked with eager anticipation. It is striking, however, that the next verse of Joel's prophecy mentions . . . the heavens and earth. . . . Certain New Testament passages (for example Luke 21:25; Matt. 24:29) relate the signs mentioned above to the second coming of Jesus Christ. Yet Joel seems to predict them as if they were to happen just before the outpouring of the Holy Spirit. Unless one interprets these signs in a nonliteral way (in which case the turning of the sun to darkness could be understood as fulfilled in the three hours of darkness while Jesus was on the cross), it would appear that Joel in his prophecy sees as coming together in a single vision what was separated by thousands of years. This phenomenon, which we may call prophetic perspective, occurs quite frequently in the Old Testament prophets.[3]

Prophetic perspective can make the interpretation of Bible prophecy difficult.[4] One of the most significant examples of prophetic perspective relates to the biblical concept of the "day of the Lord," a subject to which we now turn.

The Day of the Lord

The coming "day of the Lord" is most often spoken of as the time when God will bring swift and terrible judgment on Israel's enemies. Yet, Scripture makes clear it also will be a glorious time of salvation for God's people. This coming day of judgment and blessing was prophesied in terms of prophetic perspective. Obadiah, for example, equated the day of the Lord with the destruction of Edom, yet his prophecy obviously has greater significance. It refers as well to the future eschatological judgment of Israel's enemies (see vv. 15–16). Moreover, "Isaiah 13 . . . speaks of a day of the Lord on the not-too-distant horizon when Babylon will be destroyed (vv. 6–8, 17–22). In the same chapter, however, interspersed between descriptions of the destruction of Babylon, are references to the eschatological day of the Lord in the far distant future."[5] The text contains this insertion:

> See, the day of the LORD is coming—a cruel day, with wrath and fierce anger—to make the land desolate and destroy the sinners within it. The stars of heaven and their constellations will not show their light. The rising sun will be darkened and

the moon will not give its light. I will punish the world for its evil, the wicked for their sins. . . . Therefore I will make the heavens tremble; and the earth will shake from its place at the wrath of the LORD Almighty, in the day of his burning anger. (Isa. 13:9–11, 13)

This prediction of a day of judgment, which lay in the distant future, was intermingled with the foretelling of an immediate event.

That the day of judgment is also the day of salvation is found in a text we have already considered, Joel 2:32, where we read that all those who call on the name of the Lord will be saved—delivered from the judgment that is associated with the day of the Lord. In Malachi 4:2, the prophet told of a time before the day of the Lord in which the sun of righteousness will dawn upon all who revere God's name. But in verse 5, Malachi spoke of this as a period in which God's curse comes to fruition. As Hoekema puts it, "The day of the Lord predicted by the Old Testament prophets will be a day of judgment and wrath for some but of blessing and salvation for others."[6] Therefore, prophetic perspective appears again in a prophecy such as this, which has a double fulfillment (the coming of the messianic age with the blessings of salvation and the curses upon Israel) and a further fulfillment associated with the final judgment at the end of the messianic age (the blessing of eternal life and the curse of eternal punishment).

Old Testament prophets also spoke of the coming restoration of all things. In Isaiah 65:17, we read, "Behold, I will create new heavens and a new earth. The former things will not be remembered, nor will they come to mind." Isaiah spoke of a time when the desert will become fruitful (32:15), the wilderness will blossom (35:1), the burning sand will become a pool (35:7), and wolves and lions will lie down with lambs and goats (11:6–8).[7] This points us ahead to a time when creation will be liberated from the curse (Rom. 8:20–21) and all things will be made new (Rev. 21:5). According to George Ladd:

> The biblical idea of redemption always includes the earth. Hebrew thought saw an essential link between man and nature. The prophets do not think of the earth as merely the indifferent theater on which man carries out his normal task but as the expression of divine glory. The Old Testament nowhere holds forth the hope of a bodiless, nonmaterial, purely "spiritual" redemption as did Greek thought. The earth is the divinely ordained scene of human existence. Furthermore, the earth has been involved in the evils which sin has incurred. There is an interrelation of nature with the moral life of man; therefore the earth must also share in God's final redemption. The human heart, human society, and all of nature must be purged of the effects of evil, that God's glory may be perfectly manifested in his creation.[8]

The panoramic view of the history of redemption does indeed take us from creation to the fall of humanity, to the promise of redemption, to the renewal of all things. We again are brought back to the themes of kingdom, covenant, and consummation.

The Coming Redeemer

The entire Old Testament is filled with the expectation and promise of a coming Redeemer. He would crush the serpent but would be bruised himself. He would come from the seed of the woman (a veiled reference to the virginal conception), be the seed of Abraham, hail from the tribe of Judah, and be a descendant of David. The coming one would fulfill the offices of prophet, priest, and king, for he is the final Prophet, the great High Priest, and the conquering King. What is more, he was given titles directly connected with Yahweh, clearly pointing ahead to his coming incarnation. But the coming one also would be a suffering servant who would save his people through his suffering and death on our behalf. He was the mysterious "Son of Man" and would be associated with a coming judgment upon the nations. He would bring with him the rule or kingdom of God and would establish a new and better covenant. The coming Redeemer would restore Israel.

Much like modern dispensationalists expect Jesus to reign over the nations in the future millennial kingdom, the Jews expected the Messiah to establish a political kingdom whereby Israel would rule over the Gentile nations. This explains why the Jews rejected Jesus as their Messiah. The New Testament, however, equates Israel's restoration, prophesied in the Old Testament, with Jesus's kingdom—a kingdom not of this world (John 18:36).

The Redeemer's coming was equated with an outpouring of the Holy Spirit as well as the terrible judgment of the day of the Lord. In this case, the prophetic perspective is in effect, as the prophets saw the two comings of Christ as one event. The New Testament sees it as two events, the first and the second advent. The "age of the Spirit," the presence of the kingdom of God, and the so-called millennial reign of Christ characterize the period of time between these two comings of Christ.

In These Last Days: The Dawn of the Messianic Age

Old Testament believers were aware that God was moving history toward a goal that lay far off on the distant horizon. That goal was the coming of the promised Redeemer who would bring to fruition the prophetic expectations and hopes of the people of God.[9] As we turn our focus to the eschatological expectation of the New Testament, it is vital to notice that New Testament eschatology did not arise suddenly in a vacuum. Instead, it grew directly out of this Old Testament prophetic expectation of a coming Redeemer and a glorious age of redemption.

On the eve of the incarnation of Christ, pious Jews longed to see this promised redemption draw near. Although God had been silent since the days of Malachi nearly four hundred years earlier, by the time the New Testament era dawned, there was a widespread, eager expectation that God was about to act once again. Anthony Hoekema explains:

> We may see this eschatological hope exemplified in the aged Simeon, about whom it is said that he was looking "for the consolation of Israel" (Luke 2:25), and in Anna, the prophetess, who, after she had seen the infant Jesus, "gave thanks to God, and spoke of Him to all who were looking for the redemption of Jerusalem" (Luke 2:38).[10]

New Testament revelation opened with the strong sense that God was about to fulfill the promises anticipated under the old covenant. The promised Redeemer was about to come.

As the New Testament writers unpacked this Old Testament expectation and its fulfillment in Jesus Christ, it soon became clear that the fulfillment of the Old Testament prophecies regarding the messianic age and the blessings Christians can enjoy in the present age were a major step toward a final and glorious fulfillment to come. This is known as the *already*, the "realized eschatology," or as George Ladd speaks of it, "the presence of the future." Because of Jesus Christ and his coming, the Christian possesses the complete fulfillment and blessings of all the promises of the messianic age made under the old covenant.

But the arrival of the messianic age also brought with it a new series of promises to be fulfilled at the end of the age. The fulfilled promises pointed to a more glorious and future fulfillment. This is called the *not yet* or future eschatology. It is this already/not yet tension that serves as the basis for understanding much of New Testament eschatological expectation.

The Basic Elements of New Testament Eschatology

There are three basic elements of New Testament eschatology.[11] The first of these is that the Old Testament promise of a coming Redeemer was realized in Jesus Christ. This was a prominent theme throughout the New Testament, especially in the Gospel of Matthew.[12] Jesus's birth, life, death, and resurrection were fulfillments of Old Testament prophecies. With his first advent, the kingdom of God and the "last days" arrived, indicating that Old Testament expectation had turned to New Testament fulfillment.

The second basic element of New Testament eschatology is that what was understood as one glorious messianic age predicted in the Old Testament unfolded in two different ages: "this age" and "the age to come." This means that the coming of Jesus Christ marked the beginning of a glorious new redemptive age with a corresponding set of blessings. Yet, this new age is not fully consummated and will be fulfilled in the future. This already/not yet structure gives the New Testament a strong forward-looking focus. In the words of one writer:

> The New Testament, as well as the Old, has a strong forward look. There is a deep conviction that the redemptive workings of the Holy Spirit which are now experienced are but the prelude to a far richer and more complete redemption in the future, and that the era which has been ushered in by the first coming of Jesus Christ will be followed by another era which will be more glorious than this one can possibly be. In other words, the New Testament believer is conscious on the one hand of the fact that the great eschatological event predicted in the Old Testament has already happened, while on the other hand he realizes that another momentous series of eschatological events is still to come.[13]

Therefore, the New Testament contains a distinct and pronounced tension between what God has already done in fulfilling the promises of the Old Testament and what God will do yet in the future. This so-called already/not yet tension characterizes much of New Testament theology.[14]

The third element of New Testament eschatology is that the present blessings of the coming Redeemer are the pledge of greater blessings to come. Christ's first advent guaranteed his second coming, which includes the final judgment, the bodily resurrection, and the renewal of the heavens and the earth. Christ's first advent and the final consummation at the second mark the comprehensive fulfillment of the expectations set forth by the Old Testament prophets.

Let us now look briefly at each of these aspects of New Testament eschatology in more detail.

Jesus Christ, the Coming Redeemer

The first of these three elements, namely, that what the Old Testament promised about a coming Redeemer had come to pass, is readily apparent by the way the New Testament writers spoke of the coming of Christ. It is clear from the Gospel accounts that many details of Jesus's life and messianic mission fulfilled otherwise obscure Old Testament prophecies in stunning and exacting detail.[15]

Notice the way New Testament writers spoke of the finished work of Christ in providing all that is necessary for our redemption. "Of great importance in this connection is the application of words like *hapax* (once) and *ephapax* (once for all) to the work of Christ."[16] Peter told us, "For Christ died for sins once for all" (1 Pet. 3:18). The writer of Hebrews said, "He entered the Most Holy Place once for all by his own blood, having obtained eternal redemption" (9:12). Further, "We have been made holy through the sacrifice of the body of Jesus Christ once for all" (10:12). Jesus died for our sins and was raised for our justification, the proof that his death remits the guilt of our sins and that his victory becomes ours through faith.

The New Testament writers spoke with one voice in this regard. Jesus was the true Passover Lamb who took "away the sin of the world" (John 1:29). Paul described Jesus's death, burial, and resurrection as events that were "according to the Scriptures" (1 Cor. 15:3–8). The New Testament spoke of Jesus's redemptive work as final and complete, and we receive his saving benefits through faith alone. All the Old Testament promises of redemption were complete in Jesus Christ.

Another important connection made by New Testament writers was found in the announcement of the coming of the kingdom of God, which coincided with Jesus's first advent. According to Hoekema:

> Both John the Baptist and Jesus are said to proclaim that in the coming of Jesus the kingdom of God or of heaven is at hand (Matt. 3:2; Mark 1:15; the Greek word translated "at hand" is *engizō*). Jesus also told the pharisees that his casting out demons by the Spirit of God was proof that the Kingdom of God had come upon them (Matt 12:28). . . . In Christ's person the promised kingdom had come—although there would be a final consummation of that kingdom in the future.[17]

Even though the kingdom of God was not explicitly defined in the Old Testament, the New Testament writers linked it with the first coming of Jesus. They understood the dawn of the messianic kingdom as the revelation of righteousness and salvation, which the Old Testament writers associated with that kingdom.[18] Christ's messianic ministry advanced God's kingdom, which will never end and will conquer to the ends of the earth.

Another way New Testament writers linked the coming Redeemer with the fulfillment of Old Testament prophecy was by referring to the new messianic age as the "last days." In fact, the phrase "latter days" appears twenty-seven times in the New Testament. In several instances, the phrase was used of the end of history, but in most instances it was used of the eschatological epoch that began in the New Testament era with the coming of Jesus Christ.[19] Based on the emphasis the apostolic writers placed on the unity between the Old Testament, which had foretold the messianic age, and the revelation of the Messiah, it's clear they were conscious that the first advent marked the beginning of the last days and the dawn of the age to come.

Throughout the Old Testament, the "last days" (or "latter days") referred to a future time when Israel would experience unprecedented tribulation, including oppression (Ezek. 38:14–17), persecution (Dan. 10:14; 11:27–12:10), false teaching, and apostasy (Dan. 10:14). This horrible tribulation precedes an age of redemption in which Israel will at long last seek the Lord and be delivered. It will also be a time in which all her enemies will be judged (Hosea 3:4–5; Ezek. 38:14–23; Dan. 10:14; 11:40–45; 12:1–3). According to the Old Testament, this anticipated deliverance and judgment will come to pass through God's Messiah, who will conquer Israel's Gentile enemies and will establish a Davidic kingdom, his rule extending to the ends of the earth (Gen. 49:1–8; Num. 24:14–19; Isa. 2:2–4; Dan. 2:28–45; 10:14–21; Mic. 4:1–3).

An additional strand of data indicates that the last days include a time of great tribulation and persecution, only to be followed by a resurrection of both the righteous and the unrighteous (Dan. 11–12).[20] In light of Old Testament premessianic revelation, it is difficult to see how all these divergent themes could possibly be fulfilled by one individual, which becomes a valuable point of New Testament polemic against the Jewish concept of Messiah.

In light of the coming of Jesus Christ, the New Testament writers picked up this phrase "latter days" and used it to argue that the "last days" had arrived and would continue until the final consummation and the end of the age. "This means that the Old Testament prophecies of the great tribulation, God's deliverance of Israel from her oppressors, God's rule over the Gentiles, and the establishment of his kingdom have been set in motion by Christ's life, death, resurrection, and the formation of the Christian church."[21] As G. K. Beale points out, the resurrection marked the beginning of Christ's messianic reign, while Pentecost was the great sign of Christ's present rule. The Old Testament prophets, however, could not understand how the glorious messianic reign and rule of Christ could coexist side by side with images of persecution and tribulation.[22]

This use of the phrase "last days" as marking the dawn of the new age of redemption can be seen in Peter's Pentecost sermon (Acts 2:16–17). Peter demonstrated that the coming of Christ and his resurrection clearly meant that the last days had arrived. "The words 'in the last days' (*en tais eschatais hērmerais*) are a translation of the Hebrew words '*acharey khen*,' literally, 'afterwards.' When Peter quotes these words and applies them to the event which has just occurred, he is saying in effect, 'We are in the last days now.'"[23]

Paul used virtually identical language in several places. Galatians 4:4 is one important example: "When the time had fully come, God sent his Son."[24] The term Paul used here, translated as "fully come," is *plērōma*, which conveys the thought of fulfillment or completion.[25] In using this term, Paul meant that the coming of Jesus Christ marked the fulfillment of earlier redemptive-historical expectations.[26] Paul also said that with the coming of our Lord the "fulfillment of the ages has come" (1 Cor. 10:11). It is clear that the church is living at the end of the age, since the dawn of the messianic age eclipsed the former premessianic era.[27]

The author of Hebrews made a similar point: "But now he [Jesus] has appeared once for all at the end of the ages to do away with sin by the sacrifice of himself" (Heb. 9:26). The author used the word *synteleia*, meaning "end" or "completion." As Hoekema notes, "In the one instance where this word is used with the plural of *aiōn* (age), it means the present era."[28] The phrase is, therefore, roughly synonymous with Matthew's phrase "the consummation of the ages," or Paul's phrase "ends of the ages," or even Peter's phrase "end of the times."[29] The author of Hebrews saw the first coming of Jesus Christ as the fulfillment of the promises of complete (in the sense of "once for all") redemption made under the old covenant. The coming of Jesus marked the beginning of the end of the ages. The last days began with his coming, since Jesus was the long-expected Messiah. This explains the futility of discussing eschatology apart from the person and work of Jesus Christ.

This Age and the Age to Come

The second aspect of New Testament eschatology is that what the Old Testament writers predicted as one movement must now be seen as two stages, one present and one future. This means that the New Testament believer, "while conscious that he was living in the new age predicted by the prophets, realized that this new age, ushered in by the coming of Jesus Christ, was perceived as bearing in its womb another age to come."[30] In other words, the Old Testament conception of eschatology was linear. They thought their age of world history would give way to the age to come. Yet, in the New Testament, it became clear that the age to come was realized in principle with the coming of Jesus Christ, though the "future age and world fully realized in solid existence" awaits the parousia.[31] Throughout the messianic era, the two ages overlap.

The New Testament writers understood that believers are now in the "last days," but there is still an "age to come" in which all redemptive-historical loose ends will be tied up and the final consummation of all things, such as the resurrection of the dead, the final judgment, and the re-creation of all things, will take place. Terms used to describe this coming age include:

> "that age" (*ho aiōn ekeinos*, Luke 20:35), "the age to come" (*ho aiōn erchomenos*, Luke 18:30), and "the age to come" (*ho aiōn mellon*, Matt. 12:32). The author of Hebrews, for example, states that certain people in this day have tasted "the powers of the age to come" (*mellontos aiōnos*, Heb. 6:5).[32]

Certainly the concept of prophetic perspective must be factored in here, as the Old Testament prophets predicted future events that, when viewed from their perspectives, seemed to point to a single great event. From the perspective of the postmessianic New Testament era, clearly two advents of our Lord are in view. The first marks the beginning of the age to come, while the second indicates the end of the present "evil" age.

Our Lord contrasted these two eschatological ages in such passages as Matthew 12:32, Luke 18:29–30, and Luke 20:34–35. Paul used this formulation to describe the relationship of the present to the future in Ephesians 1:21. In numerous texts, Paul spoke of "this age" or "this world" (Rom. 12:2; 1 Cor. 1:20; 2:6–8; 3:18; 2 Cor. 4:4; Gal. 1:4; Eph. 2:2; 1 Tim. 6:17; Titus 2:12). In other texts, Paul spoke of a "kingdom of God," which in many cases is synonymous with "age to come" (1 Cor. 6:9–10; 15:50; Gal. 5:21; Eph. 5:5; 1 Thess. 2:12; 2 Thess. 1:5; 2 Tim. 4:18).[33]

Much of the structure of New Testament eschatology is to be understood in terms of the contrast between "this age," ushered in by Christ and marked by the redemptive fullness of the Holy Spirit, and "the age to come" after the *eschatos* or "the end," which will bring an end to the course of history as God finally destroys the presence of sin in the universe. Neither Jesus nor Paul spoke of the future course of biblical history as entailing an earthly millennium.

Not One Coming of the Messiah but Two

The third aspect of New Testament eschatology is that the relationship of these two ages ensures that the blessings of the present age are a guarantee of the consummation of the age to come, which will bring even greater and final blessings. This means that the first coming of Christ marked the dawn of a new eschatological age with a corresponding set of redemptive-historical blessings, while the second coming of Christ will mark the end of the present course of history, ensuring the blessings of the consummation. The first coming of Christ guarantees the second.

This point may be illustrated from such texts as Acts 1:11, where Luke stated, "This same Jesus, who has been taken from you into heaven, will come back in the same way you have seen him go into heaven." We also see this in Acts 3:20–21: "And that he may send the Christ, who has been appointed for you—even Jesus. He must remain in heaven until the time comes for God to restore everything, as he promised long ago through his holy prophets." In Ephesians 1:13–14, Paul said much the same thing: "Having believed, you were marked in him with a seal, the promised Holy Spirit, who is a deposit guaranteeing our inheritance until the redemption of those who are God's possession—to the praise of his glory." In his letter to Titus, Paul informed us that "we wait for the blessed hope—the glorious appearing of our great God and Savior, Jesus Christ" (2:13). Likewise, in Hebrews 9:27–28, we read, "Just as man is destined to die once, and after that to face judgment, so Christ was sacrificed once to take away the sins of many people; and he will appear a second time, not to bear sin, but to bring salvation to those who are waiting for him."

As Richard Gaffin points out, this aspect of New Testament eschatology is most clearly seen in Christ's resurrection from the dead in relationship to the believer's own resurrection "in Christ."

> The unity of the resurrection of Christ and the resurrection of believers is such that the latter consists of two episodes in the experience of the individual believer—one which is already past, already realized, and one which is future, yet to be realized. In the period between the resurrection and the Parousia of Christ, any believer is one who has already been raised from the dead, and is yet to be raised. . . . The distinctive notion that the *eschatos*, the "age-to-come," is both present and future, is reflected in his teaching concerning the fundamental eschatological occurrence for the individual believer: his resurrection is both already and not yet.[34]

The first coming of Christ and his resurrection ensured that in the present age Christians are already raised with him. Christ's resurrection from the dead also ensured that we believers will be raised bodily at the end of the age (1 Cor. 15:42–44).

As a result of this basic structure of New Testament eschatology, the apostolic church expected the imminent return of the Lord Jesus Christ, an event that was to be the consummation of all human history. What the Old Testament prophets had predicted came to pass in the person of Jesus, and all the promised blessings under the old covenant were fulfilled by a new and better covenant. The coming of Jesus Christ brought a new eschatological age, which is a deposit guaranteeing a glorious and tumultuous end to this age as we know it. Because our Lord has come once, he will come again and in the same manner in which he went into heaven. Maranatha!

7

Christ and the Fulfillment of Prophecy

One of the most compelling lines of biblical evidence for the amillennial position is how a number of Old Testament prophecies were fulfilled in the New.[1] Setting these matters out carefully is important when treating the subject of the millennium, especially since dispensational premillenarians insist on a literal fulfillment of these prophecies in a future millennial age.

If these prophecies have already been fulfilled in Jesus Christ, much of the dispensational case for a future earthly millennium simply evaporates. Dispensationalists tell us that these prophecies remain unfulfilled until Jesus Christ returns to earth to establish his millennial kingdom. Paul, on the other hand, told us, "What Israel sought so earnestly it did not obtain, but the elect did. The others were hardened" (Rom. 11:7). Thus, true Israel, those Jews who have embraced Jesus Christ through faith, has already received the inheritance promised God's people, since they are the children of promise (Rom. 9:6–8).

Christ, the True Israel

When we use the prophetic vision of Israel's prophets and look to the future, what do we see? The prophets anticipated a time when Israel would be restored to her former greatness. Such a prophetic vision included not only the restoration of the nation but also a restoration of the land of Canaan, the city of Jerusalem, the throne of David, and the temple. The nation had been taken into captivity, the magnificent temple had been destroyed, and the priesthood

83

had gone some five centuries before Christ's first advent, so these prophetic expectations spoke of a reversal of fortune—the undoing of calamity that had come upon the nation. In fact, with apostolic hindsight Peter told of how "the prophets, who spoke . . . searched intently and with the greatest care, trying to find out the time and circumstances to which the Spirit of Christ in them was pointing when he predicted the sufferings of Christ and the glories that would follow" (1 Pet. 1:10–12).

The prophet Isaiah spoke of a future restoration of Israel in these terms: "But you, O Israel, my servant, Jacob, whom I have chosen, you descendants of Abraham my friend, I took you from the ends of the earth, from its farthest corners I called you. I said 'You are my servant'; I have chosen you and have not rejected you" (41:8–9). The same promise was reiterated in the next chapter of Isaiah (42:1–7), when the Lord declared of his servant, "I will keep you and will make you to be a covenant for the people and a light for the Gentiles" (v. 6). Isaiah continued to speak of this servant in chapters 44 (vv. 1–2) and 45 (v. 4). Dispensationalists, who interpret such passages literally, assign the fulfillment of Isaiah's prophecies to a future earthly millennium in which Israel will coexist with Gentiles under the reign of the Davidic king.[2] Is this how the New Testament interpreted these messianic prophecies regarding the servant of the Lord? Who is this servant of the Lord—the nation of Israel or Jesus, Israel's Messiah?

The Gospel writers interpreted these prophecies from Isaiah as fulfilled in the messianic mission of Jesus. As Jesus cast out demons and healed the sick, Matthew saw in this the fulfillment of Isaiah's prophecies of a suffering servant who would take upon himself our infirmities and carry our diseases (Matt. 8:17 with Isa. 53:4). Luke spoke of both Israel and David as servants of God (Luke 1:54, 69). Yet, in Acts, Luke pointedly spoke of Jesus as the servant of God (Acts 3:13). After Jesus's crucifixion, God raised him from the dead so that people everywhere might be called to repentance (Acts 3:26). Later on, when the Ethiopian eunuch read Isaiah 53:7–8 and asked Philip to whom this prophecy referred, Philip told him that this passage was about Jesus (Acts 8:34–35). But this is not all that is in view here.

The prophet Hosea quoted God as saying, "When Israel was a child, I loved him, and out of Egypt I called my son" (11:1). But Matthew told us that Hosea's prophecy was fulfilled when Jesus's parents took him to Egypt for a time as a baby to protect him from Herod's "slaughter of the innocents" (Matt. 2:13–18). Thus, Matthew, not the "spiritualizing amillenarian" centuries later, took a passage from Hosea that referred to Israel and told his readers that it was fulfilled in Jesus Christ.

According to many New Testament writers, Jesus was the true servant, the true Son, and the true Israel of God. Recall as well that Isaiah spoke of Israel

and the descendants of Abraham as the people of God. It was through the
seed of Abraham that the nations of the earth would be blessed. Therefore,
even as Jesus was the true Israel, he was the true seed of Abraham.

Paul made this point in Galatians 3:7–8 when he said that "those who believe are children of Abraham. The Scripture foresaw that God would justify
the Gentiles by faith, and announced the gospel in advance to Abraham: 'All
nations will be blessed through you.'" Paul's words here are important for
several reasons. First, they tell us that Abraham believed the same gospel that
Paul preached to the Gentile Galatians. There has been only one plan of salvation and one gospel from the very beginning. This, of course, raises serious
questions about the dispensational theory of distinct redemptive purposes
for national Israel and the Gentiles. Paul also explained, "If you belong to
Christ, then you are Abraham's seed, and heirs according to the promise"
(Gal. 3:29). From the beginning of redemptive history, the true children of
Abraham, whether Jews or Gentiles, will be heirs of God's promise if they
belong to Jesus Christ, the true seed of Abraham.[3]

The ramifications for this on one's millennial view should now be obvious.
The New Testament writers claimed that Jesus was the true Israel of God
and the fulfillment of Old Testament prophecies. So what remains of the
dispensationalists' case that these prophecies will yet be fulfilled in a future
millennium? They vanish in Jesus Christ, who has fulfilled them.

The Land of Canaan, the City of Jerusalem, and the Mountain of the Lord

When God established his covenant with Abraham and his descendants after
him "to be your God and the God of your descendants after you," he also
promised the great patriarch, "The whole land of Canaan, where you are now
an alien, I will give as an everlasting possession to you and your descendants
after you; and I will be their God" (Gen. 17:7–8). According to classical dispensationalists, this promise was "an unconditional covenant made with Israel
and therefore cannot be either abrogated or fulfilled by people other than the
nation Israel."[4] In other words, God's unconditional promise of a land to
Abraham's descendants is everlasting and therefore can be fulfilled only by
the return of national Israel to her ancient homeland.

At first glance, this appears to be a compelling argument, especially since
the nation of Israel was formed in Palestine in 1948, amounting to a return of
the Jews to the land of their fathers. But once again the critical question is,
How did the authors of the New Testament view this prophecy?

To answer this question, we must first answer a different one. How did Israel's own prophets understand this promise of a land that God made to Abraham? Once again, returning to the words of Isaiah, we find language such as this:

"Behold, I will create new heavens and a new earth. The former things will not be remembered, nor will they come to mind. But be glad and rejoice forever in what I will create, for I will create Jerusalem to be a delight and its people a joy. I will rejoice over Jerusalem and take delight in my people; the sound of weeping and of crying will be heard in it no more. Never again will there be in it an infant who lives but a few days, or an old man who does not live out his years; he who dies at a hundred will be thought a mere youth; he who fails to reach a hundred will be considered accursed. They will build houses and dwell in them; they will plant vineyards and eat their fruit. No longer will they build houses and others live in them, or plant and others eat. For as the days of a tree, so will be the days of my people; my chosen ones will long enjoy the works of their hands. They will not toil in vain or bear children doomed to misfortune; for they will be a people blessed by the LORD, they and their descendants with them. Before they call I will answer; while they are still speaking I will hear. The wolf and the lamb will feed together, and the lion will eat straw like the ox, but dust will be the serpent's food. They will neither harm nor destroy on all my holy mountain," says the LORD. (Isa. 65:17–25; cf. 66:22)

The promise of the land in Canaan made to Abraham was reinterpreted by Isaiah to mean a new heaven and a new earth, not just the land of Canaan. This is an easy claim to make, but what is the evidence for it?

As we have seen, Joshua regarded God's promise of the land of Canaan as provisionally fulfilled when Israel took possession after the exodus (Josh. 1:2–9; 21:43). Israel's prophets, writing during the exile, when Israel had been cast from the land, universalized the promise of a land in Canaan to include a new heaven and a new earth, the fruit of the eschatological victory won by the suffering servant and conquering king.[5] Because God swore the oath of ratification in the covenant of promise, God ensured that the everlasting promise entailed by the covenant would be realized. This would be true even if God's covenant people disobeyed and lost their inheritance, receiving instead divine sanctions, such as being cast from the land.

The idea of land promised under the Abrahamic covenant was also universalized in several passages in the New Testament. In his Epistle to the Romans, Paul described the role of Abraham in redemptive history. Notice again the promise God made to Abraham: "I will establish my covenant as an everlasting covenant between me and you and your descendants after you for the generations to come. . . . The whole land of Canaan . . . I will give as an everlasting possession" (Gen. 17:7–8). In Romans 4:13, Paul saw the fulfillment of this as follows: "It was not through law that Abraham and his offspring received the promise that he would be heir of the world, but through the righteousness that comes by faith." As Robert Strimple so aptly puts it, "Where in the Old Testament do you find the promise that Paul refers to here? Nowhere if you insist on a strict literalism. But you find it in Genesis 17:8 . . . if you see that this is inspired apostolic interpretation of the Old Testament promise that Paul is giving us here."[6]

The author of Hebrews made a similar point when he wrote that ultimately Abraham was not looking just to Canaan, even though he and his descendants after him lived in the Promised Land. Abraham "was looking forward to the city with foundations, whose architect and builder is God" (Heb. 11:10). Peter also picked up on this prophetic expansion of the Promised Land when he wrote, "In keeping with his [God's] promise we are looking forward to a new heaven and a new earth, the home of righteousness" (2 Pet. 3:13). The inheritance promised to Abraham, which was couched in premessianic terms as a reference to the land of Canaan, was, after Israel took possession of the land under Joshua, subsequently reinterpreted by Isaiah, Paul, the author of Hebrews, and Peter as a new heaven and a new earth.[7]

If the New Testament writers did in fact reinterpret the promise of a land in terms of a new heaven and a new earth, this raises great difficulties for premillenarians who assign these prophecies to an earthly millennial age—a halfway consummation yet to dawn—instead of understanding these promises in terms of a new creation and the final consummation. If this interpretation is correct, amillenarians are no less literal in their hermeneutic than the New Testament writers.

This same pattern of a premessianic prophecy being reinterpreted in the New Testament also holds for those prophecies dealing with the city of Jerusalem and the mountain of the Lord. Like the prophet Isaiah, Micah gave us the following vision of what lies ahead:

> In the last days the mountain of the LORD's temple will be established as chief among the mountains; it will be raised above the hills, and peoples will stream to it. Many nations will come and say, "Come, let us go up to the mountain of the LORD, to the house of the God of Jacob. He will teach us his ways, so that we may walk in his paths." The law will go out from Zion, the word of the LORD from Jerusalem. He will judge between many peoples and will settle disputes for strong nations far and wide. They will beat their swords into plowshares and their spears into pruning hooks. Nation will not take up sword against nation, nor will they train for war anymore. Every man will sit under his own vine and

under his own fig tree, and no one will make them afraid, for the LORD Almighty
has spoken. All the nations may walk in the name of their gods; we will walk
in the name of the LORD our God for ever and ever. (4:1–5)

In this amazing vision, Micah foresaw not only a glorious time for Israel but also
a period in which the knowledge of the Lord will extend to the very ends of the
earth. Dispensationalists are clear about how this prophecy is to be interpreted.
This text, they say, along with a similar passage in Isaiah 2:2–4, refers to Israel's
future exaltation during the millennial age when the city of Jerusalem is the seat
of God's millennial government.[8] But this is an erroneous interpretation because
it ignores an important step in the interpretive process, namely, how the New
Testament writers understood this prophecy in light of the coming of Jesus Christ.

The pattern for how these premessianic images were interpreted should
now be clear. We ask one more time, What did the New Testament writers
do with these Old Testament prophecies?

The author of the Epistle to the Hebrews could not be more clear about
how he understood this prophecy. Though Old Testament prophets spoke of
the earthly city of Jerusalem, the New Testament writers did not say these
prophecies would be fulfilled in a future earthly Jerusalem. On the contrary,
the author of Hebrews said the prophecy was already fulfilled in the person
and work of Jesus Christ.

> You have not come to a mountain that can be touched and that is burning with
> fire; to darkness, gloom and storm; to a trumpet blast or to such a voice speaking
> words that those who heard it begged that no further word be spoken to them,
> because they could not bear what was commanded: "If even an animal touches
> the mountain, it must be stoned." The sight was so terrifying that Moses said,
> "I am trembling with fear." But you have come to Mount Zion, to the heavenly
> Jerusalem, the city of the living God. You have come to thousands upon thou-
> sands of angels in joyful assembly, to the church of the firstborn, whose names
> are written in heaven. You have come to God, the judge of all men, to the spirits
> of righteous men made perfect, to Jesus the mediator of a new covenant, and to
> the sprinkled blood that speaks a better word than the blood of Abel. (12:18–24)

In Jesus Christ, the heavenly Jerusalem has already come, even now.[9]

This point is especially problematic for postmillenarians who see Micah
4:1–5 and Isaiah 2:2–4 as important texts supporting the idea that a millennial
age, in which the nations will turn to Christ, is yet to dawn in this present age.
Agreeing with amillenarians that this prophecy is fulfilled before the second
advent of Jesus Christ, postmillenarians see this passage as finding fulfillment
in the last days in which "a spiritually renewed church attracts the nations

(v. 2) to the Christian faith by the vitality and depth of its worship, doctrine and life."[10] The problem with the postmillennial interpretation is simply this: If it is self-evident that this prophecy has not yet been fulfilled, why did the author of Hebrews speak of the fulfillment as a present reality? We can go a step farther. Strimple shows us that postmillenarians "must view Christ's kingly reign as a *failure* so far."[11] This, it seems to me, is highly problematic.

Yet, dispensationalists will undoubtedly remind us that the same author who said that in Jesus Christ the new Jerusalem has already come also said in the next chapter, "We are looking for the city that is to come" (Heb. 13:14). This is a problem for dispensationalists because they fail to distinguish between the earthly copy and the heavenly reality.[12] The earthly city is a redemptive-historical picture of a heavenly reality yet to come.

A word of explanation is in order. The apostle John spoke of the new Jerusalem as though it were yet future (Rev. 21:2). When we look more closely at the text, however, we see that this heavenly city is even now coming down from heaven. The new creation, which will be consummated with the coming of Christ in judgment on the last day, has already been inaugurated and is a present reality for the people of God.[13] But how can the new Jerusalem be said to be both present and future?

To understand this, we need to distinguish between the earthly copy and the heavenly reality. The author of Hebrews distinguished between earthly and heavenly things: "It was necessary, then, for the copies of the heavenly things to be purified with these sacrifices, but the heavenly things themselves with better sacrifices than these. For Christ did not enter a man-made sanctuary that was only a copy of the true one; he entered heaven itself, now to appear for us in God's presence" (9:23–24). When we speak of the premessianic prophetic expectations regarding the city of Jerusalem and the mountain of the Lord as fulfilled in Christ but awaiting a final consummation at the end of the age, we are speaking of the earthly Jerusalem serving as a type or a copy of the heavenly reality, which now is realized in principle. If true, this strikes a serious blow to the root of dispensational and premillennial expectations about Jesus reigning over an earthly kingdom from a new Jerusalem. The earthly Jerusalem was intended to point us to Jesus Christ and to serve as a shadow of the realities to come when God makes all things new.

David's Greater Son

Dispensationalists place great weight on their interpretation of the Abrahamic covenant, but the Davidic covenant is right behind it in terms of importance.[14]

Based on God's promise that he would establish the kingdom of David's son forever (2 Sam. 7:12–16), dispensationalists believe this promise was partially fulfilled in the first coming of Christ, with the final fulfillment delayed because of Israel's stubborn refusal to embrace Jesus as her messianic king. This prophecy stated that the throne of David will be established forever. Since dispensationalists believe that such prophecies must be interpreted literally, this necessitates a literal rule of Jesus Christ on the earth during a future millennial kingdom. At that time the postponed kingdom will be finally consummated. John Walvoord feels so strongly about the literal fulfillment of this prophecy that he believes amillenarians commit exegetical fraud by spiritualizing literal prophecies such as this one.[15]

Since no one wants to be guilty of such an offense, the safest course of action is to return to the New Testament interpretation of the Davidic covenant. Before we do so, we ought to note that the prophecy of 2 Samuel 7 does not stand alone. In the famous words of Isaiah 9:7, we read, regarding the coming Redeemer, that "of the increase of his government and peace there will be no end. He will reign on David's throne and over his kingdom, establishing and upholding it with justice and righteousness from that time on and forever." In Psalm 2:7–9, we find the following: "I will proclaim the decree of the LORD: He said to me, 'You are my Son; today I have become your Father. Ask of me, and I will make the nations your inheritance, the ends of the earth your possession. You will rule them with an iron scepter; you will dash them to pieces like pottery.'" That a descendant of David would return to Israel and rule over his kingdom was a major aspect of the prophetic expectation of Israel and occupied a significant role in the New Testament.

From the beginning of Jesus's messianic mission, his identity as the heir to David's throne was clearly established. In Matthew's Gospel, Jesus's link to David was established through the use of genealogy (1:1–17). In the birth narrative in Luke's Gospel, Luke informed his readers that the angel Gabriel told Mary:

> Do not be afraid, Mary, you have found favor with God. You will be with child and give birth to a son, and you are to give him the name Jesus. He will be great and will be called the Son of the Most High. The Lord God will give him the throne of his father David, and he will reign over the house of Jacob forever; his kingdom will never end. (1:30–33)

According to Matthew and Luke, the prophecies of Samuel, Isaiah, and the psalmist were fulfilled in Jesus. But how does his birth fulfill the prophecy of an everlasting kingdom?

The answer to this is also found in Luke's writings, though not in the infancy narratives. When Peter delivered the Pentecost sermon, he preached to Jews who did not yet believe that Jesus was the Christ. To make his case, he had to demonstrate that Jesus was exactly who he claimed to be. The two most effective tools to do this were the apologetic arguments from fulfilled prophecy and miracle. Therefore, Peter pointed out that the eternal kingdom promised to David's son was finally realized in the resurrection of Jesus. Because Jesus conquered death and the grave, Peter could say with confidence:

> Brothers, I can tell you confidently that the patriarch David died and was buried, and his tomb is here to this day. But he was a prophet and knew that God had promised him on oath that he would place one of his descendants on his throne. Seeing what was ahead, he spoke of the resurrection of the Christ, that he was not abandoned to the grave, nor did his body see decay. God has raised this Jesus to life, and we are all witnesses of the fact. Exalted to the right hand of God, he has received from the Father the promised Holy Spirit and has poured out what you now see and hear. For David did not ascend to heaven, and yet he said, "The Lord said to my Lord: 'Sit at my right hand until I make your enemies a footstool for your feet.'" Therefore let all Israel be assured of this: God has made this Jesus, whom you crucified, both Lord and Christ. (Acts 2:29–36)

It was in Christ's resurrection and ascension, therefore, that God fulfilled his promise that David's greater son would rule the nations with an everlasting kingdom. People's greatest foe is death, and in his resurrection Jesus emerged victorious. This is why his kingdom is everlasting and why he is both Lord and Christ. When dispensationalists complain that amillenarians spiritualize these great Old Testament prophecies by saying they are fulfilled in Jesus Christ, perhaps they should take this up with the apostles who did the very thing of which dispensationalists are so critical.

Christ, the True Temple

Jesus declared of himself, "One greater than the temple is here" (Matt. 12:6) and told the Samaritan woman that he could give her "living water" (John 4:10–14). Such declarations give us a major clue that the authors of the New Testament reinterpreted the premessianic understanding of God's temple in light of the coming of Israel's Messiah. The temple occupied a principal role in the witness of Israel's prophets regarding God's future eschatological blessing for the nation. When we see that this imagery pointed forward to Jesus, we can better understand the nature and character of the millennial age.

Let us consider the Old Testament expectations regarding the temple of the Lord. Both Isaiah 2:2–4 and Micah 4:1–5 speak of God's future blessing on Israel in the last days when his people will go up to the temple on the mountain of the Lord and learn his ways. In Isaiah 56, we read of those who hold fast to God's covenant (v. 4) and love the name of the Lord and keep his Sabbaths (vv. 6–8). God will bring them to the holy mountain and the temple, which will be a house of prayer for all nations (v. 7). A similar vision was given in Isaiah 66:20–21, which says that the Israelites will bring their grain offerings to God's temple, and he will renew his priesthood. In Zechariah's prophetic vision, we learn that one day Israel will once again offer sacrifices acceptable to God (14:16–19).

With all this prophetic expectation in the minds of Jews living in Palestine in the first century, it is no wonder that Jesus's declaration of God's judgment on the temple—"Not one stone here will be left on another; every one will be thrown down" (Matt. 24:2)—came as a shocking offense. How dare this man say that their expectation of a glorious temple was fulfilled in him! He said, "Destroy this temple, and I will raise it again in three days" (John 2:19). It was not until after Christ's resurrection that the meaning of these words became plain to his disciples. When he spoke of the destruction of the temple, he was speaking of his own body (John 2:22). This is what he meant when he said that one greater than the temple had come.

Ezekiel prophesied that the temple will be rebuilt, the priesthood will be reestablished, sacrifices will be offered, and the river of life will flow from the temple. How we interpret this prophecy will have a significant bearing on the question of a future millennial age on the earth.

It should come as no surprise that dispensationalists believe that this prophecy will be literally fulfilled in the millennial age. According to J. Dwight Pentecost:

> The glorious vision of Ezekiel reveals that it is impossible to locate its fulfillment in any past temple or system which Israel has known, but it must await a future fulfillment after the second advent of Christ when the millennium is instituted. The sacrificial system is not a reinstituted Judaism, but the establishment of a new order that has as its purpose the remembrance of the work of Christ on which all salvation rests. The literal fulfillment of Ezekiel's prophecy will be the means of God's glorification and man's blessing in the millennium.[16]

Traditional amillenarians criticize such images of perpetual animal sacrifices and temple worship after the second advent of Christ, saying this would undercut his saving work, especially since these aspects of Mosaic economy were fulfilled at Calvary.[17] So Pentecost is careful to argue that Ezekiel's prophecy is not connected to a renewed Mosaic economy but to an entirely new order, one that commemorates the saving work of Christ in the past.

But is this what the authors of the New Testament taught about these prophecies? We have already seen that the New Testament taught that Christ is the true Israel and David's greater son. The Old Testament prophecies regarding Jerusalem and the mountain of the Lord are fulfilled in Christ's church. The promise of a land, as we have seen, will be fulfilled in a new heaven and a new earth in the consummation. Likewise, the New Testament taught that Christ is the new temple and that a new order of commemoration involving the ceremonies typical of the earthly temple can only commemorate the types and shadows, not the reality. This presents a serious problem for dispensationalists, who argue, in effect, that redemptive history takes a U-turn in the millennial age, as the reality in Christ supposedly returns to the types and shadows of the Old Testament.

How, then, is the temple imagery from the Old Testament fulfilled by Jesus Christ in the New? In Exodus 40:34, we are told that the glory of the Lord filled his temple. When viewed against the backdrop of redemptive history, we see how this pointed to Pentecost, when, through the indwelling Holy Spirit, the glory of the Lord filled his true temple, the mystical body of Jesus Christ (1 Cor. 12:12ff.).[18] If Christ's body is the true temple and as Paul put it, "We are the temple of the living God" (2 Cor. 6:16), what use remains for a future literal temple? That to which the temple had pointed is now a reality through the work of the Holy Spirit. Why return to the type and shadow?

It is also clear from Hebrews 8–10 that Jesus fulfilled the priesthood typology of the Old Testament in his death, and he put an end to the sacrificial system in his own blood once and for all. The author of Hebrews said, "We do have such a high priest, who sat down at the right hand of the throne of the Majesty in heaven, and who serves in the sanctuary, the true tabernacle set up by the Lord, not by man" (8:1–2). If the reality to which the Old Testament sacrifices and priesthood pointed is found in this true sanctuary and tabernacle in heaven, why look for a return to the shadows in the form of an earthly temple, which pointed us to this heavenly scene?

Contrary to the view of dispensationalists, the prescribed New Testament commemoration of the ratification of the new covenant will not be found in a new order of temple worship, which includes a new temple, a new priesthood, and animal sacrifices, supposedly in an earthly millennial kingdom. At the Last Supper, Jesus told his disciples, "This is my body given for you; do this in remembrance of me. . . . This cup is the new covenant in my blood, which is poured out for you" (Luke 22:19–20). He instituted the divinely approved method of commemorating his sacrificial work, the sacrament of the Lord's Supper. In this way, the people of God feed on the Savior through faith and commemorate his dying on their behalf.

Jesus told the Samaritan woman that he could give her living water and that "whoever drinks the water I give him will never thirst" (John 4:14). Jesus declared that he fulfilled the image Ezekiel foretold in chapter 37 of his prophecy when he spoke of water flowing from the sanctuary.[19] If Jesus is the true temple of God, he alone gives us the "living water" that takes away the thirst of human sin and longing.

Therefore, the dispensationalists' insistence on a return in the millennial age to the types of the Old Testament sacrificial system amounts to a serious misunderstanding of the nature of redemptive history. By arguing for a new commemorative order based on Old Testament typology in the millennial age, dispensationalists see the future not as a consummation but as a return to the past. And this, of course, sadly obscures the person and work of Christ by seeing the ultimate reality not in him but in the types and shadows destined to perish when the reality entered the theater of redemption.

8

The Nature of New Testament Eschatology

In surveying the basic eschatological structure of the New Testament, I noted that biblical writers understood the course and future climax of human history as the progressive unfolding of two successive eschatological ages: "this age" and "the age to come." These two ages have a strong bearing on whether or not there will be an earthly millennium.

These two ages provide a major interpretive category for eschatology in general and the millennial question in particular. The case for amillennialism grows directly out of an understanding of these two eschatological ages.

The Two-Age Model as an Interpretive Grid

We now turn to the overall framework provided by the New Testament writers, who spoke of eschatological matters with one voice. They depicted God's sovereign control of history as distinct and successive eschatological ages known as "this age" and "the age to come." Throughout the New Testament, "this age" refers to the present course of human history, while "the age to come" refers to the age of redemption realized with the coming of Jesus Christ, his bodily resurrection, and his exaltation.

The period of time between the first and second advent of Jesus Christ— the time between the establishment of Christ's kingdom as described in the Gospels and the consummation of all things—is the same period described in Revelation 20 as a "thousand years." This means that the so-called millennium is a present reality and not a future hope. The events depicted in Revelation 20 refer not to the future but to the present. The thousand years is that same period of time in which citizens of this age await the age to come. However, given the present reality of the kingdom of God (Matt. 12:28; Luke 10:1–20; 17:20–21; Rom. 14:17) and the work of the Holy Spirit (Eph. 1:13–14), the age to come is already a present reality for believers in Jesus Christ. This tension between the already and the not yet characterizes much of New Testament eschatology as Christians await the final consummation of Christ's present kingdom on the great and glorious day of the Lord Jesus.

As Geerhardus Vos points out, "Christianity in its very origin bears an eschatological character. It means the appearance of the Messiah and the inauguration of His work." Therefore, the starting point in developing this Christ-centered eschatology is "the historico-dramatic conception of the two successive ages," which are variously designated "this age" and "the age to come."[1] According to Vos, since the very fabric of redemption itself is eschatological, the key to understanding Christ-centered eschatology is to correlate eschatological language regarding these two ages to the historical events surrounding the person and work of Jesus Christ. This will become clear when we examine phrases such as "this age" and "the age to come" and the biblical texts in which they occur.

Both Jesus and Paul repeatedly spoke of this age and the age to come as two successive and qualitatively distinct eschatological periods. In three places in the synoptic Gospels, our Lord explicitly contrasted "this age" with "an age to come." In Matthew 12:32, Jesus spoke of the impossibility of forgiveness for blasphemy against the Holy Spirit either "in this age or the age to come." In Luke 18:29–30, Jesus spoke about the kingdom of God in response to the unbelief expressed by the rich young ruler. Jesus said, "I tell you the truth, . . . no one who has left home or wife or brothers or parents or children for the sake of the kingdom of God will fail to receive many times as much in this age and, in the age to come, eternal life." In Luke 20:34–36, Jesus declared, "The people of this age marry and are given in marriage. But those who are considered worthy of taking part in that age and in the resurrection from the dead will neither marry nor be given in marriage, and they can no longer die; for they are like the angels. They are God's children, since they are children of the resurrection."

These texts make it clear that our Lord understood these two ages as successive and qualitatively distinct. This age, Jesus said, is characterized by marriage and things temporal. The age to come, on the other hand, is characterized by resurrection life and immortality. So it is impossible that natural, earthly life will continue after the general resurrection that will occur at our Lord's return (John 6:39–40, 44, 54). The idea of a general resurrection occurring at Christ's second advent presents a serious problem for premillennialists who argue that people in natural bodies continue to populate the earth during Christ's millennial rule after the resurrection of the righteous. If the age to come is the age of resurrection in which there are no marriages or sexual relationships, how can people escape this universal event and repopulate the earth after Christ returns? This is an impossibility.

Paul set out the same eschatological understanding of history in Ephesians 1:21, speaking of the present exaltation of Jesus Christ, who is "far above all rule and authority, power and dominion, and every title that can be given, not only in the present age but also in the one to come." Like Jesus, Paul saw these two ages as consecutive and distinct, though Paul added that Christ's rule is already a present reality that began with his resurrection and exaltation.[2]

The impact of this two-age eschatological framework on the question of millennialism becomes apparent when we examine how these terms are used throughout the New Testament. Whenever "this age" is used, it is always in reference to things temporal, things destined to perish. Consider the following things predicted by the biblical writers regarding this age. The end of the age will be preceded by signs (Matt. 24:3), and Christ himself will be with us until this age ends (Matt. 28:20). There are material rewards in this age (Luke 18:30), and the people of this age marry and are given in marriage (Luke 20:34). According to Mark, the present age is an age of homes, fields, and families (Mark 10:30).

Paul, on the other hand, put this in ethical terms. We are not to be conformed to the pattern of this age (Rom. 12:2), for this present age is evil (Gal. 1:4). The wisdom of this age is the godless speculation of philosophers (1 Cor. 1:20) and is characterized by rulers who do not know the truth (1 Cor. 2:6–8). In fact, Satan himself is the "god" of this age (2 Cor. 4:4), for the ways of this age are evil (Eph. 2:2). Paul exhorted those who are rich in this age not to put their hopes in their riches for the age to come (1 Tim. 6:17), for we are to live godly lives now as we await the age to come (Titus 2:12–13).

In every case, the qualities assigned by the biblical writers to this age were always temporal in nature and represented the fallen world and its sinful inhabitants awaiting the judgment to come at the Lord's return. This becomes clear when we see this age as the biblical writers intended—an age that stands in stark contrast to the eschatological age to come.

What do the Scriptures say about the age to come?[3] The Gospel writers recorded our Lord as saying that there will be no forgiveness in the age to come for speaking blasphemy against the Holy Spirit (Matt. 12:32). It is a period of judgment when the weeds will be thrown into the fire (Matt. 13:40). It is also an age of eternal life (Mark 10:30; Luke 18:30) and when there is no longer marriage or giving in marriage. It is an age, said Paul, where life is truly life (1 Tim. 6:19).

This means that the age to come is an age of eternal life and immortality. It is characterized by the realization of all the blessings of the resurrection and consummation. It is not an age in which people await the consummation. When we consider those additional texts in which Paul spoke of the consummation of the kingdom of God, the evidence against premillennialism becomes even stronger. According to Paul, evildoers will not inherit this kingdom (1 Cor. 6:9–10), while flesh and blood cannot (1 Cor. 15:50). Those who live evil lives will not enter this kingdom (Gal. 5:21) nor will the immoral (Eph. 5:5). Thus, it is clear that the age to come refers to that period of time after the resurrection, the judgment, and the restoration of all things. Those who participate in the age to come are no longer characterized by the temporal but the eternal. This point is particularly problematic for premillennialists who insist on an earthly existence in a millennial age of halfway consummation after Christ's return.[4] It also is a problem for preterists (full and partial) who see this age as the Jewish era and the age to come as that which followed God's judgment on Israel in AD 70.[5]

The inability of dispensationalists in particular to refute this argument becomes clear when we look at how they deal with the rather extensive biblical data about the two ages. As J. Dwight Pentecost argues:

> As it is used in the New Testament, according to the normal usage of the words, *this present age* refers to that period of time in which the speaker or writer then lived. As used in reference to Israel in the Gospels *this present age* referred to the period of time in which Israel was anticipating the coming of the Messiah to fulfill all her covenant promises. The coming age was the age to be inaugurated by the Messiah at His advent. In reference to the church the term *this present age* refers to the inter-advent period, that period from the rejection of the Messiah by Israel at His second coming. The phrase *coming age* could be used in its earthly aspect, to which the church will be related (as in Eph. 1:21), or in its eternal aspect (as in Eph. 2:7).[6]

But are we justified in saying that the coming age was to be inaugurated but was not because Israel rejected her Messiah? Does the age to come have an earthly aspect as well as an eternal one? Pentecost's understanding of this matter simply does not fit with the data we have already seen, and it seems as though the two ages have not been properly considered as a major interpretive grid.

Elliot Johnson has tried to weaken the thrust of this argument by pointing out that since so many interpreters of the New Testament cannot agree on what is entailed by the terms *already* and *not yet*, it must be because the terms fail to clarify what is already fulfilled and what remains yet to be fulfilled.[7]

The solution to this overstated dilemma is to connect the terms *already* and *not yet* to the more concrete terms *this age* and *the age to come*. The already refers to the eternal blessings of the age to come that are realized in the present, while the not yet refers to the blessings of the age to come to be realized in the consummation. Neither dispensationalists nor millenarians in general can account for the significance of the biblical writers' view of history as a successive unfolding of two distinct eschatological ages.

The Implausibility of Premillennialism

The Scriptures explicitly tell us that the line of demarcation between these two ages is our Lord's second advent: "The harvest [of wheat] is the end of the age, and the harvesters are angels. As the weeds are pulled up and burned in the fire, so it will be at the end of the age. . . . This is how it will be at the end of the age. The angels will come and separate the wicked from the righteous and throw them in the fiery furnace, where there will be weeping and gnashing of teeth" (Matt. 13:39–40, 49–50). This passage seems to strike a serious blow against all forms of premillennialism. Premillennialists insist that the judgment occurs at the end of the millennial age, fully one thousand years after our Lord's return.[8] Indeed, this separation of the two bodily resurrections by a one-thousand-year interval has been called the "linchpin of premillennialism."[9]

Premillenarians arrive at this conclusion, they say, because their hermeneutic is based on a literal interpretation of the Scriptures.[10] But the biblical writers clearly (literally) told us that the judgment will occur at the time of our Lord's return: "When the Son of Man comes in his glory, and all the angels with him, he will sit on his throne in heavenly glory. All the nations will be gathered before him, and he will separate the people one from another as a shepherd separates the sheep from the goats" (Matt. 25:31–32; cf. Matt. 13:40–43). Premillennialists, instead, insist that there is a one-thousand-year gap between our Lord's return and the final judgment, the millennium of Revelation 20. Premillenarians must attempt to sidestep the clear teaching of Scripture that the resurrection (1 Cor. 15:35–57; 1 Thess. 4:13–5:11; 2 Thess. 1:5–10), the restoration of all things (2 Pet. 3:3–15), and the judgment occur at the same time—at our Lord's second advent. Based on a literal reading, just where is the millennial gap in these texts? Premillenarians cannot have it both ways. Even an appeal to progressive revelation fails. If the apostle John introduced a gap in Revelation 20 to explain Jesus's earlier teaching in the Olivet Discourse, then there is also a second fall of humanity to go along with it.[11] The problem of evil in the millennial age is a serious problem for all forms of premillennialism and is a point to which we will turn shortly.

John's Gospel is equally important regarding the resurrection and the judgment, for he taught that Jesus Christ will raise his own "on the last day," because those who believe in the Son already possess eternal life. For believers in Jesus Christ, the first resurrection has already come to pass (cf. John 5:24–25 with Rev. 20:4–5). Those who are Christ's have already crossed over from death to life and will be raised at the last day (John 6:39–40, 44). When our Lord consoled Martha after the death of Lazarus, Martha said, "I know he will rise again in the resurrection at the last day" (John 11:24). When we consider Paul's comments that the sinful nature, but not the spirit, will be destroyed on "the day of the Lord" (1 Cor. 5:5); that the resurrection occurs "at the last trumpet" (1 Cor. 15:52); that "the day of the Lord" will come as a thief (1 Thess. 5:2); and that it is still future (2 Thess. 2:2), an impressive case can be made that the resurrection, the judgment, and the re-creation are all concomitant events.

This presents a serious problem for all premillennialists (whether they be dispensational, progressive, or historic) who insist on separating the resurrection and the final judgment by a future one-thousand-year earthly reign of Jesus Christ over a halfway redeemed earth. The Scriptures do not allow for such a gap nor for such unredeemed elements to exist in the age to come after the *eschaton*.

The most serious problem faced by all premillenarians is the presence of evil in the millennial age. Recall that the thousand years depicted in Revelation 20 begin with the binding of Satan when he is prevented from deceiving the nations. When the thousand years have ended, Satan is released and again deceives the nations. This culminates in a worldwide revolt against God's people and a fiery and final judgment from heaven on Satan and his cronies, the beast and the false prophet. If the thousand years do not begin until after the second coming of Christ, as premillenarians insist, then we must pointedly ask, Who are these people who are deceived and then revolt against Jesus Christ?

We have already seen from several passages in the Gospels and Paul's letters that the resurrection, judgment, and re-creation have already occurred at the coming of Christ. This age of things fallen and temporal has already come to an end. The age to come of immortality, resurrection life, and no marriage is now a glorious reality in an already/not yet scheme. The last day has already come, and our Lord has raised his own and sent those who are not his into the fires of eternal judgment. There simply cannot be people in unresurrected bodies on the earth after our Lord's return, for the wheat has already been separated from the weeds (Matt. 13:37–43), the sheep have already been separated from the goats (Matt. 25:31–46), and the elect have already been gathered from the four corners of the earth by the angelic host (Matt. 24:30–31).

Who are these people who are still on earth at the end of the millennial age who revolt against Christ? Are they the redeemed? If so, the premillennialist has just introduced a second fall of humanity into sin into the course of redemptive history. This time, however, we have a fall of glorified saints after the resurrection and the judgment. This simply cannot be, though premillennial commentators ignore the force of this, choosing instead to make the hermeneutical crux an overly rigid exegesis of the first resurrection of Revelation 20:5,[12] often overlooking the important parallel passage in John 5:24–25, which explicitly tells us when the first resurrection occurs—at the moment of conversion.

Premillennialists, who insist on a literal one thousand years in Revelation 20:2, do so even though the consequence of this exegetical decision is the revolt of the redeemed against the Redeemer in verses 7–10. This is problematic when it is debatable whether such numbers used in apocalyptic literature were intended by the author to be taken in a literal sense in the first place.[13] Is it not better to see Revelation 20 as a description of the age of the church militant and the present reign of Christ?

This is also consistent with Paul's statement to the Corinthians in which the apostle spoke of the present reign of Christ in anticipation of the final consummation. When Christ comes, so will the end. Amillenarians interpret this text as follows.

For as in Adam all die, so in Christ all will be made alive [at the resurrection]. But each in his own turn [*tagmati*]: Christ, the firstfruits [in his own resurrection power]; then, when he comes, those who belong to him [those alive and those asleep in Christ]. Then [the very next thing] the end will come [the final judgment], when he hands over the kingdom to God the Father after he has destroyed all dominion, authority and power [at his return]. For he must reign [from his coronation in his ascension] until he has put all his enemies under his feet [at the time of his return]. The last enemy to be destroyed is death [in the resurrection]. For he "has put everything under his feet." Now when it [everything] has been put under him, it is clear that this does not include God himself, who put everything under Christ. When he has done this, then the Son himself will be made subject to him who put everything under him, so that God may be in all. (1 Cor. 15:22–28)

Premillenarians see this passage as a proof text for their interpretation.[14] In 1 Corinthians 15, "Paul understood this final triumph to take place during the millennial reign of Christ . . . following His return and prior to the eternal state, a time that Revelation 20:4–6 calls the 'thousand years.'"[15] Robert Duncan Culver asks the key question in this regard, "Does Paul here speak of three redemptive-historical events?" Culver frames the matter as follows:

> Do the words . . . "Christ the firstfruits," . . . "afterward they that are Christ's at his coming" . . . [and] "then cometh the end" specify three groups in the resurrection of men?—one composed of Christ Himself, a resurrection now past; one of those who are Christ's at His parousia, yet future; and, still another at a time more remote at the "end" of the series of resurrections composed of "the rest of the dead" (Rev. 20:5). If so, then this passage clearly teaches premillennialism.[16]

But as critics of the premillennial view have long pointed out, if Paul taught such a thousand-year interval between the parousia and the end, "it seems unthinkable that Paul, if he believed in such a kingdom, should pass over it without a word."[17]

As is often pointed out by amillenarians, the word *eita* ("then") can mean "thereupon" and in no sense implies any such delay between Christ's coming and the end.[18] The implication is that the end comes immediately at the time of Christ's appearing. If true, Paul's point is that Christ's coming is accompanied by the "resurrection of Christians [and] ushers in the end, at which the main event is the handing over of the kingdom by Christ to God."[19]

Despite their professed literal method of interpretation, premillenarians must find or insert these long intervals between resurrections to support the separation of the final judgment from Christ's coming, justifying a one-thousand-year earthly millennium. And in doing so, they must live with the theological problem this creates, the presence of evil during the millennial age after Christ's return.

Consider also that Scripture may provide additional evidence for the present reign of Christ when we consider the tension between the already and the not yet and the nature of the kingdom of God—subjects to which we will turn shortly. There is also the intriguing possibility of a parallel passage to Revelation 20:1–10 found in 2 Thessalonians 2:1–12, where Paul spoke of the coming of our Lord occurring after an unprecedented apostasy and the revelation of the man of sin, all because the one who presently restrains such activity ceases to do so. Indeed, this apostasy ends, and the man of sin is destroyed by the splendor of our Lord's coming, events that sound much like those depicted in Revelation 20:7–10.[20]

A Summary of the Two-Age Model

These two eschatological ages can now be seen as the basic eschatological framework taught by both Jesus and Paul. When describing this age, the biblical writers set forth the following qualities of life:

- Matthew 12:32: There is no forgiveness for blasphemy against the Holy Spirit.
- Matthew 24:3: The end of the age will be preceded by signs.
- Matthew 28:20: Christ will be with us until the end of the age.
- Mark 10:30: The present age is an age of homes, fields, and families.
- Luke 18:30: Material rewards are given to us in this life.
- Luke 20:34: The people of this age marry and are given in marriage.
- Romans 12:2: We are not to be conformed to the pattern of this world (age).
- 1 Corinthians 1:20: Philosophy is the wisdom of this age.
- 1 Corinthians 2:6–8: Wisdom and rulers are of this age.
- 2 Corinthians 4:4: Satan, the god of this age, blinds people's minds to the truth.
- Galatians 1:4: The present age is evil.
- Ephesians 1:20–21: Christ reigns in this present age.
- Ephesians 2:2: The ways of this world (age) are evil.
- 1 Timothy 6:17: Those who are rich in this age are not to hope in their wealth for the next.
- Titus 2:12: We are to live godly lives in this present age.

Notice the qualities assigned by the different biblical writers to this present age. In every instance, the qualities mentioned are temporal in nature. These texts describe the present course of history before the return of Christ. Those things that characterize this age pass away at the return of our Lord.

Notice also the way both Jesus and Paul contrasted the two ages. This indicates that this age is not only qualitatively different from the age to come but is also marked by the presence of the age to come in some provisional but not fully consummated sense. For example, the presence of the kingdom of God and the gift of the Holy Spirit are pledges and guarantees of the glorious blessings of the age to come, which will be the inheritance of believers. Christians live in the eschatological tension during the partial overlap of the two ages as they await the arrival of the age to come in its fullness.

When examining the biblical data regarding the age to come, we find the following qualities mentioned:

- Matthew 12:32: There is no forgiveness for blasphemy against the Holy Spirit.
- Matthew 13:40: The weeds will be thrown into the fire.
- Mark 10:30; Luke 18:30: Eternal life is a reward.
- Luke 20:35: There will be no marriages or giving in marriage.
- 1 Corinthians 6:9–10: Evildoers will not inherit the kingdom of God.
- 1 Corinthians 15:50: Flesh and blood will not inherit the kingdom of God.
- Galatians 5:21: Those who live evil lives will not inherit the kingdom.
- Ephesians 1:21: Christ will reign in the age to come.
- Ephesians 5:5: Immoral people will not inherit the kingdom of God.
- 1 Thessalonians 2:12: We are encouraged to live lives worthy of the kingdom.
- 2 Thessalonians 1:5: Our faith will make us worthy of the kingdom of God.
- 1 Timothy 6:19: The coming age has life that is truly life.
- 2 Timothy 4:18: The Lord will bring us to the kingdom of God.

Here again, it is essential to observe the qualities assigned by the biblical writers to the age to come. In marked contrast to this age, the qualities assigned to the age to come are all eternal (or nontemporal) in nature. These references clearly describe the future eschatological state of believers (and nonbelievers if you factor in the references to judgment). The contrast between the two ages could not be greater.

The line of demarcation between the two ages is also clearly set forth:

- Matthew 13:39: The harvest is the end of the age, and angels are the harvesters.
- Matthew 13:40: The weeds will be burned in the fire at the end of the age (judgment).
- Matthew 13:49: The angels will separate the wicked from the righteous.

The return of Christ in his second advent is the event that marks the end of this age as we know it (with all of its temporal qualities) and commences the age to come (with its eternal qualities). Following the historic Protestant hermeneutic, which utilizes the analogy of faith, instead of the dispensational hermeneutic, in which the Old Testament is allowed to interpret the New in matters related to eschatology, this model uses clear and unambiguous texts drawn from throughout the New Testament.

In conclusion, the following points need to be made. First, both Jesus and Paul spoke of the present course of history as "this age" and the age of the consummation as "the age to come." Indeed, this was the basic eschatological understanding of history as set forth in the New Testament.

Second, the final judgment occurs when Christ returns. These texts give no hint of a delay in the judgment of unbelievers until after the thousand-year reign of Christ on the earth. The "white throne judgment" (Rev. 20:11) occurs at Christ's return, not one thousand years later. This argument makes premillennialism in any form difficult to justify solely on the basis of a "literal" reading of the thousand years of Revelation 20:1–10.

Third, since judgment occurs at the return of Christ, there can be only two categories of people after Christ's return: those who are righteous and participate in the blessings of the age to come and those who are not and are burned in the fire. This makes it difficult to argue that people are left on the earth in unresurrected bodies after Christ returns and after the judgment of all men and women.

This point is supported by the following distinctions made in the passages we have just seen between sheep and goats, wheat and weeds, and the elect and the reprobate. Those who are Christ's—the sheep, the wheat, and the elect—are raised from the dead and participate in the glories of the age to come. The goats, the weeds, and the reprobate are judged at Christ's return at the end of the age. This means that no people will be on earth in natural bodies after the event that separates the two ages: Christ's return, which is the *eschaton*.

The dispensational attempt to circumvent the thrust of this simply cannot do justice to the biblical data. The hermeneutical distinction made between the church and Israel forces dispensationalists to try to make distinct references to the church and Israel when the passages in view allow for no such distinctions. The present age is never seen as an anticipatory age but an age destined to perish. It is an evil age, though it is invaded by the messianic age (the age to come). The Messiah's coming is not part of the present age; after all, the Messiah is the one who announced to Israel that the present age was destined to perish.

The preterist contention that the overlap of the two ages is limited to the period between Christ's public ministry and AD 70 and that the end of the age occurred when Jesus came in judgment on Israel in AD 70 does not comport with the New Testament teaching about the two ages. The contrast between the two ages is not redemptive-historical but a contrast between the temporal and the eternal.

The Two-Age Model and New Testament Parallels

Other eschatological phrases that appear in the New Testament are those associated with the final day of blessing and cursing foreseen in the distant future by Israel's prophets. It is important to note the way in which these terms were used in the New Testament, specifically as they relate to the two-age model as an interpretive grid. I am thinking here of the "last day," the "day of the Lord," and the "last trumpet."

In John 6:39, we are told that Christ will raise up his own at the last day. Similarly, in verse 40 of that same chapter, John told us that those who believe in the Son will have eternal life and be raised up at the last day. In verse 44, we are told that our Lord will raise up his own on the last day. Finally, in verse 54, Jesus said, "Whoever eats my flesh and drinks my blood has eternal life, and I will raise him up at the last day." In John's mind, the last day is a day of blessing and resurrection.

But as we move farther into John's Gospel, the same phrase appears again. This time it is not limited to blessing. In John 11:24, Martha stated that she knew that Lazarus would rise in the resurrection at the last day. We are told in the next chapter (12:48), however, that those who reject Christ will be condemned at the last day. The last day will be a day not only of blessing but also of cursing.

A similar relationship holds for the phrases "day of the Lord" and "last trumpet." In Acts 2:20, Luke said there will be cosmic signs—"the sun will be turned to darkness and the moon to blood"—before the day of the Lord. In the next chapter, he told us that Jesus "must remain in heaven until the time comes for God to restore everything, as he promised long ago through his holy prophets" (Acts 3:20–21). The apostle Paul reminded his readers that the sinful nature (i.e., the flesh) but not the spirit will be destroyed on the day of the Lord (1 Cor. 5:5). Paul also said that the resurrection will occur at the last trumpet (1 Cor. 15:52). Similarly, the apostle declared that the day of the Lord will come like a thief (1 Thess. 5:2). And to correct what appeared to be a prevalent error in the Thessalonian church, Paul was forced to remind them that the day of the Lord had not already come (2 Thess. 2:2). How do these seemingly disparate texts help to answer the millennium question?

Notice that all these events (the judgment of both believers and unbelievers, the day of the Lord, the last trumpet, and the restoration of all things) occur at the same time—at the return of Christ. Nothing was said or implied to lead us to believe that Christ returns to set up his kingdom or that a one-thousand-year gap lies between his second advent and the final judgment. No such lengthy intervals are found in any passage individually or collectively. The premillennialists read these lengthy intervals into the biblical text.

As I have mentioned, amillennial commentators argue that Revelation 20:1–10 described this present period. Everything John described there is best said about this present age. Under this interpretation, the age to come is the glorious age of consummation and can have no evil in it. Historic premillennialism, on the other hand, sees the period described in Revelation 20 as future and unrelated to the present. The age to come is both present and future (as in the amillennial scheme), but historic premillennialists insist that the events of Revelation 20 take place visibly on the earth and in the heavens. Another judgment will occur at the end of this millennial period before the age to come is fully realized. For premillenarians, the events described in 1 Corinthians 15:22 and following are separated by lengthy intervals of time. Amillenarians insist that these intervals are not in the text but that historic premillennialists read them into the text.

Yet, as we have seen, the visible reality of the age to come is not yet. The New Testament writers believed in the presence of the kingdom but also saw this present kingdom as a shadow of what is yet to come in the consummation. This is the already/not yet tension that marks so much of the New Testament. The arrival of the fullness of the age to come awaits the return of Christ in blessing and curse. In terms of blessing, the age to come is an age of glorious resurrection life for those in Christ. In terms of judgment, the age to come is a time of eternal punishment for those who reject Christ. This is clearly taught in passages such as Matthew 24:50–51, for example. When we look closely at the biblical data as it relates to the kingdom of God and the age of the Spirit, we see the importance of understanding the influence of both the past and the future on the present.

Before moving on to discuss postmillennialism in relationship to the two-age model, a brief word is in order about the problems raised by the preterist understanding of the two-age model. To limit this age to the so-called Jewish era and to argue that the end of the age refers to the end of the Jewish era and the beginning of the age of the Gentiles, as do many preterists, is highly problematic.

Preterists such as J. Stuart Russell build their case on the belief that the term *aiōn* ("age") refers to an indefinite period of time, not to be confused with *kosmos* ("the world"). Therefore, say the preterists, it is improper to argue that the end of the age should be interpreted to mean the end of the world.[21]

It is the age that ends, not the world. Technically, this is true. *Aiōn* does refer to an age or a period of time, while *kosmos* does indeed refer to the world. But preterists miss the point.

As we have seen, Jesus always described this age in temporal terms—the course of daily life with homes, families, and fields. Jesus did speak of the coming desolation of Israel in Matthew 23:38 and the destruction of the temple and Jerusalem in the Olivet Discourse (Matt. 24), which came to pass as he predicted they would with the events of AD 70. But he also spoke of the age to come as a time in which "there is no marriage or giving in marriage." This can hardly be confused with the age of the Gentiles. The contrast Jesus set forth between the two ages was not strictly chronological but a contrast between two successive redemptive ages that differ from one another qualitatively, as temporal life differs from eternal. People marry and have families in this age. They will not in the age to come because they will be children of the resurrection (Luke 20:34–36).

While preterists may insist that this age ends with the destruction of Jerusalem and the end of the Jewish era, they miss the point regarding Jesus's use of *aiōn*. The way in which these two ages are used throughout the New Testament cannot be limited to historical chronology. When we come to the Olivet Discourse, we see that a redemptive-historical shift occurred with the destruction of Jerusalem and the end of the Jewish era. Yes, this destruction ushered in the time of the Gentiles. But the contrast between the two ages is a contrast between the temporal and the eternal. This age ends at the harvest, said Jesus, which is the day of final judgment when the wheat and weeds are finally separated and go to their eternal rewards. This does not refer to a temporal judgment on Israel but to the final judgment of the righteous and the unrighteous (cf. Matt. 25:31–46).[22]

To make the case that the end of the age occurred in AD 70, preterists also appeal to texts such as Matthew 16:28, in which Jesus said to his disciples, "I tell you the truth, some who are standing here will not taste death before they see the Son of Man coming in his kingdom." According to Russell, comments such as these prove that Jesus taught that his parousia would take place within the lifetime of the disciples, bringing about the end of the age.[23] But as D. A. Carson points out, the coming of the Son of Man is like the coming of the kingdom of God. It comes in stages. The kingdom of God came in the person of Jesus Christ, but that kingdom is not yet consummated. Therefore, this verse and those like it (cf. Matt. 10:23) do not teach that our Lord's second coming occurred in AD 70. Rather, Jesus was referring to the coming manifestation of his kingly reign after his transfiguration and resurrection. Our Lord's kingly rule was manifest not only in the resurrection and at Pentecost but also in the rapid expansion of the church and the mission to the Gentiles. Indeed, the disciples did not die until these things became a reality.[24] They are signs that the age to come has already dawned in the person of Jesus.

More importantly, we must ask, how does the preterist make sense of passages such as Matthew 28:20, where the promise of our Lord's continual presence with his church "to the very end of the age" undergirds his command to make disciples of all nations? Clearly, this text cannot refer to God's judgment on Israel in AD 70.

Problems for Postmillennialism

The difference of opinion between amillennialism and postmillennialism is of a decidedly different nature than the debate between amillenarians and premillennialists. In the former case, the disagreement is not about the overall structure of the eschatological framework of the New Testament and whether there are multiple resurrections and judgments separated by a future millennial age. Rather, the debate between amillenarians and postmillenarians is a more carefully nuanced difference of opinion about the essential character of the millennial age, the precise nature of the victory of the kingdom of God, and the way in which "this present evil age" comes to an end. With moderate forms of postmillennialism, the differences with amillenarians can be subtle and nonsubstantial.[25] If amillennial Christians must lament the ongoing problem of definition and mischaracterization of their viewpoint, so must postmillennialists.[26]

As Oswald T. Allis has correctly pointed out, there are at least two distinct varieties of postmillennialism. One group stands within the trajectory of Daniel Whitby and Jonathan Edwards, contending that the millennium is a literal one-thousand-year golden age for the church on the earth still yet to dawn.[27] A more moderate group sees the millennial age as involving a gradual amelioration of evil brought about by "the preaching of the gospel under the power of the Holy Spirit,"[28] a position that has much in common with amillennialism, though several important differences do indeed remain.

While amillennial Christians would level some criticisms at both pre- and those postmillenarians in the Whitby-Edwards trajectory, namely, the problems of locating the millennial age entirely in the future and of describing the millennium in largely earthly and temporal categories, the differences between amillennialism and the more moderate form of postmillennialism can be difficult to pin down. As I noted earlier, many postmillennial writers often describe this matter as a debate between "optimistic" postmillenarians

and "pessimistic" amillenarians,[29] while amillennial writers often locate the
difference of opinion in the postmillennial confusion of the already (the present blessings of the kingdom of God) and the not yet (the eternal blessings
of the consummation).[30]

Most contemporary Reformed postmillennialists are of the more moderate
variety. The first critical question to be asked of those who hold this position
is whether the Bible teaches that there will be a gradual amelioration of evil
during this present age as moderate postmillenarians argue.[31] A second and
related question is whether Jesus Christ returns to a saved world as postmillennialists such as B. B. Warfield contend.[32] Or does Christ return to save the
world as amillenarians believe?[33]

The best way to deal with these two questions is to return to the basic
eschatological framework given us throughout the New Testament. How do
postmillennial assumptions fit with this data? By looking at this question
from the perspective of the two eschatological ages given us by Jesus and
Paul, we can answer both of the preceding questions in the negative. According to the biblical evidence we have already cited regarding this age, which is
characterized by its sinful and temporal nature, Scripture indicates that this
age is not gradually transformed into the age to come on this side of Christ's
return. Neither is the evil of this age and its temporal character transformed
by the amelioration of evil, the implication of the way postmillennialists
apply texts speaking of the victory of the kingdom of God through secular,
economic, cultural, and political factors.[34] In fact, biblical writers repeatedly
stated that this age ends abruptly and cataclysmically at the second advent of
our Lord (Matt. 13:39–40; cf. 1 Cor. 15:50–57; 1 Thess. 4:17; 2 Thess. 1:7–10;
Rev. 6:12–17; 19:11–21).

Although the kingdom advances throughout this age, the final eschatological victory is won by Jesus Christ himself at his second coming (1 Cor.
15:54), not before. The expectation of this eschatological victory was Paul's
word of comfort to the Christian church in Rome in the form of the promise
that "the God of peace will soon crush Satan under your feet" (Rom. 16:20).
This referred to the cataclysmic defeat of Satan at the *eschaton* and not to a
gradual amelioration of Satan's kingdom during the course of the present age.[35]

This point, it seems to me, is problematic for all forms of postmillennialism, including the more moderate variety. Postmillenarians like to speak of
the success of the kingdom of God in the present age, and justly so. But they
do not talk much about those texts that address the nature of our Lord's
second advent—the very heart of New Testament eschatology. Such texts
make our Lord's return to a "saved" earth after a brief period of apostasy a
theological stretch.

What do we do then with the biblical texts often cited by postmillennialists regarding the advance and spread of the gospel before the return of the Lord (Pss. 2:6–9; 21:8–12; 110:1–2; Isa. 2:2–4; 9:6–7; 11:6–10)?[36] We interpret them within the broader framework of New Testament eschatology and the relationship these texts have to the tension between the already and the not yet, between the signs of the end and the suddenness of our Lord's return, between the kingdom at present and the consummation of that kingdom in the future.

It is clear throughout the New Testament that the last days commenced with the coming of Christ and his triumphant resurrection (Acts 2:17; Heb. 1:2). These last days are also the time of salvation (2 Cor. 6:2), for with the coming of Christ, the new creation began. The old had gone, and the new had come (2 Cor. 5:17). Paul said that certain blessings of the age to come, including reconciliation, were won for us by Jesus Christ through his death and resurrection (Rom. 4:25; 1 Cor. 15:20–28). Paul spoke of these blessings as the present possession of those in union with Christ, for they no longer belong to "the old," that is, this present evil age.

And yet it is equally true that these blessings are not fully realized until the consummation, when creation itself is finally released from bondage (Rom. 8:18–25) and when the earthly at last puts on the heavenly (1 Cor. 15:53). Paul said, "If we hope for what we do not yet have, we wait for it patiently" (Rom. 8:25). It is the possession of the blessings of the eschatological not yet in this evil age that gives Christians hope until these things become a visible reality at the end of the age. In fact, Paul said, God has given us his Holy Spirit, who is a deposit guaranteeing our inheritance, which is not a temporal victory in this age but our ultimate redemption (Eph. 1:13–14). It is this eschatological dimension that gave Paul a theological basis for the hope Christians need in the face of suffering until this present evil age comes to an end—"the fellowship of sharing in his [Christ's] sufferings" (Phil. 3:10).[37] Indeed, we may be, as Paul said, crushed but not perplexed. We are not abandoned or destroyed, though we may be stricken down by our enemies. As Christians, we are to "carry around in our body the death of Jesus, so that the life of Jesus may also be revealed in our body. For we who are alive are always being given over to death for Jesus' sake" (2 Cor. 4:10–12).

This does not sound like the postmillennial vision of the triumph of the kingdom in this present evil age. Paul expected that believers would at times suffer greatly at the hands of unbelievers and would not completely conquer unbelief with great political, economic, and cultural benefits until the Lord returns. This explains why Christians are to be salt and light in this age, fully confident that Christ will ultimately deliver them. Through Jesus's own resurrection and exaltation and our union with him by the Holy Spirit, all believers experience the blessings of the already as they await the not yet of the final consummation (Rom. 5:1–11).

Much the same tension between the already and the not yet may be seen in the biblical teaching regarding the kingdom of God. On the one hand, Christ's kingdom is a present reality; it arrived in Jesus's person (Matt. 3:2; Mark 1:15). It was evidenced by Christ's power over the demonic (Matt. 12:28; Luke 11:20), by the fall of Satan (Luke 10:17–20), and by miracles and the preaching of the gospel (Matt. 11:2–19). Even though the kingdom is present, it is, as Jesus said, "not of this world," for his kingdom is "from another place" (John 18:36). In fact, when the Pharisees asked Jesus when the kingdom of God would come, he replied, "The kingdom of God does not come with your careful observation, nor will people say, 'Here it is,' or 'There it is,' because the kingdom of God is within you" (Luke 17:20–21). This is why Paul could say, "The kingdom of God is not a matter of eating and drinking, but of righteousness, peace and joy in the Holy Spirit" (Rom. 14:17). The unshakable nature of this kingdom means that Christians can face what Paul called the "last days"—in which some have "shipwrecked their faith" (1 Tim. 1:19), "will abandon the faith" (1 Tim. 4:1), will persecute the church (2 Tim. 3:11), and will reject sound doctrine (2 Tim. 4:3). Paul's warnings about the future course of this age do not sound like a description of "spiritual prosperity . . . characterized by increasing peace and economic well-being,"[38] the expectations of even moderate postmillennialists.

Let us not forget that this present, spiritual kingdom also has an eschatological consummation yet to come. Thus, not every one will enter (Matt. 7:21–23), and those outside the kingdom will weep and gnash their teeth (Matt. 8:12). Only the redeemed participate in the blessings of the age to come. Indeed, the parables of the marriage feast (Matt. 22:1–14), the wheat and the weeds (Matt. 13:24–30, 36–43), the net (Matt. 13:47–50), and the talents (Matt. 25:14–30) all speak of the present spiritual kingdom as finally consummated in the age to come but not before.

Paul also made reference to this future consummation of the present kingdom as an age in which the wicked will not receive its blessings (1 Cor. 6:9; Gal. 5:21; Eph. 5:5) and that cannot be inherited by flesh and blood (1 Cor. 15:50). It is this already/not yet tension, the present spiritual kingdom in tension with the future consummated kingdom, that forms the interpretive grid through which we must interpret those texts cited by postmillenarians as describing a victory of the kingdom of God in the present. Though the kingdom of God spreads to the ends of the earth throughout the course of this present evil age, it spreads through Word and sacrament and is a spiritual kingdom "which is not of this world." When men say "here it is" or "there it is," we must say that "the kingdom of God does not come with your careful observation" (Luke 17:20).

But when the last trumpet sounds, the kingdom of the world will at long last become the kingdom of our Lord and of his Christ (Rev. 11:15). It is then, and only then, that our blessed Lord Jesus will hand his kingdom over to his Father (1 Cor. 15:24–25). Our last and greatest enemy, death, will finally be destroyed.

9

The Kingdom of God

Defined simply as God's sovereign, dynamic, and eschatological rule, even a cursory reading of the Gospels reveals that the kingdom of heaven is a central theme in Jesus's preaching.[1] In Mark's Gospel, Jesus's messianic mission commences with the declaration, "The time has come, . . . the kingdom of God is near. Repent and believe the good news!" (1:15). Matthew's Gospel summarizes the early phase of Jesus's Galilean ministry by stating that Jesus "went throughout Galilee, teaching in their synagogues, preaching the good news of the kingdom, and healing every disease and sickness among the people" (4:23).

To understand both the teaching of Jesus and the basic eschatology of the New Testament, we must understand something about the kingdom of God.

Differing Approaches to Interpreting Kingdom Language

Defining the kingdom of God is easier said than done. Since no explicit definition of this kingdom is found in either the Old or the New Testament, the kingdom of God has been interpreted in different ways depending largely on the presuppositions of the interpreter. Because dispensationalists insist on the literal fulfillment of the Old Testament prophecies regarding Israel, they also insist that the kingdom of heaven and the kingdom of God are distinct entities. For them, the kingdom of heaven is God's rule on earth and essentially has to do with the earthly theocratic kingdom promised to national Israel throughout the Old Testament.

This was the Jewish aspect of the kingdom, taught by Jesus in Matthew's Gospel, where the term was used in contrast to the more common New Testament expression "kingdom of God." Jesus offered this kingdom of heaven to Israel, but when she refused it and rejected him, the offer was withdrawn, and a new redemptive epoch began in which the kingdom is seen as a mystery.[2] The kingdom of God will not come until the millennial age dawns after Christ's second advent. For dispensationalists, then, the kingdom of God is essentially the future earthly reign of Jesus Christ in Jerusalem associated with the glories of an earthly millennial age.[3]

The interpretive pendulum has swung back and forth for a generation or so between the beliefs that the kingdom is a present reality or a future reality. However, beginning with the groundbreaking work of W. G. Kummel, the recent scholarly consensus largely contends that the kingdom, while present in some sense, nevertheless still awaits a future consummation at the second advent of Jesus Christ,[4] although the kingdom came in provisional fashion at his first advent. This interpretation of the kingdom of God fits with the categories established in the previous discussion on the two eschatological ages—this age and the age to come—and in the discussion on the present blessings of the already and the future blessings of the not yet.

In recent studies, Reformed writers have argued that the kingdom of God serves as one of the main motifs in biblical revelation. It also should serve as an organizing principle for understanding the historical outworking of the administration of this kingdom in the two main covenants found in the Bible: the covenant of works and the covenant of grace.[5] Kingdom language expresses the absolute sovereignty of God over both his creatures and his creation. It not only underlies both the covenant of works and the covenant of grace but also underlies both law (as divine command) and gospel (as divine promise). The kingdom of God is, therefore, fundamental to much of Reformed theology and should be in the foreground of any Reformed discussion of eschatology.

As Anthony Hoekema has pointed out, "The arrival of the kingdom of God, therefore, as well as its continuance and final consummation, must be seen as an essential aspect of biblical eschatology."[6] Indeed, the arrival of the kingdom in Jesus Christ is the essential category the New Testament writers used to announce that in Jesus Christ what God promised in the Old Testament came to pass.

George Ladd makes the same point: "Since the historical mission of Jesus is viewed in the New Testament as a fulfillment of the Old Testament promise, the entire message of the kingdom of God embodied in Jesus' deeds and words can be included in the category of eschatology."[7] This means that much of what

Jesus said in the Gospels has a direct bearing on our view of eschatology and is, indeed, inseparable from it. The kingdom is a fundamental eschatological category, and Jesus's fundamental message is about the kingdom.

This helps to explain the objection of Reformed theology to dispensationalism. In the dispensational understanding of eschatology, the kingdom of God is relegated to the millennial age after the second coming of Christ, effectively removing a present or realized eschatology. According to dispensationalists, this is because the kingdom of God was offered to Israel by Jesus himself, and when that offer was rejected, the kingdom was then withdrawn and postponed until Christ's second advent. This understanding of the kingdom of God does not fit at all with the presentation in the Gospels of the ministry and teaching of Jesus. Indeed, it does great harm to it.

As one example of how dispensationalists understand the coming of the kingdom, John Walvoord describes the parables of Matthew 13 in the following manner:

> Chapter 13 faces the question, what will happen when the rejected king goes back to heaven and the kingdom promised is postponed until His second coming? The concept of a kingdom postponed must be understood as a postponement from the human side and not from the divine, as obviously God's plans do not change. . . . The rejection of Christ by His own people and His subsequent death and resurrection were absolutely essential to God's program. Humanly speaking, the kingdom, instead of being brought in immediately, was postponed. From the divine viewpoint, the plan always included what actually happened. . . . In this chapter are presented in the seven parables the mysteries of the kingdom . . . a different form of the kingdom, namely the present spiritual reign of the King during the period He is physically absent from the earth, prior to His second coming. The mysteries of the kingdom, accordingly, deal with the period between the first and second Advent of Christ and not the millennial kingdom which will follow the second coming.[8]

According to Walvoord, the kingdom, though present in a mysterious form, is formally postponed until the millennial age following the second advent. Therefore, the category used by dispensationalists to understand the nature of the kingdom in the present dispensation of the church age is that of "mystery." And though, says Walvoord, God knew in advance that Israel would refuse Jesus's offer, the kingdom was postponed because Israel willfully rejected the offer. Therefore, God is delaying the kingdom for the lengthy period of time known as the church age or the "great parenthesis" between the sixty-ninth and the seventieth week of Daniel.[9] The present dispensation results from humanity's ability to frustrate God's redemptive-historical purposes.

A number of problems are raised by this interpretation of the kingdom of God. First, Walvoord argues that the kingdom is postponed until the second coming, but he says that the "mystery of the kingdom" is a present reality because Christ is reigning now in heaven. If this is true, the kingdom must be present in some sense and not postponed. There is no need to say the kingdom offer was withdrawn, except for Walvoord's presuppositions about God having different redemptive purposes for national Israel and for the Gentile nations. Is it not better to say that the kingdom has already come in Jesus Christ, although it is not yet consummated until the *eschaton*?

Second, despite Walvoord's efforts to insist that God is sovereign, the lack of human cooperation frustrated his plan, thereby forcing a delay in its inauguration for at least two thousand years. But the New Testament knows nothing of a kingdom offered and a kingdom withdrawn according to the whims of unbelieving Israel. In fact, as the New Testament era opened, we were told that the kingdom was "at hand" because Jesus Christ had come. Indeed, the apostle Paul could not be any clearer when he said that it was God's sovereign purpose in Christ from before the foundation of the world to save those whom the Father had chosen. It is difficult to develop the idea that the church age is a redemptive-historical postponement from Paul's language in Ephesians 1:3–14 (cf. 2 Tim. 1:9).

Third, we must ask, What if the Jews had accepted Christ's offer of a kingdom? According to dispensationalists, the parables of the kingdom Jesus told in Matthew 13, such as the parable of the sower and the parable of the mustard seed, are not to be understood as describing the kingdom of God brought by Jesus, the pattern God has established for this age. Instead, say the dispensationalists, they describe the "mystery of the kingdom" where Christ reigns in heaven, and the kingdom on earth is only "the number of true believers" awaiting the second coming when the kingdom will finally arrive.[10] Sad to say, such formulations make the most important parts of Christ's teaching about the course of this age unintelligible. Either the kingdom is present in some sense or it is not. If it is present, it has not been postponed.[11]

With these differences of opinion about the kingdom in mind, we now turn to the Old Testament expectation of a coming kingdom before we examine how that expectation is realized in the New.

The Old Testament Expectation of the Coming Kingdom

The New Testament opens with the annunciation of the arrival of the kingdom of God in the person of Jesus Christ (cf. Mark 1:14–15).[12] And yet, while the kingdom is proclaimed, it is never formally defined. How, then, do we define the phrase "kingdom of God" as it was used throughout the New Testament? Says Anthony Hoekema, "This is not an easy thing to do, particularly since Jesus himself never gives a definition of the kingdom. Neither do we find such a definition in the apostolic writings."[13]

Indeed, kingdom language can take on many different nuances, depending on the context and the stage of development within redemptive history. Is the kingdom of God a realm or sphere of influence, or is it a physical territory over which God exercises his rule? Or is the kingdom of God the rule or reign of God as such? Is it a place, or is it the act of reigning? As Hoekema writes, "Though occasionally the term kingdom has spatial connotations, as referring to an order of things or a state of peace and happiness, it usually describes the reign of God over his people."[14] He goes on to say:

> The kingdom of God, therefore, is to be understood as the reign of God dynamically active in human history through Jesus Christ, the purpose of which is the redemption of God's people from sin and from demonic powers, and the final establishment of the new heavens and the new earth. It means that the new age has been ushered in.[15]

George Ladd essentially concurs and states in this regard, "The kingdom of God means that God is King and acts in history to bring history to a divinely directed goal."[16] The kingdom of God is a real, though nonspatial, rule of God.

The kingdom of God is never expressly mentioned in the Old Testament.[17] Even though the term is not used, however, we do find a number of ideas repeatedly expressed throughout the Old Testament that refer to God's rule or reign.

For one thing, we are told in a number of passages throughout the Old Testament that YHWH is the great King:[18] YHWH is the "Sovereign Lord" (Deut. 9:26); YHWH was King of Israel (Deut. 9:26); YHWH is the "King of glory" (Ps. 24:10); he is "enthroned as King forever" (Ps. 29:10). Isaiah gave us a glimpse of a magnificent scene in heaven. In response, he cried out, "My eyes have seen the King, the LORD Almighty" (6:5). Later in that same prophecy, Isaiah declared that "the LORD is our king; it is he who will save us" (33:22). The prophet Zephaniah touched on the same theme when he said, "The LORD, the King of Israel is with you" (3:15). Finally, Zechariah told us that the nations will one day go to Jerusalem "to worship the King, the LORD Almighty" (14:16–17). From passages such as these, it is clear that the theme of kingship carries with it the elements of divine right and divine sovereignty as well as divine rule and authority.[19]

But this is not all. We are also told that YHWH possesses a royal throne, a symbolical seat of power from which he exercises his kingly office and function. In Psalm 9:4, the psalmist said to YHWH, "You have sat on your throne, judging righteously." In Psalm 45:6, we read, "Your throne, O God, will last for ever and ever; a scepter of justice will be the scepter of your kingdom." Likewise, in Psalm 47, which throughout speaks of YHWH as the great King over all the earth, the psalmist declared, "God reigns over the nations; God is seated on his holy throne" (v. 8). Again, in Isaiah 6:1, we are told that Isaiah saw the Lord "seated on a throne, high and exalted, and the train of his robe filled the temple." In the last chapter of his prophecy (66:1), Isaiah recorded for his readers these words of YHWH: "Heaven is my throne, and the earth is my footstool." Then in the opening chapter of Ezekiel's prophecy, we read, "Above the expanse over their heads was what looked like a throne of sapphire, and high above on the throne was a figure like that of a man" (1:26). Clearly, the picture of a throne is meant to convey regal authority and rule, just as a scepter does.

To complement these exalted royal images, a number of texts describe God's rule over what he created. In Psalm 10:16, we read of God's rule over all things, including the nations. Likewise, in Psalm 146:10, we are told that the Lord reigns forever. In Isaiah 24:23, the prophet declared that the Lord Almighty will reign on Mount Zion and in Jerusalem. A glorious declaration in Psalm 22:28 says that "dominion belongs to the LORD and he rules over the nations." God sits in the heavens and does what pleases him on the earth precisely because he is King over all things.

As George Ladd notes, however, it is also important not to overlook the idea that the King who sits enthroned in the heavens and who rules over all things is also the same one who repeatedly comes to his people in a series of divine visitations. Says Ladd:

> This idea that "the God who comes" is one of the central characteristics of the Old Testament teaching about God, and it links together history and eschatology. The whole of the history of Israel, from the birth of the nation at Mount Sinai to her final redemption in the kingdom of God, can be viewed in light of the divine visitations. . . . [There] is a distinct theology of the God who comes. God who visited Israel in Egypt to make them his people, who has visited them again and again in their history, must finally come to them in the future to judge wickedness and to establish his kingdom.[20]

The King visits his people, coming to them with all the vast benefits of his long-anticipated salvation. When the Gospels opened with the glorious declaration that the kingdom of God was at hand, this meant that God had come to his people to bring them salvation. This was the way the Gospel writers portrayed Jesus's messianic mission from the outset.

An apocalyptic version of this same theme can be found in the book of Daniel. In this, the context was one of captive Israel in Babylon. God's rule was contrasted with four world empires pictured by a great statue with a head of gold, a chest and arms of silver, a belly and thighs of bronze, and feet of clay. As Daniel interpreted this dream for King Nebuchadnezzer, it became clear that these various parts represented the Babylonian, Medo-Persian, Greek, and Roman Empires. They all will be crushed by the rock cut without hands that fell on the statue (Dan. 2:31–45) and who, we learn later, is the mysterious Son of Man (7:13–14) pictured as "a heavenly, transcendental being." The figure "assumes the royal role of the spiritual powers at work behind the earthly potentates, and his saints are given the kingly rule of monarchs under the whole heaven."[21] This served, in part, as the national expectation of Israel, when her true King did indeed come to her.

Although there was no definitive messianic consensus in Israel, several messianic expectations were widely held throughout Palestine in the days of Jesus. First, when the Messiah appeared, he would bring salvation and blessing to his people and judgment on the wicked nations that had oppressed Israel. Second, God would return this long-promised messianic king to David's royal throne. Third, this messianic king would liberate Palestine from Israel's Gentile oppressors, especially the Romans.[22] When Jesus announced that the kingdom of God was at hand, these were the expectations his hearers used to interpret his words.

But this would have been a thoroughly secularized and politicized kingdom. In many ways, it is the kingdom envisioned by dispensationalists and postmillenarians. Jesus spoke of a different kingdom, where God would bring deliverance from humanity's true enemy, the guilt and power of sin. Because Jesus did not offer the economic, political, and nationalistic kingdom so many in Israel longed for, he was put to death.

The Present Reality of the Kingdom of God

With the Old Testament background now before us, it is clear that Jesus made no offer of a national kingdom to Israel. What we do find in the Gospel accounts is Jesus's proclamation that a spiritual and nonnationalistic kingdom had drawn near because he had come. Though Israel as a whole did not embrace Jesus and his messianic mission, the kingdom he brought was a reality, nonetheless. In fact, the present reality of the kingdom is a major theme throughout the New Testament.

The New Testament opened with the proclamation of the arrival of the kingdom of God by both Jesus and John the Baptist. As shown in Matthew 3:2 and the parallel passage in Mark 1:15, even from the beginning of our Lord's public ministry, John declared, "Repent, for the kingdom of heaven is near." Whereas John said that the kingdom was about to appear in the person of the coming one, Jesus said that the time predicted by the prophets was now fulfilled in his person (Luke 4:21). The time of which Jesus spoke was the dawning of the messianic age foretold by Isaiah when the poor would have the good news preached to them. As Jesus said later in his ministry, "The kingdom of God has come upon you" (Matt. 12:28; Luke 11:20).

Some background here might be helpful. Both John the Baptist (Mark 1:15) and Jesus (Matt. 10:7) stated that the kingdom was "near." The Greek term used is *ēngiken*, which means that the kingdom has drawn near, that it is present in some sense.[23] A stronger verb is used by Jesus in Luke 11:20, *ephthasen*, meaning that the kingdom had arrived, though as Ridderbos cautions, there is really no significant difference in the meaning of the two terms.[24] The importance of this is well stated by Hoekema:

> We may say, therefore, that Jesus himself ushered in the kingdom of God whose coming had been foretold by the Old Testament prophets. We must therefore always see the kingdom of God as indissolubly connected with the person of Jesus Christ. In Jesus' words and deeds, miracles and parables, teaching and preaching, the kingdom was dynamically active and present among men.[25]

The signs of the presence of the kingdom were numerous. The first sign was that Jesus cast out demons. He said, "If I drive out demons by the Spirit of God, then the kingdom of God has come upon you" (Matt. 12:28). The demons fled from the presence of the Son of God when he confronted them. The rule of God was pushing back the frontier of darkness. How does this fit with the dispensational teaching regarding the postponement of the kingdom?

A second sign of the presence of the kingdom was that Satan fell from heaven and was bound. When the seventy-two followers returned from preaching the gospel, Jesus reported that he saw "Satan fall like lightning from heaven" (Luke 10:18). This becomes clear when cross-referenced with the binding of Satan as described in Revelation 20:1–10 and the mysterious "restrainer" of 2 Thessalonians 2:7. Not only did Satan fall from heaven and become bound, but the mystery of lawlessness was also restrained. Why? Because the kingdom of God had come.

A third sign of the presence of the kingdom was that Jesus performed miracles. Jesus replied to John the Baptist's questioning, "Go back and report to John what you hear and see: The blind receive sight, the lame walk, those who have leprosy are cured, the deaf hear, the dead are raised, and the good news is preached to the poor" (Matt. 11:4–5). It is clear that the kingdom had come in power. These miracles pointed to the arrival of the great age of salvation, which dawned because Jesus Christ had come. If Jesus could make the blind see, he can give believers the eyes of faith. If Jesus could make the lame walk, he can show sinners the way of faith and repentance. If Jesus could cure leprosy, he can remove the guilt and stain of sin. If Jesus could give hearing to the deaf, he can grant understanding into the mysteries of the gospel. And if Jesus could raise the dead, he can give new spiritual life.

Therefore, these miracles pointed to the reality of Christ's kingdom and the preaching of the good news. Says Hoekema in response, "[These] miracles were only signs; they had their limitations. For one thing, not all the sick were restored to health, and the dead who were raised still had to die. The miracles were provisional in their function, indicating the presence of the kingdom, but not yet marking its final consummation."[26] Even though these miracles were provisional, they were signs that the kingdom had come, not that it had been offered.

A fourth sign that the kingdom had arrived was that the gospel was preached to the poor. The answer Jesus gave in response to the questions of the followers of John about whether or not Jesus was the coming one was that "the good news is preached to the poor" (Matt. 11:5). Because of this preaching, Jesus said, "The kingdom of heaven has been forcefully advancing" (Matt. 11:12). This was related to our Lord's miracles, which pointed to the coming of the kingdom and to the salvation found only in Christ. Our salvation is at hand now because Christ has come and because his kingdom is present.

Fifth, the kingdom was present because Jesus forgave sins. Hoekema says:

> In the OT prophets, the forgiveness of sins had been predicted as one of the blessings of the coming Messianic age (Isa. 33:24; Jer. 31:34; Mic. 7:18–20; Zech. 13:1). When Jesus came, he not only preached about sins, he actually bestowed it. The healing of the paralytic after Jesus had forgiven his sins was proof that "the Son of man has authority on earth to forgive sins" (Mark 2:10).[27]

The fact that Jesus declared the forgiveness of sins was a sure sign that the kingdom was present. When seen against this backdrop, it is difficult to argue that Jesus took the kingdom back to heaven as dispensationalists claim.

Sixth, the kingdom was present because Jesus declared it was a spiritual kingdom. The Pharisees asked Jesus when the kingdom of God was coming. They knew what the prophets had written, and they saw that Jesus clearly connected himself and his ministry to this particular aspect of prophetic revelation. Jesus responded by saying, "The kingdom of God does not come with your careful observation, nor will people say, 'Here it is,' or 'There it is,' because the kingdom of God is within you" (Luke 17:20–21). When Pilate asked our Lord about the nature of this kingdom, Jesus said, "My kingdom is not of this world. . . . But now my kingdom is from another place" (John 18:36). Jesus's kingdom was a spiritual kingdom, completely unlike the nationalistic kingdom Israel expected. This should also be a caution to those who would see Jesus's kingdom in terms of nationalism or secular progress in economics, politics, and culture.

Many interpreters, accordingly, see the need to equate the present eschatological kingdom with the age to come.[28] In other words, when the kingdom came in the person of Jesus, the age to come also arrived, at least in some provisional sense. The consummation of that kingdom, when Jesus Christ returns to judge the world, raise the dead, and make all things new, coincides with the arrival of the age to come in all its fullness. This is why the two-age model depicts the presence of the age to come in a provisional sense during the course of this present evil age. It indicates that the presence of Jesus's spiritual kingdom, the "rule of Christ," is a reality that guarantees the consummation of the kingdom of God yet to come. This is further reflected in the Lord's Prayer, when Jesus exhorted believers to pray for the consummation of the same kingdom that dawned in his own person during his messianic mission (Matt. 6:9–13). This focus on the "other worldliness" of the kingdom was supported by the apostle Paul in Romans 14:17, when he wrote, "The kingdom of God is not a matter of eating and drinking, but of righteousness, peace and joy in the Holy Spirit." The kingdom of God, therefore, is not a place or a locality in this world, but it is the reign of Christ in the midst of his people until he makes his enemies his footstool (cf. Matt. 22:44; Mark 12:36; Luke 20:43; Acts 2:35; 1 Cor. 15:21ff.; Heb. 1:13; 10:13).

This raises serious questions about attempts to equate the kingdom of God in the New Testament with Old Testament premessianic motifs, such as a restoration of national Israel or a spatial, physical kingdom that manifests itself on this earth in a geopolitical manner. To do this is to say that the Old Testament picture of the kingdom, although a type of the glorious kingdom yet to come at the *eschaton*, is the ultimate reality. Thus, Old Testament prophecy, intended to point to the glorious messianic age, now predicts a return to the shadows and types instead of the reality to which they pointed. Ironically, dispensationalism anticipates a bleak eschatological future, since it insists on returning to Old Testament types as the ultimate reality instead of the reality they represent in the eternal state. To look for a rebuilt temple, Jesus sitting on David's throne in an earthly Jerusalem, babies being born, and daily life continuing after Christ's return empties the kingdom and the age to come of their eternal character.

Reformed Christians have insisted on the present kingdom being redemptive and spiritual in nature. Such an understanding of the kingdom as both present and future does indeed have consequences for Christian ethics, since one who has been justified should now know something about justice. Therefore, a redemptive understanding of the kingdom should lead to proper political and social actions as consequences of the present kingdom. But political and social actions in themselves cannot be tangible signs that the kingdom of God is present.

The advance of God's kingdom, while inevitable, does not guarantee that evil in society will abate as the kingdom advances. In fact, the presence of God's kingdom guarantees conflict with the forces of evil. As Jesus himself said, "Do not suppose that I have come to bring peace to the earth. I did not come to bring peace, but a sword" (Matt. 10:34). Wherever Christ's kingdom advances, Christians must do combat with our three great enemies: the world, the flesh, and the devil. The Christian hope is that one day the kingdom will be consummated and all evil will be crushed by the Lamb. But not before.

The Future Consummation of the Kingdom

The New Testament teaches that the present kingdom of God remains to be consummated. Jesus illustrated this future consummation with his frightening words in Matthew 7:21–23: "Not everyone who says to me, 'Lord, Lord,' will enter the kingdom of heaven." He was speaking of the time when the kingdom of God comes into its glorious fullness on the day of judgment. The key to understanding this is when Jesus connected the consummation of the kingdom to his own parousia and the resurrection of the dead at the end of the age. Not until Christ appears and the dead are raised will the kingdom be fully realized.[29]

We also see this linkage of the parousia and the resurrection with the future consummation of the kingdom in Jesus's discussion about Gentiles sitting at the table with Abraham, Isaac, and Jacob in the kingdom of heaven, while unbelievers "will be thrown outside, into the darkness, where there will be weeping and gnashing of teeth" (Matt. 8:11–12). This event must occur after the end of the age, for as Jesus said, "The harvest is the end of the age, and the harvesters are angels. As the weeds are pulled up and burned in the fire, so it will be at the end of the age" (Matt. 13:39–40). Jesus linked the consummation of the kingdom with the parousia and the resurrection, for this age ends on the day of God's wrath.

A future consummation of the present kingdom was a theme in several of Jesus's parables. The parable of the weeds (Matt. 13:24–30, 36–43), the parable of the net (Matt. 13:47–50), the parable of the marriage feast (Matt. 22:1–14), the parable of the ten virgins (Matt. 25:1–13), and the parable of the talents (Matt. 25:14–30) all speak of a future consummation of the present kingdom by pointing to the last day and Jesus's appearing in judgment at the end of the age.

The apostle Paul also made reference to a future consummation of the present kingdom. He reminded his readers that the wicked will not inherit the kingdom unless they are made fit by the grace of God in Jesus Christ (see 1 Cor. 6:9; Gal. 5:21; Eph. 5:5). Paul also referred to the consummation when he pointed out that "flesh and blood cannot inherit the kingdom of God" before going on to state that "the perishable must clothe itself with the imperishable, and the mortal with immortality" (1 Cor. 15:50, 53). This comes about, Paul said, because God has brought believers "into the kingdom of the Son he loves, in whom we have redemption, the forgiveness of sins" (Col. 1:13–14). Therefore, like Jesus, Paul located the consummation in the resurrection at the end of the age. Those who participate in that kingdom have been delivered from the guilt and consequences of their sins through faith in the Son of God. Because of God's saving work, which culminates in the resurrection, sinners will inherit the very kingdom that flesh and blood cannot.

The Present/Consummated Kingdom and the Already/Not Yet

It should be clear from the preceding that the kingdom of God is a present reality, though it is not yet consummated. As George Ladd notes in his book *The Presence of the Future*:

> The Kingdom of God is the redemptive reign of God dynamically active to establish his rule among men, and that this Kingdom, which will appear as an apocalyptic act, has already come into human history in the person and in the mission of Jesus to overcome evil, to deliver men from its power, and to bring them into the blessings of God's reign. The Kingdom of God involves two great moments: fulfillment within history, and consummation at the end of history.[30]

Herman Ridderbos concludes:

In this preaching [of Jesus], the element of fulfillment is no less striking and essential than that of expectation. . . . For the future and the present are indissolubly connected in Jesus' preaching. The one is the necessary complement of the other. The prophecy about the future can only be rightly viewed from the standpoint of the Christological present, just as the character of the present implies the necessity and certainty of the future.[31]

The point that Ladd, Ridderbos, and Hoekema all make is that biblical data indicates that the kingdom has both present and future elements. New Testament writers set forth a distinct tension between the present inauguration of that kingdom (the already, this age) and its future consummation (the not yet, the age to come). God does this, says Ladd, for the purpose of "preparing men for the day of judgment," as well as to exhort men to watchfulness and readiness for the end.[32]

Therefore, when viewed against the backdrop of the two-age model, it is possible to harmonize much of the data about the two ages, the present kingdom of God and its future consummation. The present reality of the kingdom demonstrates that Jesus Christ has fulfilled the Old Testament promises regarding the coming messianic age. The prospect of a future kingdom indicates that Christ's fulfillment of these Old Testament promises is typological of a more glorious and final kingdom yet to come. This tension is part of God's plan by placing believers in the position of dual citizenship. They are to live in this age but under the ethical guidelines of the age to come. While we live as citizens of this world, we should realize that our true citizenship is in heaven. Christianity itself is thoroughly eschatological.

This understanding of biblical history, and the possibility of the "present millennium," shifts the focus of the contemporary debate about the millennium from the details of future events to the present, giving life meaning and hope in the face of an uncertain future. Since history is redemptive in nature, we have God's promise that he will work everything for the good of those who love him and have been called according to his purpose (Rom. 8:28).

This model of the kingdom shows the unfortunate but necessary conflict between Reformed theology and dispensationalism. Dispensationalism, and its understanding of the postponed kingdom, flies directly in the face of the New Testament's teaching about the present reality of the kingdom. Instead, it is oriented toward a future millennium in which premessianic Old Testament motifs remain dominant. Reformed Christians contend that this destroys the biblical conception of history as taught by Jesus and the apostles. Christ's return is not the inauguration of a halfway step on the road to consummation called a millennium. Christ's return is the consummation.

10

The New Creation, the Israel of God, and the Suffering Church

Christ's Resurrection and the New Creation

When Jesus Christ rose from the dead that first Easter Sunday, a new epoch in redemptive history dawned. The empty tomb was the first concrete sign that the new creation had begun. Though this point is often overlooked when discussing the nature of the millennial age, Christ's resurrection is, in fact, central to it. This becomes apparent when we turn to the key millennial text, Revelation 20. John wrote, "Blessed and holy are those who have part in the first resurrection. The second death has no power over them" (Rev. 20:6).

In light of John's assertion, amillenarians often appeal to his Gospel, where Jesus said that those who believe in him have already "crossed over from death to life" (John 5:24). According to our Lord's own words, the first resurrection occurs in the midst of this present age, and this is not a reference to the bodily resurrection that marks the end of the age. If Christian believers have already been raised from death to life by virtue of the new birth, then in Revelation 20, John was not speaking of a future millennium but the present age. This is another serious blow to premillennialists, who argue that the first resurrection is the bodily resurrection associated with Christ's return.

An additional line of evidence from Paul's writings supports the idea that the first resurrection is connected to Christ's own resurrection. Drawing in part on the work of Reformed biblical theologians such as Geerhardus Vos and

129

Herman Ridderbos, Richard Gaffin advanced the thesis that the resurrection of Jesus Christ was much more than the vindication of his redemptive work on Calvary and proof of his deity. Rather, Christ's resurrection marked the dawn of the age to come and ushered in a new and final era of redemptive history. This, Gaffin says, was evident when Paul spoke of Christ's resurrection as the "firstfruits."

The term *firstfruits* (1 Cor. 15:20ff.) is commonly understood to mean that Christ's resurrection was chronologically prior to the resurrection of those who will rise after him. Gaffin, however, makes the case that Paul's use of the term *firstfruits* was intended to demonstrate an organic unity between Christ and his people, who have been raised with him. This means that Christ's resurrection marked the initial resurrection from a whole group to follow. As Gaffin puts it, our Lord's "resurrection is the representative beginning of the resurrection of believers."[1] All who are in Christ were raised with him when Christ rose from the dead. This is what Paul meant when he said, "As in Adam all die, so in Christ all will be made alive" (1 Cor. 15:22). This is also why Paul spoke of believers already raised with Christ and seated in the heavenlies even while they are still living on earth (Eph. 2:6; Col. 2:12–13; 3:1). Because believers have been raised with Christ and are united to him through faith, they now participate in his resurrection as citizens of the age to come.

Christ's bodily resurrection entailed two subsequent resurrections for all Christian believers. The first of these is a spiritual resurrection that occurs when believers are united to Christ through faith. This union with him also ensures their bodily resurrection at the end of the age.[2] By virtue of this first resurrection, believers now participate in the resurrection age to come (Luke 20:34–37). They await the resurrection of their bodies when the age to come is fully consummated. The chronology of this can answer questions about the nature and character of Christian existence during a possible millennial age after Christ's second coming. Is there any kind of resurrection for Christians prior to the bodily resurrection at the end of the age? If so, the first resurrection of which John spoke in Revelation 20:6 occurs in this present age, not at the beginning of a future millennium.

A clue as to how Paul understood this twofold resurrection for believers is seen in 2 Corinthians 4:16: "Though outwardly we are wasting away, yet inwardly we are being renewed day by day." Likely, Paul was speaking of the fact that believers are inwardly renewed because they have been raised with Christ. Their minds and hearts have been transformed (cf. Rom. 12:2; Eph. 3:16). But despite this inner renewal, the bodily resurrection is not yet. Barring the second coming of Christ, their bodies will die and not be raised until the general resurrection at the end of the age. But their inner beings, hearts, and

minds have already been raised, though the "flesh has not."[3] This certainly
seems to fit with Jesus's view as recorded in John's Gospel, namely, that those
who trust in him have already crossed over from death to life. Since the Scriptures teach a spiritual resurrection before the resurrection of the body, the
first resurrection in John 20:6 is the same event (regeneration or conversion)
about which Jesus and Paul were speaking in the texts we have just considered.

This same point can be seen in the use of the words *flesh* (*sarx*) and *spirit*
(*pneuma*) in Paul's writings. Although the term *flesh* can refer to the body or
even to the whole person, the term most often refers to the natural order of
everyday human life. When used in this sense, *sarx* is roughly synonymous
with this present age (*aiōn*).[4] In texts such as Romans 7:5, when the apostle
spoke of being controlled by the flesh, he meant being enslaved to something
bigger than his own sinful passions. Paul was enslaved to the present world
order and the power it exercised over him. He was enslaved because of his
orientation toward self and because he lived in a world in which everyone was
enslaved to sin and self as well.[5] An anti-Christian world order is in view in
texts such as 1 Corinthians 1:20, where Paul said that "God made foolish the
wisdom of the world."

This flesh-spirit eschatological framework explains why Paul contrasted flesh
and spirit throughout his writings.[6] This is ultimately a contrast between two
eschatological ages. This present evil age is the age of the flesh. It is destined to
pass away and does so in a sense for believers even now when they are united
to Christ through faith. This is why Paul emphasized that Christ's resurrection was "spiritual" (1 Cor. 15:46) and why the author of Hebrews spoke of
the Holy Spirit as the power of the "coming age" (6:5). As Geerhardus Vos
put it, "To belong to the world to come and to be *pneumatikos* (spiritual) are
interchangeable conceptions."[7] To be in Christ is to be freed from the bondage
of the flesh. To be spiritual is to be a citizen of the age to come and assured of
the future resurrection of the body (Eph. 1:13–14). Through the indwelling of
the Holy Spirit, the inner being is renewed. This is the pledge that the outer
being (i.e., the body) will also be raised.

The significance of Christ's resurrection cannot be limited to the impact
it has on individual Christians who are raised in him. As Gaffin reminds us,
there are cosmic implications throughout Paul's discussion of the resurrection,
but these can be seen most clearly in 1 Corinthians 15:45–49. Here we are told
that the resurrection of Jesus Christ marked the beginning of the renewal of
all creation. Jesus was called the last Adam and designated as the life-giving
Spirit.[8] The first Adam belonged to this present age; he was of the dust. But
the second Adam was the man from heaven, the one who brought about the
new age, which dawned in his very person.

Once again, it is important to consider the chronology of this. As Gaffin notes, "The order of Adam is first; there is none before him. The order of Christ is last; there is none after Christ. He is the eschatological man; his is the eschatological order."[9] Adam belongs to the world that is, Christ to the world to come. Once Jesus burst from the tomb, the age to come dawned, and the new creation commenced. Easter Sunday was the birthday of the new world. The empty tomb was the sign and seal of the new creation.

If the first resurrection of which John spoke is a spiritual resurrection, then in Revelation 20:6, John is not speaking of a future earthly reign of Christ but a present reign of Christ. This is further reinforced by Paul's argument that Christians are already raised with Christ, and while their outer bodies are dying, their inner beings are being renewed.

The Church as the Israel of God

When John Calvin first set forth his understanding of the relationship between the Old and New Testaments in chapters X and XI in book II of his *Institutes of the Christian Religion*, the link between the church and Israel was firmly established in the Reformed dogmatic tradition. As Calvin looked to the unfolding drama of redemption, he saw the following pattern:

> The Lord held to this orderly plan in administering the covenant of his mercy: as the day of full revelation approached with the passing of time, the more he increased each day the brightness of its manifestation. Accordingly, at the beginning when the first promise of salvation was given to Adam [Gen. 3:15] it glowed like a feeble spark. Then, as it was added to, the light grew in fullness breaking forth increasingly and shedding its radiance more widely. At last—when all the clouds were dispersed—Christ the Sun of Righteousness fully illumined the whole earth.[10]

This understanding of progressive revelation led Calvin to conclude that believing Israel in the Old Testament was really the church in its infancy.[11] There is one people of God in both testaments, all members of the one covenant of grace, whose one Mediator is Jesus Christ. Even though Calvin saw but one people of God throughout redemptive history, he was not ready to say that God has no more place for ethnic Israel in his redemptive purposes. Despite Israel's present unbelief, said Calvin, "for the sake of the promise, God's blessing still rests among them."[12]

Previously, we saw that Old Testament prophecies regarding the land, the temple, and the Davidic throne were fulfilled in Jesus Christ. We also saw that much of what the Old Testament predicted of Israel in premessianic terms is fulfilled in the church. This fits with the basic Reformed paradigm first set forth by Calvin. Type and shadow give way to fulfillment and the ever-increasing redemptive-historical clarity found in Jesus Christ.

We have also seen how dispensationalists are committed to a literal interpretation of Bible prophecy. They insist that Old Testament prophecies regarding national Israel will be fulfilled by the modern state of Israel, even when evidence points in a different direction. Therefore, classical dispensationalists such as Charles Ryrie take a different approach than amillenarians, arguing that the church has a "mysterious character" not revealed in the Old Testament. As Ryrie sees the matter, the church is marked off "as distinct to this age [the church age] and a mystery hidden in Old Testament times but not revealed."[13] Dispensationalists make a radical separation between God's redemptive program for national Israel and for the Gentile church. Popular writers, such as Hal Lindsey, go so far as to speak of the church age as "the great historical parenthesis."[14] Furthermore, says Lindsey, "I believe that God's purpose for Israel and His purpose for the church are so distinct and mutually exclusive that they cannot both be on the earth at the same time during the seven-year tribulation."[15] Therefore, the church age functions as plan B during this present dispensation. Israel rejected the kingdom offer made by Jesus, creating the present parenthesis phase of redemption until God again deals with ethnic Israel at the beginning of the great tribulation after the rapture of the Gentile church.

However, is it correct to say that the church was a mystery in the Old Testament? Strictly speaking, the answer is yes. There is no specific reference to the church in the Old Testament. But in a number of places, the Old Testament indicated that Gentiles will participate in the blessings God has promised to pour out on Israel in the distant future. Although the church may be a mystery of sorts, God's inclusion of the Gentiles in future eschatological blessing is not. God promised to take his redemption to the ends of the earth in the messianic age, and this includes the Gentile nations.

Recall that in both Genesis 12:3 and 22:18 God told Abraham that through his offspring all peoples and nations on earth will be blessed. The same thing can be seen in Psalm 22. According to the psalmist, "All the ends of the earth will remember and turn to the LORD, and all the families of the nations will bow down before him, for dominion belongs to the LORD and he rules over the nations" (vv. 27–28). Such language extends the blessings of the kingdom beyond the narrow confines of Israel to the nations of the earth.

The prophet Isaiah repeatedly spoke of a future time when God will give salvation to Israel. But Gentiles are also mentioned as among "his people" whom God intends to save. God said to the servant of the Lord, "It is too small a thing for you to be my servant to restore the tribes of Jacob and bring back those of Israel I have kept. I will also make you a light for the Gentiles, that you may bring my salvation to the ends of the earth" (Isa. 49:6). God said to Israel, "Arise, shine, for your light has come, and the glory of the LORD rises upon you. See, darkness covers the earth and thick darkness is over the peoples, but the LORD rises upon you and his glory appears over you. Nations will come to your light, and kings to the brightness of your dawn" (Isa. 60:1–3).[16] These assertions lead Anthony Hoekema to conclude:

> In the light of these passages one can understand the universal invitation found in Isaiah 45:22, "Turn to me and be saved, all the ends of the earth! For I am God, and there is no other." Malachi clearly predicts the worship of Israel's God by the Gentiles: "For from the rising of the sun to its setting my name is great among the nations [or Gentiles ASV], and in every place incense is offered to my name, and a pure offering; for my name is great among the nations, says the Lord of Hosts (1:11)."[17]

The Bible everywhere supports the idea of the organic unity of the people of God, despite the fact that these people are citizens of national Israel in the Old Testament and members of Christ's church in the New. Paul was emphatic about this when he declared that "there is one body and one Spirit—just as you were called to one hope when you were called—one Lord, one faith, one baptism; one God and Father of all, who is over all and through all and in all" (Eph. 4:6). Paul seemed to indicate that through the redemptive work of Christ the division of Babel (Gen. 11:1–8) gave way to the unity of a new society (Eph. 2:19–22). In all of this, the organic unity of God's redemptive-historical purposes is clearly evident.

Therefore, it is quite wrong-headed to interpret a distinction made in the Scriptures between the church and Israel—as J. Dwight Pentecost and Lewis Sperry Chafer argue[18]—as a foundational point of agreement with one of the pillars of the dispensational hermeneutic, that God has two mutually exclusive purposes for national Israel and the Gentile church. Although the church and Israel occupy different roles and stages in redemptive history, that does not constitute an argument for distinct redemptive plans for each group. In fact, the evidence shows that the opposite is the case. In Christ, God takes the two peoples and makes them one.

Paul, the zealous Pharisee turned apostle to the Gentiles, argued that a primary outcome of the ministry and death of Jesus Christ was the abolishing of any redemptive-historical superiority of Jew over Gentile. He said, "There is neither Jew nor Greek, slave nor free, male nor female, for you are all one in Christ Jesus" (Gal. 3:28). Since every pious Jew daily gave God thanks that he was not a Gentile, a slave, or a woman, these words from Paul are remarkable.[19] Christ destroys all racial, gender, and socioeconomic distinctions in his kingdom. In his letter to the Ephesians, Paul used the divided temple with its Court of the Gentiles as a backdrop to make an important point about God's redemptive-historical purposes.

> Therefore, remember that formerly you who are Gentiles by birth and called "uncircumcised" by those who call themselves "the circumcision" (that done in the body by the hands of men)—remember that at that time you were separate from Christ, excluded from citizenship in Israel and foreigners to the covenants of the promise, without hope and without God in the world. But now in Christ Jesus you who once were far away have been brought near through the blood of Christ. For he himself is our peace, who has made the two one and has destroyed the barrier, the dividing wall of hostility. (2:11–14)

It is Christ who made the two peoples, Jew and Gentile, into one. These two texts (Gal. 3:28; Eph. 2:11–14) are clear challenges to the dispensational notion of two distinct peoples of God with separate redemptive economies.[20]

A number of additional lines of evidence supporting the unity of the people of God are in the New Testament as well. The first of these is found in the biblical words used in reference to both Israel and the church. As Hoekema points out:

> The Hebrew term *qahal*, commonly rendered *ekklēsia* in the Septuagint (the Greek translation of the Hebrew Bible), is applied to Israel in the Old Testament. To give just a few examples, we find the word *qahal* used of the assembly or congregation of Israel in Exodus 12:6, Numbers 14:5, Deuteronomy 5:22, Joshua 8:35, Ezra 2:64, and Joel 2:16. Since the Septuagint was the Bible of the apostles, their use of the Greek word *ekklēsia*, the Septuagint equivalent of *qahal*, for the New Testament church clearly indicates continuity between that church and Old Testament Israel.[21]

When God's new covenant people gather for worship, that assembly is known as the *ekklēsia*—the same term used by Greek-speaking Jews of the *diaspora* of the formal religious assemblies of their fathers. Surely, this connection is not accidental.

Another important term in this regard is *temple*, which in the Old Testament pointed forward to the priestly work of Jesus Christ and was applied by New Testament writers to the church. Paul asked the Corinthian believers,

"Don't you know that you yourselves are God's temple and that God's Spirit lives in you? If anyone destroys God's temple, God will destroy him; for God's temple is sacred, and you are that temple" (1 Cor. 3:16–17). Paul also said, "We are the temple of the living God" (2 Cor. 6:16). The same idea is found in Ephesians 2:21–22, where Paul wrote, "In him [Christ] the whole building is joined together and rises to become a holy temple in the Lord. And in him you too are being built together to become a dwelling in which God lives by his Spirit." In the Old Testament, the tabernacle was that place where heaven and earth intersected, for there God chose to be present with his people and revealed his divine glory (Exod. 40). Because of Christ's redemptive work, however, the two peoples are not only made into one but also knit together into the one body of Jesus Christ. The church is now that place where God's glory resides and where God dwells with his people.[22] In this temple, there is neither Jew nor Greek, as all are living stones in Christ Jesus.

A third line of evidence is that New Testament writers saw the church as a fulfillment of Old Testament prophecies about the city of Jerusalem. The "heavenly Jerusalem" is a picture of redeemed saints, the church of the living God (Heb. 12:22). The apostle John saw a "new Jerusalem" coming down out of heaven, prepared as a bride for her husband (Rev. 21:2). This was mirrored in Ephesians 5:25–27, where Paul spoke of the church as the bride of Christ, radiant, without stain and blemish.[23]

Furthermore, Paul wrote to the Galatians, presumably Jewish and Gentile Christians, "Peace and mercy to all who follow this rule, even to the Israel of God" (Gal. 6:16). If Paul meant to say here (as the context seems to indicate, "Neither circumcision nor uncircumcision means anything; what counts is a new creation" [v. 15]) that Jew and Gentile alike are united by their participation in Christ's redemption, then together they are the true Israel of God.[24] This, of course, includes all believers who trust in Jesus Christ.

This renders the dispensational scheme of two distinct peoples of God very tenuous indeed. Walvoord knows full well the dilemma this text poses to the dispensational system:

> It has been alleged on the basis of this passage that the church as such is specifically called the "Israel of God." To this is opposed the fact that everywhere else in the Scriptures the term Israel is applied only to those who are the natural seed of Abraham and Isaac, never to the Gentiles. If it can be sustained that in this passage the church is called *Israel*, it would, of course, be an argument for the identification of the church with Israel in the present age. . . . God's blessing is declared on those who walk according to this rule (among the Galatians who were Gentiles), and also "upon the Israel of God." The use of *and* (Greek *kai*)

is difficult to explain apart from the intention of the writer to set off the "Israel of God" from those considered in the first half of the verse.[25]

Does this passage support Walvoord's contention? Hoekema argues:

> The problem with [Walvoord's] interpretation is that believing Jews have already been included in the words "all who follow this rule." The word *kai*, therefore, should be rendered *even*, as the New International Version has done. When the passage is so understood, "the Israel of God" is a further description of "all who follow this rule"—that is, of all true believers, including both Jews and Gentiles, who constitute the New Testament Church. Here, in other words, Paul clearly identifies the church as the true Israel. This would imply that promises which had been made to Israel during Old Testament times are fulfilled in the New Testament Church.[26]

As Ronald Fung points out, what is perhaps determinative of the issue is the fact that the "whoever" (*hosoi*) following this "rule" of verse 16 "would naturally include Jewish as well as Gentile Christians; moreover, particularly in light of verse 15, it is improbable that Paul, with his concern for the unity of the church (Gal. 2:2) would here single out Jewish Christians as a separate group within his churches."[27] Therefore, the Israel of God extends to all who follow this rule and who participate in the new creation, including both Jews and Gentiles.

The church is not a plan B or a contingency developed by God in hasty response to Israel's rejection of Jesus and his messianic kingdom. Matthew recorded Jesus as saying, "And I tell you that you are Peter, and on this rock I will build my church, and the gates of Hades will not overcome it. I will give you the keys of the kingdom of heaven; whatever you bind on earth will be bound in heaven; and whatever you loose on earth will be loosed in heaven" (Matt. 16:18–19). From this, it should be clear that Jesus did not consider the Gentile church an afterthought on God's part. Rather, God's purpose from the beginning was to create a church and defend it against all forms of satanic attack until Christ's second advent. Christ entrusted the keys of the kingdom and the power to bind and loose to the officers of the church.

Paul made a similar point when he said, "And God placed all things under his [Christ's] feet and appointed him to be the head over everything for the church, which is his body, the fullness of him who fills everything in every way" (Eph. 1:22–23). Christ's headship over all things is for the church. Furthermore, the church is seen as the body of Christ. These same people over whom Christ rules as head are those chosen "before the creation of the world to be holy and blameless in his sight" (Eph. 1:4).

The Suffering Church

Postmillenarians look for a glorious victory of Christ's kingdom in this present age—a victory anchored in the great success of the missionary enterprise.
But what also characterizes postmillennial expectation in distinction from
amillennialism is a corresponding Christianizing of the nations, resulting in
unprecedented gains in all spheres of life—economic, political, and cultural.
According to J. Marcellus Kik, whose book *The Eschatology of Victory* has
exercised a wide-ranging influence on American postmillenarians, the millennium "is the period of the gospel dispensation, the messianic kingdom,
the new heavens and earth, the regeneration, etc."[28] Sounding a bit like an
amillenarian, Kik believes that the millennium began at Christ's ascension
or the day of Pentecost and is not a literal one-thousand-year period. But Kik
also believes that at some point in this present age the nations will become
predominantly Christian, the kingdom of Satan will be destroyed, and peace
and truth will spread throughout the earth.[29] A golden age for the church will
be realized, which Kik characterizes as a "new earth."

Traditional postmillennial expectations raise two obvious objections. First,
it is self-evident that the stated postmillennial expectations have not yet been
realized. This raises serious questions about how postmillenarians interpret the
last two thousand years of the church's history and the spread of the gospel
into the four corners of the earth without a corresponding "Christianizing of
the nations." This point, taken by itself, does not refute postmillennialism. It
merely demonstrates that postmillennial expectations have not been realized
and that the millennium is future. Problematic? Yes. Refutation? No.

Scottish theologian John Dick wrote, "However improbable it may seem
that the whole world should be Christianized, we know that God is able
to perform what he has promised. . . . A future generation will witness the
rapidity of its progress; and long before the end of time."[30] This is a point
well taken, since amillenarians believe much the same thing about the present
age, namely, that the gospel will spread to the ends of the earth before Christ
returns. What separates amillenarians from postmillenarians is the fact that
amillenarians do not necessarily believe that things will get better for God's
people on a global scale. In fact, things may get worse.

As postmillenarians trust in God to bring about their expectations even in
the face of present and rampant evil, so too amillenarians believe that God's
kingdom will advance, even while provoking men to wrath against it. Both
amillennial and postmillennial expectations are grounded in believing God's
command to take his kingdom to the ends of the earth in the face of evidence to the contrary. The disagreement between them lies in how Christians

understand the consequences of the advance of Christ's kingdom. Will the nations be Christianized as a result of the spread of that kingdom? Or do the forces of unbelief continue to persecute the church as the kingdom advances throughout the course of the present age? Amillenarians say no to the first question but yes to the latter.

The second obvious objection to postmillennial expectation is much more serious. Does the New Testament promise Christians that God will Christianize the nations and that glorious things lie ahead for God's people in this present age? The answer to this question is no.[31] If postmillennialists are correct, you would expect Jesus to tell his church something like this: "Things will be rough in the beginning. But hang in there! All nations will come to faith in me, and there will be such cultural, economic, and political improvements that you wouldn't believe me even if I told you."

Instead, Jesus repeatedly exhorted his disciples, "Keep watch, because you do not know on what day your Lord will come. But understand this: If the owner of the house had known at what time of night the thief was coming, he would have kept watch and would not have let his house be broken into. So you also must be ready, because the Son of Man will come at an hour when you do not expect him" (Matt. 24:42–44; cf. 25:13; Mark 13:35–37). Does this warning, typical of many given by Jesus, fit with postmillennial expectations of a future golden age?

In the Olivet Discourse, Jesus declared that the gospel of the kingdom must first be preached to all nations as a testimony against them, and only then will the end come. How could Jesus say this if postmillennial expectations are found in his teaching? Furthermore, Jesus went throughout Galilee, teaching in the synagogues, preaching about the kingdom of heaven, and performing miraculous signs and wonders to confirm the truth of his preaching. Jesus told the crowds, "Blessed are those who are persecuted because of righteousness, for theirs is the kingdom of heaven. Blessed are you when people insult you, persecute you and falsely say all kinds of evil against you because of me. Rejoice and be glad, because great is your reward in heaven, for in the same way they persecuted the prophets who were before you" (Matt. 5:10–12). Is this messianic blessing of the persecuted limited to Jesus's immediate hearers, or does this expectation of persecution hold true throughout the present age?

As the apostle Paul pointed out, this present age is "evil" (Gal. 1:4). It is dominated by those whose minds are blinded by Satan, the god of this age (2 Cor. 4:4). Indeed, the two-age model presents great difficulty for postmillenarians, since the difference between the two ages is qualitative, the temporal in contrast to the eternal. There is no evidence that this present evil age is transformed into the age to come only to return to its evil characteristics in those days of apostasy before Christ returns in judgment.

Paul made it clear that Christians should expect something quite unlike postmillenarians would lead us to believe. This can be seen in two distinct lines of thinking in Paul's writings. One has to do with the characteristics of the last days. Throughout the New Testament, the last days constitute that period of time between the first and second advent of Jesus Christ. In his second pastoral letter to young Timothy, Paul gave this warning about the course of the age:

> But mark this: There will be terrible times in the last days. People will be lovers of themselves, lovers of money, boastful, proud, abusive, disobedient to their parents, ungrateful, unholy, without love, unforgiving, slanderous, without self-control, brutal, not lovers of the good, treacherous, rash, conceited, lovers of pleasure rather than lovers of God—having a form of godliness but denying its power. Have nothing to do with them. (2 Tim. 3:1–5)

Although some postmillenarians say that the "last days" is a reference to that brief period of apostasy before Christ comes back,[32] Paul more likely referred to the course of the entire interadvental age.[33] Throughout the last days, some will distort the gospel to tickle itching ears and gather followers to themselves.

In this letter to Timothy, Paul warned Christians against such false teachers, cautioning us that they will arise in our midst and that we are to have nothing whatsoever to do with them.[34] Jesus also told his disciples that one of the signs of the end is that "many false prophets will appear and deceive many people" (Matt. 24:11).

But this was not Paul's only warning to Timothy about the course of the present age. He wrote, "In fact, everyone who wants to live a godly life in Christ Jesus will be persecuted, while evil men and imposters will go from bad to worse, deceiving and being deceived" (2 Tim. 3:12–13). In order for postmillennial expectations to come to pass, such false teaching must be eliminated from the church. How can this be when Paul warned us that this lamentable state of affairs is an inevitability for Christ's church? Like Timothy, ministers of the gospel must keep their heads (2 Tim. 4:5) and use the Holy Scriptures to rebuke error and train their flocks in righteousness (2 Tim. 3:16). The situation was, apparently, so serious that Paul repeated the warning. In fact, it would get so bad, said Paul, that "the time will come when men will not put up with sound doctrine. Instead, to suit their own desires, they will gather around them a great number of teachers to say what their itching ears want to hear. They will turn their ears away from the truth and turn aside to myths"

(2 Tim. 4:3–4). Why did Paul warn us about heresy and false teaching if he saw a golden age ahead for the church in which the peril of false teaching is eliminated until a brief period of apostasy? He gave us this warning because he expected heresy and false teaching to plague Christ's church until the end of the age. We must be on our guard until the day of Christ Jesus.

The second Pauline category that is problematic for postmillenarians has to do with another important theme in his Epistles: the fact that Christ's church shares in the sufferings of its head (Phil. 3:10). As Jesus suffered and endured the shame of the cross, so will Christ's people endure the shame heaped on them by an unbelieving world (2 Cor. 1:3–11). This point is important when considering the kind of kingdom victory anticipated by the New Testament. Richard Gaffin points out the importance of this in connection with Christ's own humiliation and suffering:

> The inaugurated eschatology of the New Testament is least of all the basis for triumphalism in the church, at whatever point prior to Christ's return. Over the interadvental period in its entirety, from beginning to end, a fundamental aspect of the church's existence is (to be) "suffering with Christ"; nothing, the New Testament teaches, is more basic to its identity than that.[35]

If the church is to suffer with Christ until his return, this undercuts the triumphalism of postmillennialism. Amillenarians can explain how God's kingdom advances while God's people simultaneously "suffer with Christ" and endure the persecution of the world. Postmillenarians cannot.

Three texts in Paul's letters make this important point. The first states, "But we have this treasure in jars of clay to show that this all-surpassing power is from God and not from us. We are hard pressed on every side, but not crushed; perplexed, but not in despair; persecuted, but not abandoned; struck down, but not destroyed" (2 Cor. 4:7–9). It was Paul's calling as apostle to the Gentiles to suffer greatly, but the weakness of the vessel did not affect the glories of his message. Though the messenger of reconciliation may be oppressed and persecuted, Christ ensures the victory. This victory is paradoxical. The messenger is weak and persecuted, but the message thrives. There is certainly no Pauline expectation, implied or otherwise, that this condition will change before the return of our Lord.

A second text to consider in this regard is Philippians 3:10–11. After describing the futility of his attempts to earn favor with God based on his own efforts, Paul wrote, "I want to know Christ and the power of his resurrection and the fellowship of sharing in his sufferings, becoming like him in his death, and so, somehow, to attain to the resurrection from the dead." Paul renounced his own righteousness and embraced the righteousness of Christ through faith. He then expressed his heartfelt desire to know that, as he himself suffered, in some way he participated in Christ's own sufferings. Though these words had primary reference to his own situation, they also apply to all believers.[36] By participating in the sufferings of Christ, we are transformed into his image, a process finally completed when Christ comes again in glory.[37] This is a picture of the church militant awaiting the Lord of glory to come to its final rescue, not the triumphant church of postmillennial expectation that is at peace for centuries followed by a brief time of apostasy before the *eschaton*.

Finally, in Romans 8:17, Paul wrote, "Now if we are children, then we are heirs—heirs of God and co-heirs with Christ, if indeed we share in his sufferings in order that we may also share in his glory." In this text, the apostle anchored Christian hope—participating in Christ's glory—in Christ's sufferings. As Christians participate in Christ's own suffering through faith, they also participate in his glory. The fact that Christians will suffer may lead some who lack the eyes of faith to conclude that Christ cannot make good on his promises. But as Charles Cranfield points out, the passage has the following sense: "For the fact that we are now suffering with Him, so far from calling the reality of our heirship into question, is a pledge of our being glorified with Him hereafter."[38] To suffer with Christ does not mean the Savior has rejected us. On the contrary, he is preparing us for glory. God's purposes are advanced through means we would not expect. The signs of Christ's kingdom are an empty cross and an empty tomb. The church triumphs by suffering with Christ, not by taking dominion over the world and controlling its political institutions, economic resources, and cultural establishments.

One unifying theme in all three of these passages raises serious doubts about traditional postmillennial assumptions. This is the fact that Christians throughout this present age will suffer for Christ's sake. It is in their suffering with Christ that they will ultimately triumph. This leads Richard Gaffin to conclude:

> This mark—this *essential* mark—of the church's identity seems muted or largely ignored in much of today's postmillennialism. . . . Most assuredly, the eschatology of the New Testament is an "eschatology of victory"—victory presently being realized by and for the church, through the eschatological kingship of Christ (Eph. 1:22), but any outlook that fails to grasp that, short of Christ's return, this eschatology of victory is an eschatology of suffering—an eschatology of (Christ's) "power made perfect in weakness" (2 Cor. 2:19)—confuses the identity of the church. . . . Until Jesus comes again, the church "wins" by "losing."[39]

This is the great paradox of the kingdom. God always humbles the proud but exalts the weak and downcast. Christ's kingdom cannot be gained by prestige, power, or purity. It can be entered only when God bestows it upon whom he wills.

This means that Christ's church has triumphed, is triumphing, and will triumph in spite of its own sins and shortcomings, even in the midst of the horrible suffering, persecution, and weakness it has endured from the day of Pentecost. Christ's church triumphs only as it identifies with Christ's suffering and as her ministers boast only in the cross, the gospel of foolishness to the Greek and stumbling to the Jew.

This is but one more aspect of that biblical tension between the blessings of the already and the hope of the not yet. The kingdom of God will advance in triumph until the end of the age, even though world conditions will ebb and flow, like the birth pains Jesus described. The situation for God's people will look hopeful at certain times and in certain places. It may look utterly hopeless in others. Christ's kingdom is a glorious and present reality and will steadily advance until Jesus returns. But this can only be seen through the eyes of faith and not through the institutions it controls—a point postmillenarians fail to grasp.

11

The Antichrist

There is no topic in all of Christian eschatology that is subject to as much undue speculation as is the doctrine of the Antichrist—considered by many to be the ultimate end-times foe. Yet, when biblically considered, the Antichrist is not just a fascinating topic in its own right. Christ (the Messiah) versus the Antichrist forms one of the major subplots throughout redemptive history.[1]

No doubt, many readers are familiar with the Left Behind series of novels written by Tim LaHaye and Jerry B. Jenkins that feature a young Romanian politician named Nicolae Carpathia who suddenly rises to power over a revived Roman Empire (the EU) and then dupes Israel into signing a seven-year peace treaty. Upon entering the rebuilt temple in Jerusalem, Carpathia proclaims himself to be divine and turns on the Jews, provoking the battle of Armageddon. Although this scenario is widely accepted by many, it is not found anywhere in the Bible.

This sort of unbiblical speculation caused many of us to live in fear that our new credit card, social security number, or driver's license would have the consecutive digits 6-6-6 somewhere on them. We worried that some well-known Middle Eastern or European politician would eventually make a deal with the devil (in the person of the Antichrist) and then acquire economic and military power without limits before turning on the church and persecuting the faithful, setting the stage for the church to be rescued from such danger by Jesus Christ during the rapture.

Given all the speculation and misinformation that surrounds this topic, I humbly suggest we go back to square one and analyze what Scripture actually teaches about the Antichrist. We will proceed by taking note of the two threats raised by the Antichrist as well as the three strands of data in the New Testament associated with the Antichrist. As we do so, we will consider the biblical and theological issues that form the backdrop to this topic. Then we will look at attempts to identify him and consider his mysterious mark (666) before we offer some final conclusions.

Two Threats, Three Lines of Biblical Data

It is my contention that Christ's church will face two significant threats associated with the Antichrist. The first of these threats is internal—a series of antichrists who arise within the church and are tied to a particular heresy, the denial that Jesus Christ is God in human flesh. This internal threat has been present since the days of the apostles in the form of various heresies and will be present until the time of the end when Jesus Christ returns.

The second threat is external—the repeated manifestation of the mysterious beast throughout the course of history (as depicted in the book of Revelation), taking the form of state-sponsored heresy and the persecution of Christ's church and the people of God. In the New Testament era, the beast was the Roman Empire and its imperial cult, which demanded the worship of the state and its leader. The Roman Empire, in turn, became the epitome of all those empires that arose and will arise throughout the course of history seeking divine rights, privileges, and prerogatives that belong only to God.

It is also my contention that these two distinct threats merge into a single threat at the time of the end, taking the form of an end-times Antichrist who is revealed immediately before the return of our Lord only to be destroyed by Jesus Christ at his second advent. The Antichrist's appearance is tied to some form of state-sponsored heresy much like that of the emperor cult of ancient Rome, wherein the Roman emperor viewed himself as a deity and used the full military and economic might of the state in an attempt to impose his will—that the emperor be worshiped as a deity—on the people of God.

If there are two threats to God's people (internal and external), there are three distinct lines of evidence found in the New Testament regarding the doctrine of the Antichrist. These are the antichrists of John's Epistles, Paul's "man of sin" in 2 Thessalonians 2:1–12, and the beast and false prophet of the book of Revelation (especially Rev. 13).

Many Christians assume that these three lines of evidence refer to the same thing—an end-times Antichrist. But this connection needs to be established, not just assumed. Do these three distinct strands of biblical data reveal to us what B. B. Warfield once described as a "composite photograph" of one individual?[2] Although Warfield did not believe this was the case, I respectfully disagree. But Warfield was right to insist that each of these lines of biblical data needs to be developed independently, even as we work to put together a composite picture given us by the biblical writers.

Throughout the book of Revelation, John depicts this enemy of the church as a counterfeit Trinity of sorts—an unholy collaboration among the dragon (Satan), the beast (the state), and the false prophet (its leader), who collectively wage war on the people of God after the dragon is cast from heaven (as described in Rev. 12–13).[3] Since this Antichrist figure is a false Christ who mimics our Lord's redemptive work, he will manifest his own death, resurrection, and second advent.[4] In opposition to the city of God (the New Jerusalem), even now coming down out of heaven, the beast will seduce the harlot-city Babylon and proclaim it the "city of man." The beast's number, 666, is the number of man, indicating that the beast can never enter God's rest nor rise to deity.[5]

It is vital to notice that these events take place against the backdrop of very familiar events in the Old Testament. The moment Adam fell into sin, God promised to save the fallen race through the seed (descendant) of the woman, who would in turn crush the head of the serpent, even as his own heel was bruised (Gen. 3:15). This promise set in motion throughout the subsequent course of redemptive history the conflict between the Messiah and his chief opponent (an antichrist figure). In Genesis 4, we read that the city of man's first builder was Cain, followed by Lamech, Nimrod, and then a host of other self-deified messianic pretenders. Redemptive history is replete with satanically energized geopolitical empires that rise up to wage war on the people of God—one thinks of the pharaoh of Egypt, Nebuchadnezzer, and the emperors of Rome, to name a few—only to be crushed by the Ancient of Days (as recounted in Dan. 7:9ff.). When we take a panoramic view of redemptive history, we see that the city (Babel) on the plains of Shinar (cf. Gen. 11) has come full flower in Revelation 18 in the form of Babylon the Great only to meet its demise at the time of the end in but a single hour (Rev. 18:17).

The Christian confession that "Jesus is Lord" is the supreme offense to the beast, who craves the worship of his subjects. Whenever Christians refuse to pay this individual and his government the homage they demand, God's people will pay the price. There will be economic hardship, and the faithful, at times, will be prevented from conducting ordinary commerce (buying and selling).

Some will pay with their lives (cf. Rev. 2:10), because the beast will ruthlessly kill those who will not worship him or his image (Rev. 13:15).

Paul calls this evil end-times figure the man of sin (or the man of lawlessness) in 2 Thessalonians 2:1–12. Paul tells us that this individual arises within the church (the temple of God), proclaims himself to be God's equal, demands to be worshiped, and is empowered by Satan to perform deceptive signs and wonders.[6] The man of sin is likely connected to the end-times beast John sees, which arises from the abyss at the time of the end to do the bidding of the dragon (cf. Rev. 17:11; 20:7–10).[7] Like Paul's man of sin, the beast too craves the worship of the world's inhabitants and is empowered by his master to perform signs and wonders designed to deceive those who worship him (Rev. 13:11–18). The title given this man by Paul, *man* of sin, coupled with the fact that he is cast into the lake of fire (Rev. 19:20), points in the direction of a particular individual who is said to be revealed once empowered by the dragon at the time of the end (2 Thess. 2:3–10).

Although the Antichrist's power is economic and military, it is ultimately given him by the dragon, who is Satan (Rev. 13:2). The Antichrist will be a persecutor on the order of Pharaoh, Nebuchadnezzer, or the Roman emperor Domitian and will commit acts of blasphemy that make the desecrations and blasphemies of historical figures such as Antiochus IV, Titus, and Nero pale by comparison. Therefore, these figures from redemptive history should serve to prepare us to face the future. God destroyed them all and delivered his people from their clutches, just as he will destroy the Antichrist and deliver his church when conditions become most desperate.

This final manifestation of the Antichrist, then, is state-enforced heresy— the worship of the state and its leader—and is connected to a time of great apostasy (2 Thess. 2:3; Rev. 20:7–10). The Antichrist's final destruction is brought about by the second advent of Jesus Christ (2 Thess. 2:8; Rev. 17:14; 19:19–21; 20:7–10). Just when the hour is darkest, Christ will appear in all his glory to judge the world, raise the dead, and make all things new.

Keeping this big picture in mind, let us look in more detail at the three distinct lines of evidence in the New Testament to see if they yield a composite picture of a single individual—the Antichrist.

An Antichrist or Many Antichrists?

The term *antichrist* is used in two senses in Christian eschatology. The narrow or biblical usage of the term refers to those individuals spoken of in John's Epistles who are the manifestation of the spirit of antichrist and who deny that Jesus is God come in the flesh (1 John 2:18, 22; 4:3; 2 John 1:7). The word *antichrist* never appears in the book of Revelation. The four passages from John's Epistles that mention antichrist are as follows:

- 1 John 2:18: "Children, it is the last hour, and as you have heard that antichrist is coming, so now many antichrists have come. Therefore we know that it is the last hour" (ESV).
- 1 John 2:22: "Who is the liar but he who denies that Jesus is the Christ? This is the antichrist, he who denies the Father and the Son" (ESV).
- 1 John 4:3: "And every spirit that does not confess Jesus is not from God. This is the spirit of the antichrist, which you heard was coming and now is in the world already" (ESV).
- 2 John 1:7: "For many deceivers have gone out into the world, those who do not confess the coming of Jesus Christ in the flesh. Such a one is the deceiver and the antichrist" (ESV).

According to John, many antichrists had already come and gone by the time he wrote this epistle at some point after AD 70.[8] Until the return of Jesus Christ, John says, many more antichrists will come. In this sense, then, antichrist is a past, present, and future foe. As B. B. Warfield reminds us, John warns us about these antichrists not to satisfy our curiosity about dates and times but to prepare us to do combat with him.[9] How do we combat the spirit of antichrist? We do so with the truth of the gospel, not with the force of arms.

According to John's Epistles, many antichrists were already present in the apostolic church—the primary sign that it was "the last hour" (1 John 2:18). As seen in the passages above, John described antichrist in terms of heresy and/or apostasy, which means that antichrist is (in this sense) an internal threat that arises within the church. These antichrists are likely related to our Lord's warnings about false Christs (Matt. 24:4–5; 23–24; Mark 13:5–6; 21–22; Luke 21:8), Paul's warnings about false teachers (e.g., 1 Tim. 4:1; 2 Tim. 3:1ff.), and Peter's warning about false prophets (2 Pet. 2:1).

In this narrow sense, then, antichrist is anyone who denies that Jesus Christ is God in the flesh. The spirit of antichrist was already present during the apostolic age (1 John 4:3) and was probably tied to the secret power of lawlessness mentioned by Paul, which was already present but currently restrained (2 Thess. 2:7).[10] While the end-times Antichrist has not yet come (or has not yet been revealed), many antichrists have already made their appearance.

On the other hand, the theological use of the term *antichrist* refers to the composite picture of that eschatological individual who opposes God and persecutes God's people at the time of the end and is destroyed by our Lord at his second advent. John speaks of his personal destruction in the lake of fire in Revelation 19:20. His appearance is foretold in Paul's second letter to the Thessalonians, where he is identified as "the man of sin" (2:3), another indication that a particular individual, not an impersonal system of thought or an institution, is in view. This end-times Antichrist is described by John in Revelation 11:7, 17:8, and 20:7 as the beast who arises from the abyss at the time of the end.

In an obvious parody of the redemptive work of Christ, the beast of Revelation 11, 17, and 20 is the final manifestation (*parousia*) of the two beasts who were persecuting the church at the time John was given his vision (Rev. 13). Therefore, when we use the term *antichrist* in its broad or theological sense, we are referring to this eschatological personage who appears at the time of the end and is destroyed by our Lord at his second advent.

The Man of Lawlessness

According to Paul (2 Thess. 2:1–12), the day of the Lord had not already come (as some in the Thessalonian church had feared), because two specific events had not yet occurred: a great apostasy and the revelation of the man of sin. Even though Paul wrote 2 Thessalonians before AD 70 (about AD 50/51),[11] he was probably not referring to the events of AD 70 but to the time of the end. In verse 8, he wrote, "And then the lawless one will be revealed, whom the Lord Jesus will kill with the breath of his mouth and bring to nothing by the appearance of his coming" (ESV). The spirit of lawlessness (*anomia*) was already present when Paul wrote his letter but was presently being restrained. "For the mystery of lawlessness is already at work. Only he who now restrains it will do so until he is out of the way" (v. 7 ESV). This restraint probably refers to the preaching of the gospel and is Paul's description of the "binding" of Satan mentioned by John in Revelation 20:1–10.[12] If true, this places the binding of Satan in the present age and not in a future millennial age, as taught by premillenarians.

When the final apostasy does occur, Paul said, the revelation of the man of sin is at hand. In 2 Thessalonians 2:3–4, he wrote, "For that day will not come, unless the rebellion comes first, and the man of lawlessness is revealed, the son of destruction, who opposes and exalts himself against every so-called god or object of worship, so that he takes his seat in the temple of God, proclaiming himself to be God" (ESV). The revelation of the one (the man of sin) is connected to the other (the apostasy). These are concomitant events. Paul also connected the revelation of the man of sin to the day of judgment at the second advent (vv. 8–10). This evil man is revealed so that he (and those who follow him) will be judged, bringing history to its final culmination.

As noted above, when Paul referred to the man of sin "sitting" in the temple, he was referring to the church on earth when the apostasy occurs and when the man of sin is revealed—not to the Jerusalem temple in AD 70 (contra preterism) or to a rebuilt temple in Jerusalem at the time of the end (contra futurists, including the church fathers, dispensationalists, and historic premillenarians). The five other times Paul used the word *temple* (*naos*), it clearly referred to believers (the church), who constitute the temple of God.[13]

Paul's reference to the man of sin does not refer to the papacy, since Paul was not referring to a series of individuals who may come and go (an institution) but to a particular individual who appears at the time of the end and is destroyed by Christ at his second advent. That being said, however, Reformed theologian Louis Berkhof is correct when he speaks of "elements of Antichrist in the papacy."[14] The papacy has, at times, manifested characteristics like those described by Paul, primarily in the claim made by the Roman church that the pope is the vicar of Christ on the earth.[15] The union of pope and prince in the sixteenth century—when papal authority directed the armies of Spain, France, and Italy to wage war on Protestants in France, Belgium, and the Netherlands[16]—may serve as a type of what the end-times man of sin and his blasphemous behavior will be like.

The Antichrist and the Beast of Revelation 13

When John speaks of the two beasts in Revelation 13 (the beast from the sea and the beast from the earth), he is speaking of the Roman Empire and its imperial cult. The beast from the sea (vv. 1–10) refers to the imperial cult in Rome.[17] The key historical figure in this emperor deification and worship is Nero, under whose reign the persecution of Christians began. Nero represents all forms of wickedness and ungodliness. Nero had Peter and Paul put to death in Rome. Nero blamed Christians for the great fire that destroyed much of Rome and that began a period of ruthless persecution of Christians in Rome. Nero was censured by the Roman Senate, took his own life, but was widely rumored to have survived or to have come back from the dead.[18] The Nero *redivivus* myth underlies John's discussion of the beast and his mimicking of Christ's work of redemption—his death, resurrection, and parousia at the time of the end.

The beast from the earth (vv. 11–18) refers to the imperial cult and its priests in Asia Minor at the time John was given the series of visions we know as the book of Revelation (about AD 95).[19] The key figure in this imperial cult is the Roman emperor Domitian (the beast come back to life). Under this imperial cult, there was renewed persecution of Christians throughout the area, especially Pergamum, where Antipas had been martyred some time earlier (Rev. 2:13), and Smyrna, where Christians were facing severe economic repression and were unable to buy and sell (Rev. 2:8–11).[20] The imperial cult (including the Commune of Asia) was much more active in Asia Minor than in Rome.[21] Domitian persecuted Christians quite intensely throughout Asia Minor, especially in those years immediately before John received his vision.[22]

The identification of a city with seven hills (Rome) and a series of rulers (the caesars) in power when John received his revelation indicates that the beast was a foe persecuting the apostolic church when John was given his vision. While preterists are correct to emphasize the significance of John's statement that "the time is near" (Rev. 1:3) and to recognize that John was writing to Christians already suffering from Roman persecution, ultimately, the preterist interpretation cannot be sustained. Not only does the evidence suggest that John was given his revelation after AD 70,[23] but preterist interpretations of the beast, his image, and his number are also not exhaustively fulfilled by Nero and the events of AD 70 with the destruction of Jerusalem and its temple. Both Nero and the events associated with the destruction of the temple may point ahead to another fulfillment at the end of the age (cf. Rev. 17:9–14). This is especially the case if the beast of Revelation 17 is an eschatological figure (an eighth king) who will appear at the time of the end.[24]

Futurist interpretations of the connection between the Antichrist and the beast of Revelation 13 are highly problematic as well. The biblical data clearly speaks of antichrists and the beast as present realities during the apostolic age as well as the entire interadvental period. These images cannot be pushed ahead to the time of the end, thereby virtually ignoring the historical context of John's vision and the fact that the book of Revelation was addressed to the seven historical churches mentioned in chapters 2–3 whose members actually faced the Roman beast. The dispensational variety of futurism (the idea that the Antichrist is revealed at or about the time of the rapture and the beginning of the seven-year tribulation period in connection with a peace treaty with Israel) collapses under its own weight. There is simply no biblical evidence for such an interpretive scheme.

As we have seen, in 2 Thessalonians 2:1–12, Paul was not referring to the Jerusalem temple in any sense. He was referring to the church struggling on earth (the church militant) until the time of the end. If true, the futurist interpretation of this data means that Christians of the first century were wrong to assume that John was writing about events contemporaneous to them. John was *really* writing to people living at the time of the end, not to Christians in the first century. This, of course, is not the case.

The Mark of the Beast

The mark of the beast (the number of humanity—"perfectly imperfect") is tied to the state's usurpation of divine prerogatives and attributes. Those who take the mark of the beast do so in the context of the worship of the state and its leaders in such a way as to either deny their faith in Jesus Christ (apostasy) or confess that "Caesar is Lord" (emperor worship). The number 666 may indeed be a reference to Nero, but Nero does not exhaust what is signified, especially if the book of Revelation was written after AD 70. This mark and number are a reoccurring phenomenon, tied to any appearance of the beast seeking the worship and adoration that belong only to the true and living God.

Gematria—drawing numerical value from a word or phrase—might be in view if the number 666 is a reference to Nero.[25] But even if this is a cryptic reference to Nero, it is far more important to understand what the number means than to identify the individual to whom it refers. Six falls one short of 7 (the number of completeness). The beast mimics Christ but always falls short. Six represents fallen humanity, always laboring but never entering the Sabbath rest (the seventh day of creation typifying the eternal Sabbath rest). The triple 6s indicate the beast, who along with the dragon (Satan) and the second beast (or false prophet) mimics the Holy Trinity but is condemned to fall short of completeness. The beast can never rise above humanity to attain the deity it so desires.[26]

At the time John used this image, slaves were branded or tattooed by their owners.[27] This indicates that anyone who "takes the mark" is branded as a slave (or servant) of the beast and self-consciously renounces Christ to their eternal peril. Dispensationalists miss the point when they are preoccupied with investigating which forms of technology can be used to create body markings or a cashless society. They come closer to the truth when they warn us about government usurping its God-given role and seeking the adoration and worship owed to God by his people. The worship of the state or its leader is a real and pressing threat to all Christians. Statism can easily become false religion and idolatry whenever the state claims divine prerogatives and privileges for itself. This is the very essence of the beast. Anyone who confesses that "Caesar is Lord" is denying that "Jesus is Lord." Graphic illustrations of this are the swastika and the Nazi salute to Hitler—relatively recent manifestations of the mark.

The usurpation of divine authority by the state is seen in the efforts of the second beast (Rev. 13:11–18), who is the false prophet (Rev. 16:13), to deceive the earth's inhabitants into worshiping the beast (the state) and his image (its leader). Sadly, this phenomenon occurs throughout the interadvental age before culminating in an end-times Antichrist.

Is an Antichrist Yet to Come?

Many antichrists will come and go, but, in my opinion, the series of antichrists faced by the church from the beginning will at some point give way to the Antichrist—the final heretic, arch-blasphemer, and persecutor of God's people. According to Paul (2 Thess. 2:1–12) and John (Rev. 20:1–10), the spirit of lawlessness and Satan were already at work in the apostolic era but were restrained through the preaching of the gospel. Both Paul and John expected that restraint to be lifted immediately before Christ returns. Therefore, various beasts (governments) and their leaders and henchmen will come and go until one final manifestation of satanic rage and deception breaks out, immediately before the Lord returns.

The fact that anti-Christian empires/nations and their satanically inspired leaders come and go means that many attempts by Christians in the past to identify the beast and the Antichrist may have merit, although the date-setting that was often attached to this does not. In an age when the Roman Catholic Church was able to exert political power and papal sanction against Protestants through allied nations and their armies (e.g., Spain, Italy, France), Protestants were justified in identifying the Roman Church and those nations allied with it as the beast and the papacy as the seat of the Antichrist. And yet, the preaching of the gospel restrained these Roman Catholic nations from destroying those churches that embraced the doctrine of justification, *sola fide*. Furthermore, historical circumstances have changed greatly in the centuries that have followed. The unholy alliance between pope and prince, described above, has been replaced by the socialist democracies of the EU, which are virtually secularized and take little interest in religious matters.

Based on John's discussion of the beast and the harlot Babylon (Rev. 18), the final manifestation of the beast and its leader will not be so much a Nero *redivivus* as a beast *redivivus*. If we want to know what the Antichrist and his kingdom will be like, we need to look to the Roman Empire and the imperial cult already present in the pages of the New Testament, that took the lives of God's people and prevented them from buying and selling. This is what the final beast will seek to do—wage war on the saints because they refuse

to worship him or his blasphemous image. But the beast will be destroyed by
the Lamb, who has already overcome him! If John is clear about anything,
it is that the Lamb wins in the end, not the dragon. When Satan and his sur-
rogates wage war on the saints and kill them (Rev. 13:7), John tells us that
the saints come to life and reign with Christ for a thousand years (Rev. 20:4).
Yet, the ongoing victory of the Lamb can only be seen through the eyes of
faith until that day when Jesus returns in all his glory, accompanied by the
hosts of heaven.

Biblical Reflection, Not Speculation

One lesson we must learn is that we need to be very cautious about setting
dates and identifying particular persons as the Antichrist. The biblical writers
repeatedly spoke of things associated with the time of the end as a mystery
(1 Cor. 15:51; Rom. 11:25) or as something that requires wisdom in order to be
understood (Rev. 13:18; 17:9). We have been cautioned that this phenomenon
is connected to the great apostasy and is currently prevented from appearing
by some form of divine restraint (2 Thess. 2:1–12; Rev. 20:1–10). Only God
knows when these things will come to pass (cf. Matt. 24:36). Since God gives
his people wisdom without measure (James 1:5), we can expect that when the
time comes Christians living at the time of the end will know full well what
these prophecies mean. But not before.

We also need to learn from those sincere but futile efforts by the Puritans
and individuals such as Jonathan Edwards to tie biblical prophecy to current
events, to set dates (1866), and to identify the Antichrist by name.[28] As Bernard
McGinn correctly points out, "No age in Christian history has lacked its own
ingenious proofs of the imminence of the time of the end."[29] Yet, this is the
nature of an ongoing threat, especially when that threat is expected to come
to a dramatic and climatic end. While our forefathers may have been largely
correct in their identification of the beast as the papacy (the signs were certainly
present in some measure), it was simply not God's time for the restraint to be
lifted and the beast to pour out its final fury.

Will there be an Antichrist? Yes, there will. But we need to take note of
Anthony Hoekema's caution in this regard:

> We conclude that the sign of the antichrist, like the other signs of the times, is
> present throughout the history of the church. We may even say that every age
> will provide its own particular form of antichristian activity. But we look for
> an intensification of this sign in the appearance of the antichrist whom Christ
> himself will destroy at his Second Coming.[30]

We must be very cautious yet ever vigilant. Our focus should be on the means by which God restrains the principle of lawlessness—the preaching of the gospel—and we must not spend our energies on useless speculation, for our hope as Christians lies not in our powers of prognostication but in the ultimate and final victory of the Lamb.

Geerhardus Vos wisely cautions:

> [The prophecy of the Antichrist] belongs among the many prophecies, whose best and final exegete will be the eschatological fulfillment, and in regard to which it behooves the saints to exercise a peculiar kind of eschatological patience. The idea of Antichrist in general and that of the apostasy in particular ought to warn us, although this may not have been the proximate purpose of Paul, not to take for granted an uninterrupted progress of the cause of Christ through all ages on toward the end. The making all things right and new in the world depends not on gradual amelioration but on the final interposition of God.[31]

We long not for an earthly utopia in which the city of man becomes the city of God. The harlot Babylon cannot be fumigated and remodeled. We do not long for an earthly millennium in which a fallen world is whitewashed for a time, with sinful human nature still present beneath the serene veneer while Jesus temporarily rules the nations from his earthly throne in Jerusalem. No, we long for the same thing Abraham did—a heavenly country and a heavenly city (Heb. 11:16). As God promised Abraham, even now he is preparing this very thing for his people. When Jesus Christ returns, a new heaven and a new earth will become a glorious reality, but not before.

The New Testament never holds out the hope that Babylon (the city of man) will become the New Jerusalem (the city of God). The New Testament teaches that when the seventh trumpet sounds at the time our blessed Lord returns, then "the kingdom of the world has become the kingdom of our Lord and of his Christ, and he will reign for ever and ever" (Rev. 11:15). The dragon, the beast, the false prophet, and all who serve them will be cast into the lake of fire, no longer a threat to the peace and safety of the kingdom of God. As John says in Revelation 21, "I saw the holy city, new Jerusalem, coming down out of heaven from God, prepared as a bride adorned for her husband. And I heard a loud voice from the throne saying, 'Behold, the dwelling place of God is with man. He will dwell with them, and they will be his people, and God himself will be with them as their God'" (vv. 2–3 ESV). The great covenant promise will then finally be realized: "I will be your God and you will be my people." God will dwell in our midst, and no longer will there be any tears, sadness, or sorrow. Nor will there be any trace of the harlot Babylon.

Instead of fearing and dreading the Antichrist and worrying about the latest events in the Middle East or whether the number 666 appears on a household product ID, we should be longing for the second coming of Jesus Christ, for Satan and his cronies have already been defeated by the blood and righteousness of Jesus, although for a time they will run amuck because they know their time is short (Rev. 12:12).

Perhaps Martin Luther said it best in his famous hymn "A Mighty Fortress": "One little word shall fell him." Amen. Even so, come quickly, Lord Jesus!

12

The Blessed Hope

In the face of the prospect of continuing ungodliness, Paul gave Christians the following exhortation: "Live self-controlled, upright and godly lives in this present age, while we wait for the blessed hope—the glorious appearing of our great God and Savior, Jesus Christ, who gave himself for us to redeem us from all wickedness and to purify for himself a people that are his very own, eager to do what is good. These, then, are the things you should teach" (Titus 2:12–15). With these words, we now come to the heart of New Testament eschatology. The most significant event yet ahead in redemptive history is the second advent of Jesus Christ. The glorious appearing of Jesus Christ is the blessed hope.

Paul did not direct us to a future golden age when ungodliness will cease because of gospel progress. He did not tell us that this glorious appearance of our God and Savior will be fulfilled within the lifetimes of his hearers by the events of AD 70, when God's hand of judgment fell on Israel, Jerusalem, and the temple. Nor did Paul point us to a secret rapture in which believers are mysteriously snatched away before God's wrath is poured out upon the earth. Neither did Paul tell us that the blessed hope entails two distinct events: Christ's appearance and then, after a thousand years, the final judgment. Paul was not postmillennial. He was not a preterist. Nor was he a dispensationalist or a premillenarian. Paul looked for one climactic future event, the return of Jesus Christ, the blessed hope. It is this blessed hope that enables us to live godly and upright lives in this present age.

The second advent of Jesus Christ is central to New Testament eschatology because the Lord's return marks the final consummation of redemptive history and the dawn of the eternal state in which there are no more tears, no more suffering, and no more pain, when the old order of things finally passes away (Rev. 21:4). This present evil age will pass away in the light of the glories of the age to come when Christ makes all things new and the temporal gives way to the eternal. When Jesus Christ returns on the last day, God will raise the dead, judge the world, and renew the cosmos. This event is the final chapter in the great drama of redemption. We now turn to the specific events associated with the return of Jesus Christ: the resurrection, the judgment, and the renewal of all things.

The Resurrection

Because of Christ's victory over death and the grave that first Easter, Paul exclaimed, "Thanks be to God!" because humanity's greatest enemy, death, had been "swallowed up in victory" (1 Cor. 15:54–57). From the time death first came upon the human race in Eden as a result of Adam's fall, God's people have longed for that glorious day when the dead will be raised to live again forevermore. This hope of a bodily resurrection has always sustained the faithful in the face of death, depravation, sickness, suffering, even martyrdom. Our hope in the resurrection explains why, from the beginning of the Christian era, the Christian funeral service begins with these words of comfort from our Lord: "I am the resurrection and the life. He who believes in me will live, even though he dies" (John 11:25).

The hope of the resurrection of the dead also was an important theme in the writings of Israel's prophets. Daniel wrote:

> At that time Michael, the great prince who protects your people, will arise. There will be a time of distress such as has not happened from the beginning of nations until then. But at that time your people—everyone whose name is found written in the book—will be delivered. Multitudes who sleep in the dust of the earth will awake: some to everlasting life, others to shame and everlasting contempt. Those who are wise will shine like the brightness of the heavens, and those who lead many to righteousness, like the stars for ever and ever. But you, Daniel, close up and seal the words of the scroll until the time of the end. Many will go here and there to increase knowledge. (Dan. 12:1–4)

After a time of unprecedented distress, there will be a resurrection of the righteous and the unrighteous, both groups receiving everlasting blessing or cursing. These words are echoed by our Lord himself in John's Gospel when Jesus spoke of a time to come when "all who are in their graves will hear his voice and come out—those who have done good will rise to live, and those who have done evil will rise to be condemned" (5:28–29).

Both Daniel and Jesus spoke of one resurrection in which two distinct groups simultaneously participate—believers and unbelievers—each receiving the appropriate recompense. There is no hint anywhere in these two texts, implied or otherwise, that the resurrection of the righteous and the resurrection of the unrighteous are separated by a period of one thousand years, an essential feature of premillennialism.[1] Both Jesus and Daniel depicted the resurrection of the righteous and the unrighteous as occurring at the same time.

Like Daniel, the prophet Isaiah saw the resurrection occurring after a period of horrible anguish, a time when salvation will come to God's people. Describing this in premessianic terms, he painted a prophetic picture of a great messianic feast celebrated by all of God's people on the mountain of the Lord.

> On this mountain the LORD Almighty will prepare a feast of rich food for all peoples, a banquet of aged wine—the best of meats and the finest of wines. On this mountain he will destroy the shroud that enfolds all peoples, the sheet that covers all nations; he will swallow up death forever. The Sovereign LORD will wipe away the tears from all faces; he will remove the disgrace of his people from all the earth. The LORD has spoken. In that day they will say, "Surely this is our God; we trusted in him, and he saved us. This is the LORD, we trusted in him; let us rejoice and be glad in his salvation." (Isa. 25:6–9)

Paul quoted this text in 1 Corinthians 15:55, when, in light of Christ's resurrection, the apostle mocked death itself with the words, "Where, O death, is your victory? Where, O death, is your sting?" It is because of Christ's death and resurrection that the shroud of death is removed from God's people and the great prophetic hope of life after death is fulfilled. On that day, said Isaiah, "Your dead will live; their bodies will rise. . . . The earth will give birth to her dead" (Isa. 26:19). This resurrection hope of the prophets became a glorious reality when Jesus Christ rose from the dead that first Easter, the firstfruits of the resurrection of believers when he returns on the last day.

Based on his two letters to the church in Thessalonica, it is clear that, like Daniel and Jesus, Paul assigned the resurrection of both the just and the unjust to the last day, that time when the trumpet of God announces that the great blessing and curse have finally arrived. The apostle wrote:

> We believe that Jesus died and rose again and so we believe that God will bring with Jesus those who have fallen asleep in him. According to the Lord's own

word, we tell you that we who are still alive, who are left till the coming of the
Lord, will certainly not precede those who have fallen asleep. For the Lord
himself will come down from heaven, with a loud command, with the voice of
the archangel and with the trumpet call of God, and the dead in Christ will rise
first. After that, we who are still alive and are left will be caught up together
with them in the clouds to meet the Lord in the air. And so we will be with the
Lord forever. (1 Thess. 4:14–17)

Several things need to be noted. First, when Jesus comes back, he will indeed
"rapture" his saints from the earth. But this is not a secret rapture, which the
dispensationalists champion so militantly. The threefold annunciation of the
coming of the Lord by the loud command, the voice of the archangel, and
the trumpet of God gives the readers who take Paul literally the sense that this
event is anything but secret. As Leon Morris puts it, "I do not doubt that, if
he so chose, God could make the voice of the archangel, the shout, and the
trumpet audible only to believers. But I doubt very greatly whether that is
what Paul is saying."[2]

An indication that this is a day of cosmic significance is the fact that believers
are caught up—a word meaning to be seized by an irresistible force[3]—into the
clouds to meet the Lord in the air. Paul's reference to the air may have something to do with the fact that Satan was elsewhere described by the apostle as
the "ruler of the kingdom of the air" (Eph. 2:2). Hence, this event marks the
final defeat of Satan (cf. 2 Thess. 2:8; Rev. 20:10).[4]

The presence of the clouds recalls to mind other climactic events in redemptive history: the exodus (Exod. 13:21; 14:19), the events that transpired on
Mount Sinai (Exod. 19:16; 24:15), the filling of the tabernacle (Exod. 40:34–35),
the wanderings in the wilderness (Exod. 40:36–38), and the transfiguration
(Mark 9:7) and ascension of Jesus (Acts 1:9).[5] This event is the long-anticipated
redemptive-historical climax, not a secret rapture that is but the prelude to
the "real" second coming seven years later.

Paul said much the same when he wrote to Christians who endured great persecution and were counted worthy of the kingdom because of their suffering:

God is just: He will pay back trouble to those who trouble you and give relief
to you who are troubled, and to us as well. This will happen when the Lord
Jesus is revealed from heaven in blazing fire with his powerful angels. He will
punish those who do not know God and do not obey the gospel of our Lord
Jesus. They will be punished with everlasting destruction and shut out from the
presence of the Lord and from the majesty of his power on the day he comes to
be glorified in his holy people and to be marveled at among all those who have
believed. (2 Thess. 1:6–10)

When the Lord Jesus is revealed from heaven—the day of *apokalypsis*, which is also his parousia[6]—the dead are raised and those who persecute Christ's church are judged. Believers will be with the Lord forever, while unbelievers will be punished everlastingly. This direct linkage between the resurrection and the judgment of those who are Christ's and those who are not—depicted here as simultaneous events—raises a serious problem for premillenarians. Despite the assertions from Jesus (Matt. 13:37–43; 25:31–46) and Paul to the contrary, they insert a one-thousand-year delay between the blessing assigned to the righteous and the judgment that comes upon unbelievers.

Another important Pauline text in which the significance of the resurrection is discussed is 1 Corinthians 15:50–54:

> I declare to you, brothers, that flesh and blood cannot inherit the kingdom of God, nor does the perishable inherit the imperishable. Listen, I tell you a mystery: We will not all sleep, but we will all be changed—in a flash, in the twinkling of an eye, at the last trumpet. For the trumpet will sound, the dead will be raised imperishable, and we will be changed. For the perishable must clothe itself with the imperishable, and the mortal with immortality. When the perishable has been clothed with the imperishable, and the mortal with immortality, then the saying that is written will come true: "Death has been swallowed up in victory."

In his first letter to the Corinthians, Paul explained the nature of the resurrection body. As he had written to the Thessalonians, it is when the trumpet sounds that the dead are raised imperishable and the kingdom of God is finally consummated. Because Christ comes back and raises the dead, our mortal bodies will put on immortality, and the sting of death will give way to the triumph of resurrection.

Paul was not alone in this. John placed the resurrection on the "last day." During the discourse with the crowds who wanted to make Jesus king because he miraculously fed five thousand of them, he specifically stated that the dead are raised "at the last day" (John 6:39–40, 44, 54). The same thing was stated regarding the death of Jesus's friend Lazarus. Martha answered Jesus's question about the coming resurrection by saying, "I know he will rise again in the resurrection at the last day" (John 11:24).

It is beyond question that the resurrection of the righteous and the resurrection of the unrighteous both occur at the sound of the final trumpet, on the last day, when Jesus Christ returns in great glory. The biblical writers saw this as a source of great comfort. This is also the event that categorically marks "the end of the age" (Matt. 13:39). It is problematic, therefore, when Christians speak of Christ's return to raise the dead primarily in terms of a secret rapture—the catching away of believers—instead of focusing on the primary thrust of these texts, which is the resurrection of the dead, which occurs on that glorious day when Jesus comes again.

The Judgment

When Paul spoke of the resurrection of the righteous (1 Thess. 4:14–17), he linked the resurrection to the final judgment of both believers and unbelievers (2 Thess. 1:6–9). For unbelievers, the return of Jesus Christ is the time of judgment that is no longer delayed by the long-suffering mercies of God. At the moment when Jesus returns in all his glory at the "end of the age," the angelic legions will come and pull the weeds from among the wheat, throwing them into the fires of judgment (Matt. 13:36–43). Although this is the day of judgment for all who do evil, it is also the day when the righteous will shine in the kingdom of their Father.

That the final judgment of the righteous and of the wicked occur at the same time is also clearly depicted in Matthew 25:31–46, where Jesus spoke of the final judgment in terms of separating the sheep from the goats and assigning each group their everlasting rewards. When Jesus returns in glory with all his angels, he assigns the final outcome to both righteous and unrighteous.[7] There is no evidence here of the linchpin of premillennialism, a one-thousand-year gap between the resurrection of the righteous and the resurrection of the unrighteous.

Even as staunch a premillenarian as George Ladd is forced to admit regarding this passage, "If this is the final judgment, what do we do about the millennium? There seems to be no room for it. The author is frank to admit that if we had to follow this passage as our program of prophecy, there would be no room for a millennium. I would have to be an amillennialist."[8] How does Ladd escape this dilemma? He does so by denying that this text has anything whatsoever to do with a "program of prophecy." According to Ladd, Matthew 25:31–46 is a parable instructing Jesus's disciples about their responsibilities under the Great Commission.[9] Ladd's comments stand in contrast to those he makes elsewhere when he says that the entire premillennial system of interpretation hinges on not avoiding clear and unambiguous texts.[10]

A more plausible approach is to appeal to progressive revelation and to argue that, in Revelation 20, John reinterpreted Jesus's earlier teaching in the Gospels to allow for a one-thousand-year gap between the judgment of the righteous and the judgment of the unrighteous. But this appeal escapes neither the problem of evil intrinsic to any future earthly millennium nor the fact that John did not mention this in the text in question.[11]

The resurrection and the judgment are also linked in Revelation 20:11–15. John, when writing about the conclusion of the millennial age, when fire from heaven consumes those who rebel against Christ, depicted the final judgment in these sobering terms.

> Then I saw a great white throne and him who was seated on it. Earth and sky fled from his presence, and there was no place for them. And I saw the dead, great and small, standing before the throne, and books were opened. Another book was opened, which is the book of life. The dead were judged according to what they had done as recorded in the books. The sea gave up the dead that were in it, and death and Hades gave up the dead that were in them, and each person was judged according to what he had done. Then death and Hades were thrown into the lake of fire. The lake of fire is the second death. If anyone's name was not found written in the book of life, he was thrown into the lake of fire. (Rev. 20:11–15)

This is a picture of the final judgment when the dead will be judged according to what they have done, but the scene also assumes that the general resurrection has already occurred because the dead are in God's presence to receive their reward. There is also an indication that the cosmic renewal occurs at the same time, since John spoke of the earth and the sky fleeing from God's presence.

In the twelfth chapter of John's Gospel, Jesus, who already told us that the resurrection occurs on the last day, said that the judgment occurs at the same time: "There is a judge for the one who rejects me and does not accept my words; that very word which I spoke will condemn him at the last day" (v. 48). The day of resurrection is also the day of judgment, marking the end of unbelief and human rebellion. The trumpet has sounded. The last day has come. This present evil age has come to an end.

Having considered the biblical evidence regarding the resurrection and the final judgment, we can have no doubts that the last day, the last trumpet, the day of the Lord, the raising of the dead, and the judgment of people will be concomitant events. Jesus, John, and Paul all connected these events to Jesus's second advent. It will be the most frightening day known to humanity when kings and princes, generals and privates, rich and poor, great and small, slave and free will quake in terror and pray for rocks to fall on them to hide them from the fury of the one who sits on the throne of judgment. The great day of God's wrath has come, and who can stand (Rev. 6:15–17)? But for those who are Christ's, it is a day of blessed hope.

Cosmic Renewal

Scripture clearly teaches that the resurrection and the judgment of the righteous and the unrighteous will occur at the same time, thus eliminating the possibility of an earthly millennial age to dawn after the Lord's return. The Scriptures also teach that the second advent of Jesus Christ will be the time of cosmic renewal when every stain, hint, and trace of sin are removed from all creation. This too strikes a telling blow against most forms of premillennialism, which assign the creation of the new heaven and the new earth to after the resurrection and judgment of the wicked at the end of the millennial age.[12]

Peter taught that this cosmic renewal will occur when Christ returns, making this renewal a concomitant event with both the resurrection and the judgment (2 Pet. 3:3–15). Peter wrote, "The day of the Lord will come like a thief. The heavens will disappear with a roar; the elements will be destroyed by fire, and the earth and everything in it will be laid bare" (v. 10).

God's delay in judging the world is an act of grace, but his gracious delay becomes the occasion for unbelievers to scoff and ask, "Where is this 'coming' he promised?" (v. 4). To encourage believers in the midst of this unbelief, Peter painted a vision of the eschatological judgment to come upon the earth. Christians should not take the delay in the parousia to mean that Christ is indifferent to the plight of his people or is powerless to do anything about it. This delay in his return is because God's timing is not ours. Therefore, when Peter assigned the renewal of the heaven and the earth to the day of the Lord, he did so to make the point that the day of judgment will be the day of wrath and renewal and that those who sleep will be caught completely unaware.[13] Having this hope, he said, we are to purify ourselves in anticipation.

At the end of this exhortation, Peter mentioned Paul's teaching regarding God's patience with his fallen creatures. Though we don't know to which specific Pauline Epistle Peter was referring, we do know that in Romans 8 Paul also spoke of cosmic renewal and God's forbearance: "The creation waits in eager expectation for the sons of God to be revealed. For the creation was subjected to frustration, not by its own choice, but by the will of the one who subjected it, in hope that the creation itself will be liberated from its bondage to decay and brought into the glorious freedom of the children of God" (vv. 19–21). According to Paul, creation will be liberated from its bondage when the sons of God are revealed, demonstrating that Jesus Christ will deliver not only his people from eschatological wrath but also the created order. As sinful men and women are transformed into the image of Christ, so too creation will realize its final purpose. "The destiny of the creation and of the 'children of God,' whom Jesus gathers around him, belong intrinsically together."[14]

Since the cosmic renewal is depicted as a day of judgment for the wicked and the preparation of the home for the righteous, this too supports the idea that the resurrection, judgment, and re-creation of all things occur at Christ's second advent. He will come like a thief in the night to raise the dead (1 Thess. 5:2) and purify his creation from all traces of human sin and rebellion (2 Pet. 3:10).

A Sudden and Imminent Return, yet Preceded by Signs

One of the most difficult aspects of New Testament eschatology is the tension we find between those biblical passages that speak of the sudden and unexpected nature of Christ's return and those that teach that his return is preceded by specific signs. This tension, especially in the Olivet Discourse, has led a number of critical scholars, such as Albert Schweitzer, to assert that when Jesus's predictions of God's eschatological judgment did not come to pass, the first Christians introduced the idea of a delay in the timing of the parousia. Some Reformed Christians have found this challenge to be so serious that they have adopted a modified preterism in response.[15]

As we saw when we considered the already/not yet tension found throughout the New Testament, the tension between the signs preceding the Lord's return and its suddenness is not accidental. This is not the result of the early church trying to cover up the embarrassment of Jesus's prediction not coming to pass. This tension is by design. In fact, Jesus and Paul introduced it in several important passages, and it forms part of a distinctly Christian ethic.

The disciples asked Jesus, "Tell us, . . . what will be the sign of your coming and of the end of the age?" (Matt. 24:3). Jesus warned them about the rise of false Christs, wars and rumors of wars, famines, and earthquakes, all of which will be the beginning of birth pains (vv. 4–8). After speaking of the persecution of believers and the judgment to come upon Israel in AD 70 (vv. 9–26), Jesus said that his own coming will be like lightning suddenly and ominously flashing across the skies (v. 27). The situation will be much like it was in the days of Noah. God's people will go about their Father's business, while unbelievers will increase in wickedness. Suddenly, Jesus said, God's wrath will come upon the wicked (v. 39).[16] The signs of our Lord's coming will be present all along. Yet, lacking the eyes of faith, unbelievers will be caught completely unaware.

Paul clearly followed suit, speaking of our Lord's return as coming like a thief in the night and yet hinting at a delay in the parousia of an indeterminate period of time. To the Thessalonians, he wrote, "While people are saying, 'Peace and safety,' destruction will come on them suddenly, as labor pains on a pregnant woman, and they will not escape" (1 Thess. 5:2–3). Paul also spoke of the suddenness of our Lord's return when he wrote, "Listen, I tell you a mystery: We will not all sleep, but we will all be changed—in a flash, in the twinkling of an eye, at the last trumpet. For the trumpet will sound, the dead will be raised imperishable, and we will be changed" (1 Cor. 15:51–52). No doubt, Paul warned his readers that this great event will come when people least expect it. Therefore, Christians must be prepared. We are to live in expectation and hope of the Lord's return.

But Paul also seemed to expect a delay in the second coming. In his second letter to the Thessalonians, a congregation plagued with the erroneous teaching that the day of the Lord had already come, Paul told his readers that the day of the Lord had not come. He spoke of specific signs that will precede this event, indicating that it had not yet transpired despite disconcerting reports to the contrary. Paul told the Thessalonians "not to become easily unsettled or alarmed by some prophecy, report or letter supposed to have come from us, saying that the day of the Lord has already come. Don't let anyone deceive you in any way, for that day will not come until the rebellion occurs and the man of lawlessness is revealed, the man doomed to destruction" (2 Thess. 2:2–3). Not until the eschatological man of sin makes his entrance will the day of the Lord finally come.

If this tension between the signs that precede the coming of the Lord and the sudden nature of his coming did not make its way into the New Testament to explain Jesus's failure to return in the lifetimes of the apostles, why did this belief make its way into Christian teaching? According to George Ladd, this tension

> has as its primary purpose an ethical objective: to exhort watchfulness and readiness for the end. . . . Jesus was not interested in depicting eschatological conditions, but in preparing men for the Day of Judgment. . . . [This explains] why the seemingly contradictory emphasis on the imminence and the remoteness of the last day was designed precisely to make it impossible to know the time, but it demanded readiness for a sudden event. This is where the Gospels leave us: Anticipating an imminent event and yet unable to date its coming. Logically this may appear contradictory, but it is a tension with an ethical purpose—to make date setting impossible and therefore demand constant readiness.[17]

To Christians, the signs of the end and the tribulation the church will face throughout this present evil age are not signs of God's indifference or impotence in coming to their aid. These signs guarantee that Jesus Christ is coming to end this present age. The despair of humanity and the tumult of the earth cry out together for the redemption of all creation. The groaning of the earth tells us that all is not right and that God must intervene to undo the consequences of human sinfulness.

Notice too that both Jesus and Paul described the course of future history as being like that of birth pains. Birth pains come with greater frequency and become increasingly more intense. When birth finally arrives, the convulsions are so acute that it is virtually impossible to tell whether the next contraction will be the one that results in the blessed event or yet another ordeal to be endured with clenched teeth and fists. This is what we can expect the interadvental period to be like. Because of this tension, biblical writers repeatedly exhorted Christians to be watchful. Although specific signs precede his coming, our Lord will return like a thief in the night when we least expect him.

Therefore, God's people are to see these signs for what they are, the guarantee of the end. But to non-Christians, these same signs are seen as proof that Christ is not going to come at all. Without faith, the delay in the parousia is taken to mean that Jesus is never going to return, that life will go on as before, and that human sin and rebellion will simply go unpunished. In 2 Peter 3:1–10, the apostle taught that an interval of some duration will exist between Christ's first and second advent. In fact, the delay in our Lord's coming prompts scoffers to look at those same things that Christians regard as signs of the end and a guarantee of our Lord's return and see them as a reason to scoff. This further increases their guilt before a holy God who returns in judgment.

A Secret Rapture?

When some Christians think about eschatology, the idea of a secret rapture is usually one of the first things that come to mind. Yet, this understanding of our Lord's return is a position held by a small minority of Christians. Unfortunately, their ability to dominate popular Christian media and publishing gives the perception that the view has a greater significance than really exists. Given the popularity of the dispensationalist teaching about a secret rapture, as evidenced by the success of Tim LaHaye and Jerry B. Jenkins's Left Behind series, another response is required in addition to what has already been said.

According to J. Dwight Pentecost, the pretribulation conception rests on several essential presuppositions: (1) a "literal interpretation" of the Scriptures; (2) "The church and Israel are two distinct groups with whom God has a divine plan"; (3) "The church is a mystery, unrevealed in the Old Testament. This present mystery age intervenes within the program of God for Israel's rejection of the Messiah at His first advent"; and (4) "This mystery program must be completed before God can resume His program with Israel and bring it to completion."[18] This is an important admission, since the only way one could arrive at a secret pretribulational rapture is if these presuppositions are in place.

Since we have called into question all four of these presuppositions, it should now be clear that the dispensational framework is a house built on sand. The pretribulational rapture is not, contrary to the dispensationalist claim, inductively developed from the biblical text. It is based on a selective and a priori–laden use of the biblical data. And, if fundamental assumptions are false, it is highly likely that any conclusions reached based on them are also false.

The literalistic interpretation of the Scriptures associated with dispensationalism is highly problematic. The dawn of the messianic age and the kingdom of God does not constitute a parenthetical period in redemptive history until such a time when God is ready to deal with national Israel and finish his original plan of redemption. It is clearly prophesied in the Old Testament that God's redemptive purposes include Gentiles (Gen. 12:3; 22:18; Isa. 49:6). Therefore, the church is not a "mystery" during this age because the mystical body of Jesus Christ, the church, is the fulfillment of God's eternal purposes. If the formation of Christ's church and the salvation of the Gentiles are part of God's eternal plan (cf. Eph. 1:9–11), then the presuppositions mentioned by Pentecost are no longer viable.

How the literalistic hermeneutic of the dispensationalist determines the interpretive outcome in advance can be seen when we look at those texts that treat the second coming of Christ and how dispensationalists interpret them. To make his case for a pretribulational rapture, Pentecost lists seventeen distinctions between the rapture and the second advent, which, he says, serve as the basis for contending that there are yet two future comings of Jesus Christ.[19] When Pentecost argues that because a distinction is made in those texts discussing the return of Christ to the earth between believers being "raptured away" and a physical manifestation of Jesus Christ, this requires two mutually exclusive events separated by a seven-year tribulation. His conclusion, therefore, is highly suspect.[20] The methodology itself prevents the interpreter from looking at all the data with any semblance of objectivity. Carried through in other instances, this would, for example, force us to argue that because the Bible reveals that there are three persons called God in the Scriptures, there must be three Gods. Of course, such a conclusion can only be made by not dealing with the other important line of evidence in the Scriptures, which teaches us that God is one. But this is what dispensationalists do when looking at those texts that deal with the second advent of Jesus Christ. They downplay the importance of the texts that teach that these are different aspects of the same event.

Therefore, when the Bible speaks of Christ's second coming as one event with several elements (the catching up of believers and the bodily return of Christ), dispensationalists interpret these verses in light of an a priori distinction between the rapture and the second coming. They base this on the presupposition that the Gentile church must be removed at the start of the tribulation period. But this distinction between different aspects of the second coming in no way forces us to the conclusion that these must be two distinct events separated by a seven-year tribulation. In fact, if we look at the biblical data without dispensational presuppositions, we would never conclude that the coming of Christ consists of two separate events seven years apart, with one of them being secret.

One of the most telling criticisms is the language used by Paul in 1 Thessalonians 4:13–18, the very passage used by dispensationalists as a proof text for two comings of Jesus Christ and the secret rapture. Three times in the passage, Paul used terminology to convey the idea that Jesus Christ's return to earth will be accompanied by divine announcements that are clearly universal in nature. In verse 16, Paul mentioned that "the Lord himself will come down from heaven, with a loud command, with the voice of the archangel and with the trumpet call of God." The entire thrust of the threefold announcement is that God himself will proclaim the return of Jesus Christ so loudly that the whole world will hear. Not only so, but the world will also witness the subsequent catching away of believers (v. 17). If dispensationalists are correct in saying that this coming is a secret, then only believers will hear the divine declaration. As my colleague Ken Jones so aptly puts it, this turns the thrice-repeated announcement of Christ's return into something akin to a cosmic dog whistle. It is another example in which the champions of literal interpretation cannot take the key passage literally. What is worse, if dispensationalists are correct about a secret rapture, then Jesus does not have two advents but three.[21]

Another place where dispensational presuppositions get in the way of the clear teaching of Scripture can be seen in the specific terms used by biblical writers to describe the return of Christ. The way these terms were used excludes a dispensational understanding of the rapture. The first of these terms is *apokalypsis*, which literally means "unveiling" and refers to the removal of those things that presently obstruct our vision of Christ. The term appears in 1 Corinthians 1:7, where Paul longed for Christ to be revealed; in 2 Thessalonians 1:7, where Paul spoke of Jesus being revealed on the day of judgment; and then several times in 1 Peter, where Peter connected Christ's second coming to the final judgment (1:7), to blessing (1:13), and to when Christ's glory is finally manifested (4:13).[22]

The second key term is *epiphaneia*, a word that means "appearance" or "manifestation." It is used in reference to Christ's "coming forth out of a hidden background with the rich blessings of salvation,"[23] as when our Lord destroys the lawless one (2 Thess. 2:8). It is also used when we are instructed to fight the good fight of faith until Christ comes back (1 Tim. 6:14), when Christ comes back in judgment (2 Tim. 4:1, 8), and when Jesus appears as our "great God and Savior" (Titus 2:13).

A third term is *parousia*, which literally means "presence." It points to the coming of Christ that either precedes the presence or results in the presence.[24] In the Olivet Discourse, the term was used several times in reference to our Lord's return or coming (Matt. 24:3, 27, 37). Paul used the term in reference to Christ's return to consummate that resurrection of which he was the firstfruits (1 Cor. 15:23). Paul used the term a number of times to refer to our Lord's presence when he comes (1 Thess. 2:19), to our appearance before the Lord (3:13), to the coming of the Lord (4:15), and to the judgment (5:23). In 2 Thessalonians, Paul also used the term repeatedly in reference to the second coming (2 Thess. 2:1–9), while in James, the parousia is an object of hope (5:7–8). Peter used the term in reference to Christ's transfiguration (2 Pet. 1:16), while he placed the word in the mouths of scoffers who say, "Where is this 'coming' he promised?" (3:4). But Peter also used the term in reference to the final judgment and cosmic renewal (3:12).

Even in this brief survey, it ought to be readily apparent that these terms raise a number of difficulties for dispensationalists. All three words were used interchangeably of both the rapture and the second coming. This means that biblical writers did not distinguish between two phases of Christ's return, as dispensationalists claim. In one place, Paul used the term *parousia* to describe what pretribulationists assume to be the rapture (1 Thess. 4:15). In another, he used the same word to describe "when our Lord Jesus comes with all his holy ones" (3:13), which is the bodily return of our Lord to earth, supposedly seven years after the rapture. In still another place (2 Thess. 2:8), Paul used *parousia* "to refer to the coming at which Christ shall bring the antichrist to naught—which is not supposed to happen . . . until the Second Coming."[25]

The same thing holds true for the word *apokalypsis*. Paul used it in one place (1 Cor. 1:7) "to describe what these interpreters call the rapture: 'as you wait for the revealing of our Lord Jesus Christ.'" In another (2 Thess. 1:7–8), "the same word is used to describe what pretribulationists call the second phase of the Second Coming: 'At the revelation [*apokalypsis*] of the Lord Jesus Christ from heaven with the angels of his power in flaming fire.'"[26]

This is also the case with the term *epiphaneia*. In one place, Paul used the term in regard to what dispensationalists assume to be the rapture: "I charge you to keep the commandments without spot or blame until the appearing [*epiphaneia*] of our Lord Jesus Christ" (1 Tim. 6:13–14). In 2 Thessalonians

2:8, the apostle "uses the same word to describe the coming of Christ at which he will overthrow the man of lawlessness: 'And then shall be revealed the lawless one, whom the Lord Jesus shall . . . bring to nought by the manifestation [*epiphaneia*] of his coming.'"[27] The problem is that this event is not supposed to happen until after the seventieth week of Daniel (the so-called great tribulation) comes to an end. This means there is "no basis whatever for this kind of distinction pretribulationists make between two phases of Christ's return."[28] The dispensational theory of the secret rapture cannot be justified from the Scriptures.

The Bible teaches that though there are different aspects involved, they are all part of one event—the blessed hope—when Jesus Christ will come again on the last day to judge the world, raise the dead, and make all things new.

Part 3

EXPOSITION OF THE CRITICAL TEXTS

13

Daniel's Prophecy of the Seventy Weeks

In part 2, we established a biblical and theological framework to interpret various passages of Scripture that speak about a millennial age. In each instance, we traced a particular eschatological theme throughout the history of God's self-revelation in the Scriptures, and we glimpsed the whole panorama of redemption from Genesis to Revelation. This enabled us to evaluate our own presuppositions in light of the broader history of revelation as well as to identify how various themes are developed in the unfolding drama of redemption. We have been repeatedly reminded that the central figure in redemptive history and eschatology is none other than Jesus Christ.

With these redemptive-historical themes running throughout the entire Scriptures, we are in a position to look at the amillennial understanding of the specific passages that are most important in determining one's millennial views: Daniel 9:24–27; the Olivet Discourse (Matt. 24, Mark 13, Luke 21); Romans 11; and Revelation 20.

The dispensational interpretation of Daniel 9:24–27 is one of the pillars of their entire system. From this passage, dispensationalists develop their doctrine of a future seven-year tribulation period, which commences when the Antichrist signs a peace treaty with the nation of Israel about the time of the secret rapture. Dispensationalists use this section of Daniel to set out what they perceive to be the future course of Israel's history and God's dealings with the Gentile nations. They teach that a "great parenthesis," also known as the church age, results from the supposed gap between the sixty-ninth and the seventieth week of this prophecy.

Dispensationalists candidly admit that in the seventy-weeks prophecy, "we have the indispensable chronological key to all New Testament prophecy." This passage provides Christians with the interpretive grid to make sense of the Olivet Discourse and the greater part of Revelation.[1] Take away their interpretation of Daniel 9:24–27, and dispensationalism collapses.

The dispensational interpretation of Daniel 9 illustrates the fact that dispensationalists read the New Testament in light of the Old Testament, instead of vice versa. Sadly, this prevents them from seeing the passage for what it is, a great messianic prophecy that was fulfilled in the life and ministry of Jesus Christ. The passage reads as follows:

> Seventy "sevens" are decreed for your people and your holy city to finish transgression, to put an end to sin, to atone for wickedness, to bring in everlasting righteousness, to seal up vision and prophecy and to anoint the most holy.
>
> Know and understand this: From the issuing of the decree to restore and rebuild Jerusalem until the Anointed One, the ruler, comes, there will be seven "sevens," and sixty-two "sevens." It will be rebuilt with streets and a trench, but in times of trouble. After the sixty-two "sevens," the Anointed One will be cut off and will have nothing. The people of the ruler who will come will destroy the city and the sanctuary. The end will come like a flood: War will continue until the end, and desolations have been decreed. He will confirm a covenant with many for one "seven." In the middle of the "seven" he will put an end to sacrifice and offering. And on a wing of the temple he will set up an abomination that causes desolation, until the end that is decreed is poured out on him. (Dan. 9:24–27)

Daniel's Prayer

To understand the passage correctly, we must see it in its context. In Daniel 9:1–19, Daniel prayed for God to restore Jerusalem and the temple. The background is found in Jeremiah 25:11–14, where Jeremiah prophesied that Israel would serve the king of Babylon for seventy years until Babylon fell at the hands of her enemies and became a desolate wasteland.

When the angel Gabriel answered Daniel's prayer in verses 20–27, Jeremiah's prophecy had run its course, and the promise of restoration was about to be fulfilled. The theme of both Daniel's prayer and Gabriel's answer was YHWH's covenant with Israel, especially that God would bring to pass everything he had promised. Daniel invoked God's covenant mercies: "O Lord, the great and awesome God, who keeps his covenant of love with all who love him and obey his commands" (v. 4). Gabriel's answer pointed toward that time when God would not only restore his people but also consummate the covenant he had given Israel through Moses.[2] As Meredith Kline points out, what is striking about Daniel's prayer in verses 1–19 is the repeated use of the covenant name of God (YHWH) along with the repeated use of *adonay*, the "characteristic designation of the dominant party in the covenant." Daniel's prayer also included the fact that Israel had repeatedly broken God's covenant, and the covenant must be renewed.[3]

There is always much discussion about this prophecy given the cryptic use of "seventy weeks" or "seventy sevens" as the time frame in which the prophecy is to be fulfilled. Again, the key here is to look for other biblical-theological images that lend us help in interpretation. Since the entire prophecy was couched in covenantal imagery and language, the key to the meaning of the "sevens" is found in the sabbatical pattern established in Leviticus 25:1–4: "The LORD said to Moses on Mount Sinai, 'Speak to the Israelites and say to them, "When you enter the land I am going to give you, the land itself must observe a sabbath to the LORD. For six years sow your fields. . . . But in the seventh year the land is to have a sabbath of rest."'" In Daniel's prophecy, the first of the sevens (v. 25) comprises seven sabbatical years (forty-nine years total), which constitutes the jubilee (Lev. 25:8), in which the "seven sabbaths of years amount to a period of forty-nine years." This, in turn, preceded the fiftieth year, in which liberty was to be proclaimed "throughout the land to all of its inhabitants" (v. 10). The total period of seventy sevens in Daniel 9:24–27, therefore, constitutes ten jubilee eras, with the emphasis falling on the ultimate jubilee yet to come after 490 years had passed.[4] In other words, the messianic age.

Covenental Context for the Seventy Weeks

This certainly points us in the direction of Leviticus 25 and 26 as underlying Gabriel's prophecy in Daniel 9:20–27. For one thing, a covenantal pattern was clearly present, as seen in the covenantal use of the divine name as well as the covenant renewal and Sabbath language. For another, Daniel 9:24–27 followed the covenant administration pattern set out in Leviticus 26. Not only was the seventy-weeks structure built on the sabbath-jubilee pattern of Leviticus 25, but "Daniel 9 as a whole follows the covenant administration pattern of Leviticus 26. The prayer (vv. 4ff.) corresponds to the . . . confession of Leviticus 26:40, and the prophecy corresponds to the covenant restitution and renewal of Leviticus 26:24ff."[5] Too often, this important context is overlooked.

We should consider another important redemptive-historical connection as well. In Leviticus 26:43, the Lord declared that a time was coming when "the land will be deserted by them [the Israelites] and will enjoy its sabbaths while it lies desolate without them." The covenant curses would be meted out when God's people fell into unbelief. But later we read of this sabbatical rest for the land from the vantage point of fulfillment. Looking back, the chronicler wrote, "The land enjoyed its sabbath rests; all the time of its desolation it rested, until the seventy years were completed in fulfillment of the word of the LORD spoken by Jeremiah" (2 Chron. 36:21). When in the next verse the author stated, "In the first year of Cyrus king of Persia" (v. 22), it is clear that Israel's exile was now over, and the prophesied time of redemption had begun. Isaiah described the same event when he spoke of Cyrus, who would say of Jerusalem, "Let it be rebuilt" (Isa. 44:28).

In the same year that Cyrus issued his decree for Jerusalem to be rebuilt, Gabriel appeared to Daniel, indicating that Jeremiah's seventy years had concluded and that a new seventy weeks would begin. At the conclusion of this seventy weeks, beginning with the decree of Cyrus, would come the Anointed One, Israel's Messiah. His mission would be to "establish the new and everlasting covenant announced as the goal of the seventy weeks in the opening verse of the prophecy. In the course of His mission, He must undergo the violence of death, suffering on behalf of the 'many.'"[6] This idea is also found in Isaiah's prophecy when Isaiah spoke of the Messiah as the one who would come preaching: "The Spirit of the Sovereign LORD is on me, because the LORD has anointed me to preach good news to the poor. He has sent me to bind up the brokenhearted, to proclaim freedom for the captives and release from darkness for the prisoners" (Isa. 61:1).

But it is verse 2 of Isaiah 61 that catches our attention, tying all this together. Isaiah said that the Anointed One's mission would be to "proclaim the year of the LORD's favor and the day of vengeance of our God." The Messiah would deliver the captives and proclaim that the ultimate jubilee to which the 490 years had pointed had at long last come to fruition. Behind the Anointed One of Daniel 9:24–27 is Isaiah's suffering servant, who must be "cut off from the land of the living" so that many might be justified (cf. Isa. 53:8–11). Cyrus had issued his decree, and now Gabriel told Daniel in answer to his prayers that the new set of sabbatical years was about to begin. This time, however, the goal was the realization of all the covenant blessings of the ultimate jubilee.

Therefore, when we read of a covenant in verse 27, Kline reminds us "there should be no doubt as to its identity."[7] Dispensationalists insist that the subject of verse 27, "He will confirm a covenant with many for one seven," must refer back to the preceding *he*, that is, the ruler who would destroy the city and the sanctuary (v. 26). They, however, are in error, confusing the identity of the covenant maker, who is cut off for his people, with the Roman prince, i.e., antichrist.[8] In order to make this fit into their interpretive scheme, dispensationalists insist that the Messiah is cut off after the sixty-two sevens. An indeterminate gap of time comes between the end of the sixty-nine sevens and the seventieth seven, they say, when the one who confirms a covenant with many (Israel) arrives on the scene to do his dastardly deed. The insertion of a gap of at least two thousand years between the sixty-ninth and the seventieth week is a self-contradictory violation of the dispensationalist's professed literal hermeneutic. Where is the gap found in the text? Dispensationalists must insert it. The failure to acknowledge the obvious covenantal context of the messianic covenant maker of verse 27, who confirms a covenant with many, leads dispensationalists to confuse Christ with antichrist. A more serious interpretive error is hard to imagine.[9]

The failure of dispensationalists to see that the Messiah is spoken of in verse 27, not antichrist, stems from a serious interpretive error already made in verse 24 regarding what will be accomplished by the completion of the 490 years. In verse 24, we read, "Seventy 'sevens' are decreed for your people and your holy city to finish transgression, to put an end to sin, to atone for wickedness, to bring in everlasting righteousness, to seal up vision and prophecy and to anoint the most holy." These things must be completed during the 490 years so that the blessings will apply to God's people long after the prophecy is fulfilled.[10] These are blessings enjoyed by God's people during the ultimate jubilee to follow.

A Messianic Prophecy

Many Christians will quickly recognize that Daniel spoke prophetically of the active and passive obedience of Christ, or as Edward Young categorizes them, the "positive and negative" aspects of the Messiah's work.[11] Christ's death—his so-called passive obedience—"finished transgressions" in the sense of breaking sin's power over God's people (Rom. 6:1–2, 14), taking away sin's condemnation (5:12–19; 6:23), and atoning "for wickedness" (3:21–26). Through these acts, Jesus Christ took away all the consequences of the curse.[12]

Christ's active obedience can be seen here in reference to our Lord's threefold office of prophet, priest, and king—"to bring in everlasting righteousness" (v. 24), which Christ did through his perfect obedience as the final priest (Rom. 5:19); "to seal up vision and prophecy," which he did in his prophetic office, as Peter declared Jesus to be the greater prophet of whom Moses had spoken

(Deut. 18:15–16; Acts 3:22); and then finally "to anoint the most holy," most likely a reference to the anointing of the Messiah (Isa. 61:1; Matt. 3:16–17). These things, notes Young, "are all messianic. . . . The termination of the 70 sevens coincides then, not with the time of Antiochus, nor with the end of the present age, the second Advent of our Lord, but with his first Advent."[13]

The failure on the part of dispensationalists to see this, since they regard this passage as referring only to national Israel, not only leads to an error regarding their understanding of the future course of history but also can lead to a serious error in one's understanding of the doctrine of justification. Sadly, this can be seen when Alva McClain writes, "The fulfillment of the tremendous events in verse 24 cannot be found anywhere in known history." After all, says McClain, this prophecy has nothing to do with the church but with Israel.[14]

By reading this passage through the dispensational lens, namely, that Daniel was speaking of national Israel, not Jesus Christ, dispensationalists stumble badly in their interpretation of verse 27. They do not see covenant as an overarching redemptive-historical grid. Having inserted a gap between verse 26 and 27, because it is demanded by their hermeneutical presuppositions, they miss the obvious meaning. "The whole context speaks against the supposition that an altogether different covenant from the divine covenant which is the central theme throughout Daniel 9 is abruptly introduced here at the climax of it all."[15]

Indeed, the language throughout Daniel thoroughly supports the identification of the one who makes a covenant with the many as none other than Jesus himself. Not only did verse 25 give us a list of messianic and redemptive accomplishments associated with the coming one, but in verse 26, we read that the Anointed One will be cut off. Daniel used the verb *karat*, which was often used to describe the cutting ritual associated with the ratifications of covenants. This connects the "cutting off" of verse 26 with the confirming of a covenant in verse 27. The angel informed Daniel of this so that the disturbing cutting off of the Anointed One (v. 26) did not mean the ultimate failure of his mission. The words in verse 27 informed Daniel that the one who would be cut off nevertheless would make a covenant in the middle of the seventieth week of the prophecy.[16] Daniel could not have understood what these words entailed to New Testament writers centuries later: "While we were yet sinners, Christ died for us" (Rom. 5:8).

The Confirmation of the Covenant

It is significant that in verse 27 the angel Gabriel informed Daniel that the Anointed One would "confirm" a covenant with many. The usual verb used for the making of a covenant, *karat*, was found in verse 26. But in verse 27, the verb *gabar* was used instead, which means to "make strong, cause to prevail."[17] The use of this word is another serious blow to the dispensational interpretation that verse 27 refers to antichrist and an entirely different covenant from that implied by the use of *karat* in verse 26. The use of *gabar* illustrated that the covenant being "made strong" or "prevailing" in verse 27 meant that the covenant in verse 27 was not being made *de novo* but was a covenant being confirmed or enforced. In other words, the covenant being confirmed in the middle of the seventieth week by the Anointed One was a covenant that already existed. This is a reference to the covenant of grace that God had previously made with Abraham and now was confirmed by the Messiah on behalf of many (those redeemed by the suffering servant in Isa. 53:12). This would entail all the blessings promised in verse 24, blessings ultimately secured by the shed blood and perfect righteousness of Jesus Christ. It also meant that there was no gap between the sixty-ninth and the seventieth week, as dispensationalists argue.

This interpretation of verse 27 raises two immediate questions. First, if Christ would be cut off in the middle of the seventieth week, what would happen to the last part (three and a half years) of the final seven-year sabbatical period before the jubilee? Here again, we can see how the New Testament writers interpreted the Old Testament. In this case, we find the answer in Revelation 12:14, where John reinterpreted this three and a half years in Daniel as "a time, times and half a time." As Meredith Kline points out:

> The last week is the age of the church in the wilderness of the nations for a time, a times, and half a time (Rev. 12:14). Since the seventy weeks are ten jubilee eras that issue in the last jubilee, the seventieth week closes with angelic trumpeting of the earth's redemption and the glorious liberty of the children of God. The acceptable year of the Lord which came with Christ will then have fully come. Then the new Jerusalem whose temple is the Lord and the Lamb will descend from heaven (Rev. 21:10, 22) and the ark of the covenant will be seen (Rev. 11:19), the covenant the Lamb has made to prevail and the Lord has remembered.[18]

Therefore, Christ confirmed the covenant God made, namely, that he is our God, and we are his people. Although he has wrought the blessings of the jubilee, including forgiveness of sins and everlasting righteousness, what Christ accomplished remains yet to be consummated. The final three and a half years of the seventieth week, as interpreted by John, are symbolic of the church on earth during the entire time of its existence. It also is a reference to the tribulation depicted in Daniel.[19] This is a powerful argument in favor of the amillennial interpretation.

The final question has to do with two clauses in verse 27, "In the middle of the 'seven' he will put an end to sacrifice and offering. And on a wing of the temple he will set up an abomination that causes desolation, until the end that is decreed is poured out on him." How can an end of sacrifice be fulfilled by the death of Jesus, since Jewish sacrifices continued after Christ's crucifixion until the temple was destroyed in AD 70?

Several things can be said in response to this. For one thing, the author of Hebrews taught that Christ's death put an end to sacrifices in a religious sense. In Hebrews 9:26, we read that Christ appeared "at the end of the ages to do away with sin by the sacrifice of himself" (cf. also Heb. 7:11; 10:8–9). Once Christ ratified God's covenant on Calvary, the sacrifices that continued in the temple were an abomination to God. When Christ was cut off from his own, the temple veil was torn from top to bottom. From that moment forward, the temple became desolate, and acceptable sacrifices ceased. The events that transpired in AD 70 with the Roman assault on Jerusalem and its temple were now assured.

Daniel 9:24–27 is, therefore, a glorious messianic prophecy that does not support a dispensational interpretation. The fact that the angel Gabriel envisioned the ultimate jubilee after the 490 years were completed pointed forward to the already/not yet distinction—present blessings and future consummation. This prophecy also predicts that once the time, times, and half a time of the great tribulation are complete, the consummation will finally come, and the eternal jubilee will dawn.

14

The Olivet Discourse

In the Olivet Discourse, we find the most significant record of Jesus's teaching about the end times and the future course of human history. This discourse, recorded in Matthew 24, Mark 13, and Luke 21, is so named because Jesus gave these instructions to his disciples while they were on the Mount of Olives the night before his betrayal and arrest.

For a number of reasons, the Olivet Discourse is one of the most difficult and disputed passages in the New Testament. As D. A. Carson notes, "Few chapters of the Bible have called forth more disagreement among interpreters than Matthew 24 and its parallels in Mark 13 and Luke 21. The history of the interpretation of this passage is immensely complex."[1] How one interprets this important text will go a long way in determining one's view of the millennial age, pre-, a-, or post-.

The Olivet Discourse contains the most comprehensive comments by our Lord on the course of future history during this "present evil age" and provides us with details of his return to earth in judgment. This particular discourse is difficult to interpret because of the tension between signs that precede Christ's return and the suddenness of the coming judgment. Jesus spoke as though his parousia was simultaneously imminent and yet in the distant future. Was Jesus speaking about events that would come to pass within the lifetimes of the apostles or about his second coming in the distant future? These are vexing questions.

Having developed the broad eschatological themes found throughout the New Testament, we can look at the details of this difficult passage in light of the broader teaching of Scripture. Jesus's words did not occur in a vacuum but against the backdrop of the eschatological expectation of Israel's prophets, which he interpreted in light of his own messianic mission. This means that the Olivet Discourse took place against the redemptive-historical panorama of the two eschatological ages (two-age model) that Jesus had previously set forth. It also included a prophetic perspective, in which a prophet predicted what seemed like one event to the original audience but might entail several levels of fulfillment.

Similarities and Differences in the Synoptic Accounts

Some elements of the Olivet Discourse are common to all three Synoptic Gospels—Matthew 24, Mark 13, and Luke 21. First, we need to keep in mind that Jesus spoke these words in a definite historical context. Jesus was on the Mount of Olives speaking as God's final prophet, using the temple and the city of Jerusalem as graphic visual aids. Jesus spoke not only to his disciples about God's coming judgment on the city and the temple but also to the church awaiting the great consummation and the end of the present age many years hence.

In the discourse itself, Jesus answered his disciples' specific questions. They knew that Jesus's messianic mission had reached its climax when they left Galilee and made their way to Jerusalem to celebrate the Passover. They witnessed Jesus entering the city on Palm Sunday in messianic triumph. They saw the increasingly intense debate between Jesus and the Pharisees, which culminated in the plot to have Jesus killed. The disciples watched their mild-mannered Master drive the money changers from the temple, which he dared call his "Father's house." And they heard Jesus say these amazing words to the Pharisees: "Look, your house is left to you desolate" (Matt. 23:38). This was a clear pronouncement of judgment on Israel and its religious leaders, a statement that climaxed in Jesus's declaration that the magnificent Jerusalem temple would be destroyed and that not one stone would be left standing on another (Matt. 24:2). Obviously perplexed, the disciples asked, "When will this happen?" If the temple would be destroyed, surely, they thought, the end of the age must be at hand.

Second, we need to keep in mind that Jesus's words indicated that history is sovereignly controlled by God. It is moving toward a final climax, the consummation, which takes place at the "end of the age" (cf. Matt. 13:39–49), elsewhere called the "day of the Lord" (Acts 2:20; 2 Cor. 5:5; 2 Pet. 3:10). Jesus was not guessing about what is to come. He is the author of the future for the disciples, for Jerusalem and its temple, and for all the people of God.

Though he does not know the day or the hour (Matt. 24:36), Jesus's return in judgment is a certainty.

Third, in all three accounts, Jesus stressed both the signs that precede his second coming and the suddenness of his return. There was also a tension between the parts of the discourse to be fulfilled in the disciples' lifetimes and those that come at the end of the age. For example, Luke recounted Jesus as saying, "When you see Jerusalem being surrounded by armies, you will know that its desolation is near" (Luke 21:20). Jesus then depicted eschatological judgment: "At that time [when heavenly bodies are shaken] they will see the Son of Man coming in a cloud with power and great glory" (Luke 21:27). Another problem is determining which events would be fulfilled in AD 70 and which will be fulfilled at the end of the age.

Fourth, when Christ returns, he will gather his elect from the four corners of the earth and radically alter and shake the natural order of the heavens and earth (cf. Matt. 24:29–31; Mark 13:24–27; Luke 21:25–28; cf. also 2 Pet. 3:10). Our Lord's parousia will also be a time of judgment on all men and women (Matt. 24:37–39; Luke 17:26–27). The events to transpire will include a time of unprecedented tribulation (Matt. 24:15–22; Mark 13:14–20).

The accounts had several differences, however. Luke omitted the reference to the "abomination of desolation" but included a prediction of a siege of Jerusalem and a tremendous judgment on Israel, all of which would take place within the lifetimes of the Twelve (cf. Luke 19:41–44; 21:20–24). This reminds us that there were two distinct elements within the Olivet Discourse itself. One was historical, and these events were fulfilled with frightening accuracy when the Romans destroyed Jerusalem and its temple in AD 70. A second element was a distinctly future prediction that will be fulfilled at Christ's return at the end of the age.

It is this imminent-future tension within the text itself that forces us to deal with two critical questions: How much of the Olivet Discourse was fulfilled by the fall of Jerusalem in AD 70 (the preterist view)? How many of these events will be fulfilled in the future (the futurist view)? The way one answers these questions is the source of the preterist-futurist debate.

Yet, as already stated, some argue that this prophecy has both historical and future elements. Portions of the Olivet Discourse were fulfilled by the events of AD 70, while others remain to be fulfilled at the end of the age. Even double fulfillments may be in view here, with the events of AD 70 serving as shadows of a universal and final cataclysm at the end of the age. This is why Charles Cranfield cautions that "neither an exclusively historical nor an exclusively eschatological interpretation is satisfactory. . . . We must allow for a double reference, for a mingling of historical and eschatological."[2] If Cranfield is correct, we should avoid reducing the Olivet Discourse to a prophecy of the events of AD 70 and a local judgment on Israel, typical of preterism. We must also avoid treating the historical sections as though they are exclusively future, as is the case with many dispensational writers. In fact, the historical fulfillments may be types of future fulfillment. The difficulty in interpreting this text is in knowing which is which.

Three Schools of Thought

The Olivet Discourse served as the fifth and final discourse in Matthew.[3] In the chapter preceding it, Matthew 23, Jesus pronounced seven woes upon the Pharisees and teachers of the law and then announced that Israel would become desolate. He thus not only ensured his own death but also set the stage for what followed in Matthew 24.

Jesus described the judgment coming upon Israel as well as a day of final judgment in the future. Jesus spoke of future events that would forever change the course of redemptive history and impact Israel and all the nations of the earth. Jesus pronounced the covenant curses on Israel's religious leaders and announced that the nation would be cut off. It is easy to imagine the crowds, the disciples, the Pharisees, and the teachers of the law looking at one another and thinking, *Did we just hear this man say Israel will be left desolate?* If he was truly a prophet, Israel's Messiah, the Holy One sent from God, some wondered, then Israel faced a future judgment far greater than the Babylonian invasion six centuries earlier. But how could Israel be cut off when Jesus had just told his disciples that the purpose of his mission was to bring salvation to Israel? How did this fit with what the prophets said about the end of the age?

While these statements of Jesus only gave more ammunition to those already plotting our Lord's death, the woe and desolation he predicted must have raised countless questions in the disciples' minds. No doubt, they assumed that Jesus's entrance into Jerusalem meant that the messianic consummation was at hand. However, Jesus announced that the future would include specific events to occur within a generation: the destruction of the temple and the sacking of Jerusalem. But Jesus also spoke of greater judgment to fall suddenly upon the whole world after an indeterminate period of time. It is this built-in tension between predictions regarding the destruction of Jerusalem and its temple and future judgment, that is, the coming of the Son of Man, that causes the difference of opinion among commentators.

The Olivet Discourse began with the disciples' questions to Jesus and ran all the way through the end of chapter 24, though the three parables in chapter

25 were likely uttered at the same time and spoke to many of the same themes. The discourse can be divided into three main sections.[4] First, we have the disciples' questions to Jesus in verse 3, followed by Jesus's discussion of the signs of the end in verses 4–14. Second, we have the prophecy of great distress to come on Jerusalem in verses 15–28. Third, we have the discussion of the coming of the Son of Man coupled with the exhortation to keep watch for our Lord's return in verses 29–51. We will take each of these sections in turn as we work our way through the passage.

Although there are many interpretations of the Olivet Discourse, three schools of thought are germane to our topic.[5] The preterist view emphasizes that Jesus spoke about events associated with the destruction of Jerusalem in AD 70. Even the passages usually interpreted to describe the second coming of Christ—his "coming on the clouds of the sky, with power and great glory"— are understood to describe God's judgment on Israel before the generation then living passed away. The end of the age refers to the end of the Jewish era in AD 70.[6] A modified version of preterism is the position set forth by R. C. Sproul in his book *The Last Days according to Jesus*.[7]

A second school of thought among evangelicals is called futurism. This view sees the prophecy as referring to future events associated with the second coming of Christ. Although some of the events depicted in verses 15–28 do refer, in part, to the fall of Jerusalem, the balance of the prophecy from verse 15 on speaks of the future great tribulation. The nation of Israel will be back in the land of Palestine with a rebuilt temple only to suffer great persecution from the Antichrist after the secret rapture and the removal of Gentile believers.[8] This is the position of dispensationalists and is vividly depicted by Bible prophecy writers such as Hal Lindsey, as well as by Tim LaHaye and Jerry B. Jenkins, authors of the Left Behind series of novels.

A third school of thought sees the key to interpreting the passage in looking closely at the questions put to Jesus by his disciples.[9] They asked three specific questions of Jesus, one dealing with the destruction of the temple and two others dealing with the coming of Christ and the end of the age. It would be quite natural for the disciples to assume that the end of the age and the destruction of the temple would be the same event. But this assumption was not correct, for the destruction of the temple, cataclysmic as that would be, was not the end of the age, nor did the Lord return in AD 70. According to this view, Jesus answered these questions to correct the disciples' misconceptions. This means that the Olivet Discourse referred both to the destruction of the temple and the judgment on Israel and to a future judgment. Therefore, the passage was not exclusively future or completely fulfilled by the events of AD 70. With this view, thoroughgoing preterism and exclusive futurism both fail to sufficiently explain our Lord's words. These views assume that the disciples' questions were valid—the destruction of the temple was equated with the end of the age, and this prophecy would soon be fulfilled, as in preterism, or still awaits a future fulfillment, as in dispensationalism. The key is as simple as recognizing that what the disciples assumed to be one event might in fact be two events. Thus, our Lord's answer may be best understood as a both-and, not an either-or.[10]

The Disciples' Questions and the Signs of the End

The Olivet Discourse began when Jesus and his disciples left the temple. The immediate context was the aftermath of what Jesus had just said, pronouncing seven woes upon the religious leaders of Israel and then declaring that Israel would be left desolate. As recorded in Matthew 23:37–39, Jesus longed for Israel to repent and come to him in faith, but the people were not willing. He lamented that the house of Israel would become desolate. These difficult words certainly prompted the discussion and questions that followed.

According to Matthew 24, "Jesus left the temple and was walking away when his disciples came up to him to call his attention to its buildings" (v. 1). The temple was a magnificent structure, and the disciples regarded it with awe and reverence, especially since they were tourists in the city. Josephus notes that the temple "was built of hard, white stones, each of which was about 25 cubits (35 feet) in length, 8 in height (11 feet) and 12 in width (17 feet)."[11] The temple dominated the city's skyline and was Israel's historic and religious heart. As they left the temple grounds together, especially with what Jesus had just said to the Pharisees and teachers of the law in mind, the disciples called Jesus's attention to the magnificent buildings before them.

During his earthly ministry, Jesus had said many shocking things. But this might have been the most shocking of all: "'Do you see all these things?' he asked. 'I tell you the truth, not one stone here will be left on another; every one will be thrown down'" (v. 2). As they stood in the courtyard of this magnificent building, Jesus told them plainly that it would be destroyed so thoroughly that not one stone would be left on another. Certainly, Luke 19:43–44 is a prophetic foretelling of this event when Jesus said of Jerusalem, "The days will come upon you when your enemies will build an embankment against you and encircle you and hem you in on every side. They will dash you to the ground, you and the children within your walls. They will not leave one stone on another." When the Roman army subsequently laid siege to the city, sacked it, and destroyed the temple, Jesus's words were fulfilled in frightening exactness.

The disciples, no doubt, knew of the prophecies in Jeremiah 9 and 11 and Micah 3 that foretold the destruction of the first temple. Clearly, they thought, if this second even more glorious temple was going to be destroyed, Jesus must be speaking of the end of the age. Imagine standing in the middle of the mall in Washington, DC, looking toward the Capitol Building, the Lincoln and Washington Monuments, and the White House, and then being told that all these things would be destroyed. It would only be natural to conclude that the destruction must be equated with the end of the American republic. This is why at the first available moment of privacy the disciples sought answers from Jesus. The scene was a somber one, because from the vantage of the Mount of Olives, they had a wonderful view across the Kidron Valley of the entire temple area. We read in verse 3, "As Jesus was sitting on the Mount of Olives, the disciples came to him privately. 'Tell us,' they said, 'when will this happen, and what will be the sign of your coming and of the end of the age?'"

The questions put to Jesus by his disciples are the key to interpreting the passage correctly. For the disciples, the destruction of the temple would be such a momentous event that it must mean the end of the age was at hand.[12] This assumption is clear from the three questions they asked: When will this happen? What will be the sign of your coming? What will be the sign of the end of the age? The way the questions were phrased, the last two questions were clearly linked, the assumption being that the coming of the Lord and the end of the age would occur at the same time.[13]

Jesus answered their questions but in doing so made it plain that the coming destruction of the temple and the city of Jerusalem, while connected to God's judgment on Israel, was not the parousia or the end of the age.[14] National Israel would be cut off and her people dispersed to the ends of the earth. But another judgment will occur at the second coming of Jesus Christ, signaling the end of the age. Therefore, Jesus spoke of two judgments: a judgment to come on Israel within a single generation (the events of AD 70) and a final judgment at the end of the age (after an indeterminate period of time). What makes the prophecy difficult to interpret is determining which events belong to the destruction of Jerusalem and the temple and which belong to the future.

To answer their questions, Jesus set forth a series of signs of the end, which he described as the "beginning of birth pains" (v. 8). They not only would herald God's judgment on apostate Israel but also would characterize the entire period of time between the pronunciation of the covenant woes and Israel's being cut off and the end of the age. The "things mentioned here have characterized the entire church age, the intervening period between the first coming of Jesus and his return. The signs point to and warn of the reality of future judgment but not its time."[15] These signs were not given to us so that well-intentioned Bible prophecy experts can correlate current events to the immediate coming of Christ, nor were they limited to the forty-year period between AD 30 and AD 70.[16] Rather, they were given to comfort the disciples and the church, which would soon be born, so that even in the difficult and perplexing times that were about to begin, God's people could rest assured that he was in control. The signs of the end are not matters about which to speculate, nor are they indicators that God's world is out of control. They are signs of the certainty of Jesus Christ's second coming.[17]

Beginning in verse 4, Jesus first answered the last question put to him by the disciples about the end of the age: "Watch out that no one deceives you. For many will come in my name, claiming, 'I am the Christ,' and will deceive many." It is interesting that Jesus began with a warning about not being led astray by wild eschatological expectations. Deceivers would come, claiming to be Christ, the Messiah. Jesus is the only Christ, and all others who claim the name are, therefore, liars and imposters. An antichrist is anyone who either denies that Jesus is the Christ or claims to be Christ. When John wrote his first epistle, many antichrists had already come (cf. 1 John 4:1–3). Many zealots made messianic claims before Jerusalem fell to the Romans in AD 70 (cf. Acts 5:36–37; 21:38).[18] The early church was also plagued by primitive protognostic sects that denied that Jesus was God in the flesh. Christ's church has faced antichrists in every age. Jesus's point was that false Christs will inevitably plague God's people until the end.

Jesus then spoke of great national and political upheaval as a sign of the end. "You will hear of wars and rumors of wars, but see to it that you are not alarmed. Such things must happen, but the end is still to come. Nation will rise against nation, and kingdom against kingdom" (vv. 6–7). The tumult of the nations has always led people to speculate about the end of the world, but Jesus exhorted his disciples not to allow this to become an obstacle to faith—the nagging question about why God allows wars and the suffering and political intrigue that go with them. Men and women without faith will see this as proof either that God is all good but not all powerful or that God is not all good since he does nothing about it. Jesus, on the other hand, said that warfare and tumult, which would continue from his crucifixion to the Roman destruction of Jerusalem and will characterize the entire period be-tween his first and second coming, will be signs of his certain return. These things must happen, he said. They are signs that he himself will come at the end of the age in judgment.

Not only will there be political upheavals, but the very ground under our feet will quake and at times fail to produce sufficient food to feed us. Jesus said, "There will be famines and earthquakes in various places" (v. 7). The key here is when Jesus said, "All these are the beginning of birth pains" (v. 8). These signs not only are the beginning but also will come in greater frequency and with more intensity, all interspersed with periods of peace and prosperity. The creation travails until it too is renewed, when the curse is taken away at our Lord's return.

In verses 9–11, Jesus addressed the persecution the disciples as well as God's people must endure before the end of the age. Jesus said, "Then you will be handed over to be persecuted and put to death, and you will be hated by all nations because of me. At that time many will turn away from the faith and will betray and hate each other, and many false prophets will appear and deceive many people." Once the birth pains began—and this happened soon after our Lord's death and resurrection—Jesus's disciples would face horrific persecution from those who rejected their message. "The disciples' testimony will be for evidence against [i.e., the fact that the disciples have been condemned by them will be an incriminating evidence against them at the judgment] these rulers."[19] Because of this hatred and persecution, many of Jesus's followers will fall away. Many false prophets will come and deceive many. God's people will experience persecution throughout the entire period. Throughout the centuries, there have been countless Christian martyrs. Many thousands of Christians are martyred today in various parts of the globe. Our Lord's warning of persecution extends to those Christians who will die or be tortured this very day by the beast, who demands they renounce Christ to save their lives.

But this persecution and upheaval will be accompanied by moral calamity as well. This is why in verse 12 Jesus announced that "because of the increase of wickedness, the love of most will grow cold." As Matthew already stated, the love of God and neighbor fulfills the law. Yet, this will be lacking as evil increases. The calamity of nations, the groaning of the earth, and the persecution of God's people will inevitably lead to an increase in wickedness. While in many ways this characterized the period between our Lord's crucifixion and the destruction of the Jerusalem temple, these things have also characterized the last two thousand years of human history.[20] But in the midst of this wickedness, Christians are not to give up in despair or allow themselves to be taken in by deceivers, for, said Jesus, "He who stands firm to the end will be saved" (v. 13). Those who do not grow cold spiritually and who persevere in faith will be saved from the judgment of those who hate Christ, his gospel, and his disciples. Of course, we know from what Jesus said elsewhere that his people will persevere, because he himself will ensure this (cf. Luke 22:32).

In verse 14, Jesus gave another sign of the end of the age, which is linked to the birth of the church and the Gentile mission: "And this gospel of the kingdom will be preached in the whole world as a testimony to all nations, and then the end will come." Clearly, this sign extended not merely to the apostolic age, in which the gospel was proclaimed throughout most of the Roman Empire by AD 70 (cf. Acts 1:8). This same gospel that Jesus preached must be preached to all nations before the end of the age. This idea applies to the end of the age and the second advent, not to the events of AD 70. According to Charles Cranfield:

> The meaning of this verse is that it is part of God's eschatological purpose that before the end all nations shall have an opportunity to accept the Gospel. The interval is the time of God's patience during which all men are summoned to repentance and faith; it has for its content the church's mission to the world. That does not mean that the world will necessarily get steadily more Christian or that the end will not come until all are converted. It is a promise that the Gospel will be preached, not that it will be believed. The Disciples' witness is another characteristic of the last times.[21]

This sign clearly involves the ongoing mission of the church before the end of the age, a point Jesus repeated in his post-resurrection commissioning of his apostles to go into all the world and make disciples of all nations (Matt. 28:19). Thus, the preaching of the gospel to the ends of the earth is a sign of the end.

These signs are necessary, said Jesus, to point to the fact that one day Jesus, the Son of Man, will appear in the sky, and all nations of the earth will mourn. The Son of Man will come "with power and great glory" (v. 30), and the signs of the end guarantee that all these things will come to pass.

What, then, are we to make of the signs of the end as well as the destruction of the temple? Jesus answered the disciples' last question first by enumerating a series of signs that would characterize the entire period of time between his death and resurrection and the end of the age. Preterists, who attempt to limit these signs to the period between AD 30 and AD 70, have difficulty with the fact that the preaching of the gospel to all the nations is one of the signs of the end. There will be false Christs, wars and rumors of wars, earthquakes, famine, and horrific persecution from those who oppose the gospel between the time Jesus spoke these words and the end of the age at his second coming. These signs began after our Lord's death and resurrection but extend beyond the destruction of Jerusalem into the present age. For those without faith, the convulsion of the earth and the warfare among nations may make it seem as though God has abandoned his people or else is powerless to do anything about them (2 Pet. 3:3). But these signs of which Jesus spoke are not signs of God's absence but signs of the certainty of Christ's second coming in final judgment.

As our Lord himself commanded, this gospel of the kingdom must be preached to all nations. This too is a sign of the certainty of his coming. Instead of trying to connect the signs of the end to current events, the church is to be about its divinely commissioned task of preaching the gospel. Jesus has not called us to speculate about his coming. Instead, he has called us to persevere to the end during the calamity of nations, the groaning of the earth, the rise of false teachers, and in the face of persecution. He has called us to take the gospel to the ends of the earth. This is the task with which we must be concerned.

The Destruction of Jerusalem and the Temple

But what about the destruction of the temple? God warned Israel that "if you or your sons turn away from me and do not observe the commands and decrees I have given you and go off to serve other gods and worship them, then I will cut off Israel from the land I have given them and will reject this temple I have consecrated for my Name" (1 Kings 9:6–7). Now Jesus announced that it would happen again to the temple within the lifetimes of those to whom he spoke. The situation was exactly the same as it was in the days of the kings. God's people rejected their Messiah, the true temple. God would now reject the earthly temple. This magnificent building would be destroyed: "Not one stone here will be left on another" (Matt. 24:2).[22]

The temple was no longer a blessing but an obstacle to faith. According to Charles Cranfield, "It was not merely that the temple would soon be obsolete; it had actually become a stumbling block. The people of Israel had imagined that God could not do without His temple and that therefore they could sin in security; and now their sin was approaching its climax."[23] To the Jews, its destruction was the greatest calamity imaginable. This would be the sure sign of God's judgment on the nation. The tragedy was that Israel's hope was in an earthly temple with its rituals, animal sacrifices, and worldly splendor instead of that to which the earthly temple pointed—namely, the all-sufficient, once-for-all sacrifice for sin that our Lord himself was about to make through the shedding of his own precious blood.

In verse 15 of the Olivet Discourse, Jesus spoke of a period of great tribulation unsurpassed throughout the history of Israel. Dispensational writers argue that this passage must be interpreted in light of Daniel 9:27, which is assigned to a future seven-year tribulation period. If true, Jesus here spoke of some future event. According to John Walvoord, "Christ was not talking here about fulfillment in the first century, but prophecy to be related to His actual second coming to the earth in the future."[24]

There are, however, good reasons to think that Jesus was speaking about the events of AD 70. Recall that the disciples' questions were prompted by Jesus's comments about Israel's coming desolation and the destruction of the temple. That this was Jesus's answer to the disciples' question about the destruction of the temple is clear from the parallel passage in Luke 21:20, where Luke said, "When you see Jerusalem being surrounded by armies, you will know that its desolation is near." Roman military action associated with the destruction of the city and the desolation of the temple are clearly linked. Add to this the fact that Jesus switched subjects from the worldwide preaching of the gospel to the frightening prophecy of an abomination that would render the temple "desolate." As D. A. Carson points out, the details of what follows are too limited "geographically and culturally" to extend beyond AD 70.[25] It is clear, therefore, that Jesus was describing desolation for Israel and destruction for the temple. And what he had to say was not good news.

In Matthew 24:15, Jesus evoked a theme drawn directly from Daniel 11:31 and 12:11 that told of an idolatrous image that would be set up on the altar of the temple at the time of the destruction of the city. It was this abominable image that would render the temple "desolate."[26] The "abomination of desolation" is a Greek transposition of a Hebrew word and conveys an idea of something being detestable to God. It frequently referred to pagan gods and the articles used in connection with the worship of them.[27] As Charles Cranfield points out:

> The significance of the Hebrew participle is that the abominable thing causes the temple to be deserted, the pious avoiding the temple on its account. Daniel 12:11 appears to be fulfilled in part when Antiochus Ephiphanes set up a heathen altar in the temple in 168 BC. Jesus' use of the phrase implies that for Him the meaning of the prophecy was not exhausted by the events of Maccabean times; it still had a future reference. The temple of God must yet suffer a fearful profanation by which its whole glory will perish.[28]

When Jesus said, "So when you see standing in the holy place 'the abomination that causes desolation,' spoken of through the prophet Daniel," not only was the desolation of the temple associated with the messianic prophecy of the seventy weeks of Daniel 9 in view but so was Israel's not-too-distant past. In 163 BC, Antiochus Ephiphanes profaned the temple during the Maccabean wars by erecting a pagan statue in the Holy of Holies. Every Jew knew this story. They also knew what such an abomination entailed: the temple would be rendered "unclean." This was the image Jesus evoked to characterize what would happen to the temple again, only this time so as to make the profanation of the temple by Antiochus pale by comparison.

When Jesus evoked images from the prophecies of Daniel 9, 11, and 12, he claimed to be the true interpreter of Daniel's mysterious vision. The prophecies of Daniel about an abomination extended into the future and were not fulfilled by the events of 163 BC. When the disciples would see this abomination standing in the temple, Jesus warned, "Let the reader understand." This was, no doubt, a reference to chapter 8 of Daniel's prophecy, in which Daniel struggled to understand the meaning of the vision about the time of the end.[29] Therefore, by these words, Jesus was saying that he would explain the mysteries Daniel was never able to fully comprehend. This also meant that the desolation of the temple by Antiochus was but a foreshadowing of a future desolation that would fulfill Daniel's prophecy of the desolation of the temple. This desolation would be far more horrific and would foreshadow the coming destruction of the city of Jerusalem. This was every pious Jew's greatest fear—the temple would become desolate once again and the people of Israel would be hauled off into captivity to suffer and die in a land not their own. But this was exactly what Jesus predicted.

Jesus warned not only of a desecration of the temple but also of a great calamity to come upon the entire nation. When they saw the abomination in the temple, Jesus said in verse 16, "Then let those who are in Judea flee to the mountains." The apostolic church remembered Jesus's words. When it became clear that Rome was going to use great force to put down the ever-growing Jewish rebellion in the latter part of AD 66–67, those Christians remaining in Jerusalem did indeed relocate to the hill country to the northeast in the Transjordan, the same place where the Jews hid safely during the Maccabean wars.[30]

In fact, this crisis would come to pass so quickly and the consequences would be so great that Jesus warned his disciples, "Let no one on the roof of his house go down to take anything out of the house. Let no one in the field go back to get his cloak. How dreadful it will be in those days for pregnant women and nursing mothers! Pray that your flight will not take place in winter or on the Sabbath" (Matt. 24:17–20). We hear the echo in these words of the warning to Lot before Sodom and Gomorrah were destroyed: Don't look back! But there are cultural reasons for these words as well. Jewish dwellings of the first century were often built so that they utilized the roof area as a kind of porch. In effect, Jesus was telling them that if the abomination occurred when they were on their roofs relaxing, they were not to go down into the house to pack. They should flee and not even stop to pick up clothing. Things would be so dreadful that pregnant women and those with small children would have an especially difficult time. Jesus said that the believers should pray that this would not happen during bad weather or winter or on the Sabbath. The Sabbath observance of Jewish Christians would make travel difficult.[31]

Charles Cranfield sees the intriguing possibility of a double fulfillment in these words, connecting this with Paul's "man of lawlessness" (2 Thess. 2:3–10), which he says "strongly supports the identification of the 'abomination of desolation' with Anti-Christ."[32] This means that neither a historical nor an exclusively eschatological explanation is satisfactory, and we must allow for a double reference with a mingling of historical and eschatological.[33] Therefore, the events associated with the destruction of the temple in AD 70 become a prophetic foreshadowing of an eschatological fulfillment at the end of the age, when in the midst of the great apostasy, the antichrists (i.e., the beast and the man of sin) demand worship for themselves, profaning God's temple, which is the church. This is a possibility that awaits final confirmation when the end itself comes upon us.

One of Jesus's most problematic statements is the following: "For then there will be great distress [literally, "great tribulation"], unequaled from the beginning of the world until now—and never to be equaled again" (Matt. 24:21). The reason this is so problematic is that Jesus spoke of the tribulation to come as so great that nothing has or will ever equal it, past or future. This statement leads a number of commentators to argue that tribulation of this magnitude obviously has not happened yet and cannot refer to the events of AD 70.[34] But this ignores the fact that Jesus's prophetic warning clearly referred to the destruction of Jerusalem, precisely because it was the very gravity of this tribulation yet to come that explains why Jesus forcefully warned people to flee from Jerusalem when they saw the abomination in the temple. The reason people were to flee the city was that the horrors to come upon Jerusalem in AD 70 would be the worst that Jerusalem had ever experienced. They would be greater than those associated with the destruction of the temple in 583 BC and the desolation of 163 BC at the hands of Antiochus Epiphanes. This would be Israel's darkest hour. Desolation would fall on the city and the temple, and the people would be dispersed to the ends of the earth.

Anyone who has ever read Josephus's description of the Roman siege of Jerusalem, including the great famine and infant cannibalism, cannot help but be moved by the unspeakable horrors the people endured while the Roman army crushed the revolt and burned the temple to the ground. In fact, once the temple burned—accidentally and against Titus's orders—the soldiers were so eager to retrieve the gold that had melted and had flowed into the cracks between the stones that they overturned the huge stones of the burned-out building. As Jesus himself had predicted, not one stone was left standing upon another.

Yet, Jesus continued to speak not of the final judgment at the end of the age but of God's grace in restraining the evil forces that would fall on the inhabitants of Jerusalem. In verse 22, Jesus said, "If those days had not been cut short, no one would survive, but for the sake of the elect those days will be shortened." Even as Israel would become desolate and the temple destroyed, God would shorten the days of judgment for the sake of his elect, a reference to Christians living in Jerusalem at the time of the city's destruction. Israel would be cut off and the Jews dispersed, but God would preserve his people, even under the worst circumstances.

Yet, the possibility of double fulfillment surfaces again. Is this prophecy of horrible tribulation limited to the destruction of Jerusalem and the events of AD 70? Indeed, it is possible that the events of AD 70 pointed beyond historical fulfillment to the great tribulation to be faced by God's people during the apostasy, which will come immediately before the end of the age. As Cranfield notes:

> The Divine judgments in history are, so to speak, rehearsals of the last judgment, and the successive incarnations of anti-christ are foreshadowings of the last supreme concentration of the rebelliousness of the devil before the end. So for us the fulfillment of these verses is past, present and future, and are rightly included under the heading "signs of the age" or "characteristics of the last times." The key to their understanding is the recognition that there is here a double reference. The impending judgment on Jerusalem and the events connected with it are for Jesus as it were a transparent object in the foreground through which He foresees the last events before the end, which they indeed foreshadow.[35]

If Cranfield is correct, Jesus was using prophetic perspective by setting forth impending prophetic fulfillments as pointers to a cataclysmic period of tribulation associated with the loosing of Satan at the end of the age (2 Thess. 2:3–12; Rev. 20:7–10). If prophetic perspective is in view here, then the prediction of the destruction of Jerusalem and the desecration of the temple presents us with the frightening image of an unprecedented period of persecution of the people of God immediately before the return of the Lord. Such days will likewise be cut short for the sake of his elect by the coming of Jesus Christ.

In verse 23, Jesus returned to the theme he addressed earlier in verse 4, the inevitable appearance of false Christs and deceivers who will plague God's people. By returning to this theme in connection with the judgment to come on Israel, Jesus made the point that the destruction of the temple and the city would not be the parousia or the end of the age. The presence of false Christs would be a threat to Christ's church, even after the temple was destroyed.[36] Jesus said, "At that time, if anyone says to you, 'Look, here is the Christ!' or, 'There he is!' do not believe it." The judgment on Israel in AD 70 would be a breeding ground for messianic pretenders, and Jesus warned believers not to be taken in by them.[37] These false messiahs would have the appearance of God's blessing, and they would attempt to lead God's people away from their Savior. Jesus himself warned, "For false Christs and false prophets will appear and perform great signs and miracles to deceive even the elect—if that were possible. See, I have told you ahead of time. 'So if anyone tells you, "There he is, out in the desert," do not go out; or, "Here he is, in the inner rooms," do not believe it'" (vv. 24–26). But, Jesus said, it is not possible for God's elect to be ultimately deceived, for they will be able to discern such false teachers and deceivers. The very manner of their being "out in the desert" or in a secret place shows that they are liars. We are commanded to have nothing whatsoever to do with them.

In verse 27, Jesus said his coming will not be a secret or isolated event. "For as lightning that comes from the east is visible even in the west, so will be the coming of the Son of Man." This challenges the idea of a secret rapture, since Christ's coming was depicted as a single, visible appearance (not two comings with one being secret).

It also demonstrates the implausibility of preterism. Jesus's point was simply that his own parousia at the end of the age "will happen in such a sudden and dramatic way [that it is] incapable of being missed."[38] This point certainly mitigates the preterist notion that Jesus's parousia occurred in AD 70 and that his coming in the clouds was limited to God's judgment on Israel.[39] Indeed, the precise point Jesus made was that we are not to listen to claims that Christ has already come, no matter how many miracles the claimants may perform. His coming will not be an isolated, secret, or local event but will be witnessed by the entire world. Every eye will see him. The disciples asked Jesus what the sign of his coming would be. And this was his answer: "As lightning that comes from the east is visible even in the west, so will be the coming of the Son of Man" (v. 27). His coming will be an unmistakable event, like lightning flashing across the sky, impossible to miss.

In Luke's account of this same event (Luke 17:37), the disciples asked Jesus at this point where this would happen. They obviously realized that Christ's coming could not be limited to the destruction of Jerusalem. Jesus answered, "Wherever there is a carcass, there the vultures will gather" (Matt. 24:28). The image of flesh-eating birds gorging on the dead is an image drawn from Habakkuk 1:8 and Job 39:27–30. It likely refers to the day of judgment at the end of the age when the Son of Man returns in the clouds with power and great glory.[40]

Christ's Return

Matthew 24:29–51 constitutes the third section of the Olivet Discourse, in which Jesus spoke directly to the disciples' question about his coming at the end of the age. Having made it clear that the destruction of Jerusalem and the temple was not the end of the age, Jesus now answered the disciples' question about the timing and nature of his coming. Jesus had described the signs of his coming. Now he spoke of his coming itself.[41]

The critical matter here is, How is what follows connected to the preceding? Jesus stated in verse 29, "Immediately after the distress of those days the sun will be darkened, and the moon will not give its light; the stars will fall from the sky, and the heavenly bodies will be shaken." Was Jesus speaking of the destruction of the temple in AD 70 when he said, "Immediately after the distress of those days" and giving credence to the preterist view? Or was Jesus speaking of the tribulation during the entire period from the days of his death and resurrection to the destruction of the temple and extending on into the present age?

There are good reasons to embrace the latter position and to believe Jesus was speaking about his second advent at the end of the age. For one thing, Matthew's use of the word *eutheōs* ("immediately") seems to connect this to what follows (the second advent) and not to what precedes (the fall of Jerusalem).[42] This gives the passage the meaning that "immediately after the days of that sustained persecution characterizing the interadvental period comes the Second Advent."[43] In addition, "those days" is an Old Testament expression used extensively throughout the prophets with which Jesus identified himself (Jer. 3:16, 18; 31:29; 33:15; Joel 3:1; Zech. 8:23). "After the distress" appears to be a restatement of all the judgments previously mentioned. In other words, after the distress of the "signs of the end," which we know from elsewhere to be the "last days" (Acts 2:17; Heb. 1:2) and "this age," then comes the end.

It is also clear that Jesus's words echoed the words of Isaiah 13, which spoke of the day of the Lord as characterized by cosmic signs and final judgment.

> See, the day of the LORD is coming—a cruel day, with wrath and fierce anger—to make the land desolate and destroy the sinners within it. The stars of heaven and their constellations will not show their light. The rising sun will be darkened and the moon will not give its light. I will punish the world for its evil, the wicked for their sins. (Isa. 13:9–11)

The prophet pictures a day of judgment yet to come on the world, a day in which the heavens themselves will convulse. This cannot be said about the destruction of the temple and Jerusalem in AD 70. Isaiah's words make it difficult to localize this to events surrounding the desolation of Israel. These signs are cosmic, universal, and associated with final judgment.[44] Jesus not only echoed the words of Isaiah but also magnified and applied these words to himself.

But why would Jesus say that his coming will occur immediately after the "distress of those days"—i.e., the suffering of God's people throughout the interadvental period? In verse 36, Jesus said, "No one knows about that day or hour, not even the angels in heaven, nor the Son, but only the Father." Jesus must have meant that his coming could not be fulfilled by the events of AD 70. He had just told his disciples the exact time when Jerusalem and the temple would be destroyed—when they saw the abomination that makes desolate standing in the temple. When that happened, it would be time to flee. But now Jesus was obviously speaking of an event about which no one can know the day or the hour except his Father in heaven. Clearly, the subject has shifted from the events associated with the destruction of the temple to the end of the age.

The reason Jesus did this was surely intentional. He set forth the tension between the signs that precede his coming and the suddenness of his coming so that his people would live every moment in light of the promise of his coming. Yet, not knowing the day or the hour when he will come again, we are to live every moment to the fullest, going about our divinely mandated tasks of fulfilling the cultural mandate—marrying, raising our families, fulfilling our callings, and taking the gospel to the ends of the earth. This is the same tension we find throughout the New Testament between the already and the not yet. The signs that point to the certainty of our Lord's return stand in direct contrast to the teaching about the suddenness and unexpected nature of his return, about which no one knows the day or the hour.[45] Jesus's point was that his coming will shake the very heavens, picking up on the earlier image he gave of lightning flashing from east to west in verse 27. When Jesus returns, "the sun will be darkened, and the moon will not give its light; the stars will fall from the sky, and the heavenly bodies will be shaken" (v. 29).

In verse 30, Jesus went on to say, "At that time the sign of the Son of Man will appear in the sky, and all the nations of the earth will mourn." Jesus then defined in the next verse what he meant by this "sign of the Son of Man," but what is important to note here is that he was now speaking of the final judgment—"all the nations of the earth will mourn" at the very sight of his coming. Here, Jesus's words echoed the prophecy found in Zechariah 12:10: "They will look on me, the one they have pierced, and they will mourn for him as one mourns for an only child, and grieve bitterly for him as one grieves for a firstborn son." The nations will weep when he appears because it is the day of judgment, and the Judge is the one whom the nations crucified. Jesus died for the sins of the world, but the nations, just like Israel, rejected him. And on that day, they will be absolutely undone.

But what will be the sign of his coming? In verses 30–31, Jesus told us, "They will see the Son of Man coming on the clouds of the sky, with power and great glory. And he will send his angels with a loud trumpet call, and they will gather his elect from the four winds, from one end of the heavens to the other." It should be clear that when Jesus spoke of his coming as occurring "immediately after the distress of those days," it could not be confined to God's judgment on Israel.[46] For one thing, "at that time" (or "and then") indicates the end itself has come and is not just a reference to the signs that precede it.

Christ returns with the heavenly host and gathers his elect from the four corners of the earth.[47] His coming will be heralded by cosmic signs and the trumpet call of God, the sign of final judgment. In that day, the great prophecy of Daniel 7:13 will be fulfilled: "In my vision at night I looked, and there before me was one like a son of man, coming with the clouds of heaven. He approached the Ancient of Days and was led into his presence." This is the day when the trumpet sounds and the angels gather God's elect from the ends of the earth.

As Paul explained, "This will happen when the Lord Jesus is revealed from heaven in blazing fire with his powerful angels. He will punish those who do not know God and do not obey the gospel of our Lord Jesus" (2 Thess. 1:7–8). The trumpet call of God was an important theme in Paul's writings, for the trumpet will announce the long-expected day of resurrection. Paul also told us that the resurrection will occur "in a flash, in the twinkling of an eye, at the last trumpet. For the trumpet will sound, the dead will be raised imperishable, and we will be changed" (1 Cor. 15:52). Paul also said, "For the Lord himself will come down from heaven, with a loud command, with the voice of the archangel and with the trumpet call of God, and the dead in Christ will rise first" (1 Thess. 4:16). This will be the day of judgment and resurrection, not the tribulation to come on Israel in AD 70.

Returning to a theme he used just a day or so earlier, Jesus now spoke again of the fig tree in verses 32–33. It made a perfect object lesson in that context. "Now learn this lesson from the fig tree: As soon as its twigs get tender and its leaves come out, you know that summer is near. Even so, when you see all these things, you know that it is near, right at the door." In a world dominated by agriculture, the images Jesus used were familiar and powerful. When the fig tree buds and produces leaves, summer is near but has not yet arrived. Likewise, when the signs of the end are present, the coming of the Son of Man is imminent and inevitable, even though he himself has not yet appeared in his glory. From the fall of Jerusalem until this very moment, the entire universe groans, longing for the coming of the Son of Man to make all things new.

The signs he gave tell us that he is right at the door. But he has not yet come in power and great glory.

In verse 34, Jesus said, "I tell you the truth, this generation will certainly not pass away until all these things have happened." Since Jesus had just told his disciples that his coming was near but not yet, he then told them that all "these things," i.e., all the signs of which he had spoken, would come to pass before the generation to whom Jesus was speaking passed away.[48] If, as our dispensational friends argue, Jesus was speaking about Israel during the seven-year tribulation period and that this reference to the fig tree points to the birth of the nation of Israel, then Jesus never does answer the disciples' question about the destruction of the temple.[49]

In fact, since Israel became a nation in 1948, over sixty years have gone by—far more than a generation.[50] I have numerous books in my library by dispensational writers that define a generation as thirty years, then thirty-three, then forty. But Jesus was speaking to his disciples and answering their query. He was not speaking about the birth of the modern nation of Israel. In fact, the signs of the end were present from the beginning, and the temple was destroyed with Jerusalem becoming desolate exactly as he predicted.

But what did Jesus mean when he said that "this generation," i.e., his con-temporaries, would not pass away until all these things were fulfilled? Is this not an argument that this section of the discourse refers to the destruction of Jerusalem in AD 70, as preterists contend?[51] Jesus told his disciples that all the signs he had just described would be present and that the temple would be destroyed in a time of unprecedented tribulation. But those are "signs of the end," and even though the fig tree was ripe, the end was not yet. As Cranfield has noted, the signs of the end are also signs to the disciples that the end is not yet.

Let us also not overlook the following in verse 35. Only God in human flesh could predict the future of human history, much less utter the follow-ing sentence: "Heaven and earth will pass away, but my words will never pass away." This was perhaps our Lord's strongest assertion of deity yet. His words will never pass away, though the heavens and earth will. The reason Jesus could speak of the future with such certainty is because his words are the words of God.

Yet, while the signs of the end can be known and to some degree understood, the timing of our Lord's return remains a mystery—intentionally so. Jesus clearly said in verse 36, "No one knows about that day or hour, not even the angels in heaven, nor the Son, but only the Father."

In verses 37–44, Jesus now comes to the reason why he leaves his disciples with the tension between the signs that precede his coming and the suddenness and unexpected nature of his return. God's people are to be ready for the return of Jesus Christ. Jesus says to us his people, watch!

In verses 37–39, Jesus once again returned to the past—the course of redemptive history—to explain the future. He said, "As it was in the days of Noah, so it will be at the coming of the Son of Man. For in the days before the flood, people were eating and drinking, marrying and giving in marriage, up to the day Noah entered the ark; and they knew nothing about what would happen until the flood came and took them all away. That is how it will be at the coming of the Son of Man." In the days of Noah, God's judgment was swift and universal—the deluge destroyed the earth and all its inhabitants. Jesus's use of this event lends weight to the argument that he was speaking of final judgment upon the wicked, not a temporal judgment upon unbelieving Israel. Though the signs of his coming are present for everyone to see, the nations will go about their business, oblivious to the signs of the times and the certainty of final judgment. Non-Christians will be swept away in the judgment, not realizing what is happening to them until it is too late.

In verses 40–41, Jesus spoke about this judgment in more detail: "Two men will be in the field; one will be taken and the other left. Two women will be grinding with a hand mill; one will be taken and the other left." Indifferent to the fate that will befall them, people will go about their everyday activities, preoccupied with the things of this world, and will be caught unaware by the judgment. Humanity will be separated into two categories. Those who are taken away, presumably believers, are the elect and are gathered from the four corners of the earth by the legions of the heavenly host who accompany the Son of Man at his coming.

In verse 42, we now come to the applicatory section of the Olivet Discourse: Jesus's exhortation to his disciples to watch for his coming. He couched this exhortation in the tension between the signs that precede his coming and the unexpected suddenness of his return. In light of everything he had just told them, Jesus said, "Therefore keep watch, because you do not know on what day your Lord will come." Rather than focusing on the date of Christ's coming, the disciples are to concentrate on being ready at any time, since it would be impossible to know the date of his coming. Watch, Jesus said. Keep vigil. Be alert.

To make this case more powerfully (vv. 43–44), Jesus used a simple analogy. "But understand this: If the owner of the house had known at what time of night the thief was coming, he would have kept watch and would not have let his house be broken into. So you also must be ready, because the Son of Man will come at an hour when you do not expect him." Yes, signs will precede his coming, but it still will be unexpected. Since we do not know when the "thief" is coming, we must be watchful all the time, ever diligent, ever hopeful.

What does the Olivet Discourse mean for us? With the advantage of two thousand years of hindsight, we can see how Jesus's words to his disciples came to pass exactly as he said. The nation of Israel was cut off and left desolate, the Jews dispersed into all the earth, and only now have they returned to their ancient home. The city of Jerusalem was destroyed, as was Herod's magnificent temple, by Rome's army in AD 70; not one stone was left on another. It was a time of tribulation unsurpassed in Israel's history. But Jesus's words have not passed away. The signs of the end of the age continue on to the present day. There are wars and rumors of wars, earthquakes, false messiahs, and persecution and martyrdom of God's people. All the while, the gospel is being preached to all nations as Jesus said it would. God's kingdom advances without fail.

Jesus's words about his coming were put in such a way as to create a tension between the signs preceding his coming and the fact that his coming will be sudden and unexpected. As the disciples were to watch for the abomination that makes desolate, so too God's people are to watch for the sign of the Son of Man. For two thousand years, people have gone about their business, just as in the days of Noah. Non-Christians see the signs of the end, but they laugh and scoff. "Where is this coming that Jesus promised?" they ask. But as the city of Jerusalem and the temple were utterly destroyed, so will it be on the day of judgment.

15

Romans 11

When the apostle Paul wrote his letter to the church in Rome and stated that it was his heart's desire and prayer to God for his fellow citizens of Israel to be saved, the question of Israel's place in redemptive history took on major importance (Rom. 10:1). Paul's poignant question, "Did God reject his people?" (Rom. 11:1) is still a critical issue in the contemporary debate about a millennial age. Is there a distinct role for national Israel in the future course of redemptive history? If so, what is the nature of that role? Does a future role for ethnic Israel lend support to the possibility of a future earthly millennial age?

Most premillenarians and postmillenarians contend that in Romans 11 Paul taught that national Israel has a place in God's future redemptive purposes, and this role lends support for a future earthly millennium. According to amillenarians, on the other hand, Paul did not specifically address the subject of a millennium in Romans 11.[1] He did, however, speak directly regarding the future role of Israel in God's redemptive purposes, the only place in Scripture where he explicitly did so.[2] Nor did Paul tell us in Romans 11 when the things mentioned in this passage will come to pass, although he linked them to Israel's eschatological fullness, a topic of some debate.[3] Amillenarians disagree about whether Israel has a future place in redemptive history. Some say Israel does have a role,[4] while others say Israel will have no distinctive future.[5] However, neither camp sees this issue as ultimately determinative of one's millennial view.[6] Some post-Holocaust Jewish writers, as well as certain evangelicals, have argued that denying a future role for ethnic Israel and equating the church with

Israel is at the root of contemporary anti-Semitism.[7] It must be pointed out that even those Reformed amillenarians who do not see a distinct future for ethnic Israel have held out the likelihood of the conversion of large numbers of ethnic Jews before the return of Christ.[8]

The Millenarian Interpretation

There are a number of interpretations of this passage. According to dispensational premillenarians, "In Romans 11 it is shown that God has taken the nation of Israel out of the place of blessing temporarily, but will restore them to that place of blessing when His program for the church is terminated."[9] This, dispensationalists say, is an argument in favor of the so-called divine parenthesis in which God deals exclusively with the Gentiles.[10] After God removes the Gentile church from the earth in the rapture, he will return to dealing with the nation of Israel at the beginning of the tribulation. The fullness of the Gentiles will have come in, Israel's hardness of heart will be taken away, and the seventieth week of Daniel's prophecy will begin.

For dispensationalists, the future role for Israel described in Romans 11 supposedly guarantees Israel's place in the kingdom of God as well as fulfills the covenantal promise of a land that God made to Abraham.[11] This creates a scenario in which dispensational premillenarians are able to look to the land promises in the Abrahamic covenant as still applying to the nation of Israel, undergirding their argument for the necessity of a future millennial kingdom. This is also why dispensationalists so ardently defend the proposition that ethnic Israel has a future in God's economy against those amillenarians who do not see a future role for ethnic Israel. If it can be shown from this text that "all Israel" refers to the full number of the elect[12] or the sum total of all "true Israelites"[13] and not ethnic Israel, the case for dispensational premillennialism is seriously weakened. The importance of this to the defense of premillennialism can be seen when S. Lewis Johnson sets up a false dilemma by arguing that "if ethnic Israel has a future in biblical teaching, then how is it possible to deny to her a certain preeminence in the kingdom of God?"[14] Based on dispensational presuppositions, if one can prove a future for national Israel, then one can prove the premillennial interpretation of the kingdom.

But as Stanley Grenz correctly points out, "this hope" for the future role of Israel does not require "an earthly millennial reign of Christ, for the conversion of Israel could just as easily prepare for the inauguration of the eternal state as for an earthly golden age."[15] From an amillennial perspective, the future role of Israel in Romans 11 has little effect in determining one's view of the millennium. But for dispensationalists, a future role for Israel and the continuity of the land promise are essential to an earthly kingdom that comes to fruition in a future millennial age.

George Ladd, a historic premillenarian, takes a markedly different approach to the passage than dispensationalists. Ladd's view is that Israel does have a distinct role in the future of redemptive history. He understands Paul's argument in Romans 11 as follows. It is the present rejection of Israel that leads to the message of reconciliation going out to the Gentile world. But Israel's future restoration, connected by Paul to the resurrection from the dead, will bring countless new blessings to the Gentiles. "Paul does not here tell us when or how this era of blessing will occur," says Ladd. Neither "does Paul explain how the salvation of Israel is accomplished." It is clear, however, that Israel's salvation must come to pass in the same way in which salvation has come to the Gentiles, "through saving faith in Jesus as the crucified Messiah."[16] Furthermore, once the nation is converted, Israel will not have a separate theological existence; believing Jews will be brought into the church. Ladd concludes by pointing out that "Paul does not add here the thought that through this salvation of Israel, a new wave of life will come to the whole world; his concern at this point is only the destiny of Israel."[17] This view not only flies in the face of both dispensational and postmillennial interpretations of the passage but also provokes the wrath of certain dispensationalists who accuse Ladd of the greatest of interpretive sins: "spiritualizing the text."[18]

A future role for national Israel is also essential to postmillennialism.[19] According to postmillenarians, Romans 11 is a depiction of the conversion of Israel, which marks the beginning of the future millennial age. John Jefferson Davis explains that "Paul thus looks forward to a time when the nation of Israel will recognize her true Messiah and enjoy the blessings of salvation in Jesus Christ."[20] This is cited as evidence of the great missionary success for the church, indicative of the Christianizing of the nations. Some postmillenarians see Paul's reference to the "full number of the Gentiles" in verse 25 as a proof text for the postmillennial expectation that "the entire Gentile world will be converted to faith in Jesus Christ" and that "the conversion of Israel will result in an era of great blessing for the entire world."[21] Postmillennialists do not believe that this entails the conversion of every Jew and Gentile, but the postmillennial vision does see the vast majority of the world's inhabitants coming to faith in Jesus Christ. When Paul spoke of the salvation of Israel and the full number of the Gentiles, this is taken as evidence in favor of the postmillennial position.

The place of Paul's discussion about the future of Israel as recorded in Romans 9–11 and its relationship to the rest of the epistle is the subject of much scholarly debate.[22] The arguments raised in the first eight chapters force the apostle to answer the question as to whether ethnic Israel has any future in God's purposes. God was justifying Gentiles on the basis of faith in a Jewish Messiah and including them in the same covenant he had made with Abraham. *Kristallnacht* and the horrible events of the Holocaust, coupled with the formation of the modern nation of Israel in 1948, continue to thrust the future of Israel to the fore. There is no escaping the subject. Amillenarians must be prepared to answer the charge that it is "supressionist" or "replacement" theology, which contends that Israel has been cut off, no longer elect and superseded by the church, that opens the door to modern anti-Semitism.[23] The answer to these charges is found in Romans 11, where Paul set out the future course of redemptive history for Israel. It was Paul, the apostle to the Gentiles, who told us Gentiles that God's call is irrevocable (v. 29) and that "all Israel will be saved" (11:26).

Before we turn to the passage itself, several matters that specifically relate to the millennial question need to be considered. As Robert Strimple points out, the passage is quite remarkable for what it does not say. For one thing, Paul made no mention of the Jews returning to the Promised Land, nor do we find any reference to a millennial kingdom in which Jesus rules the earth as a Davidic king during an earthly millennium. Nor do we find any reference made by Paul to a postmillennial golden age in which the world will be largely Christianized.[24] One would certainly think that since Paul is addressing the subject of Israel's future and if Israel's future entailed the things dispensationalists and postmillenarians claim that it does, this would be the ideal time for Paul to mention them. But he does not. Whatever role ethnic Israel will or will not play in the future has no direct bearing on the millennial question when viewed from an amillennial perspective. Paul limits his discussion to Israel's future, and that future is in no way tied to an earthly millennium.

The Context: Is God Faithful to His Promise?

A striking feature of Romans 9 is the marked difference in outlook from chapter 8. In the first eight chapters of this epistle, Paul discussed the grace of God in Jesus Christ as it related to the justification and sanctification of ungodly Jews and Gentiles. The contemplation of Christ's justifying righteousness received through faith alone led Paul to the glorious doxological heights of Romans 8:28–39. But in chapter 9, the whole tenor changed dramatically as Paul spoke of the great sorrow and unspeakable anguish in his heart (v. 2). Why? Because his Jewish people were "cut off" from Christ. Grieved by Israel's condition, Paul must deal with the question of whether Israel's place in God's redemptive economy had come to an end.

Paul was not the only New Testament writer to speak of Israel's barrenness. The spiritual condition of Israel was a theme throughout the Gospels and Acts, when it was made plain that the covenant curses had come on Israel because she had rejected her Messiah. When the Gospels and Acts were written, Israel stood squarely under the judgment of God. What the writers of the Gospels and Acts did not address was the question of Israel's future status, i.e., the question of whether the present condition of cursing would give way to a time of blessing when ethnic Israel would once again be restored to God's favor. It fell to Paul in Romans 9–11 to speak directly to the subject of Israel's future.

Much more is at stake in this discussion than the matter of Israel. Ultimately, this is a question of God's faithfulness. What follows has been called Paul's "apologetic" for the faithfulness of God in the face of accusations that God had not fulfilled his promises to Israel.[25] In Romans 9:3–5, Paul recounted how Israel had received countless blessings from God—the covenants, the patriarchs, the law, adoption as sons, and the temple. From Israel came the human ancestry of Christ. Therefore, the critical question here was, If the gospel went first to the Jews and only then to the Gentiles, why did Israel not embrace the Messiah? Why is Israel now under God's judgment instead of his blessing? Has God not kept his promises? Has he changed his purposes?

Paul's answer was that God is faithful. His Word has not failed. The interpretive key is the second clause of Romans 9:6, where Paul said, "For not all who are descended from Israel are Israel." Here Paul introduced an important distinction between "Israel" in a broader sense ("all who are descended from Israel") and Israel in a narrower sense ("are Israel"). Paul's point was simply this. God has been faithful to this more narrowly defined Israel, frequently spoken of by commentators as "spiritual" Israel in contrast to "physical" Israel,[26] or "true Israel" in contrast to "Jewish Israel."[27] True Israel has been the object of his mercy and has been chosen to be the recipient of God's amazing grace.[28] The critical question at this juncture is, Who composes "true Israel"? True Israel may indeed refer to the messianic community, both Jews and Gentiles who believe in Christ. In Galatians 4:28, Paul spoke of all Christians as "children of promise," like Isaac. In Philippians 3:3, Christians are called "the circumcision." In Galatians 6:16, Paul explicitly called the church "the Israel of God." Furthermore, in Romans 4:16, Paul spoke of all who believe, Jews and Gentiles, as "Abraham's offspring."[29]

Nevertheless, there are good reasons to believe that in Romans 11 Paul was speaking of "true Israel" as a distinct group within the larger body of ethnic Jews (national Israel). Romans 9–11 was a discussion of the future of ethnic

Israel in light of the nation's present condition. In the first five verses of Romans 9, Paul focused on the blessings God had given to Israel throughout her long and illustrious history. Furthermore, in what followed, Paul explained the difference between the larger and the narrower body in terms that strictly applied to ethnic Israel. Throughout this section, Paul carefully distinguished between Israel and Gentiles, as in Romans 9:24, where God's purposes for elect Jews were both compared and contrasted with those of elect Gentiles. Finally, the citations taken from Isaiah (Isa. 1:9; 10:22–23) in Romans 9:27–29 refer to a believing remnant within Israel.[30] Therefore, I understand Paul's reference to a narrower body within ethnic Israel to refer to a remnant of believing Jews within the larger body of nonbelieving Jews. Based on this distinction, "true Israel" must be the same body as the "remnant chosen by grace" of Romans 11:5. But the reference to "all Israel" in Romans 11:26 must refer to ethnic Israel, the broader group, if Paul used these terms consistently throughout the course of his argument.[31]

True Israel

This important distinction between a broader and a narrower Israel can be seen in the opening section of Paul's three-chapter discussion of the future role of Israel. He made a distinction between those who are Jews by birth (biological children of Abraham through the line of Isaac and Jacob) and those who are Jews by virtue of faith in Christ (children of the promise). Therefore, "true Israel" stands over against ethnic Israel, who, while biological descendants of Abraham, are not true children of Abraham. Paul put it this way in verses 7–8: "Nor because they are his descendants are they all Abraham's children. . . . It is not the natural children who are God's children, but it is the children of the promise who are regarded as Abraham's offspring."

Who are these "children of the promise"? These are the recipients of God's grace. Therefore, "all that true Israel can ever say about its existence as God's people is that it was chosen by God and is the recipient of his love and mercy."[32] This remarkable emphasis on divine mercy becomes clear in Romans 9:10–24, where Paul described the divine election of Jacob and the passing over of Esau based on God's sovereign purposes and not because of anything good he saw in either individual. As Paul put it in verse 16, "It does not, therefore, depend on man's desire or effort, but on God's mercy."

In Romans 9, Paul established the principle of salvation based on divine election—not faith or good works—as well as the principle that there remains an elect remnant within ethnic Israel. Then in Romans 10, the apostle hammered home the point that there is but one gospel and that the believing remnant of Israel will be delivered from the guilt and power of sin in the same manner as believing Gentiles. Israel's problem, said Paul, was not a lack of zeal but a lack of knowledge. As a result, Israel tried to establish a righteousness of its own through works of law rather than through receiving the righteousness of Christ by faith (Rom. 10:2–4). Though the gospel was preached to them, "not all the Israelites accepted the good news" (10:16). This was part of the divine purpose so that as Gentiles come to faith in Israel's God, they might in turn provoke Israel to envy. God is gracious, and Israel is stubborn (Rom. 10:19–21).

This takes us to Romans 11 and the critical question in the opening verse, "Did God reject his people?" This theme, in fact, dominates the entire chapter.[33] In verses 1–6, Paul dealt with ethnic Israel in relation to the existence of a believing remnant. In light of Paul's question about the fate of ethnic Israel, the fact that he was both a Jew and a believer in Jesus Christ made clear what his answer would be. No, there is even now a "remnant chosen by grace" (v. 5). Therefore, God is not finished with Israel. But as O. Palmer Robertson points out, it is important to make sure that we understand Paul's question correctly. The question is not to be understood as, Has God cast off ethnic Israel with respect to his special plan for the future? but rather, Has God cast off ethnic Israel altogether?[34] It is important not to prejudice Paul's answer—"By no means! I am an Israelite myself" (11:1)—by asking the wrong question. The question is not to be understood in the sense of, Does Israel have any future? but rather, Has God already cast Israel off? The rhetorical question and the immediate answer tell us clearly that, no, God has not rejected Israel. As proof of this, Paul appealed to his own status as a Jew who also believed in Jesus Christ. This means that "Romans 11 deals with the place of Israel in the redemptive purposes of God at the present time, not at some future time."[35] But I, for one, am not so sure that Paul's initial focus on Israel's situation at that time prevented him from also focusing on Israel's future later in the same chapter.[36]

As David Holwerda notes, since Paul offered himself and all other Jewish Christians as proof that God had not cast off ethnic Israel, "We err if we assume that the significance of the remnant pertains only to the elect individuals who constitute the remnant. Paul is not implying that the remnant alone is Israel and no one else."[37] Therefore, the fact that a remnant still existed was no insignificant matter. For Paul, this was proof that God had not cast off Israel entirely. In fact, such a contention undergirded the largely apologetic argument about God's faithfulness. This is why "Paul points to himself and other Jewish Christians as evidence that God has not withdrawn his grace from Jewish Israel. This remnant is a sign that God is still faithful to his election of Jewish Israel." Despite his own personal despair over Israel's condition, "Paul himself is a hopeful sign that God has not rejected his disobedient people because Paul also was in an active state of disobedience when God's grace was given to him."[38] Even as God had miraculously transformed Paul from the most ferocious of wolves into the tamest of sheep, God can do the same with ethnic Israel despite her unbelief. The arch-persecutor of Christ's church was now the apostle to the Gentiles. This gave Paul hope for his people and explained why the apostle stated that a remnant had been chosen by grace, and hence, if by grace, then not by works (v. 6). Because of his grace and mercy, God may yet transform this stubborn and obstinate nation into a people who embrace the promise. This had been the case with Paul. It has been the case with the Gentiles. It will yet be the case with Israel.

But in verses 7–10, Paul dealt with the grim reality of the situation at that time. The elect—the remnant chosen by grace, including the apostle Paul—had obtained the promise, but the others (ethnic Israel) were hardened. The verdict of the prophets had come to pass. "God gave them a spirit of stupor, eyes so that they could not see and ears so that they could not hear to this very day" (v. 8). Paul knew that what the prophets foretold was now a reality. Israel was barren. And it cut him to the quick.

In verses 11–32, Paul wrapped up his discussion of Israel's future role in redemptive history, once again addressing Israel's condition, only this time the apostle did so in light of the redemptive-historical implications that Israel's situation had for the Gentiles. "Did they [Israel] stumble so as to fall beyond recovery?" Paul asked, once again answering his own question with the emphatic declaration, "Not at all!" Because of the hardening that had come upon Israel, "salvation has come to the Gentiles to make Israel envious" (v. 11). Israel's barrenness had brought great blessing to the Gentiles. It was all for a purpose.

The Non-Millenarian View

A clear pattern now begins to emerge in these verses, a redemptive-historical oscillation between the glorious blessings of God's mercy that extend first to the Gentiles and then, in turn, rebound to the Jews, only to rebound back to the Gentiles.[39] The key question for interpreters of Romans 11 to resolve is whether this oscillation is to be understood as a pattern limited to "true Israel" throughout the age or a process that reaches a climax in the salvation of "ethnic Israel" immediately before the return of Christ.

In verse 11, we are told that while Israel stumbled, they did not "fall beyond recovery." This is an important indication that the present judgment on the nation is not final. Because of Israel's sin, salvation came to the Gentiles. And this salvation came for the express purpose of making Israel envious. In verse 12, this oscillating pattern continues. This time, Israel's sin was described as bringing blessing to the Gentiles, while Israel's loss became the Gentiles' gain. But as the redemptive-historical pendulum swings back the other way, Israel's fullness will, in turn, serve to bring greater riches to the Gentiles.[40]

In verse 15, Paul's redemptive-historical pendulum continues to swing between blessings for Gentiles and blessings for Israel. This time Paul wrote, "If their rejection is the reconciliation of the world, what will their acceptance be but life from the dead?" How could Paul equate Israel's future acceptance with the resurrection? John Murray interpreted Paul's phrase "life from the dead" as a figurative expression of an unprecedented time of gospel expansion that results from "the reception of Israel again into the favour and blessing of God."[41] Postmillenarians have seized on this interpretation and argued that a future reversal of Israel's present fortune is an argument in favor of Israel's conversion, marking the dawn of an era of unprecedented blessings for the whole world.[42] But this argument is ultimately self-refuting. If the fullness of the Gentiles and the fullness of Israel have already been ushered in, how could a golden age follow with even greater fullness?[43] The postmillennial interpretation is highly problematic for another reason. Israel's acceptance does not mark the beginning of a golden age. Israel's conversion will be a sign that this present evil age is about to come to an end.

In the absence of any evidence to the contrary, the best interpretation of the connection between Israel's acceptance and life from the dead is still the traditional one. This view holds that Israel's acceptance is in some way connected to the general resurrection at the end of the age.[44] As Douglas Moo points out, "Therefore, as Israel's trespass (vv. 11–12) and 'rejection' (v. 15) trigger the stage in salvation history in which Paul (and we) are located, a stage in which God is specifically blessing Gentiles, so Israel's 'fullness' (v. 12) and 'acceptance' (v. 15) will trigger the climactic end of salvation history."[45] This places the time of Israel's acceptance immediately before the return of Christ and the bodily resurrection. As C. K. Barrett puts it, "The full conversion of Israel therefore stands on the boundary of history."[46] Geerhardus Vos sees the conversion of Israel and its connection to the general resurrection as "the beginning of the closing act of the eschatological drama."[47] This is a major obstacle to both pre- and postmillennialism, which see this "acceptance of Israel" as connected to a future millennial age. For Paul, the conversion of Israel (her "fullness") will be the herald of the consummation to come. The acceptance of Israel and the resurrection at the end of the age are inextricably linked.

Further evidence that Paul was addressing the subject of a future for ethnic Israel can be drawn from his assertion in verse 16 that an important theological relationship existed between the present harvest—the conversion of Jews to faith in Jesus Christ, the believing remnant—and the eschatological hope for ethnic Israel.[48] As Paul saw things, the remnant of Jewish believers made up the firstfruits of a much larger harvest. "Just as Jesus Christ, as the firstfruits of those who have died, represents and guarantees the resurrection of those who belong to him (1 Cor. 15:23), so the elect remnant of Jewish Israel represents and assures the eschatological salvation of Jewish Israel."[49] The presence of a believing remnant, then, guarantees a future conversion of Israel.

Paul connected this eschatological hope to the covenant, as seen in the fact that the root—Abraham and the patriarchs—remained holy, not because of works righteousness or human merit but because the root itself was holy, grounded in the perfect righteousness of Jesus Christ. Therefore, even though ethnic Israel had been disobedient and had fallen under God's curse, if God chooses to regraft the members of ethnic Israel back into the righteous root, even the disobedient members of ethnic Israel can be reckoned as "righteous." This is what God did with the Gentiles when he justified the ungodly (Rom. 4:5). God can do the same with ethnic Israel if he so wishes, since none of this depends on human righteousness but on God's electing grace and mercy.

In verses 16–24, Paul described the course of redemptive history in botanical terms, using the metaphor of Israel as an olive tree drawn from the Old Testament (cf. Ps. 52:8; Hos. 14:6). God had planted Israel, his olive tree, in the midst of the nations as a witness of his grace and mercy.[50] When Israel fell into unbelief and disobedience, God sovereignly grafted the Gentile branches into the righteous root, not because of anything meritorious in the Gentiles' behavior but because of his great love and mercy. Therefore, even though the Gentiles are now grafted into the olive tree (Israel), they are there only because of the goodness and mercy of God. Because this was God's doing in the first place, the Gentiles are not to be arrogant about their own righteousness in contrast to Israel's. Nor are they to have an attitude of superiority over unbelieving Jews. If God broke off Jewish branches when they fell into unbelief and sin, he can do the same with Gentiles if they become proud or boastful. Indeed, noted Paul, since the Gentiles were "wild by nature," it will be that much easier for God to graft back in the natural branches, i.e., ethnic Israel. But for ethnic Israel to be grafted back into the olive tree, it will take nothing less than a sovereign act of God's mercy producing Israel's conversion.

All Israel Will Be Saved

The climax of Paul's discussion that began in chapter 9, and certainly the most disputed section in Romans 11, comes in verses 25–26, where Paul wrote, "I do not want you to be ignorant of this mystery, brothers, so that you may not be conceited: Israel has experienced a hardening in part until the full number of the Gentiles has come in. And so all Israel will be saved." Four critical points need to be discussed here, and we will take them in order.

The first of these points is found in verse 25, where Paul spoke of the future of Israel in terms of a "mystery." The context is important. Paul told us that Israel had stumbled but not fallen (v. 11). This in turn led to the blessings of reconciliation going to the Gentiles (vv. 12, 15). But Israel's decrease will reverse itself and become "fullness" (v. 12), and the nation's present rejection will give way to acceptance (v. 15). Then in verses 16–24, Paul gave a clear theological justification for God to graft natural branches back into the root. In context, this mystery must in some way be related to the future restoration of Israel. What followed, therefore, was the content of the mystery so that Paul's readers would neither be ignorant nor conceited.[51] Paul's interpreters debate about the heart of the mystery Paul was revealing. Was it Israel's hardening, the fullness of the Gentiles, or the salvation of all Israel?

The second point has to do with Paul's assertion that "Israel has experienced a hardening in part" (v. 25). This was probably not what Paul had in mind when he spoke of a mystery but rather had to do with the fact that in verses 7–10 Paul already told us of this hardening. God used Israel's barrenness through unbelief to be the means of blessing for the Gentiles. Indeed, the fact that a remnant remained at all (true Israel) called attention to the fact that ethnic Israel did not believe the gospel and would not come to faith in Jesus Christ until the situation changed.

And what was this change? This was the mystery Paul would now reveal, namely, the reversal of fortune for Israel. Douglas Moo frames the matter as follows: "What stands out in vv. 25b–26a, what Paul has not yet explicitly taught, and what entails a reversal in current Jewish belief, is the sequence by which 'all Israel' will be saved: Israel hardened until the Gentiles come in and in this way all Israel being saved."[52] Since Israel was hardened toward her Messiah, what would change the barrenness into the fullness and acceptance of Israel Paul depicted? It had to do with a change in the status of the Gentiles and the removal of Israel's hardness of heart.

This takes us to the third point, and that is the meaning of the phrase "until the full number of the Gentiles has come in" (v. 25). Most commentators agree that Paul's use of "until" (*achri*) has temporal significance and is intended to mark that period of time when Israel's hardening ends and her fullness and acceptance begins.[53] Others, however, such as O. Palmer Robertson, insist that the term has an eschatological significance and is indicative of a condition that continues until the end.[54] The key here is Paul's phrase "the full number of the Gentiles." According to Anthony Hoekema, "The fullness here . . . must be understood in an eschatological way: the full number of Gentiles God intends to save. When that number of Gentiles has been gathered in, it will be the end of the age."[55] Based on this interpretation, when the full number of elect believers among the Gentiles has come in, then Israel's hardness will be removed, and Israel will attain the promised fullness and acceptance shortly before the return of Jesus Christ. This interpretation also comports with Jesus's words that after God's judgment falls on Israel and her people are scattered among the nations, "Jerusalem will be trampled on by the Gentiles until the times of the Gentiles are fulfilled" (Luke 21:24). Once the times of the Gentiles are fulfilled, God will remove Israel's present hardness of heart, and the nation will at long last return to her Messiah.[56]

This takes us to the fourth and final point, which concerns the phrase "and so all Israel will be saved" (v. 26). Amillenarians disagree about the meaning of this phrase depending on their understanding as to whether ethnic Israel does or does not have a distinct role in future redemptive history. For those who do not think Israel has a distinct future role (i.e., the so-called Dutch school), houtōs ("and so") is taken to mean that with the coming of the fullness of the Gentiles, "and in this manner," all Israel will be saved. "All Israel" is most often understood to mean the elect individuals within the community of Israel, "the sum total of all the remnants throughout history."[57]

For those amillenarians who see a future for ethnic Israel, houtōs is taken in a similar fashion to mean "and in this way," i.e., linking the salvation of all Israel to the process outlined in verses 11–24 and summarized in verse 25, namely, Israel being hardened in part until the full number of the Gentiles has come in.[58] The difference lies not in seeing houtōs in a temporal manner as is sometimes charged.[59] Indeed, there is no evidence that the term has this meaning.[60] Rather, the difference between the two interpretations has to do with the meaning of "all Israel."

Amillenarians who see a future for ethnic Israel believe that the key to interpreting the phrase correctly lies not so much in the precise meaning of houtōs but in the context. The context dictates that "all Israel" should be understood in the same manner as it was set forth in Romans 9:6, in which ethnic Israel ("all Israel") was clearly set apart from the believing remnant ("not all Israel"). Since "all Israel" has now been saved in this manner—i.e., after the hardening in part has been lifted and the fullness of the Gentiles has come in—"all Israel" should, therefore, be understood as "Jewish Israel in its eschatological fullness."[61] In other words, once God's grace removes Israel's hardness of heart, Israel's barrenness gives way to fullness, and rejection becomes acceptance. The natural branches are now regrafted into the righteous root. Just as the ungodly Gentiles have been justified by faith alone in Jesus Christ, so too will unbelieving Jews come to faith and be declared righteous. This depends on God's mercy, not man's desire or efforts. As Vos so aptly puts it, the salvation of ethnic Israel is the beginning of the end for the great eschatological drama.

A number of objections have been raised against this interpretation by those amillenarians who do not think that Romans 11 depicts a distinct future for ethnic Israel. Some have argued that the nature of Israel's hardening implies a connection to reprobation; therefore, such a hardening cannot be "lifted." According to Robertson, "If a day is coming in which the principle of reprobation is to be inactive among Israel, then it must be assumed that every single Israelite living at the time must be saved."[62]

Robertson's assumptions have several serious problems. Paul was clear that Israel's hardening had brought the nation to the point of stumbling, not falling. Indeed, the way in which Paul spoke of Israel being hardened "until" the fullness of the Gentiles comes in quite likely indicates a reversal of fortune. The Greek construction supports this, and in verses 11–24, Paul already led us to expect a tremendous reversal of Israel's present condition.[63]

Furthermore, it should be clear to every Calvinist who has tried to defend a doctrine of particular redemption against a universal atonement that "all" oftentimes means something less than "all inclusive." In the context of Romans 9–11, especially when viewed against the background of Jewish sources and the Old Testament, "all Israel" has a corporate "significance, referring to the nation as a whole and not to every single individual who is a part of the nation."[64] "All Israel," therefore, means something like the vast majority or a great number. Once the fullness of the Gentiles comes in, God will bring the vast majority of ethnic Jews to faith in Christ. And this is the harbinger of the end of the age.

Another argument that "all Israel" refers to the sum total of the believing remnant and not ethnic Israel has been raised by Anthony Hoekema. Hoekema argues that if "all Israel" is understood as ethnic Israel, the analogy of the olive tree breaks down, since this would seem to require two different olive trees—one for Israel and one for Gentiles—and two different methods of salvation.[65] But Paul's whole point was that while there were two kinds of branches, Jews (natural branches) and Gentiles (wild branches), there was only one root. The natural branches that have been broken off, as well as the wild branches of the Gentiles, must be grafted in by God. When the fullness of the Gentiles comes in and Israel's hardness of heart is removed, ethnic Jews will be saved in the same way in which the members of the present believing remnant were saved, only in such great numbers that Paul could say "all Israel" will be saved.

Yet, a third objection is that since the gathering of the fullness of the Gentiles takes place during the present age and not just at the end time, why, then, should the fullness of Israel be different?[66] Paul appealed to the redemptive-historical pendulum swinging back and forth between Israel's barrenness and blessings for Gentiles, which in turn will lead to even greater blessings for Israel. This is, Paul said, a mystery about which he did not want his Gentile readers to be ignorant. Jews and Gentiles are grafted into the same root and are made righteous before God by the same means. Paul's point was that Israel's barrenness will be reversed. Although the roles of Jews and Gentiles are inextricably bound together throughout redemptive history, it is only when the fullness of the Gentiles comes in that "all Israel" will be saved. Even though Israel's fullness is of the same kind as that of the Gentiles, it comes immediately before the end, unlike that of the Gentiles.

Throughout this entire section of Romans, Paul described an oscillation between the hardness of Israel, which in turn produces the fullness of the Gentiles, which in turn produces a jealousy that one day will lead to the fullness of Israel. If all Paul wanted to tell us here was that God was going to save the sum total of elect Jews throughout the ages, then "the salvation of Jewish Israel will be limited forever to a remnant."[67] It is difficult to see how this could produce the doxological comments that end Paul's discussion. Furthermore, what followed Paul's assertion in Romans 11:26 that "all Israel will be saved" lends additional support to the idea that "all Israel" is more than the remnant.

Just as he had done in each of the prior sections of his argument, Paul appealed to the Old Testament texts. "The deliverer will come from Zion; he will turn godlessness away from Jacob. And this is my covenant with them when I take away their sins" (11:26–27; Isa. 27:9; 59:20–21). Dispensationalists interpret this to be the second advent of Christ, when individual Jews will be saved at or before the beginning of the tribulation period.[68]

Commentators are divided as to whether Paul's reference to the deliverer coming out of Zion is a reference to Christ's first advent[69] or to his parousia, when he comes from the heavenly Zion at the end of the age.[70] Though this is a difficult point to decide, the fact that the latter view seems to drive a wedge between the manner of salvation associated with the fullness of the Gentiles and that which Israel will enjoy immediately before the consummation is an argument for the former. Paul, therefore, probably "understands the future tense of the Isaiah prophecy as fulfilled in the first coming of Christ, which set in motion the apostolic mission of the Church."[71] This seems to fit best with what is said in verses 30–32, where Paul spoke once again of the oscillation between blessings for Gentiles and Jews. God had mercy on the disobedient, first on the Gentiles and then on the Jews. These blessings are connected directly to the preached Word (Rom. 10:17) and serve to indicate that Jew and Gentile are justified in the same way.

This is the complete opposite situation of what one would normally expect. One would think that salvation would go to Israel and then to the Gentiles. In fact, salvation went to the Gentiles because Israel did not believe. The present condition of Israel's barrenness ("now" in Rom. 11:30) resulted in God's mercy going out to the Gentiles. But God's mercy, now extended to the Gentiles, will one day rebound back to Israel.[72] On that day, Paul said, "All Israel will be saved."

From this it is clear that Israel's rejection is neither total (vv. 1–10) nor final (vv. 11–32). Paul began Romans 9 with a heartfelt lament for the state of his people. By the time he ended his discussion of Israel's future in Romans 11 and considered the glorious possibility that God was not finished with Israel, Paul's heart was stirred to a glorious doxology.

> Oh, the depth of the riches of the wisdom and knowledge of God!
>> How unsearchable his judgments,
>> and his paths beyond tracing out!
> "Who has known the mind of the Lord?
>> Or who has been his counselor?"
> "Who has ever given to God,
>> that God should repay him?"
> For from him and through him and to him are all things.
>> To him be the glory forever! Amen. (vv. 33–36)

Is there a future for ethnic Israel? Paul's answer was yes. And the presence of a believing remnant was proof. But the future salvation of Israel is not connected to a future millennial kingdom. It is connected to the end of the age. When all Israel is saved, the resurrection is at hand.

16

Revelation 20:1–10

The Issues at Stake

Revelation 20 is the most important biblical passage dealing with the subject of the millennium and is the only place in the Bible that specifically mentions the "thousand years." Advocates of each of the millennial positions surveyed—a-, pre-, and post—offer their own distinctive interpretations of this passage, but none of them enjoys an unqualified consensus among the majority of Christians.[1]

In line with their a priori commitment to a literal interpretation of Scripture, the critical issue for dispensationalists is that the symbols and numbers in Revelation 20 are to be "interpreted according to their natural meaning unless the context clearly indicates otherwise."[2] When the apostle John said Satan is bound with a chain, dispensationalists assume he meant a real chain. When John said the devil is bound for a thousand years, some believe John meant a literal one thousand years and that God's adversary is physically restrained. If these symbols are not taken in their literal sense, dispensationalists fear they can be twisted to mean just about anything. This raises the question of genre, i.e., the style of writing and how we are to interpret the highly symbolic language of apocalyptic and prophetic literature, such as that in the book of Revelation. Therefore, we must address whether John intended us to understand the symbols he used literally.

For premillenarians, including classical dispensationalists, progressive dispensationalists, and historic premillenarians, the major interpretive issue has to do with the fact that what is depicted in Revelation 20 is yet future and will not occur until after the return of Christ and the first resurrection. Revelation 20 and the so-called millennial reign of Christ, both logically and chronologically, follow Revelation 19, which depicts the second coming of Christ in judgment. Since the second coming *precedes* the millennial reign, the *pre*millennial interpretation of the events in Revelation 20 is the biblical one. If true, this is an important argument in favor of premillennialism.[3]

Postmillenarians agree with premillenarians that the events of Revelation 19 precede the events of Revelation 20. For certain varieties of postmillennialism, many of whom adopt the historicist interpretation of much of what is set forth by John in Revelation, the Apocalypse is seen as a theological map that charts the future course of church history. For many postmillenarians, the Revelation 19:11–16 description of Jesus Christ riding the white horse of judgment is symbolic of the triumph of the gospel throughout the church age and the means by which the nations are Christianized,[4] not the second coming at the end of the age. They base this on Hebrews 4:12, which speaks of the Word of God, living and active, a double-edged sword. When in Revelation 19:15 we are told that "out of his [Jesus's] mouth comes a sharp sword with which to strike down the nations," postmillenarians take the Hebrews text as the interpretive key. This means that Revelation 19:11–16 is a depiction of the church age and occurs in history, the gospel continuously going forth in power.[5] This interpretation, while markedly different in detail from that of premillennialism, nevertheless concurs with it in that the material in Revelation 19 is chronologically prior to the events in Revelation 20. These particular postmillenarians do not see the second coming of Christ occurring until the middle of Revelation 20 (vv. 11ff.). Amillenarians disagree with this interpretation. To settle this interpretive difference, we must analyze the literary relationship between Revelation 19 and 20.

Another approach to this passage is that of preterism, which sees the events depicted in the book of Revelation as a prophecy referring to God's judgment on Jerusalem through the events of AD 70. Critical to this approach, which interprets Revelation as speaking of events that come to pass within the lifetimes of the apostles, is a defense of the pre–AD 70 authorship of the book of Revelation and the identification of Babylon the Great with apostate Israel.[6] In marked contrast to the dispensationalists, who assign all of these things to the future, preterists assign them to the apostolic era before the fall of Jerusalem. For preterists, the cataclysmic judgment does not come at the future second advent of Christ; it came with the death and resurrection of his first coming. It was at the cross that Christ defeated Satan. Therefore, with the coming of the kingdom, Jesus Christ has progressively bound Satan through the worldwide preaching of the gospel and the expansion of Christ's church.

For those preterists who are postmillennial, this will go on until the nations of the world are Christianized. According to Revelation 20:7–10, Satan is released immediately before the end during a time of brief apostasy.[7]

This has structural affinities with amillennialism—i.e., that Satan is bound with the coming of Christ, that the first resurrection is not a reference to the general resurrection, and that what is described in Revelation 20 has to do with the present. However, amillenarians, generally speaking, do not see Babylon the Great as Israel, nor do they see the images of judgment throughout Revelation as exhausted by the events of AD 70. This overrealized eschatology leaves no place for the eschatological tension of the already/not yet or the present-but-not-yet-consummated kingdom language found throughout the New Testament. This tension is relieved when preterists assign these things to the years before the fall of Jerusalem.

How Are We to Understand the Symbols in Revelation?

Revelation is a book much like Ezekiel, Daniel, or Zechariah, combining distinct and unique biblical genres for the purpose of explaining the course of redemptive history from God's perspective. In a sense, Revelation is a New Testament commentary on those redemptive-historical themes left open-ended by the Old Testament prophets, viewed in the greater light of postmessianic revelation. John told us that some things mentioned in this book "call for wisdom" to be understood correctly (Rev. 13:18; 17:9). God promises a great blessing to those who read "the words of this prophecy," as well as to those "who hear it and take to heart what is written in it, because the time is near" (Rev. 1:3). Given the fact that the author himself told us that this book was about things soon to transpire, we should be skeptical about extreme futurist interpretations of this book.

Revelation is a book that contains three distinct literary elements: apocalyptic, prophecy, and epistle.[8] In one sense, Revelation was an epistle to which the author, John, attached his name. But it was much more than your average letter. Defining "apocalyptic" has become a difficult task since it not only is a unique genre of ancient Near-Eastern literature but also is repeatedly utilized by the biblical writers in a distinctly eschatological sense. An apocalyptic writer makes use of symbols and numbers to depict in word pictures the great conflict between the forces of evil and righteousness that underlie the tumult of nations and empires. In apocalyptic literature, the course of world history is cast so as to depict the present age as evil and destined to pass away. This world stands in marked contrast with the world to come and the expectation that God will intervene in human history to establish his kingdom in all of its fullness.[9]

The key to understanding the writer's interpretation of history is to understand the symbols he uses. John did not intend for us to understand them literally. Admittedly, this can be tough going for modern Americans, since the symbols John used were probably immediately understood by Jewish Christians living when the book was written toward the end of the first century. They knew the Old Testament much better than we, and they intuitively knew where to look for the wisdom for which John called. As moderns, unfamiliar with what these things meant in the first-century world, we must be careful not to read apocalyptic literature without due regard for the historical context. To argue, as one popular dispensational writer has, that the locusts of Revelation 9:3 are a premodern depiction of Bell UH-1B Huey helicopters is surely to wrongly divide the Word of truth.[10] Rather, a Christian should look to Exodus 10:1–20 and Joel 1:2–2:11 for interpretive help with the meaning of the locusts in Revelation. In agrarian societies, nothing was more destructive than locusts, which destroyed everything in sight. The first-century reader knew that locusts were symbols of judgment, not pictures of an unknown future technology.

A prophet, on the other hand, is understood to speak as a divine representative. When apocalyptic writers describe the future, their writing becomes a form of prophecy. At this point, it should be easy to see how the lines between apocalyptic and prophecy blur, especially since both these elements are obviously present throughout the book of Revelation.[11] Given the fact that Revelation is apocalyptic in character, prophetic in authority, and epistolary in style, it is apparent that its symbols will be intelligible only against the backdrop of the broader biblical revelation of the Old Testament. Though some premillenarians contend that it is better to start with Revelation itself when seeking to answer the millennial question, given the need to understand how these symbols are to be understood in their historical context, we must be ever mindful that the thought world of the original author was the Old Testament.[12]

Although the Old Testament should be our interpretive anchor when reading Revelation, nevertheless, John was also fully aware of the military power, cultural influence, and political intrigue of ancient Rome. Rather than reading Revelation as though it was written to Christians living at the beginning of the twenty-first century, we need to understand what the symbols and numbers would have meant to the original audience. This is why we look to the Old Testament to see what these images meant there so that these symbols will have continued meaning for Christians in all ages. They continually point us to Jesus Christ and his saving work on our behalf.

When dispensationalists appeal to the literal meaning of the text in Revelation 20, there is a certain attraction to their argument, especially when theological liberals have in many instances ignored the plain teaching of Scripture through the use of a nonliteral hermeneutic. All Bible-believing Christians take the text of Scripture seriously and are rightly suspicious of those who do not. Some argue that if we do not interpret the symbols literally, then we can simply reshape them, like a wax nose, however we wish. But the literal interpretation of a biblical passage is not as easy as dispensationalists would lead us to believe, especially in a book like Revelation.

Charles Ryrie tells us that we should give every word the same meaning it has in normal usage, whether we employ it in writing, speaking, or thinking.[13] But as Vern Poythress points out, "Words, but not sentences, have a literal or normal meaning. Moreover, for both words and sentences context is all-important in determining meaning at any given point in the act of communication."[14] The context in Revelation 20 is not historical narrative but apocalyptic prophecy. When John told us in Revelation 20:1 that he "saw an angel coming down out of heaven, having the key to the Abyss and holding in his hand a great chain," are we to understand this literally? Does the angel have hands in which he holds a literal key and a literal chain? John Walvoord, consistent with his dispensational presuppositions, says yes.[15] But when we look at the passage closely, we are alerted by both the literary genre of the book itself and the immediate context, which tells us this vision is full of symbols such as chain, abyss, dragon, and serpent. Although in his vision John might have seen all these things, the context tells us that the things he saw are symbolic of something else.[16]

We need to consider four levels of communication. The first level of communication, the *linguistic*, has to do with the words themselves. At the level of his vision, John reported that an angel revealed these things to him, i.e., the images of a chain, an angel, a key, and so on. So he wrote down what the angel told him. The second level of communication is called the *visionary* level, what he saw. At a third level, the *referential* level, the vision points to the actual historical referents of the images in the vision, i.e., the actual dragon, an actual serpent, the reality of the abyss, the passage of a thousand years, people raised from the dead, etc. The fourth level is the *symbolic* level. What do the images in the vision symbolize, if anything?[17] After all, the context itself, not the whims of modern interpreters of John's visions, has led us to expect that the things revealed by the angel in the vision symbolize something beyond the historic reference point.

Some say the problem with dispensationalists is they move directly from the linguistic level to the referential level without acknowledging either a visionary or a symbolic level of communication in Revelation.[18] This is particularly problematic in Revelation 20, where the literary genre as well as the immediate context should tell us that in addition to the linguistic and referential meanings there are also visionary and symbolic meanings. When John said two times in this section, "I saw" (*eidon*), which he used throughout the book to indicate symbolic visions (cf. Rev. 4:1ff.; 10:1–3; 13:1–3; 14:1; 17:1–3), we should realize that what follows cannot be collapsed into linguistic and referential levels.[19] The image of an angel with a chain and a key points to something beyond the referential level, to other biblical-theological themes elsewhere in Scripture.

Dispensationalists are to be commended in their desire to defend the inspiration and authority of the Bible. However, the great irony is that by denying a symbolic level of communication in Revelation 20, the dispensationalists end up not interpreting the passages as the original author intended. They have forced the literalistic sense, i.e., the linguistic and referential sense, on a passage that is a vision with a highly symbolic meaning. Nevertheless, the warning about the wax nose of interpretation according to the whims of the interpreter should be heeded. Keeping this in mind drives us to the only authoritative source for determining the meaning of these symbols: the rest of Scripture, especially the Old Testament. This is why historic Protestants do not insist on the literalistic interpretation, as do dispensationalists, but on the analogy of faith, whereby Scripture interprets Scripture.

Recapitulation: How Are Revelation 19 and 20 Related?

Not only is it problematic to interpret the symbols used in apocalyptic literature literally, but it is also problematic to read the book of Revelation chronologically. When reading historical narrative, you start at the beginning and read through the narrative until you come to the end. The events described therein more or less follow a chronological sequence. Not so with apocalyptic literature such as the book of Revelation. Revelation contains a series of visions, each of which functions like a different camera angle looking at the same event. Therefore, the order in which the various visions contained in Revelation are recounted by John does not necessarily reflect the order of historical occurrence of the reality those visions symbolize.[20] This is what is known as "recapitulation," in which the same basic pattern is repeated in a variety of formulations.[21] Put more simply, the visions were arranged topically, not chronologically. Although the cycles of judgment in Revelation increase in intensity as the return of our Lord draws near, the vision described in Revelation 20 might come to pass at the same point in history as previous visions in the book. Revelation 20 may, in fact, not be describing events that come chronologically after those recorded in Revelation 19 but events that are contemporaneous with them.[22]

The fact that Revelation is a series of consecutive visions, each depicting the course of the present age from a different perspective (recapitulation), should warn us. We are not to read Revelation with the assumption that because something appears in an earlier chapter, the historical fulfillment of that vision must occur in history prior to that which is revealed in later chapters.

But this sounds so theoretical. Is there concrete evidence for this? As William Hendriksen points out, "A careful study of chapter 20 will reveal that this chapter describes a period which is synchronous with that of chapter 12."[23] This can be clearly demonstrated by simply comparing Revelation 12:7–11 with Revelation 20:1–6.[24]

The obvious parallelism between chapters 12 and 20 of Revelation is important for a number of reasons. For one thing, this means that Revelation 12 and 20 are both speaking about the present period of time. Although they are not identical, "they depict the same events and mutually interpret one another."[25] If true, this is a serious blow to all forms of premillennialism, which place the events of Revelation 20 chronologically after the return of Jesus Christ described in Revelation 19. If John was giving a series of visions, depicting the present age from different theological vantage points, and if Revelation 12 and 20 describe the same events from different perspectives, then the thousand years of Revelation 20 is a description of a present millennial age rather than a future earthly millennium.

Revelation 12:7–11	Revelation 20:1–6
(1) heavenly scene (v. 7)	(1) heavenly scene (v. 1)
(2) angelic battle against Satan and his host (vv. 7–8)	(2) presupposed angelic battle with Satan (v. 2)
(3) Satan cast to earth (v. 9)	(3) Satan cast into the abyss (v. 3)
(4) the angels' evil opponent called "the great dragon, . . . that ancient serpent called the devil or Satan, who leads the whole world astray" (v. 9)	(4) the angels' evil opponent called "the dragon, that ancient serpent, who is the devil, or Satan," restrained from "deceiving the nations anymore" (vv. 2–3), to be released later "to deceive the nations in the four corners of the the earth" (vv. 3, 7–8)
(5) Satan "is filled with fury, because he knows that his time is short" (v. 12)	(5) Satan to be "set free for a short time" after his imprisonment (v. 3)
(6) Satan's fall, resulting in the kingdom of Christ and his saints (v. 10)	(6) Satan's fall, resulting in the kingdom of Christ and his saints (v. 4)
(7) the saints' kingship, based not only on the fall of Satan and Christ's victory but also on the saints' faithfulness even to death in holding to "the word of their testimony" (v. 11)	(7) the saints' kingship, based not only on the fall of Satan but also on their faithfulness even to death because of their "testimony for Jesus and because of the word of God" (v. 4)

The main premillennial defense against this is to say that no such recapitulation exists. According to George Ladd, "No such indication [of recapitulation] is to be found. On the contrary, chapters 18–20 appear to present a connected series of visions. Chapter 18 tells of the destruction of Babylon; chapter 19 tells of the destruction of the beast and the false prophet; and chapter 20 moves on to tell of the destruction of Satan himself."[26] I will simply ask the reader to evaluate Ladd's contention in light of the obvious parallels between Revelation 12 and 20 that we have just observed.

This is such an important point for premillenarians that they dig in their heels in the face of the challenge raised by amillenarians. Stanley Grenz agrees with Ladd's assessment but moves the defensive line to the nature of the relationship between Revelation 19 and 20: "Of the parallels proposed by amillennial expositors, the break between chapters 19 and 20, demanded by this eschatological system, is most problematic. Such a break seems to be unwarranted by the text."[27] Craig Blaising says much the same thing: "The visions of 19:11–21:8 are structured in a unified sequence. There is no structural indication of a major break within this sequence recapitulating pre-Parousia conditions."[28] If premillenarians are correct, Revelation 19:11–21 teaches that a great battle occurs at the second advent of Jesus Christ, followed by one thousand years of peace (Rev. 20:1–6), which, in turn, ends in yet another battle, which culminates in the final judgment. But this exposes one of the most serious weaknesses of premillennialism, namely, the presence of evil among the redeemed during the millennial age, provoking the final eschatological battle.

Indeed, there are a number of reasons to believe that the two battles depicted in Revelation 19:11–21 and Revelation 20:7–10 are one and the same event, each depicted from a different redemptive-historical angle. The battle of Revelation 20:7–10 is a recapitulation of the battle recorded in Revelation 19:11–21, not a different battle that occurs one thousand years later. These are two pictures of the same conflict. If this case can be made with any degree of probability, it goes a long way toward establishing amillennialism as the biblical understanding of the millennial age.

Two main lines of argument support recapitulation in Revelation 19:11–21 and Revelation 20:7–10.[29] The first has to do with an interpretive problem associated with the judgment on the nations mentioned by John in Revelation 19:15 and Revelation 20:3. The second line of argumentation has to do with the similarities between the two great battles mentioned in both passages.

In Revelation 19:14–15, we read the following: "The armies of heaven were following him, riding on white horses and dressed in fine linen, white and clean. Out of his mouth comes a sharp sword with which to strike down the nations. 'He will rule them with an iron scepter.'" Clearly, this is a picture of divine judgment on the nations at our Lord's second advent. But in Revelation

20:1–3, we are told that Satan is bound for the express purpose of being prevented from deceiving the nations. Which nations? we must ask. According to the premillennial interpretation, these nations have just been judged by Christ at his second advent. What remains of the nations to be protected from satanic deception?

Again, the scope of the problem for those who hold a sequential relationship between Revelation 19 and 20 becomes clear when we examine the role of the nations throughout the book of Revelation. In Revelation 13, we read that the dragon gave the beast his authority (v. 2) to rule over every tribe, people, language, and nation (v. 7). The result of this satanic empowering of the beast is that "all inhabitants of the earth will worship the beast" (v. 8) because they are deceived by the false signs and wonders of his supreme lieutenant, the false prophet. Then in Revelation 16:13–16, we read of how the kings of the whole earth are gathered for battle at Armageddon "on the great day of God Almighty" (v. 14). This is the day, John said, when Jesus returns like a thief in judgment (v. 15).[30]

Therefore, when we read in Revelation 19:19, "Then I saw the beast and the kings of the earth and their armies gathered together to make war against the rider on the horse and his army," it is clear who these people are. These are those "who had received the mark of the beast and worshiped his image" (Rev. 19:20), i.e., the nations. At this time, we are told, the beast and the false prophet are captured, and the two of them are thrown alive into the "fiery lake of burning sulfur" (v. 20). Indeed, "the rest of them were killed with the sword that came out of the mouth of the rider on the horse, and all the birds gorged themselves on their flesh" (v. 21). Clearly, Revelation 13, 16, and 19 depict the same event, yet another strong indication of recapitulation in this epistle. What is depicted in Revelation 16 and 19 is judgment day. This is when Jesus Christ returns in wrath to judge the nations, raise the dead, and make all things new.

The problem that this raises for premillenarians is quite serious but is often overlooked by capable premillennial interpreters.[31] If Christ judges the nations at his second advent as depicted in Revelation 19:11–21, how does this relate to John's subsequent reference to the nations in Revelation 20:1–3? As R. Fowler White points out, the problem for the premillenarian is simply that "it makes no sense to speak of protecting the nations from deception by Satan in 20:1–3 after they have just been both deceived by Satan (16:13–16) and destroyed by Christ at his return in 19:11–21."[32] In light of the broader eschatology of the New Testament, the most plausible explanation is that Revelation 19:11–21 depicts the same event as Revelation 20:7–10. The premillennial attempt to argue that the nations mentioned in

Revelation 20:3 are the survivors of the great battle in 19:11–21 is contrived at best.[33]

God's restraint of satanic deception of the nations (Rev. 20:1–3) is a description of the present age of gospel preaching and is not a reference to a future millennium. This is the gospel dispensation when Satan is bound, and the gospel will go to the ends of the earth until the thousand years are over (Acts 17:30–31; Eph. 3:4–6). Only then is God's restraint of Satan lifted so that he can deceive the nations and organize them against Christ's church, the supreme act of rebellion that brings about the final judgment.

The second line of evidence in favor of recapitulation in Revelation 19:11–21 and 20:7–10 has to do with the similarities between the two battles here depicted by John. One reason for the similarity no doubt has to do with the fact that in both texts John drew heavily on the imagery of the prophecy of Ezekiel 38 and 39, which describes the eschatological defeat of the mysterious Gog and Magog.[34] In Ezekiel 39:17–20, the prophet Ezekiel foretold of a gruesome scene in which wild animals and birds are summoned to feast on the remains of God's defeated enemy, Gog, chief prince of Meshech and Tubal. The birds and animals, said Ezekiel, "will eat the flesh of mighty men and drink the blood of the princes of the earth. . . . At my table you will eat your fill of horses and riders, mighty men and soldiers of every kind, declares the Sovereign LORD" (Ezek. 39:18–20).

In Revelation 19:17–18, John described the following scene: "And I saw an angel standing in the sun, who cried in a loud voice to all the birds flying in midair, 'Come, gather together for the great supper of God, so that you may eat the flesh of kings, generals, and mighty men, of horses and their riders, and the flesh of all people, free and slave, small and great.'" The similarity between the visions of John and Ezekiel are obvious. The birds and animals are summoned to feast on God's enemies, crushed by the divine warrior. In fact, John's vision ends in verse 21 with the stark declaration that after divine judgment was meted out on the beast and the false prophet, and after the rest [of the nations] were killed, "all the birds gorged themselves on their flesh." The prophecy has become a reality. There can be little doubt that the prophecy of Ezekiel 38–39 is fulfilled by the events of Revelation 19:11–21 at the time of our Lord's second advent.[35]

It is also vital to notice in Revelation 20:7–10 that when the thousand years are over and the nations rebel against God's city and people, the rebels are referred to as Gog and Magog and are gathered together for battle in such numbers that John said "they are like the sand on the seashore."[36] This points to the fact that the visions in Revelation 19:11–21 and Revelation 20:7–10 are of the same battle, and the burden of a second fall of the human race into sin during the millennial age associated with premillennialism is eliminated. This time, when God's judgment by fire falls on the rebellious nations, we learn that the devil himself is destroyed, just as the beast and the false prophet had been. John was not separating the judgment of the beast and the false prophet from that of the devil by a thousand-year reign extending from the time of the second coming to the final judgment after the millennial age. Rather, we are given two different camera angles of the same event.

In both Revelation 19:20 and Revelation 20:9–10, the fire of God's judgment consumes his enemies. One vision depicts the judgment on the nations, the beast, and the false prophet. The other depicts the judgment on the nations and on Satan himself. Both groups are said to experience the final and eternal wrath of God through the means of burning sulfur. As R. Fowler White concludes, "If John expected us to interpret the revolts in Revelation 19 and 20 as *different episodes* in history, we could hardly expect him to describe them in language and imagery derived from the *same episode* in Ezekiel's prophecy."[37] Given the weight and strength of these two lines of evidence, it is clear that the battles in Revelation 19:11–21 and Revelation 20:7–10 are one and the same.

Yet, one more line of evidence supporting recapitulation in the book of Revelation remains to be mentioned. In Revelation 15:1 and 8, we are told that there are seven plagues to come that "complete" *(etelesthē)* God's wrath on the earth.[38] With the sixth bowl, the dragon, the beast, and the false prophet gather the kings of the earth together for battle (Rev. 16:12–14). This, of course, is what is described in Revelation 19:19, when the beast gathers the kings of the earth for the battle. With the seventh bowl, Revelation 16:17–21, we read of an angelic announcement informing us that "it is done!" God's wrath is complete. The result, John said, is a massive earthquake that splits the great city into three parts, while destroying the cities of the nations. "Every island fled away and the mountains could not be found" (Rev. 16:20). This occurs at the same time the nations are struck down in Revelation 19:15. Therefore, what is depicted here from a cosmic perspective is the means by which this is done—the altering of the natural order by a great earthquake.

The point is simply this. If Revelation 19:19–21 and 20:7–10 depict different battles, fully one thousand years apart, why has not the seventh bowl fulfilled God's wrath against his enemies? By itself, this is troubling for premillenarians, who argue that God's wrath is poured out again at the end of the millennium. Add to this the fact that the premillenarian must see Revelation 20:7–10 as involving the redeemed and a partially redeemed earth, and the problem is greatly magnified. It makes far more sense to see each of these visions as a depiction of the course of the present age, which will come to the final consummation when God's wrath is poured out on his enemies.

Various Interpretations of Revelation 20

Because of the unique literary genre of the book of Revelation and the extensive use of apocalyptic symbolism throughout, any exposition of Revelation 20 should take place with the broader eschatology of the New Testament firmly in mind. Several factors that we have already considered serve as the background for the proper interpretation of this passage. From our evaluation of the two eschatological ages in part 2 (the two-age model), it is clear that only glorified saints can be on the renewed earth after the return of Jesus Christ. It also should be clear that, according to the *analogia fidei*, we must interpret unclear or difficult passages of Scripture in light of clearer ones. This is especially the case with apocalyptic literature. Before we look at the details of the passage, we need to examine the serious questions regarding the various interpretations of this passage.

Because the bodily resurrection and the final judgment take place at the return of Christ (according to the two-age model), there is no possibility of a post–second advent millennial age populated by people in nonresurrection, perishable bodies (cf. 1 Cor. 15:42). The mortal, the apostle said, must first put on immortality (1 Cor. 15:53). This also means that there cannot be another resurrection at a later period, as premillenarians argue.

The idea of a millennial age dominated by a return to the Old Testament redemptive economy is also problematic.[39] While premillenarians tell us that what is depicted here is a golden age on a partially renewed earth after Christ's second advent, postmillenarians see this period as a golden age for Christ's church during this present evil age in which the nations are Christianized and the vast majority of the earth's citizens come to faith in Jesus Christ. Both forms of golden-age millennialism build their cases on the assumption that what is depicted in Revelation 20 is like that foretold in the second chapter of Isaiah when the nations "beat their swords into plowshares and their spears into pruning hooks. Nation will not take up sword against nation, nor will they train for war anymore" (v. 4).

The amillennial position, on the other hand, interprets this period of one thousand years as anything but a golden age in which lions and lambs play together. This period is marked by conflict, martyrdom, and revolt against God. Revelation 20 depicts the church militant, not the church triumphant. What is described in Isaiah 2:4 has to do with the renewed earth, not the millennial age. The description in Revelation 20 is much more likely a description of this present evil age rather than a future millennium. There is a real millennium despite the *a*millennial nomenclature. The millennial age in which Christ rules, however, is a present reality and not a future hope.

Amillennial interpreters of Revelation 20 see the passage as the weak link in any form of premillennialism. If the premillennial position is correct, the golden age of the millennium, in which Christ reigns for one thousand years, ends with glorified men and women revolting against the visible rule of Christ when Satan is released from the abyss at the end of that time. When viewing this conception of the future millennial age through the analogy of faith, the idea of a second fall at the end of the millennium is so highly problematic that most amillennial interpreters rule out any form of premillennialism a priori. A fall of glorified humanity into sin after Christ's second advent means that eternity is not safe from apostasy and the spontaneous eruption of sin in the human heart. This is why the amillennial interpretation of Revelation 20 attempts to build on clear texts in the Gospels and Paul's epistles. Amillenarians interpret the symbolic and apocalyptic language used by John in Revelation in light of how these symbols were used elsewhere in Revelation and throughout the Bible.

Revelation 20 can be divided into three sections.[40] Verses 1–3 deal with the binding of Satan, while verses 4–6 deal with the saints in heaven, the first resurrection, and the second death. The third section, verses 7–10, describes the rebellion that transpires when the thousand years are over and Satan is released from the abyss. We now turn to an examination of these verses.

Revelation 20:1–3

The language of Revelation 20 is highly symbolic. According to William Hendriksen, "John sees an angel coming down out of heaven. He has a key with which he is going to lock the abyss (cf. 9:1, 11). This abyss is a deep hole provided with a shaft (9:1), and with a lid. This lid can be unlocked (9:2), locked (20:3), and even sealed (20:3). Bear in mind, that all this is symbolism."[41] To interpret the symbols correctly, the vision of Revelation 20, specifically the mention of the angel and the abyss, must be seen against the backdrop of prior visions in which the same symbols appear.

The first interpretive question, then, has to do with the identity of the two central figures in view, the serpent and the angel. The identity of the serpent is straightforward, since the text itself identifies him for us. The ancient serpent, the dragon, we are told, is the devil or Satan. *Dragon (drakōn)* comes from an Old Testament word for an evil sea monster who symbolizes the nations who terrorize Israel. "Often the wicked kingdom of Egypt is portrayed by this emblem. God is spoken of as defeating Pharaoh as a sea dragon at the exodus deliverances and at later points in redemptive history."[42] The dragon's home is the sea, which in the ancient world was understood to be the place of monsters, storm, and tempest (Rev. 12:15; 13:1) and which explains why in the New Jerusalem "there was no longer any sea" (Rev. 21:1). The dragon's final abode is the lake of fire, far removed from the people of God.

The identity of the angel is more problematic and is often understood to be Christ himself[43] or perhaps Michael the archangel (cf. 2 Pet. 2:10–12; Jude 9). The identity of the angel should be determined in light of the meaning of the other symbols involved in this vision, specifically the abyss and the key. According to Revelation 8:6 and 9:1–2, angels serve as "Christ's intermediaries executing his authority over demonic beings in the realm of the dead."[44] Since there is nothing in Revelation 20 to indicate otherwise, a similar thing is likely in view here. But this particular angel has a key, probably the same key mentioned in chapter 1 by Christ himself. "I am the Living One; I was dead, and behold I am alive for ever and ever! And I hold the keys of death and Hades" (v. 18). The risen Christ holds these keys in his hand because he alone is victorious over death and the grave. When this angel appears, he has a key to the abyss, a symbolic indication that Christ's authority extends over the demonic and the realm of the dead.[45] The angel is most likely not Christ himself but an angelic intermediary exercising Christ's authority over death and the grave. This fits with Paul's assertion that a mysterious restrainer prevents the lawless one from appearing until immediately before the final judgment (2 Thess. 2:7–10).

The real interpretive debate, however, is over the specific action taken by the angel in verses 2–3. "He seized the dragon, that ancient serpent, who is the devil, or Satan, and bound him for a thousand years. He threw him into the Abyss, and locked and sealed it over him, to keep him from deceiving the nations anymore until the thousand years were ended." The meaning of this declaration has produced no end of discussion.

The first issue to be dealt with is the matter of the thousand years. Faithful dispensationalist scholar that he is, John Walvoord sees the years mentioned by John as a literal one thousand years.[46] Historic premillenarian George Ladd, on the other hand, contends that "it is difficult to understand the thousand years for which he was bound with strict literalness in view of the obvious symbolic use of numbers in the Revelation. A thousand equals the third power of ten—an ideal time."[47] Even though, unlike premillenarians, postmillenarians locate the millennial age prior to the return of Christ, they also generally agree with Ladd's assessment. According to J. Marcellus Kik, "The term thousand years in Revelation twenty is a figurative expression used to describe the period of the messianic-Kingdom upon earth. It is that period from the first Advent of Christ until his Second Coming."[48] Amillenarians generally agree with this assessment, seeing the thousand years as a symbolic number, spanning the entire church age.

There are good reasons not to take John's reference to the thousand years literally. For one thing, numbers are always used symbolically throughout the book.[49] Ladd is probably correct when he indicates that ten to the third power, i.e., one thousand, symbolizes an ideal period of time, a time of completion. In addition, the immediate context and the figurative nature of many words used by John, such as *chain, abyss, serpent, beast,* and so on, should remind us that numbers are also symbolic of something else. There are solid theological reasons as well. In Revelation 2:10, we are told that certain Christians were to endure a trial of ten days' length. For enduring such a trial, they "will receive the reward of a millennial reign. This intensifying of ten to a thousand together with the lengthening of the days to years, might suggest that present momentary affliction results in greater glory even in the intermediate state prior to eternal glory."[50]

It is clear, then, that the thousand years begin with the binding of Satan. But what does this binding of Satan entail? Does this mean that Satan is prevented from engaging in all evil activity? And if, as amillenarians claim, the millennial age is a present and not a future reality, how can Satan be bound when there is obviously so much evil in the world? At first, this seems like a formidable objection to the amillennial view. But once we look closely at what John actually taught about the binding of Satan, the notion of Satan being bound in the present age becomes an argument in favor of the amillennial position.

The amillennial interpretation of the binding of Satan is simply this. With the first advent of Jesus Christ and the coming of his kingdom, Satan was, in some sense, bound from the beginning of our Lord's messianic ministry. According to verse 3, Satan was thrown into the abyss for a very specific reason, namely, "to keep him from deceiving the nations any more until the thousand years were ended. After that, he must be set free for a short time."[51] What this binding of Satan means is that, after the coming of the long-expected Messiah, Satan lost certain authority that he possessed prior to the life, death, burial, resurrection, and ascension of the Savior. It does not mean that all satanic operations cease during the millennial age, as many opponents of amillennialism mistakenly assume.[52] The binding of Satan simply means that Satan cannot deceive the nations until he is released at the end of the millennial age.

The first place to look for help in interpreting the meaning of the binding of Satan is earlier passages within the book of Revelation itself. As seen in Revelation 9, the abyss is symbolic of death and Hades. G. K. Beale points out, "The abyss is one of the various metaphors representing the spiritual sphere in which the devil and his accomplices operate. [Revelation] 9:1–11 portrays an angelic being (probably the devil) using 'the key of the shaft of the abyss,' opening the abyss, and releasing demonic creatures so that they torment unbelievers on earth."[53] If Christ takes authority over this realm through his death and resurrection, as stated in Revelation 1:18, then the binding of Satan "is a direct result of Christ's resurrection."[54] Once Jesus rose from the dead, the devil was bound in the abyss. In the light of Christ's triumph, he cannot deceive the nations until he is released.

The imagery that Satan is presently bound means that he cannot deceive God's people en masse, nor can he attack the covenant community with relative impunity, as he did before the coming of the Messiah. This is evident by reviewing the broad course of redemptive history. Satan deceived Adam in Eden, resulting in sin and the curse of death coming on the entire human race. Through the agency of Israel's pagan neighbors, Satan prevented the nation from fulfilling its assigned role in the Promised Land as a light to the nations. Adam desired to be like God. Israel desired to be like her pagan neighbors.

When Jesus began his messianic mission in Galilee, he "went throughout Galilee, teaching in their synagogues, preaching the good news of the kingdom, and healing every disease and sickness among the people" (Matt. 4:23). His preaching led to repeated conflicts with Satan and his demonic minions, which characterize the Gospel narratives. But once Christ died for sinners and overcame Hades itself, the conflict with Satan changed. Now, we are told, the gates of hell will not prevail against Christ's church (Matt. 16:18). Although Satan remains a fierce foe, persecuting God's people as he is allowed, he cannot triumph because he is bound until released at the end of the millennial age.

This interpretation certainly fits with the language we find throughout the New Testament that speaks of Christ's cross and empty tomb as indicative of Christ's triumphal victory over Satan. This victory is evident in Colossians 2:15, where Paul wrote that "having disarmed the powers and authorities, he made a spectacle of them, triumphing over them by the cross." As Arthur Lewis points out, this binding of Satan can be seen throughout the ministry of the Messiah.

> When Jesus drove out the demons, He actually proclaimed His authority over Satan and the arrival of His kingdom. He said, "How can one enter a strong man's house unless he first binds the strong man?" (Matt. 12:29). As the disciples also found success in casting out demons, the Lord exclaimed: "I saw Satan fall like lightning out of heaven" (Luke 10:18). This was a metaphoric way of saying that the devil's power had been overcome by the king's envoys. We know that Satan was cast down when Christ was lifted up (John 12:31); thus it was Calvary's victory that broke the grip of the devil on men and nations. The Gospels clearly teach that the devil's control and power over the peoples of the world has been weakened since the first advent of Christ (cf. Heb. 2:14).[55]

Although Satan is bound during the present age, this does not mean he ceases to be the "god of this age" who blinds "the minds of unbelievers" (2 Cor. 4:4), "the ruler of the kingdom of the air" (Eph. 2:2), and the one who "prowls around like a roaring lion looking for someone to devour" (1 Pet. 5:8). Satan continues to do all of these things. The amillennial interpretation of Revelation 20 does not deny this.

John did tell us, however, that a bound Satan is prevented from deceiving the nations until he is released (cf. 2 Thess. 2:1–12). The point of John's vision was that the angel restrains Satan's evil activities. His binding does not eliminate them. Even though Satan is presently bound and cannot deceive the nations, he remains a dangerous foe, the same way in which a mortally wounded animal is far more dangerous than a healthy one. But however we understand this binding of Satan, we need to be faithful to two distinct but complementary lines of biblical data.

The first line of data emphasizes a decisive defeat of Satan by Jesus Christ. This defeat at the cross and empty tomb guarantees Satan's eventual and final end. Indeed, the binding of Satan is a continuous activity through the preaching of the gospel in which Christ's followers make disciples of all nations (Matt. 28:19). It is the light of the gospel that exposes the darkness of satanic deception. It is the preaching of Christ crucified that sets men and women free and liberates them from the basic principles of this world (Gal. 4:9).

The second line of biblical data is that Satan still rages against Christ and his kingdom in this age in some limited but nevertheless sinister fashion. Although his power to deceive is bound by the truth of the gospel, his fury is not. As William Hendriksen reminds us, a savage animal may be bound with a chain, but this in no way prevents him from doing great damage to anything still within the radius of his reach.[56]

What did John mean when he said that at the end of the thousand years Satan must be released? How does the "release" of Satan for a "short time" figure in? In fact, it makes perfect sense according to the amillennial model, while serving as a serious interpretive problem for all forms of premillennialism. As Arthur Lewis says:

> John makes it very clear in his final book that Satan's area of power is closely guarded and controlled by God. Only after an angel with a key opens the "bottomless pit" can the demons come out (9:2–6). The Beast has to be brought up from the pit at God's command (11:7–8). He is later allowed to make war on the saints (13:7). All of this language supports the secondary line of thought in the New Testament, which states that in some very real sense the devil is "bound" and no longer free to deceive the nations as he did before Christ.[57]

When Satan is released, the rebellion of the nations in Revelation 20:7–10 occurs, and the beast deceives the nations (Rev. 13). Once the divine restraint is lifted, the lawless one suddenly appears, accompanied by lying signs and wonders (2 Thess. 2:1–12). The release of Satan at the end of the millennial age is itself a strong argument in favor of the amillennial interpretation of Revelation 20:1–3. The binding of Satan for a thousand years and his subsequent release surely belong to the present age and not to that period after Christ returns to judge all people, raise the dead, and make all things new.

Revelation 20:4–6

As we turn our attention to the second section of Revelation 20, verses 4–6, the focus shifts from the dragon and the abyss to the life and rule of saints in heaven. What is depicted in verses 4–6 is a result of the binding of Satan in verses 1–3 and is, as we have seen, a recapitulation of the same events described in Revelation 12:7–11. While Satan is bound and his power of deception restrained, Christ's saints are victorious. Christ's victory over death and the grave is now theirs, since he alone possesses the key to Hades and the abyss. In his resurrection, Jesus Christ is the firstfruits of the same resurrection harvest in which his saints will also rise. As Paul said, "If we died with him, we will also live with him; if we endure, we will also reign with him" (2 Tim. 2:11–12).

The scene in Revelation 20:4–6 should be seen as one in which judgment has been executed on the serpent, enabling God's saints to reign.[58] As Richard Bauckham puts it, "Those whom the beast put to death are those who will truly live—eschatologically, and that those who contest his right to rule and suffered for it are those who will in the end rule as universally as he—and for much longer: a thousand years!"[59]

The scene of the heavenly reign of Christ's saints is important, given the historical situation in which Revelation was written. At the time when John wrote this epistle, Christians were under horrible persecution at the hands of the pagan Roman Empire.[60] John was writing largely to give them hope in the midst of their trials at a time when martyrdom was all too common. By the time Revelation was written, Stephen, James, Paul, and Peter had already died martyrs' deaths. The seven letters to the churches in Revelation 2–3 describe a situation in which false doctrine and persecution were becoming increasing threats to God's people scattered throughout Asia Minor. The binding of Satan coupled with the description of the present reign of God's saints would have been of comfort to God's people then undergoing great tribulation from within and without.

A number of interpretive questions raised by verses 4–7 need to be answered. The first of these has to do with the location John described. Verses 1–3 describe the abyss, that is, the realm of death and Hades, but where does the scene in verses 4–6 take place? It is clear from the text that the thousand-year reign occurs where the thrones are, for we read, "I saw thrones on which were seated those who had been given authority to judge" (v. 4). The answer is simple: the thrones are in heaven.

It should come as no surprise to the reader that dispensationalists interpret John's words literally. Walvoord argues that those reigning with Christ are

> the twenty-four elders who are said to reign on earth (5:10). This correlates with the prophecy of Christ recorded in Luke 22:29–30. . . . The judgment here predicted may be considered a general one involving several phases of divine judgment at this stage in world history. . . . The implication in the latter part of verse 4 is that the tribulation saints resurrected from the dead are also judged and rewarded. If the saints of the Old Testament are raised at this time, they too may be the objects of divine judgment and reward.[61]

This is yet another indication of the dispensational propensity to interpret the New Testament in light of the Old. For one thing, Revelation 5:10 is a vision associated with the new creation, not an earthly millennium.[62] Instead of *the* resurrection, Walvoord tells us that multiple resurrections are in view.[63] Walvoord's interpretation is based on the presupposition of the truth of the dispensational interpretation of Daniel 9:24–27, which argues for a seven-year tribulation period preceding the second advent and the millennial age. As we have seen, Walvoord's presuppositions cannot be sustained.

Throughout the book of Revelation, the thrones of Christ and his people are invariably said to be in heaven (Rev. 1:4; 3:21; 4:2ff.; etc.). The scene is in heaven, therefore, not on earth, a serious blow to the dispensational interpretation. Because of the heavenly location, "There can be little doubt that the portrayal of beings sitting on 'thrones' is not intended to express the literal idea of people sitting on actual pieces of furniture and ruling from there. This is, rather, a figurative way of saying that they reign over a kingdom."[64] If true, this raises another series of questions. Who are these people? And what kind of judgment do they exercise?

John told us that the people who reign while Satan is bound are those who did not worship the beast or his image (v. 4). This most likely includes those who were killed "because of the word of God and the testimony they had maintained" (Rev. 6:9), as well as those who died of natural causes "in the Lord" (Rev. 14:13).[65] They have been given authority to judge, John said, which conveys the idea of

God's people joining the heavenly court where thousands upon thousands of angels attend the Ancient of Days waiting for the books to be opened (Dan. 7:9–10). According to Daniel, the beast "was waging war against the saints and defeating them, until the Ancient of Days came and pronounced judgment in favor of the saints of the Most High, and the time came when they possessed the kingdom" (Dan. 7:21–22). From this it is clear that when Satan is bound, not only do the saints possess the kingdom (Christ's) but judgment is also passed on their enemy on their behalf.[66] The reign of saints depicted in Revelation 20:4–6, therefore, fulfills the prophecy of Daniel 7 and is of "a thousand years" duration.

It is also important to notice that the thousand-year reign takes place where the disembodied souls of the martyrs are (in heaven) in contrast to the abyss. Furthermore, these souls reign during the entire period of time when Satan is bound from the resurrection of Christ until the thousand years are over, when Christ returns in judgment and to raise the dead (Rev. 20:7–10). After Christ returns, disembodied souls no longer reign, because after the resurrection, body and soul are reunited when the perishable becomes imperishable. Once this occurs, the saints will reign not for one thousand years but "for ever and ever" (Rev. 22:5). This is what John was getting at when he said, "To him who overcomes, I will give the right to sit with me on my throne, just as I overcame and sat down with my Father on his throne" (Rev. 3:21).

In addition to this, "the thousand year reign also occurs where Jesus lives, for we read, 'And they lived and reigned with Christ.' . . . Where does Jesus live? Clearly it is in heaven. . . . We may safely say, therefore, that the thousand year reign takes place in heaven."[67] All of this is a powerful argument in favor of the amillennial position, namely, that what is depicted in Revelation 20:4–6 belongs to the present, not the future.

The next interpretive matter to be addressed—and certainly among the most hotly disputed in all Scripture—has to do with the nature of the first resurrection mentioned by John in Revelation 20:4–6 and the meaning of the word *ezēsan*, translated by the phrase "they came to life" (v. 4). As George Ladd correctly notes, "This is the most important word in the entire passage. The exegete must decide whether or not it means resurrection; and upon this decision will be determined how he interprets the entire passage."[68] As a premillenarian, Ladd understands this resurrection to be the bodily resurrection associated with the return of Jesus Christ as described in Revelation 19, not a "spiritual resurrection" associated with conversion or the death of Christians. As usual, Ladd's words are direct and to the point:

> In Revelation 20:4–6, there is no such contextual clue for a similar variation of interpretation. The language of the passage is quite clear and unambiguous.

There is no necessity to interpret either word spiritually in order to introduce meaning to the passage. At the beginning of the millennial period, part of the dead come to life [the martyrs]; at its conclusion, the rest of the dead come to life. There is no evident play on words. The passage makes perfectly clear sense when interpreted literally.[69]

Ladd quotes Henry Alford's famous defense of premillennialism:

If, in a passage where *two resurrections* are mentioned, where certain [*psychai ezēsan*] at the first, and the rest of the [*nekroi ezēsan*] only at the end of a specified period after that first,—if in such a passage the first resurrection may be understood to mean *spiritual* rising with Christ, while the second means *literal* rising from the grave;—then there is an end of all significance in language, and Scripture is wiped out as a definite testimony to any thing.[70]

Since two resurrections are mentioned here, and one of them is bodily, both resurrections must be bodily resurrections, according to Ladd. The first resurrection includes believers at the return of Christ. The second resurrection includes unbelievers at the end of the thousand years. This is the natural result of understanding the events depicted in Revelation 20 as occurring after those in Revelation 19. This is the sine qua non of all forms of premillennialism. Premillennialism stands or falls at this very point.[71]

How, then, do amillennial Christians understand the "first resurrection"? Because it is clear that the reign of the saints is in heaven during the present age, the "first resurrection" mentioned by John must be an event occurring prior to the return of Christ when the bodily resurrection takes place at the end of the age (cf. 1 Cor. 15:35–57; 1 Thess. 4:13–18). The critical phrase, "they came to life and reigned with Christ," has been variously interpreted by amillennial Christians as either the believers' conversion and spiritual reign with Christ (the position of Augustine[72] and Calvin[73]) or the believers' death and translation to heaven, where they reign with Christ. This is the position taken by Hendriksen,[74] Beale,[75] B. B. Warfield,[76] and Meredith Kline, whose treatment of the two resurrections will be set forth in some detail to follow. Based on either of these views, then, the first resurrection is spiritual and not bodily and occurs before, not after, the second advent.

Premillenarians, such as Ladd and Alford, think the meaning of *ezēsan*, "they came to life," is ironclad evidence in favor of their position. The coming to life of the rest of the dead, as mentioned in verse 5, is supposedly physical, but such is not the case. Even though the word for "resurrection" (*anastasis*) appears forty-one times in the New Testament in reference to physical resurrection, the word occurs but once in Revelation, which also happens to be the only instance in the

Scriptures where it is used with the ordinal *first*. Furthermore, the verb "to live" (*zaō*) is much more fluid in its meaning. In Revelation, it can mean a physical resurrection (Rev. 1:18, for example) or even physical existence of some sort (cf. Rev. 16:3). More often the verb is used in reference to "spiritual existence," as in passages such as Revelation 3:1, where it clearly refers to spiritual life.[77] When John reported seeing those who "came to life," he may have been referring to a spiritual existence brought about by conversion or the death of believers.

As Beale points out, "But most striking is the observation that elsewhere in the NT *anastasis* and *zaō* (or the cognate noun *zōē*, or "life") and synonyms are used interchangeably of both spiritual and physical resurrection within the same immediate contexts."[78] In Romans 6:4–13, Paul spoke about Christ being "raised from the dead" (*anastasis*) so that "we too may live a new life" (*zōē*). The apostle told of being united to Christ in his resurrection and that we will also live with him. Therefore, the words *life* and *resurrection* can be used together to contrast a spiritual with a physical state of affairs.

There is another important exegetical reason to believe that John had in mind here two different kinds of resurrection: a spiritual and a physical resurrection. This has to do with the contrast John made between the "first resurrection" and the "second death" in verse 6. John's use of these terms has been discussed in some detail by Meredith Kline, whose exegesis of this text is helpful in answering the premillennial insistence that the two resurrections mentioned in the passage must be the same kind and therefore are both bodily resurrections. According to Kline, the evidence indicates the contrary. John was contrasting two kinds of resurrections, a spiritual resurrection (the first resurrection) and a bodily one: "The rest of the dead did not come to life until the thousand years were ended" (v. 5). When John spoke of the "first resurrection," he did not mean the first in a series of resurrections of the same kind; rather, he indicated a difference of kind with the resurrection that follows. As Kline points out:

> One of the critical points in the exegesis of Revelation 20 is the interpretation of *prōtos* [first] in the phrase, "the first resurrection" (v. 5). Premillenarians understand it in the purely sequential sense of first in a series of items of the same kind. They interpret both "the first resurrection" and the resurrection event described in verses 12 and 13 of this chapter as bodily resurrections. The contextual usage of *prōtos*, however, does not support such an exegesis; it rather points compellingly to an interpretation of the "first resurrection" found in (so-called) amillennial exegesis.[79]

If it is true that *prōtos* may not necessarily have a sequential meaning, this undercuts the premillennial contention that both resurrections mentioned by John must be bodily. The term *prōtos* may, in fact, refer to a difference in kind rather than reflect a purely sequential order. If the first resurrection is of a different kind than the second, this is a compelling argument for the amillennial position rather than an impediment to it, as premillenarians claim.

In order to establish this point more firmly, we turn to evidence of how the adjective *first* is used within the book of Revelation. The term *prōtos* appears in the next chapter, Revelation 21, where John's use of the term is illustrative as to how the term is to be understood in chapter 20. According to Kline:

> *Prōtos* does not merely mark the present world as first in a series of worlds and certainly not as first in a series of worlds all of the same kind. On the contrary, it characterizes this world as different in kind from the "new" world. It signifies that the present world stands in contrast to the new world order of the consummation which will abide forever.[80]

Then in Revelation 21:1, *prōtos* does not mean the first in a sequence of the same thing. In fact, it refers to a difference in kind, i.e., something that passes away and is replaced, such as the first heaven and earth. The contrast is not between a first earth and a second earth of the same kind. Rather, John contrasted a fallen creation and a redeemed heaven and earth.

Further illumination of this point is found when we consider John's use of the term *second* in Revelation 21, which functions in a sense as an alternate term for *new* in the same chapter. Verse 8 mentions the "second death," which is identified with the fiery lake of burning sulfur and is the opposite of the death that belongs to the order of "first things" depicted in verse 4, namely, that which results in the first resurrection. Therefore, the words *second* and *new* serve as an antithesis of the "first" (*prōtos*). "Whatever accounts for the preference of 'first' over 'old' in describing the present world, the use of 'first' naturally led to the use of 'second' alongside of 'new' for the future world, particularly for the future reality of eternal death for which the term 'new' with its positive redemptive overtones would be inappropriate."[81] The "first" heaven and earth pass away to be replaced by a "second," or new, heaven and earth. Clearly, then, the terms do not indicate sequence but contrast.

The difficulties this represents for premillenarians should now be apparent. According to Kline:

> In this antithetical pairing of first death (an expression virtually contained in verse 4) and "second death" (v. 8), Revelation 21 confronts us with the same idiom that we find in Revelation 20 in the "first resurrection" (vv. 5, 6) and the second resurrection (an expression implicit in this chapter). The arbitrariness of the customary premillennial insistence that "the first resurrection" must be

a bodily rising from the grave if the second resurrection is such is exposed by the inconsistent recognition by premillennial exegesis that, although the first death is the loss of physical life, the "second death" is death of a different kind, death in a metaphorical rather than literal physical sense.[82]

Therefore, while insisting on understanding these two resurrections as both bodily resurrections, premillenarians are forced to spiritualize the second death. But the second death is not the death of the body. It is something far worse.

At this point, it is helpful to consider other passages in the New Testament in which these same terms appear. How are they used elsewhere in the Scriptures? When we turn to the book of Hebrews, the terms *first* and *new* are used to distinguish between the Mosaic economy of God's redemptive covenant and that same covenant under its messianic administration (cf. Heb. 8:7–8, 13; 9:1, 15, 18; 10:9). It is interesting to note that the new covenant is also called the "second" (10:9). If two major redemptive covenants—the Mosaic covenant and the new covenant—can be contrasted with the same terms, *prōtos* and *new*, this certainly strengthens the case that John did the same thing in Revelation 20 and 21, contrasting two kinds of resurrection. As Kline points out, although in Revelation 20 and 21 "the term 'second' appears along with 'new,' it is 'new' that predominates the counterpart to 'first.' Accordingly, the significance of 'first' in this context is not so much priority in a series but opposition to the idea of 'new.'"[83] This means that *prōtos* functions as the equivalent for *old*, which is traditionally the term applied to the Mosaic covenant, i.e., the old covenant.

There are other instances of *prōtos* being used in this sense in the New Testament as well. Once again, the sequence of two events of the same kind is not in view, but the contrast between these two events is. Paul contrasted the first man Adam (1 Cor. 15:45) with the second Adam (or man) from heaven. When Paul spoke of Adam as the first man and Christ as the second man, Paul was not thinking of Adam being the first in a series of "Adams" and Christ being the first in a series of "Christs." Surely, Paul made the point that Adam and all those he represents stand in contrast to the second man Christ and all those he represents.[84] Adam was from earth; Christ is from heaven. Adam stands at the head of the human race; Christ stands at the head of the redeemed. Death, sin, and weakness characterize Adam and his descendants, while Christ stands at the head of those raised from the dead.[85]

By now it should be clear that the terms *first* and *second* often refer to differences of kind, particularly in contrasting the old order—this present age, the *first* (in the sense of what was here and will pass away)—with that of the *second* or *new*, that which we have seen is the age to come, eternal, resurrection life. Properly understood, this distinction means that in Revelation 20 and 21, John intended us to see these two resurrections not as two bodily resurrections but two different orders or kinds of resurrection. This leads Kline to conclude:

> "The first resurrection" is not, therefore, the earliest in a series of resurrections of the same kind, not the first of two (or more) bodily resurrections. The antithetical usage of *prōtos* in this context requires a conclusion diametrically opposite to the customary premillennial assumption. If the second resurrection is a bodily resurrection, the first resurrection must be a non-bodily resurrection. . . . Proper decipherment of "the first resurrection" in the interlocking schema of first-(second) resurrection and (first)-second death is now obvious enough. Just as the resurrection of the unjust is paradoxically identified as "the second death" so the death of the Christian is paradoxically identified as "the first resurrection." John sees the Christian dead (v. 4). The real meaning of their passage from earthly life is to be found in the state to which it leads them. And John sees the Christian dead living and reigning with Christ (vv. 4, 6); unveiled before the seer is the royal-priestly life on the heavenly side of the Christian's earthly death. Hence the use of the paradoxical metaphor of "the first resurrection" (vv. 5 ff.) for the death of a faithful believer. What for others is the first death is for the Christian a veritable resurrection![86]

This, then, is a strong argument in favor of understanding the first resurrection in Revelation 20:4–6 as a spiritual resurrection, specifically, the death of believers and their entrance into heaven, where they now reign with Christ until the thousand years are over. Christ then returns in glory to raise the dead, judge the world, and make all things new.

When believers are converted and then taste death, they participate in the first resurrection (a spiritual resurrection) so that they might be raised bodily at the end of the age. As John said, "The second death has no power over them" (v. 6). When they die, they reign with Christ as they await the bodily resurrection at the end of the age. But when unbelievers die (the first death), they will experience the second death when they are raised unto everlasting punishment. The contrast between the two kinds of resurrection is now obvious. For Christians, death is really a resurrection unto life. For non-Christians, death entails a resurrection unto the second death.

What, then, do we do with those texts that seem to suggest the first resurrection occurs at the time of conversion? John 5:24–25 is an important passage in this regard. John wrote, "I tell you the truth, whoever hears my word and believes him who sent me has eternal life and will not be condemned; he has crossed over from death to life. I tell you the truth, a time is coming and has now come when the dead will hear the voice of the Son of God and those who hear will live." John stated that believers presently have eternal life.[87] Believers have already crossed over from death to life; hence, a resurrection of some sort has already occurred, even while believers are still living. Paul made a similar point when he stated that believers are made alive with Christ, raised with Christ, and presently seated with Christ in the heavenlies (Eph. 2:5–6; Col. 2:12).

This lends support to the notion that the first resurrection occurs at the time of a believer's conversion. As Leon Morris notes, this is a Johannine pattern.

> The implications of the present possession of eternal life are brought out in the assurance that its possessor "cometh not into judgment." This is the usual Johannine thought that judgment is something that takes place here and now. The man who accepts the way of darkness and evil has already been judged. His judgment lies in that fact. So with the man who has eternal life. His vindication is present in the here and now. He has already passed out of the state of death, and has come into life.[88]

A second point John makes is that when the dead hear the voice of the Son of God, they will live. Again, the imagery is that of those who are spiritually dead coming to life through the means of the life-giving Word of God. As D. A. Carson notes, John makes use of the resurrection imagery here in a twofold sense. The first sense is in reference to the already and is strictly spiritual (as we have seen); the second is in reference to a physical resurrection in the not yet.

> The tension inherent in Christian eschatology between what belongs to the "already" and what belongs to the "not yet" is teased out in this and the following verses. For the expression a time is coming and has now come cf. 4:23. By verse 28, where the eschatology is oriented entirely toward the future, the "time" or the "hour" is coming; John does not say it "now is." Here, however, the coming hour already is: the resurrection life for the physically dead in the end time is already being manifest as life for the spiritually dead. It is the voice of the Son of God (or his word cf. v. 24; 6:63, 68; 11:43) that calls forth the dead, and those who hear will live. Such a voice, such a life-giving word, is nothing other than the voice of God (cf. Isa. 55:3), whose vivifying power mediates the life-giving Spirit (cf. 3:3, 5, 7; 7:37–39) even to dry bones (Ezek. 37).[89]

This adds strong support to Kline's argument that the two resurrections in Revelation 20 are of different kinds in which the old order (a spiritual resurrection) is contrasted with the new (the bodily resurrection). It is also evidence that this is a Johannine pattern of sorts and can be seen in his Gospel in addition to Revelation.

This leads me to conclude that the first resurrection is the believers' regeneration. But as G. K. Beale points out, this is not necessarily incompatible with Kline's view, especially if regeneration is seen as the preconsummate phase pointing to the consummate literal resurrection.[90] Christians are both spiritually raised from death to life at the moment of regeneration and spiritually raised from earth to heaven at the time of death. The one is necessarily connected to the other.

Revelation 20:7–10

As we have seen, verses 7–10 recapitulate John's discussion of Christ's return in judgment depicted in Revelation 19:11–21. John is describing that time when the thousand years are over and God's restraint of Satan is ended. In Revelation 19, we learned of the fate of the beast and the false prophet, while in chapter 20, we learn of the fate of Satan himself. All of these events coincide with the great apostasy immediately before the end of the age (2 Thess. 2:1–12), and that is the occasion for Christ's return in final judgment, when the beast mercilessly makes "war against the saints" (Rev. 13:7). The amillennial interpretation of this passage is that John was depicting the kingdom of God coming in glory, crushing all forces of unbelief once and for all.[91] This is nothing less than the glorious victory of the consummation. On this day, the kingdoms of the world become the kingdom of our God and of his Christ. This is the end of the age, when the temporal gives way to the eternal.

Revelation 20:7–10 raises a number of problems for all millenarians, whether they be pre- or post-. For premillenarians, what is depicted here is especially problematic, given the fact that the satanically inspired revolt of the nations John described occurs after the general resurrection and when there cannot be people in natural bodies on earth or people on earth who have not passed through the final judgment. Who are these people who revolt against Christ? Who are these who are consumed by fire? Are these people in unresurrected bodies? If so, where do they come from? How do they pass through the judgment at the beginning of the millennial age? Are these people the redeemed? Such is unthinkable. The presence of evil in the millennial age is a problem from which all forms of premillennialism cannot escape.

For postmillenarians, on the other hand, Revelation 20 is equally problematic. As Meredith Kline points out, "Revelation 20:7–10 by itself refutes the postmillennial projections, for it is evident there that the nations of the world have not become officially Christianized institutions during the millennium."[92] How can such a thing happen if Christ's kingdom has truly transformed the political, cultural, and economic affairs of all the nations? The global revolt betrays the postmillennial insistence that the nations of the earth will be Christianized. The extent of evil depicted here means that whatever Christianizing of the nations has taken place is more shallow than deep.

In verse 7, we are told that when the thousand years are over Satan is released from the abyss, from the realm of death and Hades, which has served as his prison during the gospel era.[93] What John prophesied in verses 1–3 is now fulfilled. The divine restraint upon his abilities to deceive the nations now lifted, Satan goes out to the ends of the earth to deceive the nations and gather them for battle (v. 8). The number is not small—they are like the sand on the seashore. This is a fulfillment of the prophecy against Gog and Magog in Ezekiel 38–39. In Ezekiel's prophecy, Gog and Magog are Israel's great enemies to the north, while in Revelation 20:7–10, they represent the nations from the four corners of the earth—a Semitic expression for the whole earth. Having been deceived by Satan, they gather together to wage war on God's people.[94]

This is the third time in the book of Revelation that John made reference to the Ezekiel prophecy (cf. Rev. 16:14–16; 19:17–21), the focus this time being the defeat of Satan himself. In verse 9, allusions to the Ezekiel prophecy continue. Ezekiel described God's enemies descending on the land, where they will fall in utter defeat as a direct result of God's judgment (39:11–20). John universalized Ezekiel's prophecy when he described the unbelieving hordes coming against the camp of God's people, a clear allusion to the Israelites encamped in the wilderness of the Sinai during the exodus. The camp of the saints is the same place as the city God loves. This is the church, the true Israel.[95]

Before the rebels can destroy God's people, he will destroy them instead. According to John, "Fire came down from heaven and devoured them" (v. 9). Just as God delivered Elijah from the wicked king Ahaziah with fire from heaven (2 Kings 1:10–14), he will now deliver his people from Gog and Magog, consuming them with fire. This is the fate that awaits the dragon, the serpent, the devil, the archenemy of Christ and his people. John said, "And the devil, who deceived them, was thrown into the lake of burning sulfur, where the beast and the false prophet had been thrown" (Rev. 20:10). Unlike the thousand years—the period limited to the time between the first and second advent of Christ—the devil's torment knows no end, since it will continue forever and ever.

It should now be clear that John was depicting the final consummation and that this event occurs at the same time as the second advent of Christ (Rom. 16:20; 2 Thess. 2:8), when the beast and the false prophet are judged (Rev. 19:20). There is no gap of a thousand years between the judgment on the beast and the false prophet and that of Satan, as demanded by premillennialism. John was describing the same event from different camera angles, if you will. In Revelation 19:20, the camera is looking at the beast and the false prophet, while in 20:7–10, the camera focuses on God's judgment on Satan. This is the same event, and both things occur at the same time.

Premillenarians must take a completely different approach, seeing the revolt depicted in verses 7–10 as evidence of the latent human propensity to sin, even after the return of Christ and under the best of all conditions. According to George Ladd, verses 7–8

> suggest the reason for the temporal reign of Christ during the millennium. A burning theological question is the justice of God in judgment and in condemnation. . . . In the present instance, even after Christ has reigned over men during the millennium, when the deceiver is set free from his prison, he finds the hearts of men still responsive to his seductions. This makes it plain that the ultimate root of sin is not poverty or inadequate social conditions or an unfortunate environment; it is the rebelliousness of the human heart. The millennium and the subsequent rebellion of men will prove that men cannot blame their sinfulness on their environment or unfortunate circumstances; in the final judgment, the decrees of God will be shown to be just and righteous.[96]

Ladd candidly acknowledges that the premillennial position must allow for a satanically inspired rebellion against Christ after his millennial reign. Yet, he does not seem to realize how serious a challenge this represents to his own view. Who are these people who revolt? How can people in natural bodies be on earth after the judgment?[97] What about the premillennial contention that this is a partially renewed earth in which redeemed and nonredeemed people intermingle?[98] To provide answers to these questions, one must do as Ladd does and insert a one-thousand-year gap between Christ's second advent and the judgment, and this after having just argued that the key to interpreting Revelation 20:1–10 is to interpret the first resurrection literally. If judgment day and the second advent occur at the same time, all forms of premillennialism collapse.

The dispensational premillennial interpretation adds a number of distinct features to the traditional premillennial interpretation, radically altering it. According to John Walvoord:

> A brief survey of the Scripture bearing upon the millennial kingdom described here . . . serves to justify the literal interpretation of the thousand years. John in his vision in Revelation does not occupy himself with the details of the millennial kingdom but only with the fact and duration of it. The character of Christ's reign

on earth is fully described in many Old Testament passages such as Isaiah 2:2–4;
11:4–9; Psalm 72, and from many others. From these scriptures it may be seen that
Jerusalem will be the capital of the millennial kingdom (Isa. 2:3) and that war
will be no more (Isa. 2:4). . . . The prominence of Israel in the millennial scene
is evidenced in many passages in the Old Testament. . . . Israel then is rejoined
to God in the symbol of marriage, being transformed from an unfaithful wife
to one who reciprocates the love of Jehovah. Gentiles who share in the kingdom
blessings have unparalleled spiritual and economic benefits, and the thousand-
year reign of Christ is a time of joy, peace, and blessing for the entire earth.[99]

Walvoord goes on to describe the events surrounding Gog and Magog,
denying that these two terms have anything to do with Ezekiel 38 and 39,
for if they did, this would put the so-called Russian invasion of Israel in the
millennium, again indicative of how dispensational presuppositions require
a certain outcome even before an evaluation of the data. "Ezekiel's battle
probably occurs before the millennium, whereas this occurs after the thousand
years have been finished. The number of those who rebel against God and
follow Satan is described as innumerable 'as the sand of the sea.' Thus the
last gigantic rebellion of man develops against God's sovereign rule in which
the wicked meet their Waterloo."[100] Like Ladd, Walvoord sees the destruction
of Satan occurring at the end of the millennial age, one thousand years after
the destruction of the beast and the false prophet (Rev. 20:10). For Walvoord,
the rest of Revelation 20 describes the "great white throne" judgment, the
second resurrection of the unbelieving dead, the second death, and then the
establishment of the new heaven and the new earth.

I simply ask, Is this what John said? If not, what did John say? I remain
satisfied that only the amillennial interpretation of Revelation 20:1–10 lets John
speak in the light of his own thought world, and that, of course, is the Old
Testament now fulfilled by Christ. John was not describing an earthly scene
at all. The scene takes place first in the abyss (vv. 1–3) and then in heaven (vv.
4–6) before shifting to earth in verses 7–10. John was not describing a time
of universal peace and brotherhood, although he did describe a time when
Satan's ability to deceive the nations is curtailed. Instead, John was describing
the present reign of Christ's saints and the final consummation of all things
when, in the end, the ultimate enemy of Christ and his people, Satan, finally
gets everything that is coming to him.

Part 4

AWAITING THE BLESSED HOPE

17

Signs of the End

Anthony Hoekema reminds us, "The expectation of Christ's Second Advent is a most important aspect of New Testament eschatology—so much so, in fact, that the faith of the New Testament is dominated by the expectation. Every book of the New Testament points us to the return of Christ and urges us to live in such a way as to be always ready for that return."[1] In light of this expectation, one pressing question remains to be answered: What remains in biblical prophecy yet to be fulfilled before the Lord's return? The purpose of this chapter is to address this important question.

To offer an answer to this question, we must begin with an investigation of the so-called signs of the end as taught by Jesus and the apostles. Based on this investigation, we can identify three distinct categories of signs of the end found throughout the New Testament. These categories can be designated as follows: (1) those signs of the end that are specific to the apostolic age, (2) those signs of the end that characterize the entire interadventual age, and (3) those signs of the end that herald the end of the age and the second advent of Jesus Christ. We now take up these three categories in order.

Signs of the End That Are Specific to the Apostolic Age

The first group of signs of the end—those specific to the apostolic age—are signs witnessed by our Lord's disciples, who are included among "this generation." "This generation" refers to those people living when Jesus spoke and to whom his words specifically applied.[2] Because these signs are unique to the apostolic era, they indicate that with the coming of Jesus Christ and the dawn of the messianic age, redemptive history reaches the critical point that we may identify as "the beginning of the end." In other words, the presence (and fulfillment) of these particular signs tells us that redemptive history has entered its final phase—that period of time between the first and second advent of Jesus Christ (the so-called interadventual age). These particular signs and their fulfillment also guarantee our Lord's return at the end of the age.

As we consider this first group of signs, the critical biblical text that comes to mind is Matthew 24:33, where Jesus said to his disciples, "Truly, I say to you, all these things will come upon this generation" (Matt. 23:36 ESV). As mentioned in the discussion of the Olivet Discourse (chap. 14), a number of signs were given by Jesus to his disciples (i.e., "these things"). Some of these signs (the first group identified above) began to manifest themselves during the lifetimes of the disciples and were fulfilled by the events associated with the fall of Jerusalem and the destruction of the temple in AD 70. Other signs began to appear during the lifetimes of the apostles but continue to characterize the entire interadventual age (category 2 above).[3]

Four specific signs of the end given by Jesus to the disciples were fulfilled in their lifetimes and especially by the events of AD 70.

The first of these signs was the presence of false prophets and the arrest and persecution of the Twelve (cf. Matt. 24:4–5; 9–14; Mark 13:9–13; Luke 21:12–19). As the Olivet Discourse began to unfold, Jesus warned his disciples, "See that no one leads you astray. For many will come in my name, saying, 'I am the Christ,' and they will lead many astray" (Matt. 24:4–5 ESV). In Matthew 24:9–13, Jesus spoke directly to the fate of those sitting with him on the Mount of Olives as he described the events surrounding the fall of Jerusalem.

> Then they will deliver you up to tribulation and put you to death, and you will be hated by all nations for my name's sake. And then many will fall away and betray one another and hate one another. And many false prophets will arise and lead many astray. And because lawlessness will be increased, the love of many will grow cold. But the one who endures to the end will be saved. (ESV)

Jesus's words echoed a previous warning about false prophets that he gave to the disciples earlier in his messianic mission. "Beware of false prophets, who come to you in sheep's clothing but inwardly are ravenous wolves. You will recognize them by their fruits" (Matt. 7:15–16 ESV). In fact, the words of Matthew 24:11 restate the opening words of the discourse, where Jesus told the disciples to expect false messiahs (Matt. 24:4–5).[4] Proof that this portion of Jesus's warning was fulfilled in the lifetimes of the disciples can be found in Josephus's description of a number of messianic pretenders arising during this period[5] and in Acts 5:36–37, where we read of two false messiahs: Judas the Galilean and Theudas.

In light of the fact that eleven of the twelve disciples are presumed to have died as martyrs (only John lived into old age as an exile on the Isle of Patmos),[6] Jesus's words have a certain poignancy about them. In the book of Acts, we read that shortly after Pentecost Peter and John and other apostles were arrested for proclaiming the resurrection of Jesus Christ (Acts 4:1–4; 5:17ff.). James, one of the Twelve, son of Zebedee and not the brother of our Lord, was killed by Herod about AD 40 (Acts 12:1–5). The persecution promised by Jesus began in earnest when his disciples began preaching the gospel he had commissioned them to preach (cf. Matt. 28:18–20).

The second of the signs of the end specific to the apostolic age was Jesus's prediction of a Roman siege of the city of Jerusalem, the so-called times of the Gentiles (cf. Luke 19:41–44; 21:24). In Luke 19:41–44, Jesus predicted the Roman siege with a remarkable specificity:

> And when he [Jesus] drew near and saw the city, he wept over it, saying, "Would that you, even you, had known on this day the things that make for peace! But now they are hidden from your eyes. For the days will come upon you, when your enemies will set up a barricade around you and surround you and hem you in on every side and tear you down to the ground, you and your children within you. And they will not leave one stone upon another in you, because you did not know the time of your visitation." (ESV)

The horrific events associated with the fall of Jerusalem were recounted in great detail by Josephus[7] and constituted the greatest calamity ever to have come upon the city of Jerusalem (cf. Matt. 24:21). The usual Roman tactics to capture an occupied strong point (like Jerusalem) involved encircling it, cutting off supplies of food and water, and then building large siege towers from which Roman archers could pick off at will those moving about below. Siege warfare was a labor-intensive operation, but the Roman engineers had the time and the material resources to carry it out. This tactic drastically reduced Roman casualties associated with a frontal assault on a fortified defensive position.

The detail in which Jesus predicted the fall of Jerusalem to the Romans (and their siege tactics) is striking, especially in light of the additional details offered in Luke 21:24, where Jesus told the disciples, "They will fall by the edge of the sword and be led captive among all nations, and Jerusalem will be trampled underfoot by the Gentiles, until the times of the Gentiles are fulfilled" (ESV).

The first portion of Jesus's prediction about the fate of Jerusalem was framed in language that echoed a number of Old Testament prophecies about God's future judgment on Israel (e.g., Jer. 20:4–6; 39:1–10; 52:5–10).[8] No doubt, this portion of Jesus's prophecy referred to the Roman siege and subsequent occupation of the city. When Jesus spoke of the Jews being led captive among the nations, he was describing the Roman army taking thousands of Jews prisoner, as well as the sack of Jerusalem and the looting of the temple, infamously depicted on the famed Arch of Titus in the city of Rome.[9]

But Jesus also spoke of the fulfillment of the "times of the Gentiles" (or nations) as comprising the limit of Jerusalem's suffering. This was similar to Paul's point in Romans 11:25–27, where he stated, "I do not want you to be unaware of this mystery, brothers: a partial hardening has come upon Israel, until the fullness of the Gentiles has come in. And in this way all Israel will be saved" (ESV).[10] From what Jesus and Paul both affirmed, there will be an extended period in redemptive history in which the Gentile mission predominates until such time as God's redemptive pendulum swings back in the direction of Israel.[11] This particular portion of Jesus's discussion of the signs of the end (the end of the time of the Gentiles) falls under category 3.

The third sign of the end to be fulfilled in the apostolic age was closely related to the second and had to do with the destruction of the city of Jerusalem and the temple in AD 70 (cf. Matt. 24:1–2, 15–22; Mark 13:1–2, 14–20; Luke 19:43–44; 21:20–24). As the Olivet Discourse opened, Jesus's disciples were in awe of the temple and nearby buildings. We read, "Jesus left the temple and was going away, when his disciples came to point out to him the buildings of the temple. But he answered them, 'You see all these, do you not? Truly, I say to you, there will not be left here one stone upon another that will not be thrown down'" (Matt. 24:1–2 ESV). In fact, Jesus went on to tell them:

> So when you see the abomination of desolation spoken of by the prophet Daniel, standing in the holy place (let the reader understand), then let those who are in Judea flee to the mountains. Let the one who is on the housetop not go down to take what is in his house, and let the one who is in the field not turn back to take his cloak. And alas for women who are pregnant and for those who are nursing infants in those days! Pray that your flight may not be in winter or on a Sabbath. For then there will be great tribulation, such as has not been from the beginning of the world until now, no, and never will be. And if those days had not been cut short, no human being would be saved. But for the sake of the elect those days will be cut short. (Matt. 24:15–22 ESV)

The destruction of Jerusalem and its temple constituted what may be the greatest cataclysm in all of redemptive history. As D. A. Carson points out, these events are so specific "that they must be related to the Jewish War."[12] After describing the way in which many Christians who heeded Jesus's warning escaped from Jerusalem in the years and months preceding the Roman offensive, Eusebius concluded, "Anyone comparing our Savior's words with the rest of the historian's record of the war cannot fail to be astonished or to confess the divine character of the Savior's prediction."[13]

The fourth sign of the end specific to the apostolic age was the desolation to come upon Israel. In Matthew 23:37–39, Jesus told his disciples:

> O Jerusalem, Jerusalem, the city that kills the prophets and stones those who are sent to it! How often would I have gathered your children together as a hen gathers her brood under her wings, and you were not willing! See, your house is left to you desolate. For I tell you, you will not see me again, until you say, "Blessed is he who comes in the name of the Lord." (ESV)

Having pronounced seven woes on the scribes and Pharisees in Matthew 23:1–36, Jesus uttered what amounted to his final public words to the people of Israel, as the Olivet Discourse that followed was given in private.[14] Since the city of Jerusalem was symbolic of the entire nation, Jesus was informing the people that his messianic mission would suffer the same fate as those prophets whom God had sent throughout the nation's history to call his people to repentance. Jesus predicted that after the fall of Jerusalem, Israel's house (i.e., the temple) would be left desolate, the supreme sign of God's judgment on the nation. The focus here was not so much on the destruction of the temple (as in points 2 and 3 above) but on the fact that God's presence would depart from it as a form of judgment.[15]

With Jerusalem sacked and the temple destroyed, it was only a matter of time before Israel came under complete Gentile domination (the so-called times of the Gentiles) and the Jews then living in the area were dispersed throughout much of the Mediterranean world. Although a great tragedy (the ancient people of God coming under covenant judgment), Herman Ridderbos reminds us that Jesus's words also pointed ahead to the end of the age.

> One day, however, Jerusalem will see Jesus again; and then she shall say, "Blessed is he who comes in the name of the Lord." Here Jesus was speaking of His coming in glory, His Parousia. It is not without reason that He expressed the homage that then will be given to Him in the same words with which He had been welcomed into Jerusalem shortly before (Matt. 21:9). For when He comes in glory, everyone will be forced to acknowledge what some had cried out loudly during the Triumphal Entry . . . that Jesus is indeed the King sent by God.[16]

Signs of the End That Characterize the Entire Interadvental Age

The next group of signs of the end are those that characterize the entire inter-adventalperiod (category 2). As with the signs in the first group (those specific to the apostles), these signs of the end also began to manifest themselves during the lifetimes of the disciples. Yet, unlike the first group of signs, these signs were not fulfilled during the lifetimes of the apostles (i.e., with the events of AD 70) but may be said to characterize the entire period of time between the first and second advent of Jesus Christ.

Jesus spoke of these signs as the beginning of the birth pains of the end of the age. Our Lord's use of the birth pain analogy indicates that an extended period of suffering and tribulation must run its course before culminating in the birth of a new created order (the final consummation).[17]

The birth pain metaphor must be understood in light of what motherhood meant to a Jewish woman. The travail of childbirth marked the end of barren-ness (often considered a social stigma and matter of disgrace) and promised the realization of that for which she hoped.[18] Such signs speak of (and indeed guarantee) the certainty of our Lord's return and final judgment but do not indicate when these events will occur—only that they will.[19]

Earlier, Jesus had spoken of the final consummation in Matthew 19:28, where he stated, "Truly, I say to you, in the new world, when the Son of Man will sit on his glorious throne, you who have followed me will also sit on twelve thrones, judging the twelve tribes of Israel" (ESV). The birth pains that began during the apostolic age will culminate in the final consummation of all things (i.e., the new world—*tē palingenesia*) when Jesus returns to judge the world (2 Thess. 1:6–7), raise the dead (Acts 24:15), and make all things new (2 Pet. 3:10). These signs extend from individual families (Matt. 10:34–37) to nations (Matt. 25:32) and even to the natural order (cf. Rom. 8:20–21).[20] In 1 Thessalonians 5:3, Paul used the same analogy to emphasize the tumultuous and unexpected arrival of the end of the age when he stated, "While people are saying, 'There is peace and security,' then sudden destruction will come upon them as labor pains come upon a pregnant woman, and they will not escape" (ESV).

Four signs of the end of this type are found in the New Testament. As with the previous category, several of them are interconnected.

The first of those signs of the end that characterize the entire period of time between Christ's first coming and his second advent involves the presence of false Christs (as predicted by Jesus in Matt. 24:3–6, 10–11; Mark 13:3–8; Luke 21:7–8), coupled with the rise of a series of antichrists within the churches who seek to lead many astray (1 John 2:18–19; 4:3; 2 John 7). As we saw in the previous category of signs, our Lord warned his disciples, "Many will fall away and betray one another and hate one another. And many false prophets will arise and lead many astray" (Matt. 24:10–11 ESV). Many scholars believe that this sign of the end—the presence of false Christs—is closely associated with the spirit of antichrist present in the apostolic church.[21]

According to John, an antichrist is anyone "who [does] not confess the coming of Jesus Christ in the flesh" (2 John 7 ESV). In this strict sense, an antichrist is anyone who teaches falsely about the identity of Jesus Christ—who is God manifest in the flesh (cf. John 1:1–17). Elsewhere, John said, "Every spirit that does not confess Jesus is not from God. This is the spirit of the antichrist" (1 John 4:3 ESV). Such an antichrist "denies that Jesus is the Christ" and in doing so "denies the Father and the Son" (1 John 2:22 ESV). John also described these antichrists as "deceivers [who] have gone out into the world" (2 John 7 ESV). For John, the explanation of the antichrist phenomenon is as simple as it is tragic. "They went out from us, but they were not of us; for if they had been of us, they would have continued with us. But they went out, that it might become plain that they all are not of us" (1 John 2:19 ESV).

The appearance of false Christs (as Jesus predicted) and a series of antichrists (as John mentioned in his epistles) not only is one of the birth pains of the end but also gives his readers an important indicator of the times in which they live. "Children, it is the last hour, and as you have heard that antichrist is coming, so now many antichrists have come. Therefore we know that it is the last hour" (1 John 2:18 ESV). John informed his readers that antichrist, "which you heard was coming and now is in the world already," is not a future but a present foe (1 John 4:3 ESV). Although many think of antichrist as the final end-times foe, John revealed that many antichrists were already present during the apostolic era. In fact, anyone who denies that Jesus is the Christ is such an antichrist, and their very presence in the church is an indication that the last hour (that last period of redemptive history before the consummation) has already begun. The fact that antichrists were already present when John wrote his epistles at some point after AD 70 is an indication (if not a warning) that such antichrists will continue to arise throughout the interadvental period until culminating in a final Antichrist[22] immediately before our Lord's return (see category 3 below).

The second of the signs of the end—the presence of false teachers and false doctrine—that characterize the entire interadvental age bears some similarity to the previous sign (the warning about false Christs, as foretold by Jesus, and the spirit of antichrist mentioned by John). However, I see Paul's warning of the presence of false doctrine and those who teach it in the churches, as mentioned in his second letter to Timothy, as a sign more broadly conceived than the presence of false Christs and the denial of Christ's deity associated with antichrists. In 2 Timothy 3:1–5, Paul's focus was the great moral and ethical difficulties facing the church throughout the interadvental age. In 2 Timothy 3:1–5, Paul warned Timothy (and us):

> But understand this, that in the last days there will come times of difficulty. For people will be lovers of self, lovers of money, proud, arrogant, abusive, disobedient to their parents, ungrateful, unholy, heartless, unappeasable, slanderous, without self-control, brutal, not loving good, treacherous, reckless, swollen with conceit, lovers of pleasure rather than lovers of God, having the appearance of godliness, but denying its power. Avoid such people. (ESV)

When Paul spoke of the "last days" (the only time this phrase was used in this way by Paul), he was saying that his own contemporary state of affairs (the presence in the churches of the various attitudes spelled out above) was an indicator of the approach of the end.[23] Geerhardus Vos contends that "the characteristic feature of these New Testament applications of the phrase [last days] consists in the idea accompanying them that the writers and readers are conscious of the last days being upon them, or at least close at hand."[24] In other words, the time frame of the "last days" extends from Paul's own day until the end of the age.[25] The entire period between Christ's first advent and his second will be "difficult times" (*kairoi chalepoi*) characterized by the behavior described by Paul to Timothy.

In fact, Paul had already warned Timothy that "the Spirit expressly says that in later times some will depart from the faith by devoting themselves to deceitful spirits and teachings of demons" (1 Tim. 4:1 ESV). This statement is quite similar to his comments in 2 Thessalonians 2:3, 9, where Paul cautioned the Thessalonians that the day of Lord "will not come, unless the rebellion [*apostasia*] comes first, and the man of lawlessness is revealed, the son of destruction. . . . The coming of the lawless one is by the activity of Satan with all power and false signs and wonders" (ESV). Paul understood that the "last days" (exemplified by behavior he himself had witnessed [2 Tim. 3:1–5]) would culminate in a final apostasy and with the appearance of the man of lawlessness—the final Antichrist. The difficult times described by Paul to Timothy extend from the apostolic era until the time of the end and culminate in a great apostasy and with the manifestation of the man of sin (the Antichrist)—signs that herald the end of the age (see category 3 below).

The third group of signs of the end tied to the interadvental age were mentioned by Jesus in the course of several verses in the opening portion of the Olivet Discourse (Matt. 24:3–8; Mark 13:3–8; Luke 21:7–11). "And you will hear of wars and rumors of wars. See that you are not alarmed, for this must take place, but the end is not yet. For nation will rise against nation, and kingdom against kingdom, and there will be famines and earthquakes in various places. All these are but the beginning of the birth pains" (Matt. 24:6–8 ESV).

At first glance, the mention of these particular signs of the end (wars and rumors of wars, earthquakes, and famine) is surprising since these things have all been part of human history since the fall of the human race. On closer inspection, however, it becomes clear that these particular signs serve an important theological purpose. The presence of wars and natural disasters serves to remind us that the dawn of the messianic age is not yet the end. In fact, the presence of these signs constitutes proof that a final consummation awaits until Jesus's kingdom is fully realized with the resurrection and final judgment at the end of the age.

When Paul described the course of the interadvental age in general terms in 1 Corinthians 15:24–26, he too indicated that the end (consummation) will not come until the general resurrection at the end of the age. Paul wrote, "Then comes the end, when he delivers the kingdom to God the Father after destroying every rule and every authority and power. For he must reign until he has put all his enemies under his feet. The last enemy to be destroyed is death" (ESV). The presence of famine and natural disasters, including earthquakes, and the reality of continuing warfare among the nations after the coming of the Messiah should serve "not to curb enthusiasm for the Lord's return but to warn against false claimants and an expectation of a premature return based upon misconstrued signs."[26] The Messiah has come and inaugurated his kingdom. But the Messiah must return at the end of the age to consummate that kingdom! The presence of war, famine, and earthquakes throughout the entire interadvental period tells us that the consummation is still yet to come.

The theological point is that these signs of the end do not tell us *when* the end will come, only that it will. Although contemporary prophecy pundits are oftentimes unable to resist the temptation to do so, it is important to realize that Jesus did not predict specific wars, earthquakes, and natural disasters— only that the effects of the fall will remain with us until his second advent. Therefore, when we see the nations wage war on one another, when we feel the ground shake under our feet, we know that these things will continue until the end. But they also tell us that the end is coming. And this knowledge should give us confidence in God's purposes in the face of difficult times and tribulation around us.

An additional factor that merits consideration is that the use of the birth pain analogy by Jesus and Paul may indicate that these particular signs (war and natural disaster) may intensify before the end. If so, this parallels the various seal and trumpet judgments depicted in the book of Revelation that occur throughout the entire present age but seem to intensify at the time of the end.[27] As Geerhardus Vos once put it, "As the reign of truth will gradually be extended, so the power of evil will gather force towards the end. The making of things right and new in the world depend not upon gradual amelioration but on the final interposition of God."[28] Things may not get better before the end. In fact, it is likely they will get worse.

The fourth and final sign of the end that characterizes the entire interadventental age is the persecution of believers. Paul warned Timothy:

> Indeed, all who desire to live a godly life in Christ Jesus will be persecuted, while evil people and impostors will go on from bad to worse, deceiving and being deceived. But as for you, continue in what you have learned and have firmly believed, knowing from whom you learned it and how from childhood you have been acquainted with the sacred writings, which are able to make you wise for salvation through faith in Christ Jesus. All Scripture is breathed out by God and profitable for teaching, for reproof, for correction, and for training in righteousness, that the man of God may be competent, equipped for every good work. (2 Tim. 3:12–17 ESV)

Paul's warning about the reality of persecution facing the followers of Jesus brings to mind several supporting lines of evidence found elsewhere in the New Testament. The first is Paul's own experience as an apostle, as described in passages such as 2 Corinthians 11:23–29:

> Are they servants of Christ? I am a better one—I am talking like a madman— with far greater labors, far more imprisonments, with countless beatings, and often near death. Five times I received at the hands of the Jews the forty lashes less one. Three times I was beaten with rods. Once I was stoned. Three times I was shipwrecked; a night and a day I was adrift at sea; on frequent journeys, in danger from rivers, danger from robbers, danger from my own people, danger from Gentiles, danger in the city, danger in the wilderness, danger at sea, danger from false brothers; in toil and hardship, through many a sleepless night, in hunger and thirst, often without food, in cold and exposure. And, apart from other things, there is the daily pressure on me of my anxiety for all the churches. Who is weak, and I am not weak? Who is made to fall, and I am not indignant? (ESV)

There can be little doubt that Paul's own experience as an apostle convinced him that suffering and hardship were, for many, part and parcel of the Christian life. To follow Christ and to live a godly life often provoke non-Christians to anger. In fact, Paul reminded the Thessalonian Christians, "We kept telling you beforehand that we were to suffer affliction, just as it has come to pass, and just as you know" (1 Thess. 3:4 ESV).

Second, Paul's warning to Timothy also calls to mind the words of our Lord that the Christian life entails "cross bearing" (Matt. 16:24) and inevitable hatred from the world. Jesus told the Twelve, "If the world hates you, know that it has hated me before it hated you. If you were of the world, the world would love you as its own; but because you are not of the world, but I chose you out of the world, therefore the world hates you" (John 15:18–19 ESV). In his comments on this passage, John Calvin cautioned, "The Gospel cannot be proclaimed without the world straightway going mad. Hence it will never be possible for godly teachers to avoid the world's hatred."[29]

Third, in Revelation 7:14, John spoke of the interadvental period as a time of "great tribulation" (*thlipseōs tēs megalēs*), likely the same period of time Paul described to Timothy as a period of "great difficulty" (cf. 2 Tim. 3:1 ESV). This period of tribulation extends from Christ's first advent to his second. As G. K. Beale (and others) point out, John's reference to a great tribulation is drawn from Daniel 12:1, where Daniel spoke of the time of the end as one in which God's people are persecuted for their loyalty to YHWH. "At that time shall arise Michael, the great prince who has charge of your people. And there shall be a time of trouble, such as never has been since there was a nation till that time. But at that time your people shall be delivered, everyone whose name shall be found written in the book" (ESV). According to Beale, such "tribulation consists of pressures to compromise faith, these pressures coming both from within the church through seductive teaching and without from overt oppression."[30]

In Revelation 7:14, the "great tribulation" refers to the persecution that comes on the followers of Jesus because of their testimony about the person and work of their Savior. In Revelation 13, this tribulation takes the form of persecution of Christians by the Roman state (the beast) and its emperor (the false prophet). The military and economic might of Rome is directed against the people of God—who refuse to worship the state or its leader, who have been empowered by the dragon. In this sense, Rome serves as the epitome of all those God-hating empires that arise throughout the interadvental pe-riod and claim divine rights and prerogatives for themselves and who see the people of God as subjects unwilling to pay them the homage they think they are due. When viewed from the broader perspective of the New Testament as a whole, it is clear that this period of tribulation began with the suffering of Jesus himself, is present throughout the entire interadvental period as the church preaches the gospel to the nations, and will reach its zenith at the time of the end (cf. Rev. 20:7–10).[31]

The presence of those signs of the end that characterize the entire inter-advental period (category 2) present a number of interpretive problems for futurists, who tend to push the signs of the end off until the days immediately preceding our Lord's return, as well for those who contend that the events of AD 70 fulfilled the signs of the end in their entirety (i.e., preterists).

The presence of specific signs of the end that characterize the course of redemptive history between Christ's first and second advent indicates that as the church engages in its missionary outreach, God's people will face false Christs and antichrists, they will witness great difficulties arising in their midst stemming from the immorality among their members, they will endure the horrors of wars and natural disasters, and they will endure periods of intense persecution depicted by John as the "great tribulation." The presence of these signs of the end eliminates any secularist dream of an earthly utopia as well as challenges the postmillennial expectation of the conversion of the nations, producing a golden age of cultural, economic, and political transformation before our Lord's return.[32] As Vos points out, "The trouble is that . . . certain types of post-millennialism leave too little room for eschatology."[33] Given the reality of this category of signs of the end, I wholeheartedly concur with Vos's assessment. The signs of the end do not point to a golden age for the church as a whole during the interadvental age but seem to indicate alternating periods of blessing and tribulation—the eschatological tension between the already and the not yet.

Signs of the End That Herald the End of the Age and the Second Advent of Jesus Christ

The third category of signs of the end are those that herald the end of the age and the second advent of Jesus. These are the signs that tell us our final redemption is drawing near. Three specific signs of the end fall into this category.[34] Several of these signs are discussed in some detail elsewhere in this volume, so I will briefly summarize them here.

The first sign that heralds the end of the age is that the gospel is preached to the ends of the earth. In Matthew 24:14, Jesus told his disciples, "This gospel of the kingdom will be proclaimed throughout the whole world as a testimony to all nations, and then the end will come" (ESV). This establishes the church's missionary charter, which is anchored in the Great Commission (cf. Matt. 28:18–20). This sign is also an indication that at some point the church's Gentile mission will be largely completed, and this period of time may correspond with the "times of the Gentiles" discussed previously (cf. Luke

21:24). When commenting on the parallel passage in Mark's Gospel (13:10), Charles Cranfield stated:

> The meaning of this verse is that it is part of God's eschatological purpose that before the End all nations shall have an opportunity to accept the gospel. The interval is the time of God's patience during which men are summoned to repentance and faith; it has for its content the church's mission to the world. That does not mean that the world will necessarily get steadily more Christian or that the End will not come till all men are converted. It is a promise that the gospel will be preached, not that it will necessarily be believed. The disciples' witness is another characteristic of the last times.[35]

The sign that the gospel must be preached to all nations before the end can come establishes the church's mission to preach the gospel to the ends of the earth. This sign is the only one directly tied to the activity of Christ's church. Sadly, those Christians who are interested in Bible prophecy often devote themselves to discerning the signs of the times, even though Jesus made it clear that "concerning that day and hour no one knows, not even the angels of heaven, nor the Son, but the Father only" (Matt. 24:36 ESV). The one sign of the end Jesus gave, however, that falls into the realm of the church's responsibility is that the gospel will be proclaimed to the nations before the Lord returns. If we truly desire the return of our Lord, then our energies should be devoted to missions and evangelism, not to undue speculation and date-setting, striving to discern the identity of the Antichrist, or claiming that specific natural disasters and wars were foretold by Jesus and the apostles.

The second sign of the end that signals the return of Jesus Christ was given by the apostle Paul in Romans 11:25–26, where he described the future course of redemptive history, specifically, the future role of Israel during the interadventual age in light of God's redemptive purposes for both Jew and Gentile. Since I spent considerable time on this matter in chapter 15, I will briefly summarize that material here. In Romans 11:25–26, Paul told his readers, "Lest you be wise in your own sight, I do not want you to be unaware of this mystery, brothers: a partial hardening has come upon Israel, until the fullness of the Gentiles has come in. And in this way all Israel will be saved" (ESV). I understand the salvation of "all Israel" to refer to national Israel (i.e., the Jews), indicating a dramatic change in God's redemptive purposes when the "fullness of the Gentiles has come in," or, as Jesus put it in Luke 21:24, "until the times of the Gentiles are fulfilled" (ESV).

According to this view, the church's evangelistic mission centering on the Gentiles begins to dramatically shift toward the conversion and evangelism of Jews at the time of the end. The conversion of Israel (not each and every Jew living but a substantial number of Jews) to faith in Jesus Christ (being regrafted into the righteous root, who is Jesus Christ, to use Paul's metaphor in Romans 11:17–24) is a harbinger of the end. The conversion of the Jews is therefore a significant sign that our Lord is soon to return to bring about the final consummation of all things. As Paul put it in Romans 11:15, "What will their acceptance mean but life from the dead?" (ESV). The salvation of "all Israel" (Israel's reconciliation) is tied to the general resurrection at the end of the age when Jesus returns in glory.[36] This means that the conversion of Israel is a sign that the end of the age is at hand.

The third sign of the end that signals the return of the Lord is a great apostasy among the ranks of professing believers, tied directly to the appearance of the man of sin (i.e., the Antichrist), who is the final eschatological enemy of the church. This matter is also discussed in detail elsewhere in this volume, so I will briefly summarize here the material developed in chapter 11.

In 2 Thessalonians 2:1–12, Paul informed the Thessalonians that the day of the Lord had not yet come because the rebellion (*apostasia*) had not yet occurred and the man of sin had not yet been revealed (v. 3). According to Paul, the revelation of the latter (the man of sin) will occur in conjunction with a final outbreak of satanic activity. Paul wrote:

> And then the lawless one will be revealed, whom the Lord Jesus will kill with the breath of his mouth and bring to nothing by the appearance of his coming. The coming of the lawless one is by the activity of Satan with all power and false signs and wonders, and with all wicked deception for those who are perishing, because they refused to love the truth and so be saved. Therefore God sends them a strong delusion, so that they may believe what is false (vv. 8–11 ESV).

Paul's prediction of a great apostasy is directly tied to the appearance of the Antichrist (the lawless one), which, in turn, corresponds with the release of Satan from the abyss, as described in Revelation 20:7–10. This connection is often overlooked but once established serves to tie the events predicted by Paul (a final apostasy, the revelation of the man of sin, and the outbreak of satanic activity) to the release of Satan from the abyss and the deception of the nations depicted by John as occurring immediately before the return of Jesus Christ.

> And when the thousand years are ended, Satan will be released from his prison and will come out to deceive the nations that are at the four corners of the earth, Gog and Magog, to gather them for battle; their number is like the sand of the sea. And they marched up over the broad plain of the earth and surrounded the camp of the saints and the beloved city, but fire came down from heaven and

consumed them, and the devil who had deceived them was thrown into the lake of fire and sulfur where the beast and the false prophet were, and they will be tormented day and night forever and ever. (Rev. 20:7–10 ESV)

To summarize, then, the appearance of this final Antichrist (Paul's man of sin) is the culmination of that series of antichrists described by John who have plagued the church from the beginning. The satanic activity associated with the appearance of the final Antichrist corresponds to the release of Satan from the abyss, is also tied (as either cause or effect) to a time of great apostasy in the church, and is said by Paul to immediately precede the return of Jesus Christ, who will destroy the man of sin when he appears. "And then the lawless one will be revealed, whom the Lord Jesus will kill with the breath of his mouth and bring to nothing by the appearance of his coming" (2 Thess. 2:8 ESV).

Therefore, before the Lord returns, the gospel must be preached worldwide, there will be a massive conversion of Jews to faith in Jesus Christ, and the church will experience a time of great apostasy and satanic activity tied to the revelation of the final Antichrist, who appears only to be destroyed by Jesus Christ at his second advent.

The Tension between the Imminence and the Delay of Christ's Second Advent

One of the remarkable consequences arising from Jesus's and the apostles' teaching about the signs of the end as found throughout the New Testament is the tension created by the presence of specific signs that clearly precede the end (the three categories set out in the preceding) and the rapidity at which the second advent can come to pass.

The tension between signs preceding the end and the suddenness and surprise associated with our Lord's return is found within the Olivet Discourse (and discussed previously). Jesus spoke of those signs that precede his coming as something of which his disciples were to be aware. "From the fig tree learn its lesson: as soon as its branch becomes tender and puts out its leaves, you know that summer is near" (Matt. 24:32 ESV). Yet, the same disciples were also told in the same discourse that the Lord can return suddenly with great surprise:

> For as were the days of Noah, so will be the coming of the Son of Man. For as in those days before the flood they were eating and drinking, marrying and giving in marriage, until the day when Noah entered the ark, and they were unaware until the flood came and swept them all away, so will be the coming of the Son of Man. Then two men will be in the field; one will be taken and one left. Two

women will be grinding at the mill; one will be taken and one left. Therefore, stay awake, for you do not know on what day your Lord is coming. But know this, that if the master of the house had known in what part of the night the thief was coming, he would have stayed awake and would not have let his house be broken into. Therefore you also must be ready, for the Son of Man is coming at an hour you do not expect. (Matt. 24:37–44 ESV)

There can be no doubt that the tension between the signs preceding the end and the suddenness of the Lord's return is intentional. On the one hand, the surprise associated with the time of the end should prevent date-setting, although, sadly, many have ignored Jesus's words in this regard. It is hard to escape the directness of Jesus's words, "But concerning that day and hour no one knows, not even the angels of heaven, nor the Son, but the Father only" (Matt. 24:36 ESV). We do not know when the Lord will return. On the other hand, the presence of such a tension should prevent idleness on the part of God's people. We must constantly be watching for the Lord's return and yet be about the business God has assigned to us (Matt. 24:42–44). At a practical level, this means God's people should preoccupy themselves with fulfilling the Great Commission and not with how the Bible supposedly predicts specific wars, earthquakes, or natural disasters.

The tension between the signs of the end and the suddenness of the Lord's return mirrors, in many ways, the already/not yet tension found throughout the New Testament. As G. K. Beale has pointed out, the Old Testament writers speak frequently of the "latter days," but it is not until Jesus Christ comes and begins to fulfill this Old Testament expectation (the already; cf. Gal. 4:4–6) that he, in turn, points God's people to a final consummation at the end of the age (the not yet). What begins in the first century continues on until Jesus Christ's second advent.[37] Many Christian writers have sought to understand this tension in terms of the Allied invasion of Europe on D-day (June 6, 1944). With the success of the Allied landings, there was little doubt that Germany would eventually be defeated. But the war lasted nearly a year after D-day. As Oscar Cullman put it, "The hope of the final victory is so much more vivid because of the unshakably firm conviction that the battle that decides the victory has already taken place."[38] With Christ's death and resurrection, the final victory is assured. But the end has not yet come.

Although many Christians believe the Lord can return at any moment, as we have just observed, certain signs remain to be fulfilled before the Lord returns. But how can the Lord return at any moment when these things must still come to pass? In light of those signs of the end that herald our Lord's return (category 3), it is quite plausible that the events associated with the end of the age and the return of Jesus Christ can come to pass very quickly. Birth pains can lead rapidly to delivery. Great apostasy in the church, a dramatic increase in satanic activity, the rise of the Antichrist, and the conversion of the Jews can all come to pass with great speed once Satan is released from the abyss (Rev. 20:7–10) and the restrainer ceases his restraining work (2 Thess. 2:5–8).

In light of the fact that specific signs of the end remain to be fulfilled (category 3) before the Lord's return, Anthony Hoekema suggests that we not speak of our Lord's return as "imminent" (i.e., as though it can occur at any moment) but as "impending."[39] This, I think, is a wise approach. As the Lord of history, God alone ordains our days and final destinies. When the time of the end has come, it is reasonable to conclude that the events associated with our Lord's return can come to pass in a very short period of time. But the fact remains that the signs of the end have not yet been fulfilled and must be before Jesus returns.

When speaking of the appearance of the Antichrist, Geerhardus Vos is correct when he reminds us that the best interpreter of those signs that herald the end is their actual fulfillment.[40] When these signs actually begin to manifest themselves, there will be no question about whether or not this is "really" the end. God's people will know that the end of the age is at hand and that our redemption draws near. There will be no doubt.

So What, Exactly, Is Fulfilled, and What Remains to Be Fulfilled?

We have now reached a point where we can summarize which of the signs of the end have been fulfilled and which signs remain yet to be fulfilled.

Category 1: The signs of the end fulfilled in the lifetimes of the apostles

- The events associated with the founding of the church and the persecution of the apostles and earliest Christians
- The destruction of Jerusalem, the temple, and the desolation (fulfilled with the events of AD 70)
- The continuing spread of Christianity to the ends of the earth (cf. Matt. 13:31–32; Acts 1:8) underway by the close of the apostolic era

Category 2: The signs of the end that characterize the course of the interadventual period

- Wars and rumors of wars (ongoing)
- Earthquakes and other natural disasters (ongoing)

- The presence of antichrists, false teachers, heresy, and the persecution of God's people (ongoing)

Category 3: The signs of the end that herald the end of the age and the return of Jesus Christ

- The spread of the gospel to the ends of the earth (as a condition of the end) and the salvation of all God's elect (ongoing, time of fulfillment unknown)
- The conversion of Israel as the fullness of the Gentiles comes in (ongoing but not yet fulfilled)
- A great apostasy within the church and the appearance of the man of sin (the Antichrist), tied to the release of Satan from the abyss, where he had been bound so as to prevent him from deceiving the nations (not yet fulfilled)

What Can We Say about the Signs of the End?

- The signs of the end do not tell us when Jesus will return, only that he will.
- As we consider the signs of the end, our methodology must be grounded in the analogy of faith (Scripture must be allowed to interpret Scripture). Current events cannot tell us what the Bible means when speaking of the various signs of the end. But the Bible does tell us that all these signs point ahead to the end of the age and the return of Jesus Christ.
- The Bible does not predict specific events (specific antichrists, wars, famines, earthquakes, etc.), but it does tell us to expect all these things and worse, because these things are characteristic of this age as it awaits the age to come.
- No one knows the day or the hour of our Lord's return. If anyone claims otherwise, they are lying or deceived.
- We are to do as our Lord commands and endeavor to fulfill the Great Commission until he comes.
- We are to eagerly keep watch and pray for our Lord's return. The Bible speaks of our Lord's return as the blessed hope (Titus 2:13). The early church prayed for this great event (1 Cor. 16:22), and the final benediction of the book of Revelation exhorts us to seek the Lord's return (Rev. 22:20).

18

Evaluating Millennial Options

In part 1, we surveyed the major millennial positions and discussed the underlying hermeneutical issues that contribute to the distinctives of each of these views. In part 2, we developed a comprehensive biblical-theological backdrop to better illumine the Bible's teaching about the millennial age. In part 3, we surveyed several of the critical biblical passages that have an important bearing on the subject. So far in part 4, we have identified the signs of the end and considered how to interpret them. We are now in a position to briefly summarize the major interpretive problems to be faced by pre-, post-, and amillenarians.

Throughout this volume, I have been defending the amillennial understanding of the millennial age and related issues. An astute reader will no doubt ask, If the case for amillennialism is so compelling, why aren't all Christians convinced? There are a number of reasons why this is the case. One reason for this lack of greater acceptance is the fact that amillenarians do not relate current events to the Bible. Instead, the amillennial interpretation flows from a distinctive, comprehensive Reformed theology. Therefore, amillennialism will never be as compelling a system as dispensationalism. In the hands of able communicators, such as Tim LaHaye and Jerry B. Jenkins, John Hagee, Jack Van Impe, Dave Hunt, and Hal Lindsey, the dispensational understanding of prophetic biblical texts can be applied to virtually any geopolitical crisis mentioned on the evening news. If these men are correct, the secret rapture may occur at any moment. The Antichrist may soon be revealed and take his place on the global scene. This creates a compelling sense of urgency that makes a more theologically grounded system like amillennialism seem almost irrelevant to everyday Christian living.

The solution to this particular dilemma is for amillenarians to do a better job of communicating that the imminent return of Jesus Christ to judge the world, raise the dead, and make all things new lies at the heart of their own eschatological system. As Jesus exhorted us, "Keep watch, because you do not know the day or the hour" (Matt. 25:13). We obey this exhortation in part by stressing the immediacy of the blessed hope, our Lord's return for those who are his own. This is a central tenet of amillennialism in particular and Christian eschatology in general. Amillenarians anticipate the second coming of the Lord every bit as much as dispensationalists do.

Another reason why amillennialism is not widely accepted among American evangelicals is that far too often people simply dismiss amillennialism without much consideration. This is, in part, because so many popular Bible teachers and prophecy experts contend that amillenarians do not take the prophetic passages of the Bible seriously. Others label amillennialism anti-Semitic because amillenarians supposedly replace Israel with the church. Amillennialism has gotten a great deal of bad press, much of it quite unjustified.

Because amillennialism has this kind of reputation among many Christians who are interested in Bible prophecy, it is often dismissed out of hand by people who have never seriously considered the position to be a viable option. This is a lamentable situation. From years of lecturing and teaching on this topic in Christian circles, I can tell you this is often the case. But this should not surprise us, since investigating a new and controversial eschatological position always involves a risk. Oftentimes, people become comfortable with one particular millennial position—usually the one they embraced when they first became a Christian—and then they dig in their heels when their view is challenged. This tendency is part of fallen human nature. We do not find it easy to objectively evaluate matters we feel strongly about with open minds and without prejudice.

So whether or not I have convinced you, it is my hope that you examine amillennialism with an open mind in the light of the biblical data we have just considered. I would also ask that you give due consideration to the major problems associated with other millennial positions, a subject we will now briefly consider.

Evil in the Millennium? The Problem with Premillennialism

No doubt, the great strength of premillennialism is its apparently straight-forward reading of Revelation 19 and 20. If John depicted the second advent of Jesus Christ in Revelation 19 and described the millennial reign of Christ that follows in chapter 20, he established a form of premillennialism. On the face of things, this seems like a formidable argument in favor of premillennialism. Therefore, when amillenarians attempt to challenge this point by contending that Revelation 20 is part of a different vision that recapitulates the events depicted in Revelation 19, we run headlong into the premillennial argument that amillenarians spiritualize the Bible. Premillennialists say we do not take John seriously when he spoke of a literal thousand years and a bodily resurrection (the first resurrection) associated with the second coming of Jesus Christ. A literal reading of the text makes far more sense to Christians who are rightly suspicious of those who twist biblical texts to suit their own ends. A complicated argument for reading apocalyptic literature in what appears to be a nonliteral way faces an uphill struggle from the outset. Thus, it is easy for premillenarians to dismiss amillennialism as a viable alternative because it, apparently, does not comport with the plain sense of the critical millennial passage.

However, the premillennialist interpretation creates more serious theological problems than it solves, problems that are often overlooked by premillenarians. Suppose, for the sake of argument, we grant that the premillennial understanding of the millennial age is the biblical one. What are the consequences of this interpretation of Revelation 20:1–10?

If premillennialism is true, this means that Jesus Christ returns to judge the world in Revelation 19 and sets up his millennial reign in Revelation 20. But what happens at the end of Christ's millennial rule over the earth? According to Revelation 20:7–10, Satan is released from the abyss and immediately goes out to the four corners of the earth to deceive the nations (those same nations that have already been judged, according to Revelation 19:15). Satan organizes them for battle against the camp of God's people and the city God loves, i.e., Jerusalem. This revolt ends when fire comes down from heaven and consumes the rebels along with the devil, who deceived them. But the question remains, Who are these people who are deceived by Satan, who then revolt against God, only to be consumed by fire from heaven?

According to premillenarians, one group of people on earth during the millennial age are the redeemed. No one believes it is possible for people who were raised from the dead in the general resurrection and are now glorified to participate in a revolt like the one depicted in Revelation 20. Therefore, those who revolt during the millennium must be individuals who were not raised from the dead or who did not go through the judgment when Christ returned to earth when the millennial age began. On the one hand, dispensationalists believe that these are individuals who come to faith after the rapture and survive the great tribulation and the wrath of the Antichrist. On the other, historic premillenarians believe that these are people living at the time of our Lord's return who are not raised from the dead or judged and who subsequently repopulate the earth during the millennial age.

This conception of the millennial age is highly problematic, despite the apparent literal reading of Revelation 20. According to premillenarians, the millennium is a period in which people who were raised from the dead and now live on the earth in resurrected bodies coexist with people who were not raised from the dead and remain in the flesh. How can this be? Where does Scripture teach such a mixture of resurrected and unresurrected individuals? As we have seen, the New Testament writers all anticipated the final consummation at the time of our Lord's second advent. They did not anticipate a halfway step of an earthly millennium before the final consummation such as that associated with all forms of premillennialism.

Perhaps even more problematic is the dilemma raised by the premillennial insistence that people in natural bodies live on the earth alongside Christ and his resurrected saints. How do people living on the earth at the time of Christ's second coming escape the resurrection and the judgment? The Scriptures are very clear that Christ returns to judge the world, raise the dead, and renew the cosmos. According to Paul, dead believers are raised at Christ's coming. Living believers are caught up to meet the Lord in the air. This includes all believers, whether living or dead (1 Thess. 4:15–17). But those who are not Christ's, we are told, face his wrath and are taken to face final judgment (Matt. 24:37–41). This includes all unbelievers living at the time of our Lord's return.

Therefore, premillenarians must explain the identity of these people in unresurrected bodies living during the millennium. How do they account for people who are not judged or raised from the dead at the time of our Lord's second advent? This is especially problematic since Jesus himself taught that in the age to come his people will all be children of the resurrection (Luke 20:34–38). Furthermore, Paul stated that "flesh and blood cannot inherit the kingdom of God" (1 Cor. 15:50). The temporal has passed away; hence, people in natural bodies cannot repopulate the earth after the second coming.

Premillenarians attempt to deal with the problem of evil and apostasy during the millennial age by contending that the final judgment does not take place until after the thousand years have passed. Passages such as Matthew 25:31–46 explicitly teach that the final judgment occurs when our Lord returns, but premillenarians argue that there is a gap of one thousand years between our Lord's return and the final judgment. They insist that their interpretation is based on a literal interpretation of the Scriptures and a reluctance to spiritualize prophetic portions. So now we must ask our premillennial friends the obvious question: Where is the one-thousand-year gap between Christ's return and the final judgment taught in the Scriptures? It is not there. The gap must be inserted even though doing so violates the plain sense of the passage and the premillennial insistence on a literal interpretation.

Therefore, the apparent strength of premillennialism is actually its biggest weakness. If premillenarians are correct about their reading of Revelation 20, Jesus rules on the earth over people in resurrected and unresurrected bodies during the millennial age. Our Lord's millennial rule ends with a massive satanic deception of the nations and a revolt against Christ and his church after Jesus has reigned on the earth for a thousand years. If true, this millennial apostasy is tantamount to a second fall. Not even resurrected and glorified saints are safe from the future wrath of Satan and the unbelieving nations. Although at first glance premillenarians may appear to have the plain sense of the passage on their side, the consequences of the premillennial interpretation cannot be easily dismissed.

We have already demonstrated in some detail in part 3 that the premillennial reading of Revelation 20 does not make the best sense of the passage. A second reading of the passage is in order, especially given the nature of apocalyptic literature. The scene in Revelation 20 is indeed a recapitulation of Revelation 19 and, as such, constitutes a new vision distinct from that in Revelation 19. The language of Revelation 20 is highly symbolic, depicting not a future state of affairs but the present victory of Christ, who ensures that his people come to life and reign with him in heaven, despite the persecution and martyrdom faced by the faithful on the earth. Elsewhere, the New Testament speaks of a coming apostasy at the end of the age (2 Thess. 2:1–12). The same event was likely depicted by John from a different perspective in Revelation 20:7–10.

The interpretive choice is obvious. Either we see John's depiction of the millennium as a description of the present reign of Christ and the triumph of God's people over those who seek to destroy them (amillennialism), or we must see Revelation 20 as depicting a millennial age after Christ's return in which people coexist in resurrected and unresurrected bodies and which ends in a satanically energized apostasy. This scenario will be interrupted by fire from heaven that consumes the rebellious apostates who have lived under Christ's earthly rule only to fall victim to satanic deception (premillennialism). The presence of evil and the mixing of redeemed and unredeemed individuals on the earth during the millennial age make the premillennial interpretation highly untenable.

Is the Millennium Characterized by a Return to Old Testament Types and Shadows? The Problem with the Dispensational Interpretation of the Millennium

Dispensationalists face not only the problem of evil and apostasy during the millennial age but also additional problems created by their modifications of traditional premillennialism.

The problem with the dispensational interpretation of the millennium has to do with its understanding of the flow of redemptive history. Throughout the Old Testament, Israel's prophets foretold the coming messianic age in terms of their times and places in the unfolding drama of redemptive history, particularly the types and shadows associated with messianic anticipation. But Old Testament types and shadows were subsequently reinterpreted in the New Testament in the greater light of Christ's first coming. What was promised in the Old Testament was fulfilled in Jesus Christ. Because of this, the New Testament writers anticipated the final consummation at our Lord's return. They did not anticipate an earthly rule of Jesus Christ understood in terms of Old Testament types and shadows, which had passed away.

For example, when Israel's prophets spoke of Israel's restoration, the New Testament contended that this promise was fulfilled in Jesus Christ, the true Israel. When Israel's prophets spoke of the land of Canaan, the city of Jerusalem, and the mountain of the Lord, New Testament authors pointed out that these themes were fulfilled in Christ and his church. In many instances, they did so as a polemic against Jews who did not accept Jesus as Israel's Messiah. The literal interpretation of these Old Testament messianic passages was supplied by the New Testament. Therefore, Old Testament prophetic expectation must not be the basis for understanding the eschatology of the New. To understand biblical teaching about the millennium, we must determine how the New Testament applied messianic typology to Jesus Christ and how he fulfilled the Old Testament messianic expectations, thereby guaranteeing his second advent and the final consummation.

What is especially problematic about the dispensationalists' understanding of the millennial age is their belief that there will be a return to the types and shadows of the Old Testament. Since Christ fulfilled these particular prophetic expectations, how can dispensationalists justify their belief that the future millennial age will be characterized by a redemptive economy of types and shadows? This premessianic Old Testament millennial expectation, complete with restored temple worship and the reinstitution of animal sacrifices, can only be justified by a redemptive-historical U-turn. According to dispensationalists, type and shadow are fulfilled in Jesus Christ, who in the millennial age supposedly reinstitutes the same types and shadows that have passed away. This is highly problematic and does great violence to the overall thrust of biblical history. This peculiar feature of dispensationalism explains the rise of progressive dispensationalism, which seeks to avoid this aspect of traditional dispensationalism.

This supposed return to type and shadow during the millennial age is seen in the dispensational interpretation of the Abrahamic and Davidic covenants. When dispensationalists contend that the land promise of the Abrahamic covenant was not fulfilled until Israel was reborn as a nation and returned to her ancient homeland in Palestine in 1948, they run headlong into Paul's assertion that the Abrahamic covenant was fulfilled in Jesus Christ. Even Gentiles who embrace the messianic promise through faith are Abraham's children and members of this covenant (Rom. 4:1–25; Gal. 3:15–29). It was Paul who spiritualized the promise of a land in Palestine, which originally extended from the Nile River in Egypt to the Euphrates River (Gen. 15:18), to now include the whole world (Rom. 4:13).

This same tendency to ignore the way in which the New Testament writers applied Old Testament messianic expectations to Christ can be seen in the dispensational insistence that Christ has not yet fulfilled the Davidic covenant of 2 Samuel 7 since, supposedly, this will not occur until the millennial age, when Jesus rules the earth from David's throne in Jerusalem. But the writers of the New Testament could not be any clearer when they teach that this prophecy was fulfilled at the time of our Lord's resurrection and ascension, when God raised Christ from the dead and exalted him on high by seating him at his right hand in heaven. This event, Peter said, fulfilled God's messianic promise to David that one of his own descendants would sit on his throne (Acts 2:30–35). In fact, because Jesus fulfilled this promise, Peter urged his fellow Jews that first Pentecost Sunday to "repent and be baptized" (v. 38).

Finally, the dispensationalist interpretation of redemptive history hinges on a distinctive reading of the great messianic prophecy in Daniel 9:24–27, which supposedly places the seventieth week of Daniel in the future. As we have seen in part 3, Daniel's prophecy was gloriously fulfilled in Jesus Christ, who in his active and passive obedience put an end to sin, atoned for wickedness, brought in everlasting righteousness, sealed up the vision and prophecy, and anointed the most Holy Place (v. 24). Since the Messiah was cut off in the middle of the seventieth week and made a covenant with his people (vv. 26–27), Christ fulfilled the seventy weeks prophecy at his first advent. Therefore, there is no future seven-year tribulation period, as taught by dispensationalists, nor does the Bible anticipate a peace treaty between the Antichrist and the nation of

Israel. These are both essential features of the dispensationalist's expectation for the future.

Because of these factors, amillenarians believe that the dispensational understanding of redemptive history in general and the millennial age in particular is seriously flawed. The millennial age is not depicted in the Bible as a return to the types and shadows of the Old Testament, complete with temple worship and animal sacrifices, while Jesus rules the earth from David's throne in Jerusalem. Instead, the biblical data demonstrates that the millennium is this present age, in which Jesus Christ rules the earth from heaven and in which his saints, who do not worship the beast or his image, triumph in death when they come to life and reign with Christ for a thousand years. The millennial reign of Christ is a present reality.

Does the New Testament Anticipate a Golden Age for the Church? The Problem with Postmillennialism

Since postmillenarians believe that Jesus Christ returns after the millennial age, they do not face the serious problems associated with premillennialism, namely, the presence of evil during the millennial age and the presence of resurrected and unresurrected individuals coexisting on earth after Christ's second advent. In this regard, postmillennialism and amillennialism have much in common. But some important differences do remain.

The most serious interpretive problem associated with postmillennialism has to do with the nature of the New Testament's expectation for the future. Does the New Testament anticipate a future golden age for Christ's kingdom in which the nations are effectively Christianized, resulting in economic, cultural, and religious advances unsurpassed in human history? Or does the general eschatological expectation of the New Testament center on Christ's direct intervention in a wicked and unbelieving world like in the days of Noah (Matt. 24:37–38)? Postmillenarians anticipate the former, while amillenarians expect the latter.

When the debate is framed as a contrast between postmillennial optimism or amillennial pessimism, postmillennial criticisms often have great rhetorical effectiveness, especially with optimistic Americans. But such criticism fails to take into account that amillenarians are optimistic about the kingdom of God. It is the kingdoms of this world that give amillenarians pause. Defining this debate in terms of *ethos* (optimism versus pessimism) overlooks the complexity of the exegetical issues in view and the nature of New Testament eschatology.

As we have seen, New Testament writers did not anticipate a millennial age to dawn on the earth but instead anticipated an eschatological age to come in which the temporal gives way to the eternal, as sinful flesh gives way to resurrection life. Although the kingdom of God is a present reality through the reign of Christ and the outpouring of the Holy Spirit, the full realization of the blessings of the age to come is not a gradual or progressive process. The full realization of such blessings will be wrought by Jesus Christ at his second advent and not through a gradual eclipse of evil and the cessation of unbelief.

Yes, Satan is restrained throughout this present age through the preaching of the gospel. Yes, Christ's kingdom goes forth in power as men and women are transformed into the image of Christ, becoming salt and light, and therefore influencing the surrounding culture for Christ wherever they are. But there is no biblical evidence that the nations of the earth as a whole will become Christianized. In fact, just the opposite appears to be the case. After all, we read the great lament of our Lord, "When the Son of Man comes, will he find faith on the earth?" (Luke 18:8). Indeed, the Bible teaches that Christ will judge the nations when he returns because of their unbelief and hostility toward his kingdom (Matt. 25:31–32; Rev. 19:15; 20:11–12). It is difficult to attribute this deplorable condition to a brief period of apostasy after Jesus Christ and his saints have ruled over these nations for a thousand years and, according to postmillennial expectations, the nations have become Christianized. Therefore, postmillennial expectations do not fit easily with the New Testament's emphasis on our Lord's return to judge the unbelieving world.

Postmillenarians must face other difficult problems as well. For one thing, if postmillennial expectations are correct, when does the millennial age begin? If the millennium begins with the conversion of Israel and the Christianizing of the nations brought about by the binding of Satan, we can only conclude, since obviously Israel has not been converted and the nations of the earth have not been Christianized, that the millennial age has not yet commenced. Indeed, the nagging question remains, If postmillenarians are correct about their millennial expectations, what does this say about the progress of the kingdom thus far? Must we speak of the history of the church to date as an abject failure, although a golden age presumably lies ahead? Of course not. But this is the direction in which postmillennial expectations push us.

Another issue raised throughout the New Testament is the expectation—indeed the warning—that Christ's church will be a suffering church because heresy and false teaching will rise from within and because Christ's enemies will persecute his people from without. The New Testament is replete with warnings about false gospels (Gal. 1:6–9) and false apostles (2 Cor. 11:13–15). We are warned that perilous times will characterize the last days, when people love money, power, and pleasure (2 Tim. 3:1ff.) more than the Savior. Does the New Testament teach that these things will cease once the millennial age begins? Or does the New Testament teach that Christians will face these things throughout the age until the return of our Lord? Postmillenarians believe the former, while amillenarians believe the latter.

Furthermore, what are we to make of the great theological paradox taught throughout the New Testament that it is in our own suffering and weakness that Christ's grace and power are magnified? In the critical millennial text, Revelation 20, John made this very point. While the dragon makes war on the saints and appears to conquer them (Rev. 13:7), those who refuse to worship him and are put to death because of their testimony for Jesus (Rev. 20:4) "came to life and reigned with Christ for a thousand years." Satan cannot win. When he wages war on the saints and appears to have conquered them, he is actually being defeated. As John told us, those whom the serpent puts to death come to life and reign with Christ.

Therefore, postmillenarians are absolutely correct to be optimistic about the triumph of Christ's kingdom and the influence of Christianity on the cultures of the world. But postmillenarians err when they attempt to locate the triumph of the kingdom in the Christianizing of the nations and the economic, cultural, and religious progress associated with an earthly millennium. Christ's kingdom is not of this world. But one day, John said, the kingdoms of this world will "become the kingdom of our Lord and of his Christ" (Rev. 11:15). That day will come when Jesus Christ returns, but not before.

Did Christ Come Back in AD 70? The Problem with Preterism (Full and Partial)

Paul warned Christ's church about two men, Hymenaeus and Philetus, whose false teaching was spreading among the churches like gangrene. And what was the nature of their heresy? According to Paul, "They say that the resurrection has already taken place" (2 Tim. 2:17–18), and to say that the resurrection has already taken place is to say that the resurrection is spiritual and not bodily. Paul could not be any clearer that the resurrection of believers is like that of Christ—a resurrection of the body (cf. 1 Cor. 6:14; 15:35–49; Phil. 3:20–21). These words eliminate so-called full preterism as a viable eschatological option for Christians. This is because full preterists teach that the resurrection— which, they say, is not bodily but spiritual—has already occurred. To teach, as full preterists do, that Christ has already returned and that the resurrection occurred in AD 70 at the time of the destruction of Jerusalem is heresy, according to the apostle Paul.[1]

Partial preterists, however, do not believe that the second coming and the resurrection occurred in AD 70, although they do believe Jesus came back in judgment on Israel (a parousia) to bring about the end of the Jewish age (this age) and to usher in the age to come. According to many partial preterists, this view resolves the tension found throughout the New Testament between the texts that teach that Jesus and his apostles expected our Lord to return within the lifetimes of the apostles then living and the texts that say he will return at the end of time to judge the world, raise the dead, and make all things new. But to teach that our Lord returned in judgment in AD 70 and will again at the end of time creates serious interpretive problems. The belief that Jesus does not return once but twice—once in judgment on Israel (a local coming) and a second time to raise the dead and judge the nations (a cosmic coming)—not only teaches multiple comings of the Lord but also does not comport with the teaching of Jesus and the apostles regarding this age and the age to come.

The New Testament does indeed present us with a pronounced eschatological tension between things that were already fulfilled in Jesus Christ and things that remain to be fulfilled, such as the resurrection of the body. As we saw in the Olivet Discourse, Jesus taught that his coming is both imminent ("this generation will not pass away") and distant (the parable of the ten virgins). He also taught that specific signs will precede his coming and yet that his coming will occur when we least expect it, apparently, after a delay of an indeterminate period of time. This tension between signs and the suddenness of our Lord's return prevents two potential problems: date-setting and idleness. Christians must be aware of the signs of the times yet not grow weary if our Lord's coming is delayed. Jesus told us we must watch and not fall asleep.

In Paul's writings, we see much the same thing with his stress on the already and the not yet (Rom. 8:23–25)—i.e., those present blessings that are ours in Christ but are not yet the full blessings of the consummation. For example, Paul said that those who are in Christ through faith have already been raised with him and are seated in the heavenlies (Eph. 2:6), even though the redemption of our bodies (the resurrection) has not yet occurred. When it does occur, we will possess glorified bodies of flesh and bone, just as that of Jesus (cf. Luke 24:38–39; Phil. 3:20–21).

Although it is a central feature of New Testament eschatology, the tension between the already and the not yet raises several difficult interpretive questions. Partial preterists attempt to solve this problem by emphasizing that this age ended in AD 70 and that Christ came back in judgment on Israel at that time, bringing in the age to come. The tension between the already and the not yet is removed by stressing the fulfillment of all Christ's eschatological promises within the generation of his disciples. Thus, full preterists leave no place for eschatology, while partial preterists greatly reduce it. In addition, this leaves open the possibility of interpreting those passages that speak of a new heaven and a new earth as applying to the present age (e.g., Isa. 2:2–4). This fits nicely with postmillennial assumptions about a future golden age occurring before our Lord's return. This explains, in part, why many postmillenarians also embrace a partial preterist interpretation of the issues surrounding our Lord's return and the millennial age.

But preterists are not alone in their discomfort with the eschatological tension found throughout the New Testament. Dispensationalists attempt to eliminate the influence of the already and the not yet on eschatology by going in the opposite direction. Futurists emphasize that the fulfillment of Christ's promises to his disciples will occur in the last days immediately before the Lord's return as well as in the millennium that dawns after the second advent. But this overlooks the teaching of Jesus, who said, "This generation will certainly not pass away" (Matt. 24:34), and John, who said, "The time is near" (Rev. 1:3).

The tension between the already and the not yet is an important feature of New Testament eschatology, and we should not attempt to eliminate it. Rather, we should adopt a millennial position that best comports with it. The ability to do this is one of the great strengths of the amillennial understanding of the millennial age, since it not only makes the best sense in light of biblical teaching regarding the two eschatological ages but also keeps the already and the not yet in their proper perspectives.

Partial preterists must face the problem that the New Testament does not teach that Jesus came back locally in judgment on Jerusalem in AD 70. In the Olivet Discourse, Jesus himself spoke of his coming as visible ("As lightning that comes from the east is visible even in the west") and in cosmic terms ("The sun will be darkened, and the moon will not give its light; the stars will fall from the sky, and the heavenly bodies will be shaken" [Matt. 24:27, 29]). Although it is clear that Israel's desolation was completed by the events of AD 70, the Bible does not teach a coming of Christ in judgment that is invisible and localized to Jerusalem. Christ's coming is the day of judgment on the nations when the inhabitants of the earth, great and small, cower in fear (Rev. 6:15–17).

Perhaps the most serious problem associated with all varieties of preterism is the failure to acknowledge that the end of this age and the dawn of the age to come are not mere shifts in redemptive history. There is no doubt that the events of AD 70 did, in part, fulfill our Lord's words to his apostles of imminent judgment on Israel. But the destruction of Jerusalem and its temple did not mark the end of the age; the final consummation will (Matt. 13:40). The events of AD 70 did not mark the dawn of the age to come; the final consummation will (Luke 20:35). The events of AD 70, while vital to the course of redemptive history, did not constitute our Lord's parousia or the judgment. The contrast between this age and the age to come is a contrast between things eternal and things temporal. This contrast presents a major problem for preterist interpreters, who seek to limit this shift to the destruction of Jerusalem. The two ages are not merely two periods in redemptive-historical time but two distinct eschatological epochs, with the age to come not being fully realized until our Lord's second advent.

What about the Spiritualization of Prophecy, the Binding of Satan, and the Nation of Israel? Potential Problems with Amillennialism

Even though I believe amillennialism is the biblical understanding of the millennial age, amillenarians must also face the logical consequences of their interpretations. A number of potential interpretive problems have been raised by proponents of other views in response to amillennialism.

Dispensationalists charge that amillenarians spiritualize the prophetic parts of the Bible, but we have seen that it is the dispensationalists who read the Bible incorrectly (i.e., literalistically). When amillenarians allow the New Testament interpretation of Old Testament millennial expectations to stand, ironically, they end up taking a more literal reading of the critical texts than do dispensationalists. While premillenarians insist that their reading of Revelation 19 and 20 is the plain sense of the passages, we have seen that Revelation 20 actually recapitulates Revelation 19. Furthermore, if the premillennial position is correct, then premillenarians face an even bigger problem, the presence of evil in the millennial age after Christ has returned for the resurrection and the judgment.

Another common objection raised against the amillennial position is that amillenarians teach that Satan is presently bound, even though the New Testament also teaches that Satan is the "god of this age" who blinds the "minds of unbelievers" (2 Cor. 4:4) and "prowls around like a roaring lion looking for someone to devour" (1 Pet. 5:8). Given the great evil found throughout the world, how can amillenarians teach that Satan is presently bound and expect anybody to take them seriously?

The apostle John told us in Revelation 20 what this binding of Satan actually entails. Confined to the abyss, the devil is no longer free to deceive the nations until he is released before the end (20:3). This does not mean that the binding of Satan prevents all forms of satanic activity in this age. In fact, John also told us that it is precisely because Satan has been cast down (bound to the abyss) that he is filled with fury because he knows his time is short. Jesus Christ crushed the serpent's head. The Savior made a "public spectacle" of him on Calvary (Col. 2:15). Defeated and humiliated, the devil is enraged and is now behaving like a wounded animal trying to avoid capture. But Satan's continuing attempts to organize the nations against Christ and his kingdom are restrained until he is released from the abyss. Only then can he organize the nations in revolt against Christ, bringing about the apostasy predicted by John and Paul.

Another interpretive consequence amillenarians must face is the fact that the nation of Israel presently exists in Palestine. Although there is no necessary connection between the birth of the modern nation-state of Israel and the truth or falsity of amillennialism—indeed, some amillenarians see a future role for the nation of Israel while some do not—some see the birth of Israel as a powerful argument against the amillennial interpretation. Part of the reason this is an issue is because two leading proponents of the Dutch school of amillennialism from a previous generation, Louis Berkhof and Herman Bavinck, both argued that one of the sure signs that dispensationalism was false was the dispensationalists' assertion that Israel would become a nation again.[2] When Berkhof completed his venerable *Systematic Theology* in 1939, the restoration of Israel looked like an impossibility. Berkhof could not have foreseen the events of World War II, the Holocaust, and the formation of the state of Israel in 1948 and surely overstated his case. According to dispensationalists, the return of Jews to their ancient homeland confirms the dispensational reading of biblical prophecy as well as refutes the amillennial view that the Abrahamic covenant was fulfilled in Christ.

In our exposition of Romans 11 (part 3), we pointed out that some amillenarians believe there is no future role for Israel in biblical prophecy. They feel that "all Israel" in Romans 11:26 refers to the full number of the elect or to the sum of the believing remnant throughout the age. Others believe there will be a mass conversion of ethnic Jews in the days before our Lord's return once the fullness of the Gentiles has come in. In either case, amillenarians believe that the formation of the nation of Israel in 1948 is not related to the fulfillment of the Abrahamic covenant but to God's mysterious providential purposes for world history. Neither do amillenarians believe that Paul said anything about a millennial age in Romans 11, the only passage in the New Testament in which Paul specifically addressed the subject as to whether the nation of Israel will play a role in the future of redemptive history.

But even if the land promise of the Abrahamic covenant has already been fulfilled, it is quite remarkable that the Jews have returned en masse to their ancient homeland. This is a fact that cannot be easily dismissed by amillenarians. Israel is a nation again. The Jews as a people are largely gathered together in one place. Amillenarians need to offer a cogent explanation for this amazing historical development, although we must be careful not to allow current events to determine our interpretation of a given biblical text. The answer to this problem was supplied for us by Paul in Romans 11.

In Romans 11, the apostle Paul did not teach that the birth of the modern nation of Israel is related to the fulfillment of the Abrahamic covenant or to an earthly millennial age. Instead, the birth of the nation of Israel must be seen in relationship to Paul's expectation regarding the conversion of the vast majority of ethnic Jews living in the last days to faith in Jesus Christ immediately before his return to earth. Israel's reconciliation to God, Paul said, is nothing less than a veritable resurrection from the dead (Rom. 11:15). Israel stumbled, Paul said, but did not fall beyond recovery (11:11). Indeed, if God can justify sinful Gentiles through faith in Jesus Christ, he can do the same with those Jews who embrace the Messiah through faith alone (11:17–24). This means that the rebirth of the nation of Israel is almost certainly connected to the desire and anguish that filled Paul's heart, namely, the salvation of his people, the Jews. With this in mind, there can be little doubt that any future mass conversion of Israel (ethnic Jews) would be greatly facilitated by the rebirth of the nation of Israel and the relocation of significant numbers of Jews to a single country. Although this is not connected to the fulfillment of the Abrahamic covenant, it certainly falls within the mysterious providence of God, the full meaning of which cannot be understood until redemptive history unfolds beyond its present stages of development.

Final Thoughts

Since I was born and bred a dispensationalist, my own conversion to amillennialism was a slow and difficult process. I know from firsthand experience that wrestling with these issues is not easy. But after weighing the evidence for amillennialism, I found the case to be compelling, if not overwhelming. Not only does amillennialism make the best sense of the eschatological expectations of the New Testament writers, but it also eliminates some things that always troubled me about dispensationalism and premillennialism. Why was the millennium characterized by a return to types and shadows? If Jesus is the true temple, why would the temple be rebuilt during the millennium? Why would animals be sacrificed during the millennial age when Christ's death on the cross did away with them? How can there be people on earth in unresurrected bodies after Christ comes back and raises the dead? Why are those who claim to take prophetic passages literally forced to insert gaps in Daniel's prophecy of the seventy weeks and in Jesus's teaching about judgment occurring at his second coming? These things bothered me for some time, and the more questions I asked of my pastors and teachers, the more troubling the answers became.

It came as a great surprise during my seminary days when I discovered that amillenarians do take prophetic passages quite literally and that the dispensational hermeneutic drove me to literalistic interpretations of passages that were otherwise interpreted in the New Testament. For a time, I considered postmillennialism because of its objection that amillenarians teach that the millennial age is a period of defeat for the church, which leads Christians to neglect the cultural mandate. I eventually became convinced that postmillenarians could not sustain the heart of their position, which is that the New Testament anticipates a golden age ahead for the church in which the nations of the earth will be Christianized. The failure of some amillenarians to take their responsibility for the cultural mandate seriously is not a biblical argument against amillennialism. It is an embarrassing reminder that we are all sinners and many of us fail to live up to our own theological expectations. The history of western civilization has shown that Christian influence on the surrounding culture is pronounced at times and in full eclipse during others. But this is what we find throughout the New Testament, especially in light of the tension between the already and the not yet. As the kingdom of God advances, it provokes two distinct reactions. The first is a distinct Christian influence on the surrounding culture, while the other is a pronounced satanic counterreaction, producing the persecution of God's people and great opposition to the preaching of the gospel.

The New Testament, however, teaches that immediately before the end, God will cease to restrain Satan, and things will go from bad to worse. It is in the tumult of these days that Jesus Christ will return to raise the dead, judge the world, and make all things new. This is not only the heart of the Bible's teaching about the future but also the heart of amillennial prophetic expectation.

Although the differences among Christians about the nature of the millennial age are not "salvation" issues, they do affect how we understand large sections of the Bible and our expectations for the future. So despite the sentiments of "panmillenarians," who avoid taking a millennial position because they are sure things will simply "pan out" in the end, this is an important debate and worthy of our consideration in the light of Scripture.

Despite our many differences and the sometimes contentious and heated nature of this debate, we should not lose sight of this most important point:

All premillennial, postmillennial, and amillennial Christians long for the day when our Lord Jesus Christ returns for his people and puts an end to sin and suffering. This is the blessed hope, and in that day we shall be like him. There will be no more curse, and all things will be made new. Therefore, it is fitting that we end this study with Paul's prayer in 1 Corinthians 16:22: "Maranatha! Come, O Lord!"

Notes

Preface to the Expanded Edition

1. http://kimriddlebarger.squarespace.com/a-reply-to-john-macarthur/. A revised version of MacArthur's lecture can be found here: John MacArthur, "Does Calvinism Lead to Futuristic Premillennialism?" in John MacArthur and Richard Mayhue, *Christ's Prophetic Plans: A Futuristic Premillennial Primer* (Chicago: Moody, 2012), 141–59. The reader may also wish to consult the response to MacArthur written by Samuel E. Waldron, *MacArthur's Millennial Manifesto: A Friendly Response* (Owensboro, KY: Reformed Baptist Academic Press, 2008).

2. MacArthur, "Does Calvinism Lead to Futuristic Premillennialism?" 153–55.

3. It is only by ignoring this well-known fact of historical theology that Barry Horner can make the following accusation: "[Riddlebarger's] claims [i.e., that amillennialism is by and large the historical eschatological position of both Catholic and Protestant Christianity] call for a response that clearly exposes the shameful legacy of historic amillennialism which really is the eschatology of Roman Catholicism." See Barry E. Horner, *Future Israel: Why Christian Anti-Judaism Must Be Challenged* (Nashville: B & H Academic, n.d.), 148.

4. For a contemporary statement of covenant theology and a comprehensive discussion of the biblical basis for these assertions, see Michael S. Horton, *God of Promise* (Grand Rapids: Baker, 2006).

Introduction

1. See, for example, Anthony Hoekema, *The Bible and the Future* (Grand Rapids: Eerdmans, 1982); and Cornelis P. Venema, *The Promise of the Future* (Carlisle, PA: Banner of Truth, 2000).

2. These include Robert G. Clouse, ed., *The Meaning of the Millennium: Four Views* (Downers Grove, IL: InterVarsity, 1977); and Darrell L. Bock, ed., *Three Views on the Millennium and Beyond* (Grand Rapids: Zondervan, 1999).

Chapter 1: Defining Our Terms

1. Anthony Hoekema, *The Bible and the Future* (Grand Rapids: Eerdmans, 1982), 1.

2. Ibid.

3. Geerhardus Vos, *Biblical Theology* (Grand Rapids: Eerdmans, 1977), 80.

4. Hoekema, *Bible and the Future*, 173.

5. Richard A. Muller, *Dictionary of Latin and Greek Theological Terms* (Grand Rapids: Baker, 1985), 66–67.

6. According to Heinrich Schmid, "The following are mentioned as chiliasts: The Jews, Cerinthus, Papias, Joachim (Abbot of Floris), the Fanatics and Anabaptists, [and] Casp. Schwenkfeld. . . . A distinction is also made between gross and subtle chiliasm. The former estimates the millennium as happy, because of the illicit pleasure of the flesh; the latter, because of the lawful and honorable delights of both body and soul. . . . But both are rejected." See Heinrich Schmid, *Doctrinal Theology of the Evangelical Lutheran Church* (Minneapolis: Augsburg, 1961), 650.

7. Hoekema, *Bible and the Future*, 164n3.

8. Cf. Kenneth L. Gentry, *Before Jerusalem Fell: Dating the Book of Revelation* (Atlanta: American Vision, 1998); and Gentry, *The Beast of Revelation* (Tyler, TX: Institute for Christian Economics, 1994).

9. J. Stuart Russell, *The Parousia: The New Testament Doctrine of Our Lord's Second Coming* (Grand Rapids: Baker, 1999), 538–54.

10. See, for example, Kenneth L. Gentry, "A Postmillennial Response to Craig A. Blaising," in *Three Views on the Millennium and Beyond*, ed. Darrell L. Bock (Grand Rapids: Zondervan, 1999), 237; and R. C. Sproul, *The Last Days according to Jesus* (Grand Rapids: Baker, 1998), 24–26.

11. William E. Cox, *Biblical Studies in Final Things* (Phillipsburg, NJ: Presbyterian & Reformed, 1966), 1.

12. George E. Ladd, *A Commentary on the Revelation of John* (Grand Rapids: Eerdmans, 1987), 12. This is also the position taken by "progressive dispensationalists." See Robert Saucy, *The Case for Progressive Dispensationalism* (Grand Rapids: Zondervan, 1993).

13. Ladd, *Commentary on the Revelation of John*, 11.

14. G. K. Beale, *The Book of Revelation*, The New International Greek Testament Commentary (Grand Rapids: Eerdmans, 1999), 3–49; and Richard Bauckham, *The Climax of Prophecy: Studies in the Book of Revelation* (Edinburgh: T & T Clark, 1993), 1–117.

Chapter 2: A Survey of Eschatological Views

1. See John F. Walvoord, *The Millennial Kingdom* (Grand Rapids: Zondervan, 1959); and J. Dwight Pentecost, *Things to Come* (Grand Rapids: Zondervan, 1978).

2. See, for example, Charles Ryrie, *Dispensationalism Today* (Chicago: Moody, 1965), 48–64.

3. John F. Walvoord, *The Rapture Question* (Grand Rapids: Zondervan, 1979), 270.

4. See, for example, John F. Walvoord, "The New Testament Doctrine of the Kingdom," in *Vital Prophetic Issues*, ed. Roy B. Zuck (Grand Rapids: Kregel, 1995), 128–46.

5. Pentecost, *Things to Come*, 512–31.

6. Note the debate among dispensationalists about whether this is a heavenly or an earthly state. See Craig A. Blaising, "Premillennialism," in *Three Views on the Millennium and Beyond*, ed. Darrell L. Bock (Grand Rapids: Zondervan, 1999), 182–86.

7. The success of Hal Lindsey's book is truly phenomenal. *The Late Great Planet Earth*, as of 2003, has sold more than ten million copies and has gone through 140 printings. In fact, it was the bestselling book in the United States in the 1970s.

8. Jonathan Bing, "Christian Book Series a Revelation for Bantam," accessed February 12, 2002, www.variety.com.

9. See Timothy P. Weber, *Living in the Shadow of the Second Coming* (Grand Rapids: Zondervan, 1983).

10. See, for example, Robert Saucy, *The Case for Progressive Dispensationalism* (Grand Rapids: Zondervan, 1993). See also Craig A. Blaising and Darrell L. Bock, *Progressive Dispensationalism* (Wheaton: Victor, 1993); and Blaising and Bock, eds., *Dispensationalism, Israel, and the Church: The Search for Definition* (Grand Rapids: Zondervan, 1992).

11. Blaising, "Premillennialism," 182ff.

12. R. L. Thomas, "Progressive Dispensationalism," in *Dictionary of Premillennial Theology*, ed. Mal Couch (Grand Rapids: Kregel, 1996), 98–99.

13. See, for example, Charles Ryrie's criticism of progressive dispensationalists in the foreword of Wesley R. Willis and John R. Master, eds., *Issues in Dispensationalism* (Chicago: Moody, 1994), 21–23.

14. Robert B. Strimple, "An Amillennial Response," in *Three Views on the Millennium and Beyond*, ed. Darrell L. Bock (Grand Rapids: Zondervan, 1999), 256–57.

15. Also but oftentimes inaccurately known as "posttribulational premillennialism." Some hold to a dispensational hermeneutic and are posttribulational. But generally speaking, historic premillenarians reject the dispensational hermeneutic.

16. Representative treatments of historic premillennialism include George E. Ladd, *The Blessed Hope* (Grand Rapids: Eerdmans, 1956); Ladd, *Crucial Questions about the Kingdom of God* (Grand Rapids: Eerdmans, 1952); and J. Barton Payne, *The Encyclopedia of Biblical Prophecy* (Grand Rapids: Baker, 1980).

17. For the relevant citations, see R. Ludwigson, *A Survey of Bible Prophecy* (Grand Rapids: Zondervan, 1979), 127ff. The work of Charles E. Hill casts the millennial expectation of the church fathers in a new light. Hill argues that early chiliasm and orthodox nonchiliasm coexisted in the apostolic church. See Charles E. Hill, *Regnum Caelorum* (Oxford: Clarendon, 1992).

18. See John W. Montgomery's article on the millennium in *International Standard Bible Encyclopedia*, ed. G. W. Bromiley (Grand Rapids: Eerdmans, 1986), s.v. "Millennium, The."

19. John Jefferson Davis, *The Victory of Christ's Kingdom* (Moscow, ID: Canon, 1996), 10–11.

20. J. Marcellus Kik, *The Eschatology of Victory* (Phillipsburg, NJ: Presbyterian & Reformed, 1971), 4.

21. Ibid., 205.

22. Kim Riddlebarger, "Princeton and the Millennium: A Study in American Post-millennialism," the Alliance of Confessing Evangelicals, accessed August 7, 2002, www.alliancenet.org.

23. Kenneth L. Gentry marshals a list of figures from church history who were supposedly postmillennial. See Gentry, "Postmillennialism," in *Three Views on the Millennium and Beyond*, ed. Darrell L. Bock (Grand Rapids: Zondervan, 1999), 14–19. Surely we would be wise to heed the warning offered by Richard Muller: When we ask historical figures to answer modern debates, such as the millennial question, which they never were directly asked nor answered, we inevitably "accommodate" these men to meet the needs of our own age and situation. See Richard A. Muller, *The Unaccommodated Calvin* (New York: Oxford University Press, 2000), 14.

24. Riddlebarger, "Princeton and the Millennium."

25. Kik, *Eschatology of Victory*, 3–14; and Greg Bahnsen, "The Prima Facie Acceptability of Postmillennialism," *Journal of Christian Reconstructionism* 3, no. 2 (1976–77): 66–67.

26. Anthony Hoekema, *The Bible and the Future* (Grand Rapids: Eerdmans, 1982), 175ff.

27. See J. Stuart Russell, *The Parousia: The New Testament Doctrine of Our Lord's Second Coming* (Grand Rapids: Baker, 1999), 139–40; and Charles Hodge, *Systematic Theology*, vol. 3 (Grand Rapids: Eerdmans, 1979), 800ff.

28. See the helpful study by George M. Marsden, *Fundamentalism and American Culture* (New York: Oxford University Press, 1980). See also Weber, *Living in the Shadow*.

29. Richard Gaffin argues that Warfield said nothing that was incompatible with classical amillennialism, simply that there was no nomenclature yet for amillennialism, as the term did not come into use until the 1940s. See Richard B. Gaffin, "Theonomy and Eschatology," in *Theonomy: A Reformed Critique*, ed. William S. Barker and W. Robert Godfrey (Grand Rapids: Zondervan, 1990), 198–99. Charles and A. A. Hodge slightly moderated the postmillennialism they inherited from Jonathan Edwards. B. B. Warfield wore the postmillennial label, but he adopted amillennial exegesis of most of the key texts and effectively cut the exegetical underpinnings out from under the postmillennialism he espoused. Warfield left few postmillennial adherents behind at Princeton, most being won to amillennialism by his friend and comrade Geerhardus Vos, a leading defender of amillennialism. See my essay "Princeton and the Millennium."

30. See, for example, Greg Bahnsen, *Theonomy in Christian Ethics* (Phillipsburg, NJ: Presbyterian & Reformed, 1977); and Rousas John Rushdoony, *The Institutes of Biblical Law* (Phillipsburg, NJ: Presbyterian & Reformed, 1984).

31. See full citation in note 19.

32. One of amillennialism's staunchest critics states that "its most general character is that of a denial of a literal reign of Christ upon the earth." This demonstrates how dispensationalists and amillenarians differ over Christ's fulfillment of Old Testament prophecies regarding David's greater son. See Walvoord, *Millennial Kingdom*, 6.

33. Walvoord, *Millennial Kingdom*, 59ff.

34. Ibid., 61.

35. See Hal Lindsey, *The Rapture* (New York: Bantam, 1983), 30.

Chapter 3: How Do We Interpret Bible Prophecy?

1. Charles Ryrie, *Dispensationalism Today* (Chicago: Moody, 1965), 86–89.

2. Ibid., 46.

3. John F. Walvoord, *The Millennial Kingdom* (Grand Rapids: Zondervan, 1959), 128–33.

4. Ryrie, *Dispensationalism Today*, 91. See also Thomas D. Ice, "Dispensational Hermeneutics," in *Issues in Dispensationalism*, ed. Wesley R. Willis and John R. Master (Chicago: Moody, 1994), 45–46.

5. Walvoord, *Millennial Kingdom*, 59–60.

6. Hal Lindsey, *The Rapture* (New York: Bantam, 1983), 30.

7. Ryrie, *Dispensationalism Today*, 4.

8. Ibid., 96–97.

9. Robert B. Strimple, "Amillennialism," in *Three Views on the Millennium and Beyond*, ed. Darrell L. Bock (Grand Rapids: Zondervan, 1999), 84–100.

10. Richard B. Gaffin, "Theonomy and Eschatology," in *Theonomy: A Reformed Critique*, ed. William S. Barker and W. Robert Godfrey (Grand Rapids: Zondervan, 1990), 216–17.

11. Strimple, "Amillennialism," 84–100.

12. Richard A. Muller, *Dictionary of Latin and Greek Theological Terms* (Grand Rapids: Baker, 1985), 33.

13. Floyd Hamilton, "The Basis of Millennial Faith," in *Amillennialism Today*, ed. William E. Cox (Phillipsburg, NJ: Presbyterian & Reformed, 1966), 24–25, 53–54.

14. The title of John Walvoord's commentary on Daniel bears this out. See Walvoord, *Daniel: The Key to Prophetic Revelation* (Chicago: Moody, 1977).

15. F. F. Bruce, *Commentary on the Book of Acts*, New International Commentary on the New Testament (Grand Rapids: Eerdmans, 1981), 310.

16. C. I. Scofield, ed., *The Scofield Reference Bible* (New York: Oxford University Press, 1909). In the *New Scofield Reference Bible* of 1967, the note is changed to read, "This important passage shows God's program for this age. . . . James declares that Amos 9:12 shows that, at the return of Christ, there will not only be believing Jews . . . but believing Gentiles." Cf. E. Schuyler English, ed., *The New Scofield Reference Bible* (New York: Oxford University Press, 1967). I ask the reader, Is this what James is saying?

Chapter 4: The Covenantal Context of Old Testament Eschatology

1. Geerhardus Vos, *Biblical Theology* (Grand Rapids: Eerdmans, 1977), 5–8.

2. Jürgen Moltmann, *The Theology of Hope* (San Francisco: Harper & Row, 1980), 16.

3. See, for example, John Murray, *Redemption, Accomplished and Applied* (Grand Rapids: Eerdmans, 1980).

4. William J. Dumbrell, *The Search for Order: Biblical Eschatology in Focus* (Grand Rapids: Baker, 1994), 9.

5. Meredith G. Kline, *By Oath Consigned* (Grand Rapids: Eerdmans, 1967), 16.

6. Ibid.

7. Dispensationalists do not see this promise as fulfilled when Israel entered Canaan after her exile in the wilderness. This is fulfilled, they say, only when the nation of Israel regains the land before the tribulation. According to John Walvoord, the amillenarian position regarding this promise of a land is indicative of the fact that the "amillenarian position is often distinguished for its blindness to facts which would upset its own argument." See John F. Walvoord, *The Millennial Kingdom* (Grand Rapids: Zondervan, 1959), 178.

8. Kline, *By Oath Consigned*, 14–22.

9. For classic statements of the Reformed conception of the covenants, see Francis Turretin, *Institutes of Elenctic Theology*, vol. 2, trans. George Musgrave Giger, ed. James T. Dennison (Phillipsburg, NJ: Presbyterian & Reformed, 1994), 169–269; Herman Witsius, *The Economy of the Covenants between God and Man* (Escondido, CA: den Dulk Foundation, 1990); and Louis Berkhof, *Systematic Theology* (Grand Rapids: Eerdmans, 1986).

10. Meredith G. Kline, *Kingdom Prologue* (Overland, KS: Two Age, 2000), 15–22.

11. John Walvoord argues that "covenant theology is definitely the product of theological theory rather than biblical exposition. . . . The specific formulas of the covenants are inductions from Calvinist theology which go beyond the Scriptures," citing Charles Hodge's comment that the covenant of works is a deduction from Scripture. See Walvoord, *Millennial Kingdom*, 88. It is noteworthy that, given Walvoord's criticism that the Reformed notion of a covenant of works has no biblical support, the Scripture index in *Millennial Kingdom* makes no reference to Hosea 6:7 and Romans 5:12–19, key passages underlying the Reformed understanding of the covenant of works.

12. B. B. Warfield, "Hosea VI.7: Adam or Man?" in *Selected Shorter Writings of Benjamin B. Warfield*, ed. John E. Meeter, vol. 1 (Phillipsburg, NJ: Presbyterian & Reformed, 1970), 116–29.

13. Meredith G. Kline, "Gospel until the Law: Rom. 5:13–14 and the Old Covenant," *Journal of the Evangelical Theological Society* 34, no. 4 (December 1991): 433ff.

14. Herman Bavinck, "Herman Bavinck on the Covenant of Works," in *Creator, Redeemer, Consummator: A Festschrift for Meredith G. Kline*, ed. Howard Griffith and John R. Muether, trans. Richard B. Gaffin (Greenville, SC: Reformed Academic Press, 2000), 169–85.

15. For a history of the Reformed understanding of the relationship of the Mosaic covenant to the covenant of works and the covenant of grace, see Mark W. Karlberg, "Reformed Interpretation of the Mosaic Covenant," *Westminster Theological Journal* 43 (1980): 1–57.

Chapter 5: These Things Were Foretold

1. Anthony Hoekema, *The Bible and the Future* (Grand Rapids: Eerdmans, 1982), 5.

2. Scholars in the Reformed tradition insist on the progressive unfolding of redemptive history as progressive stages of the covenant of grace. Dispensationalists see each period of redemptive history as a separate epoch, each with distinctive and different "economies." See Charles Ryrie, *Dispensationalism Today* (Chicago: Moody, 1965), 31. The Reformed objection is that dispensationalism disrupts the unity of the covenant of grace. Progressive dispensationalism attempts to mitigate the emphasis on discontinuity between the testaments. See John S. Feinberg, ed., *Continuity and Discontinuity* (Westchester, IL: Crossway, 1988); and Craig A. Blaising and Darrell L. Bock, eds., *Dispensationalism, Israel, and the Church: The Search for Definition* (Grand Rapids: Zondervan, 1992).

3. See Herman Ridderbos, *Paul: An Outline of His Theology* (Grand Rapids: Eerdmans, 1975), 53. Ridderbos's point that we should not treat Paul as a theologian of aeons is well taken, though the danger in this is mitigated by keeping Christ's person and work at the center of Paul's eschatological thought, as Ridderbos counsels.

4. Meredith G. Kline, *Kingdom Prologue* (Overland, KS: Two Age, 2000), 1.

5. Hoekema, *Bible and the Future*, 5.

6. Meredith G. Kline, *The Structure of Biblical Authority* (Grand Rapids: Eerdmans, 1981), 181–95.

7. Willem A. Vangemeren, *Interpreting the Prophetic Word* (Grand Rapids: Zondervan, 1990), 309.

8. Hoekema, *Bible and the Future*, 7.

9. J. Dwight Pentecost, *Things to Come* (Grand Rapids: Zondervan, 1978), 117ff.

10. William L. Lane, *Hebrews 9–13*, Word Biblical Commentary (Dallas: Word, 1991), 271.

11. George Eldon Ladd, *The Presence of the Future* (Grand Rapids: Eerdmans: 1981), 72.

12. Notice that terms used in the Old Testament exclusively of Israel (e.g., "chosen people," "royal priesthood," "holy nation") are applied directly to the people of God in the New Testament, that is, the church.

13. Here we are told that there is no longer any distinction between Jew and Greek, etc., and, more importantly for our discussion, if you are in Christ, then you are Abraham's seed and an heir according to the promise. There is no hint here of the Gentiles serving as the plan B people of God, typical of classical dispensationalism.

14. Here the image is one of "spiritual fulfillment," whereby the heavenly promise of a new Mount Zion is equated directly with the church.

Chapter 6: According to the Prophets

1. Geerhardus Vos calls this "one of the most difficult things in the interpretation of prophecy in the Old Testament and New Testament alike." See Geerhardus Vos, *Biblical Theology* (Grand Rapids: Eerdmans, 1977), 290.

2. Classical dispensationalists, such as J. Dwight Pentecost and John Walvoord, assign the fulfillment of this prophecy to the future millennium, apparently ignoring Peter's declaration in Acts 2:28ff. that this was being fulfilled on the day of Pentecost. See J. Dwight Pentecost, *Things to Come* (Grand Rapids: Zondervan, 1978), 486.

3. Anthony Hoekema, *The Bible and the Future* (Grand Rapids: Eerdmans, 1982), 9.

4. Herman Ridderbos counsels us to see that such prophecies are "something different than a diary of future events. . . . The function of prophecy is consequently not that of a detailed projection of the future, but is the urgent insistence on the certainty of the things to come. This explains why, at the end of the vista, the perspective is lacking. The prophet sees all kinds of events that will come, and he sees in all of them the coming of God. But he cannot fix a date for the events, he cannot distinguish all phases in God's coming. To him it is one great reality." See Herman Ridderbos, *The Coming of the Kingdom* (Phillipsburg, NJ: Presbyterian & Reformed, 1962), 524–25.

5. Hoekema, *Bible and the Future*, 9.

6. Ibid., 10–11.

7. Ibid., 11.

8. Ladd, *Presence of the Future*, 59–60.

9. Hoekema, *Bible and the Future*, 13.

10. Ibid.

11. These criteria are set out in ibid., 15–22.

12. See, for example, Donald A. Hagner, *Matthew 1–13*, vol. 33A, Word Biblical Commentary (Dallas: Word, 1993), liii–lxxiii; and R. T. France, *Matthew*, Tyndale New Testament Commentaries (Grand Rapids: Eerdmans, 1985), 38–56.

13. Hoekema, *Bible and the Future*, 13.

14. See Oscar Cullman, *Salvation in History*, trans. S. G. Sowers (New York: Harper & Row, 1967), 172; Geerhardus Vos, *The Pauline Eschatology* (Grand Rapids: Baker, 1979), 1–41; Ladd, *Presence of the Future*, 307–328; and Greg K. Beale, "The Eschatological Conception of New Testament Theology," in *Eschatology in Bible and Theology*, ed. Kent E. Brower and Mark W. Elliot (Downers Grove, IL: InterVarsity, 1997), 11–52.

15. Hoekema, *Bible and the Future*, 15; and Cornelis P. Venema, *The Promise of the Future* (Carlisle, PA: Banner of Truth, 2000), 25.

16. Hoekema, *Bible and the Future*, 15.

17. Ibid., 16. It is difficult for dispensationalists to explain the words of Jesus and John the Baptist on this point. Pentecost insists that the kingdom was offered to the Jews and was rejected by them, so the offer was withdrawn. The coming of the kingdom is postponed until the millennium. But the biblical writers tell us that the kingdom is "at hand" in the person of our Lord Jesus Christ. There is no hint of an "offer" of a kingdom anywhere in the New Testament. Nor is there any indication in the Gospels that the kingdom is to be postponed. The consummation of the present kingdom is future. Jesus is said to have brought the kingdom with him. Regarding this point, Pentecost says, "The offer of the kingdom was a contingent offer . . . to Israel. . . . Because of their [the Jews'] announced rejection of Him, . . . the withdrawal of the kingdom is recorded." See Pentecost, *Things to Come*, 453, 463. Yes, Israel rejected her king, but how does this support the idea of a postponed kingdom?

18. Ridderbos, *Coming of the Kingdom*, 3–8.

19. Beale, "Eschatological Conception," 13.

20. Ibid., 14.

21. Ibid.

22. Ibid., 15.

23. Hoekema, *Bible and the Future*, 16.

24. It is difficult to square this concept with the dispensational understanding of an "offer" of a kingdom to Israel contingent upon Israel's obedience. Paul set this out very clearly: "When the time had fully come, God sent his Son, born of a woman, born under law, to redeem those under law, that we might receive the full rights of sons. Because you are sons, God sent the Spirit of his Son into our hearts. . . . Since you are a son, God has made you also an heir" (Gal. 4:4–7). This text follows Paul's declaration that there is no longer Jew nor Greek in the church (Gal. 3:28). If the kingdom is offered and then rejected with the blessings of the promise now temporarily going to the Gentiles, the whole unity of the covenant promise as portrayed here makes little sense. The divine plan was from the beginning for the "children of Abraham" to be heirs, those who would receive the promise by faith.

25. Ronald K. Fung, *The Epistle to the Galatians*, The New International Commentary on the New Testament (Grand Rapids: Eerdmans, 1988), 183–84.

26. Herman Ridderbos, *Paul: An Outline of His Theology* (Grand Rapids: Eerdmans, 1975), 44–45; and James D. G. Dunn, *The Theology of Paul the Apostle* (Grand Rapids: Eerdmans, 1998), 143–44.

27. Ridderbos, *Paul*, 52; and Vos, *Pauline Eschatology*, 26.

28. Hoekema, *Bible and the Future*, 19.

29. F. F. Bruce, *The Epistle to the Hebrews*, The New International Commentary on the New Testament, rev. ed. (Grand Rapids: Eerdmans, 1990), 231.

30. Hoekema, *Bible and the Future*, 18.

31. See Vos, *Pauline Eschatology*, 38.

32. Hoekema, *Bible and the Future*, 18.

33. For the connection between "kingdom of God" and "age to come," see Vos, *Pauline Eschatology*, 36–41.

34. Richard B. Gaffin, *Resurrection and Redemption: A Study in Paul's Soteriology* (Phillipsburg, NJ: Presbyterian & Reformed, 1987), 60.

Chapter 7: Christ and the Fulfillment of Prophecy

1. I am indebted to Robert B. Strimple for much of this material. See Robert B. Strimple, "Amillennialism," in *Three Views on the Millennium and Beyond*, ed. Darrell L. Bock (Grand Rapids: Zondervan, 1999), 84–100.

2. See John F. Walvoord, *The Millennial Kingdom* (Grand Rapids: Zondervan, 1959), 302–4; and J. Dwight Pentecost, *Things to Come* (Grand Rapids: Zondervan, 1978), 503–8.

3. As Strimple reminds us, a word of clarification is in order. "We [amillenarians] say: 'Yes, the nation of Israel was the people of God in the old covenant. Now in the new covenant the believing church is the people of God.' And thus we quickly run past (or we miss the blessed point entirely) the fact that we Christians are the Israel of God, Abraham's seed, and the heirs to the promises, only because by faith, we are united to him who alone is the true Israel, Abraham's one seed." See Strimple, "Amillennialism," 89.

4. Pentecost, *Things to Come*, 84ff.

5. J. Alec Motyer, *The Prophecy of Isaiah* (Downers Grove, IL: InterVarsity, 1993), 522ff.

6. Strimple, "Amillennialism," 90.

7. Ibid., 90–91.

8. Walvoord, *Millennial Kingdom*, 321–22.

9. William L. Lane, *Hebrews 9–13*, Word Biblical Commentary (Dallas: Word, 1991), 459ff.

10. John Jefferson Davis, *The Victory of Christ's Kingdom* (Moscow, ID: Canon, 1996), 34.

11. Robert B. Strimple, "An Amillennial Response," in *Three Views on the Millennium and Beyond*, ed. Darrell L. Bock (Grand Rapids: Zondervan, 1999), 61.

12. Strimple, "Amillennialism," 92.

13. G. K. Beale, *The Book of Revelation*, The New International Greek Testament Commentary (Grand Rapids: Eerdmans, 1999), 1044–45.

14. See Walvoord, *Millennial Kingdom*, 194ff. Walvoord indicates that the interpretation of kingdom promises made to David in the Old Testament is a defining point between dispensationalists and amillenarians. Says Walvoord, "Accepting as literal those prophecies which do not affect the premillennial argument and spiritualizing all others, [amillenarians] are able with a straight face to declare that the Old Testament does not teach a millennial kingdom on earth."

15. Ibid., 200.

16. Pentecost, *Things to Come*, 531.

17. Oswald T. Allis, *Prophecy and the Church* (Phillipsburg, NJ: Presbyterian & Reformed, 1945), 245ff.

18. Meredith G. Kline, *The Structure of Biblical Authority* (Grand Rapids: Eerdmans, 1981), 194.

19. Leon Morris, *The Gospel according to John*, The New International Commentary on the New Testament (Grand Rapids: Eerdmans, 1971), 259–61.

Chapter 8: The Nature of New Testament Eschatology

1. Geerhardus Vos, "Eschatology of the New Testament," in *Redemptive History and Biblical Interpretation*, ed. Richard Gaffin (Phillipsburg, NJ: Presbyterian & Reformed, 1980), 25–28.

2. "The terminology and structure involved in this contrast play a large part in the apostle's thought." See Andrew T. Lincoln, *Paradise Now and Not Yet* (Cambridge, UK: Cambridge University Press, 1981), 170ff. Geerhardus Vos also sees this as a fundamental structure in Paul's thought in *The Pauline Eschatology* (Grand Rapids: Baker, 1979), 1–41.

3. "The age to come," it has been noted, is a technical term in Jewish eschatology, designating the final state after the messianic reign. Cf. Herman Strack and Paul Billerbeck, *Kommentar zum Neuen Testament aus Talmud und Midrasch*, vol. 4, pt. 2 (Munchen: C. H. Beck'sche Verlagsbuchhandlung, 1922), cited in Robert H. Gundry, *The Church and the Tribulation* (Grand Rapids: Zondervan, 1973), 142.

4. Cf. George Ladd's tacit admission of the difficulty this raises for premillennialism in *A Commentary on the Revelation of John* (Grand Rapids: Eerdmans, 1987), 262ff.

5. Kenneth L. Gentry, "A Postmillennial Response to Craig A. Blaising," in *Three Views on the Millennium and Beyond*, ed. Darrell L. Bock (Grand Rapids: Zondervan, 1999), 237. Cf. Jonathan Seraiah, *The End of All Things* (Moscow, ID: Canon, 1999), 41–43.

6. J. Dwight Pentecost, *Things to Come* (Grand Rapids: Zondervan, 1978), 131–32.

7. Elliot E. Johnson, "Prophetic Fulfillment: The Already and the Not Yet," in *Issues in Dispensationalism*, ed. Wesley R. Willis and John R. Master (Chicago: Moody, 1994), 188.

8. Harold W. Hoehner, "Evidence from Revelation 20," in *A Case for Premillennialism: A New Consensus*, ed. Donald K. Campbell and Jeffrey L. Townsend (Chicago: Moody, 1992), 262; George E. Ladd, *A Commentary on the Revelation of John* (Grand Rapids: Eerdmans, 1987), 269ff.; Charles Ryrie, *The Basis of the Premillennial Faith* (Neptune, NJ: Loizeaux Brothers, 1953) 153–54; and John F. Walvoord, *The Millennial Kingdom* (Grand Rapids: Zondervan, 1959), 333ff.

9. Stanley Grenz, *The Millennial Maze* (Downers Grove, IL: InterVarsity, 1992), 128.

10. Elliot Johnson, "Premillennialism Introduced: Hermeneutics," in *A Case for Premillennialism: A New Consensus*, ed. Donald K. Campbell and Jeffrey L. Townsend (Chicago: Moody, 1992), 15–34; Ladd, *Commentary on the Revelation of John*, 266; Ryrie, *Basis of Premillennial Faith*, 34–47; and Walvoord, *Millennial Kingdom*, 128–33.

11. See, for example, Craig A. Blaising, "Premillennialism," in *Three Views on the Millennium and Beyond*, ed. Darrell L. Bock (Grand Rapids: Zondervan, 1999), 200ff.

12. Ladd, *Commentary on the Revelation of John*, 266ff.

13. G. K. Beale, *The Book of Revelation*, The New International Greek Testament Commentary (Grand Rapids: Eerdmans, 1999), 58–64, 1017–21.

14. Progressive dispensationalists such as Craig Blaising contend that 1 Corinthians 15:23–24 teaches three stages of resurrection, "Christ, those who belong to Christ (raised) at his coming, and the end." This, says Blaising, allows room for John (in Revelation 20) to reinterpret the earlier revelation in the Gospels and epistles in which Jesus's coming is connected to the resurrection and the final judgment. "The grammar of the text allows the possibility of an interval of a reign of Christ between the resurrection of believers and the final resurrection" at the end of the millennium. See Blaising, "Premillennialism," 203–4.

15. D. Edmond Hiebert, "Evidence from 1 Corinthians 15," in *A Case for Premillennialism: A New Consensus*, ed. Donald K. Campbell and Jeffrey L. Townsend (Chicago: Moody, 1992), 225–34.

16. Robert Duncan Culver, *Daniel and the Latter Days* (Chicago: Moody, 1977), 29.

17. C. K. Barrett, *The First Epistle to the Corinthians* (New York: Harper & Row, 1968), 356. See Vos's extensive discussion of this in his *Pauline Eschatology*, 236–46.

18. W. D. Davies, *Paul and Rabbinic Judaism* (Philadelphia: Fortress, 1980), 293.

19. Barrett, *First Epistle to the Corinthians*, 356.

20. Cf. Jay Adams, *The Time Is at Hand* (Phillipsburg, NJ: Presbyterian & Reformed, 1970), 23ff.

21. J. Stuart Russell, *The Parousia: The New Testament Doctrine of Our Lord's Second Coming* (Grand Rapids: Baker, 1999), 23.

22. See, for example, Donald A. Hagner, *Matthew 1–13*, vol. 33A, Word Biblical Commentary (Dallas: Word, 1993), 391–95.

23. Russell, *Parousia*, 29. Other texts often cited in this debate include Matthew 10:23; Mark 8:38, 9:1; and Luke 9:26–27.

24. See D. A. Carson, *Matthew*, vol. 8, The Expositor's Bible Commentary, ed. Frank E. Gaebelein (Grand Rapids: Zondervan, 1984), 250–53, 380–82.

25. For example, as an amillennial Christian, I heartily agree with much of what John Jefferson Davis has to say about the advance of the kingdom of God in his *Victory of Christ's Kingdom* (Moscow, ID: Canon, 1996), especially pages 60ff. I agree with Vos, however, that the Scriptures teach that "as the reign of the truth will gradually be extended, so the power of evil will gather force towards the end" (Vos, *Pauline Eschatology*, 135). It seems to me that this is Paul's point in 2 Thessalonians 2:1–12. Postmillenarians, on the other hand, must concede that a great apostasy occurs before the second advent (cf. Davis, *Victory of Christ's Kingdom*; and

Greg Bahnsen, "The Prima Facie Acceptability of Postmillennialism," *Journal of Christian Reconstructionism* 3, no. 2 [1976–77]: 63).

26. Bahnsen, "Prima Facie Acceptability," 48–105, especially 56–60.

27. See Oswald T. Allis, *Prophecy and the Church* (Phillipsburg, NJ: Presbyterian & Reformed, 1945), 4–5; Daniel Whitby, *Paraphrase and Commentary on the New Testament, With a Treatise on the True Millennium* (London: William Tegg, 1899), 1117–34; and Jonathan Edwards, *Apocalyptic Writings* (New Haven: Yale University Press, 1977). It is the insistence on the conversion of Israel and the overthrow of the Antichrist one thousand years before the Lord's return that led the Protestant orthodox to speak of this form of postmillennialism as *chilasmus subtilis*. See Richard A. Muller, *Dictionary of Latin and Greek Theological Terms* (Grand Rapids: Baker, 1985), 66–67.

28. J. Marcellus Kik, *The Eschatology of Victory* (Phillipsburg, NJ: Presbyterian & Reformed, 1971), 4; and Davis, *Victory of Christ's Kingdom*, 81ff. Kik argues that the thousand years of Revelation 20 is "that period from the first advent of Christ until his second coming" (205). Bahnsen concurs. See "Prima Facie Acceptability," 63. This clearly distinguishes this variety of postmillennialism from the view of Whitby and Edwards.

29. Kik, *Eschatology of Victory*, 3–14; and Bahnsen, "Prima Facie Acceptability," 66–67.

30. See Anthony Hoekema, *The Bible and the Future* (Grand Rapids: Eerdmans, 1982), 175ff.

31. Bahnsen, "Prima Facie Acceptability," 66–67.

32. B. B. Warfield, *The Plan of Salvation* (Grand Rapids: Eerdmans, 1980), 99–103; Warfield, "Jesus Christ the Propitiation for the Whole World," *Expositor* 21 (1921): 241–53; and Warfield, *The Saviour of the World* (New York: Hodder & Stoughton, 1914), 129.

33. As Geerhardus Vos puts it, "The making all things right and new in the world depends not on gradual amelioration but on the final interposition of God." See Vos, *Pauline Eschatology*, 135.

34. Davis, *Victory of Christ's Kingdom*, 10–11.

35. See C. E. B. Cranfield, *The Epistle to the Romans*, vol. 2, The International Critical Commentary (Edinburgh: T & T Clark, 1979), 803. Though postmillenarians do believe in a great apostasy before Christ's return, this does not sufficiently explain how the present evil age could be completely transformed by the kingdom of God only to become essentially evil again during the brief period of apostasy. John Jefferson Davis (see *Victory of Christ's Kingdom*, 74) sees Paul's mention of the future crushing of Satan as a statement foretelling the victory of Christ's kingdom before his second advent. But John places this final crushing of Satan at the *eschaton* (Rev. 20:7–10). Cranfield sees Paul's reference to the crushing of Satan not as something predicated of the present age but as referring to the final eschatological victory of God over Satan.

36. Such texts are effectively summarized by Davis in *Victory of Christ's Kingdom*.

37. Richard B. Gaffin, "Theonomy and Eschatology," in *Theonomy: A Reformed Critique*, ed. William S. Barker and W. Robert Godfrey (Grand Rapids: Zondervan, 1990), 210–11.

38. Davis, *Victory of Christ's Kingdom*, 10.

Chapter 9: The Kingdom of God

1. George Ladd defines the kingdom of God as follows: "The Kingdom of God is the redemptive reign of God dynamically active to establish his rule among human beings, and that this Kingdom, which will appear as an apocalyptic act at the end of the age, has already come into human history in the person of Jesus to overcome evil, to deliver people from its power, and to bring them into the blessings of God's reign." See George Ladd, *A Theology of the New Testament*, rev. ed. (Grand Rapids: Eerdmans, 1993), 89–90.

2. See John F. Walvoord, "The New Testament Doctrine of the Kingdom," in *Vital Prophetic Issues*, ed. Roy B. Zuck (Grand Rapids: Kregel, 1995), 128–46.

3. Ladd, *Theology of the New Testament*, 57.

4. W. G. Kummel, *Promise and Fulfillment: The Eschatological Message of Jesus* (London: SCM, 1981).

5. Meredith G. Kline, *Kingdom Prologue* (Overland, KS: Two Age, 2000), 1.

6. Anthony Hoekema, *The Bible and the Future* (Grand Rapids: Eerdmans, 1982), 41.

7. Ladd, *Presence of the Future*, 325–26.

8. John F. Walvoord, *Matthew: Thy Kingdom Come* (Chicago: Moody, 1974), 96–97.

9. See, for example, Alva J. McClain, *Daniel's Prophecy of the 70 Weeks* (Grand Rapids: Zondervan, 1969), 31–45.

10. Walvoord, *Matthew*, 102.

11. At this point, the dispensationalist distinction between the "kingdom of God" and the "kingdom of heaven" should be discussed. As Hoekema notes, "It must be maintained that kingdom of heaven and kingdom of God are synonymous in meaning. Since the Jews avoided the use of the divine name, in later Jewish usage the word heaven was often used as a synonym for God; because Matthew was writing primarily for Jewish readers, we can understand his preference for this expression." See Hoekema, *Bible and the Future*, 44.

12. There are several excellent treatments of the kingdom of God and eschatology: Ladd, *Presence of the Future*; Herman Ridderbos, *The Coming of the Kingdom* (Phillipsburg, NJ: Presbyterian & Reformed, 1962); and Hoekema, *Bible and the Future*, 41–54.

13. Hoekema, *Bible and the Future*, 44.

14. Ibid.; also see Ladd, *Presence of the Future*, 134–38, for exegetical data.

15. Hoekema, *Bible and the Future*, 45.

16. Ladd, *Presence of the Future*, 331.

17. C. C. Caragounis, "Kingdom of God/Kingdom of Heaven," in *Dictionary of Jesus and the Gospels*, ed. Joel B. Green and Scot McKnight (Downers Grove, IL: InterVarsity, 1992), 417.

18. Cf. ibid.

19. Ladd, *Presence of the Future*, 47.

20. Ibid., 48–51.

21. Caragounis, "Kingdom of God," 418. Cf. Ridderbos, *Coming of the Kingdom*, 6–7.

22. Caragounis, "Kingdom of God," 418–20.

23. Ridderbos, *Coming of the Kingdom*, 40–41. According to Kummel, "New Testament usage is therefore completely uniform as regards the temporal use of *engus:* it denotes that an event will happen soon, by which it is meant or presumed that there will not be a long time to wait before it happens." See Kummel, *Promise and Fulfillment*, 20.

24. Ridderbos, *Coming of the Kingdom*, 41.

25. Hoekema, *Bible and the Future*, 43.

26. Ibid., 47.

27. Ibid.

28. Geerhardus Vos, *The Pauline Eschatology* (Grand Rapids: Baker, 1979), 36–41.

29. Ridderbos, *Coming of the Kingdom*, 518–23.

30. Ladd, *Presence of the Future*, 218.

31. Ridderbos, *Coming of the Kingdom*, 468.

32. Ladd, *Presence of the Future*, 328.

Chapter 10: The New Creation, the Israel of God, and the Suffering Church

1. Richard B. Gaffin, *Resurrection and Redemption: A Study in Paul's Soteriology* (Phillipsburg, NJ: Presbyterian & Reformed, 1987), 34.

2. Ibid., 60.

3. Ibid., 61–62.

4. Ibid., 107.

5. Douglas Moo, *The Epistle to the Romans*, The New International Commentary on the New Testament (Grand Rapids: Eerdmans, 1996), 418–19.

6. For a list of texts, see Gaffin, *Resurrection and Redemption*, 70, 109.

7. Geerhardus Vos, "Paul's Eschatological Concept of the Spirit," in *Redemptive History and Biblical Interpretation*, ed. Richard Gaffin (Phillipsburg, NJ: Presbyterian & Reformed, 1980), 117.

8. Gaffin, *Resurrection and Redemption*, 78–85.

9. Ibid., 85.

10. John Calvin, *Institutes of the Christian Religion*, ed. John T. McNeill and Ford Lewis Battles (Philadelphia: Westminster, 1960), II.x.20.

11. Ibid., II.xi.2.

12. Ibid., IV.xvi.14.

13. Charles Ryrie, *Dispensationalism Today* (Chicago: Moody, 1965), 136.

14. Hal Lindsey, *The Rapture* (New York: Bantam, 1983), 69.

15. Ibid., 69–70.

16. Summarized from Anthony Hoekema, *The Bible and the Future* (Grand Rapids: Eerdmans, 1982), 214–15.

17. Ibid.

18. J. Dwight Pentecost, *Things to Come* (Grand Rapids: Zondervan, 1978), 201–2; and Lewis Sperry Chafer, *Systematic Theology*, vol. 4 (Grand Rapids: Zondervan, 1980), 47–53.

19. Ronald K. Fung, *The Epistle to the Galatians*, New International Commentary on the New Testament (Grand Rapids: Eerdmans, 1988), 175.

20. Pentecost comments on this passage: "The objection is sometimes raised that God has forever broken down the barrier that separates Jew and Gentile and makes them one. This view arises from a failure to realize that this is God's purpose for the present age, but has no reference to God's program in the millennial age" (Pentecost, *Things to Come*, 528). Two factors must be pointed out. First, the whole point of the passage refutes Pentecost's presupposition that God has two redemptive programs, but Pentecost dismisses those texts that argue against his position. Second, on the dispensational scheme, the millennium is a retreat to a divided people of God, in effect, an undoing of what Christ died on the cross to establish. This is highly problematic.

21. Hoekema, *Bible and the Future*, 215.

22. Ibid.

23. Ibid.

24. According to Calvin, Paul "calls the Church, which was composed equally of Jew and Gentile, the Israel of God." See John Calvin, *The Epistles of Paul to the Romans and Thessalonians*, trans. R. MacKenzie (Grand Rapids: Eerdmans, 1979), 255.

25. John F. Walvoord, *The Millennial Kingdom* (Grand Rapids: Zondervan, 1959), 169–70.

26. Hoekema, *Bible and the Future*, 197. F. F. Bruce notes that the phrase "the Israel of God" may be related to Paul's knowledge of the nineteenth benediction: "He would have been familiar with a prayer which asks God for peace . . . and mercy on us and on all Israel. . . . If so, the words 'and so on the Israel of God' would have come readily from his tongue. F. Mussner (*Galaterbrief*, 417 n. 59) probably indicates the true sense when he identifies the Israel of God here with πᾶς Ἰσραήλ [all Israel] of Romans 11:26. For all his demoting of the law and the customs, Paul held good hope of the ultimate blessing of Israel. They were not all keeping in line with 'this rule' yet, but the fact that some Israelites were doing so was in his eyes a pledge that this remnant would increase until, with the ingathering of the full tale πλήρωμα [fullness] of Gentiles, 'all Israel will be saved.' The invocation of blessing on the Israel of God had probably an eschatological perspective." See F. F. Bruce, *The Epistle to the Galatians* (Grand Rapids: Eerdmans, 1982), 274–75.

27. Fung, *Epistle to the Galatians*, 310–11. Cf. E. P. Sanders, *Paul, the Law, and the Jewish People* (Philadelphia: Fortress, 1983), 174.

28. J. Marcellus Kik, *The Eschatology of Victory* (Phillipsburg, NJ: Presbyterian & Reformed, 1971), 17.

29. Ibid., 16–17.

30. John Dick, *Lectures on Theology* (New York: Robert Carter, 1852), 156.

31. Postmillenarians often cite New Testament texts such as Matthew 13:31–33 dealing with the spread of the kingdom to support postmillennial expectations. Cf. John Jefferson Davis, *The Victory of Christ's Kingdom* (Moscow, ID: Canon, 1996), 49ff.

32. Ibid., 72–78.

33. J. N. D. Kelly, *A Commentary on the Pastoral Epistles* (Grand Rapids: Baker, 1981), 193.

34. Paul gives a similar warning: "The Spirit clearly says that in later times some will abandon the faith and follow deceiving spirits and things taught by demons. Such teachings come through hypocritical liars, whose consciences have been seared as with a hot iron. They forbid people to marry and order them to abstain from certain foods, which God created to be received with thanksgiving by those who believe and who know the truth. For everything God created is good, and nothing is to be rejected if it is received with thanksgiving, because it is consecrated by the word of God and prayer" (1 Tim. 4:1–5).

35. Richard B. Gaffin, "Theonomy and Eschatology," in *Theonomy: A Reformed Critique*, ed. William S. Barker and W. Robert Godfrey (Grand Rapids: Zondervan, 1990), 210–11.

36. Peter T. O'Brien, *Commentary on Philippians*, New International Greek Testament Commentary (Grand Rapids: Eerdmans, 1991), 41.

37. Seyoon Kim, *The Origin of Paul's Gospel* (Grand Rapids: Eerdmans, 1981), 326.

38. C. E. B. Cranfield, *Epistle to the Romans*, vol. 1, The International Critical Commentary (Edinburg: T & T Clark, 1979), 407–8.

39. Gaffin, "Theonomy and Eschatology," 215–16.

Chapter 11: The Antichrist

1. This chapter is a summation of the material in my book *The Man of Sin: Uncovering the Truth about the Antichrist* (Grand Rapids: Baker, 2006).

2. B. B. Warfield, "Antichrist," in *Selected Shorter Writings of Benjamin B. Warfield*, vol. 1, ed. John E. Metter (Phillipsburg NJ: Presbyterian & Reformed, 1980), 356.

3. Vern S. Poythress, *The Returning King: A Guide to the Book of Revelation* (Phillipsburg, NJ: Presbyterian & Reformed, 2000), 139–43.

4. G. K. Beale, *The Book of Revelation*, New International Greek Testament Commentary (Grand Rapids: Eerdmans, 1999), 690ff.

5. Ibid., 718–28.

6. Throughout his letters, Paul speaks of the church as the temple of God (1 Cor. 3:16–17; 6:19; 2 Cor. 6:16; Eph. 2:21; 2 Thess. 2:4).

7. Dennis E. Johnson, *Triumph of the Lamb* (Phillipsburg, NJ: Presbyterian & Reformed, 2001), 189–90.

8. On the dating of John's Epistles, see D. A. Carson, Douglas Moo, and Leon Morris, *An Introduction to the New Testament* (Grand Rapids: Zondervan, 1992), 451.

9. Warfield, "Antichrist," 358.

10. G. K. Beale, *1–2 Thessalonians*, IVP New Testament Commentary Series (Downers Grove, IL: InterVarsity, 2003), 218–19.

11. Carson, Moo, and Morris, *Introduction to the New Testament*, 347–48.

12. Beale, *1–2 Thessalonians*, 215–18.

13. See the discussion of this in ibid., 206–11.

14. Louis Berkhof, *Systematic Theology* (Grand Rapids: Eerdmans, 1986), 702.

15. Henry Denzinger, *The Sources of Catholic Dogma*, trans. Roy J. Deferrari (St. Louis: B. Herder, 1957), s.v. "The Roman Pontiff," Systematic Index, 15.

16. The Duke of Alba, for example, was responsible for the death of many thousands of Reformed Christians. See Henry Kamen, *The Duke of Alba* (New Haven: Yale University Press, 2004), 91–94. Kamen lists the dead in the range of just over one thousand, while Philip Schaff puts the number at one hundred thousand, which is surely an exaggeration. See Philip Schaff, *Creeds of Christendom* (Grand Rapids: Baker, 1983), I.503n2.

17. Beale, *Book of Revelation*, 684.

18. Richard Bauckham, *The Climax of Prophecy: Studies on the Book of Revelation* (Edinburgh: T & T Clark, 1993), 407ff.

19. For a discussion of the date of the book of Revelation, see Riddlebarger, *Man of Sin*, 179–91.

20. Beale, *Book of Revelation*, 707ff.

21. G. B. Caird, *The Revelation of Saint John* (London: A & C Black, 1966), 171.

22. Ibid., 166.

23. Riddlebarger, *Man of Sin*, 179–91.

24. Beale, *Book of Revelation*, 875–78.

25. Bauckham, *Climax of Prophecy*, 384ff.

26. Beale, *Book of Revelation*, 722–25.

27. Ibid., 715.

28. Jonathan Edwards, *Apocalyptic Writings*, ed. Stephen Stein, Works of Jonathan Edwards, vol. 5 (New Haven: Yale University Press, 1977), 129. Cf. George M. Marsden, *Jonathan Edwards: A Life* (New Haven: Yale University Press, 2003), 87–89; and Bernard McGinn, *Antichrist: Two Thousand Years of the Human Fascination with Evil* (New York: Columbia University Press, 2000), 239–40.

29. McGinn, *Antichrist*, xx.

30. Anthony Hoekema, *The Bible and the Future* (Grand Rapids: Eerdmans, 1982), 162.

31. Geerhardus Vos, *The Pauline Eschatology* (Grand Rapids: Baker, 1979), 133–35.

Chapter 12: The Blessed Hope

1. Incredibly, John Walvoord contends that Daniel's prophecy of the resurrection concerns "Old Testament saints" and that "the church, the body of Christ, is not included in any of these resurrections [Dan. 12:2 and Rev. 20:4]." See John F. Walvoord, *The Blessed Hope and the Tribulation* (Grand Rapids: Zondervan, 1976), 38–39.

2. Leon Morris, *The First and Second Epistles to the Thessalonians*, The New International Commentary on the New Testament, rev. ed. (Grand Rapids: Eerdmans, 1991), 145.

3. Ibid.

4. F. F. Bruce cautions not to press this too far, however. Cf. F. F. Bruce, *1 and 2 Thessalonians*, Word Biblical Commentary (Waco: Word, 1982), 103.

5. John Stott, *The Gospel and the End of Time: The Message of 1 and 2 Thessalonians* (Downers Grove, IL: InterVarsity, 1991), 104.

6. Bruce, *1 and 2 Thessalonians*, 150.

7. To avoid the implications of the final judgment occurring at the second advent, Walvoord contends that Matthew is referring to "the judgment of the living who are on earth at the time of the second coming of Christ in respect to their entrance into the millennial kingdom." See John F. Walvoord, *Matthew: Thy Kingdom Come* (Chicago: Moody, 1974), 200. But Walvoord's interpretation flies directly in the face of verse 46, in which Jesus speaks of this judgment as unto everlasting punishment and blessedness. When Walvoord states that the "judgment in view here is not a final judgment, but is preparatory to establishing the kingdom of righteousness and peace" (p. 202, i.e., an earthly millennium), he is clearly in error.

8. George Eldon Ladd, *The Last Things* (Grand Rapids: Eerdmans, 1978), 100.

9. Ibid., 101.

10. George E. Ladd, *A Commentary on the Revelation of John* (Grand Rapids: Eerdmans, 1987), 266.

11. Craig A. Blaising, "Premillennialism," in *Three Views on the Millennium and Beyond*, ed. Darrell L. Bock (Grand Rapids: Zondervan, 1999), 200ff.

12. Progressive dispensationalists argue that "the millennium is a goal in history, although not its final form. To include a new heaven and earth does not itself logically entail an exclusion of

a millennium." New Testament revelation serves to enhance Old Testament expectations. The point of difference between progressive dispensationalists and amillenarians is whether there is such a transitional state—i.e., an earthly millennium—between Christ's second advent and the creation of a new heaven and a new earth. See Craig A. Blaising and Darrell L. Bock, "Assessment and Dialogue," in *Dispensationalism, Israel, and the Church: The Search for Definition* (Grand Rapids: Zondervan, 1992), 391.

13. Richard J. Bauckham, *Jude, 2 Peter*, Word Biblical Commentary (Waco: Word, 1983), 321ff.

14. Peter Stuhlmacher, *Paul's Letter to the Romans* (Louisville: Westminster/John Knox, 1994), 134.

15. R. C. Sproul, *The Last Days according to Jesus* (Grand Rapids: Baker, 1998), 11–26.

16. The depiction Jesus gives here of the days before his return is obviously contrary to postmillennial expectations.

17. Ladd, *Presence of the Future*, 328.

18. J. Dwight Pentecost, *Things to Come* (Grand Rapids: Zondervan, 1978), 193.

19. Ibid., 206ff. The reader may be interested in the debate over this between Gundry and Walvoord. See Robert H. Gundry, *The Church and the Great Tribulation* (Grand Rapids: Zondervan, 1973), especially pages 158–62, and Walvoord's response in *Blessed Hope and the Tribulation*.

20. Notice that the terms *separate* and *distinct* have different meanings. A single event—in this case the return of Christ—might have multiple elements. To distinguish is to merely identify these various elements and their relationship to one another. To separate includes a much more radical action, in the case in view here, changing the category of a single event with multiple components into multiple events with single components.

21. This same difficulty must be faced by so-called moderate preterists, who tell us that the parousia of our Lord already occurred in AD 70. To avoid the error of Hymeneaus and Philetus, who were teaching that the resurrection had already come and was therefore not a bodily resurrection (cf. 2 Tim. 2:17–19), they also argue that the second coming and the resurrection have not yet occurred. If the parousia actually occurred in AD 70 and if the second coming of Christ is still yet to come, how many comings of the Lord are there?

22. Louis Berkhof, *Systematic Theology* (Grand Rapids: Eerdmans, 1986), 695.

23. Ibid.

24. Ibid.

25. Anthony Hoekema, *The Bible and the Future* (Grand Rapids: Eerdmans, 1982), 166.

26. Ibid.

27. Ibid.

28. Ibid.

Chapter 13: Daniel's Prophecy of the Seventy Weeks

1. Chapters 4–19, to be exact. See Alva J. McClain, *Daniel's Prophecy of the 70 Weeks* (Grand Rapids: Zondervan, 1969), 10.

2. Meredith G. Kline, "The Covenant of the Seventieth Week," in *The Law and the Prophets: Old Testament Studies Prepared in Honor of Oswald Thompson Allis*, ed. John H. Skilton (Phillipsburg, NJ: Presbyterian & Reformed, 1974), 454–55.

3. Ibid., 456–57.

4. Ibid., 459.

5. Ibid., 461.

6. Ibid., 461–62.

7. Ibid., 463.

8. McClain, *Daniel's Prophecy*, 49ff.; and John Walvoord, *Daniel: The Key to Prophetic Revelation* (Chicago: Moody, 1977), 231ff.

9. Contra Thomas Edward McComiskey, "The Seventy 'Weeks' of Daniel against the Background of Ancient Near-Eastern Literature," *Westminster Theological Journal* 47 (1985): 18–45.

10. Edward J. Young, *The Prophecy of Daniel* (Carlisle: Banner of Truth, 1978), 197.

11. Ibid., 197ff.

12. Ibid., 199.

13. Ibid., 201.

14. McClain, *Daniel's Prophecy*, 35–36. Walvoord says that the prophecy is fulfilled in relation to the consummation but not before. See Walvoord, *Daniel*, 223.

15. Kline, "Covenant of the Seventieth Week," 463.

16. Ibid.

17. Ibid., 465.

18. Ibid., 469.

19. G. K. Beale, *The Book of Revelation*, The New International Greek Testament Commentary (Grand Rapids: Eerdmans, 1999), 669.

Chapter 14: The Olivet Discourse

1. D. A. Carson, *Matthew*, vol. 8, The Expositor's Bible Commentary, ed. Frank E. Gaebelein (Grand Rapids: Zondervan, 1984), 488.

2. C. E. B. Cranfield, *The Gospel according to St. Mark*, The Cambridge Greek Testament (New York: Cambridge University Press, 1983), 401–2. This is also the position of Anthony Hoekema, *The Bible and the Future* (Grand Rapids: Eerdmans, 1982), 137ff.; and H. N. Ridderbos, *Matthew: Bible Student's Commentary*, trans. Ray Togtman (Grand Rapids: Zondervan, 1987), 442–43.

3. Donald A. Hagner, *Matthew 1–13*, vol. 33A, Word Biblical Commentary (Dallas: Word, 1993), li.

4. D. A. Hagner, *Matthew 14–28*, Word Biblical Commentary (Dallas: Word, 1995), 684.

5. Carson's discussion of the history of interpretation of the Olivet Discourse is helpful. See Carson, *Matthew*, 488–95.

6. J. Stuart Russell, *The Parousia: The New Testament Doctrine of Our Lord's Second Coming* (Grand Rapids: Baker, 1999), 13–122. According to postmillenarian J. Marcellus Kik, all of the Olivet Discourse from verses 1–35 refer to the destruction of Jerusalem. It is not until verse 36, says Kik, that Matthew's focus shifts to the second coming. See Kik, *The Eschatology of Victory* (Phillipsburg, NJ: Presbyterian & Reformed, 1971), 158. Cf. also R. T. France, *Matthew*, Tyndale New Testament Commentaries (Grand Rapids: Eerdmans, 1985), 335–36.

7. R. C. Sproul, *The Last Days according to Jesus* (Grand Rapids: Baker, 1998), 29–48.

8. John F. Walvoord, *Matthew: Thy Kingdom Come* (Chicago: Moody, 1974), 179–95.

9. Carson, *Matthew*, 495; and Hagner, *Matthew 14–28*, 683–87.

10. According to Dale Allison, "In Matthew . . . this age and the age to come seemingly overlap. Although the consummation lies ahead, although this age is still full of tribulation, and although the Christian casts his hope upon the future coming of the Son of man, saints have already been raised, the Son of man has already been enthroned in the heavenly places, and the resurrected Jesus is ever present with his followers (28:20)." See Dale C. Allison, *The End of the Ages Has Come* (Philadelphia: Fortress, 1985), 49–50.

11. Cited in William Lane, *The Gospel according to Mark*, New International Commentary on the New Testament (Grand Rapids: Eerdmans, 1982), 451.

12. Hagner, *Matthew 14–28*, 688.

13. Ibid.

14. According to Cranfield, "That it would be natural for the Disciples to assume that the destruction of the temple would be part of a complex of events leading to the end is likely. The disciples, excited and disturbed by Jesus' prediction, want to know when the temple is to be destroyed and what is the sign by which they may know the final consummation is approaching. They want to be told what will be the 'sign'—that is, they want an infallible means of recognizing the approach of the end; they want in fact to be relieved from having to 'watch.'

But instead of a single sign, Jesus gives them a multiplicity of 'signs.' The purpose of which is not to impart esoteric information but to strengthen and sustain faith." See Cranfield, *Gospel according to St. Mark*, 393–94.

15. Hagner, *Matthew 14–28*, 692.

16. Contra J. Stuart Russell, who states, "The prophecy on the Mount of Olives is one connected and continuous discourse, having exclusive reference to the approaching doom of Jerusalem and Israel." Cf. Russell, *Parousia*, 140.

17. Cranfield says these are signs that the end is not yet since there is "much that has still to happen before the consummation of all things." See Cranfield, *Gospel according to St. Mark*, 394.

18. France, *Matthew*, 337–38.

19. Cranfield, *Gospel according to St. Mark*, 397.

20. This, of course, explains why postmillenarians such as Kik must limit the first thirty-five verses of Matthew 24 to God's judgment on Israel prior to AD 70. If the birth pains of which Jesus is speaking extend beyond AD 70 into the present age, Jesus's assertion that moral conditions will grow worse is contrary to the postmillennial expectation of a Christianized world.

21. Cranfield, *Gospel according to St. Mark*, 399. Kik, for one, argues that the prophecy is fulfilled before AD 70, when, for example, it is declared in Acts 2:5 that Jews from every nation under heaven were present for the Pentecost sermon. Not only does this limit the gospel mission to Israel, in contrast to Matthew 28:19, which extends to all nations, but it is much more likely that this declaration means something like "from every land where there were Jews." See F. F. Bruce, *The Acts of the Apostles*, 3rd. ed. (Grand Rapids: Eerdmans, 1990), 116.

22. The Greek sentence contains double negatives, indicating that the temple will be totally and completely destroyed.

23. Cranfield, *Gospel according to St. Mark*, 392.

24. Walvoord, *Matthew*, 185. He also contends that this will be the fulfillment of Daniel 9:27, which dispensationalists assign to an end-times antichrist. Says Walvoord, "According to Daniel 9:27 and Matthew 24:15, the dictator in the Middle East desecrates the Jewish temple of that day, stops the sacrifices, and begins worldwide persecution of the Jew." John F. Walvoord, *The Blessed Hope and the Tribulation* (Grand Rapids: Zondervan, 1976), 132. Jesus says nothing here about a Middle East dictator.

25. Carson, *Matthew*, 499.

26. Hagner, *Matthew 14–28*, 699–700.

27. Cranfield, *Gospel according to St. Mark*, 404.

28. Ibid.

29. Hagner, *Matthew 14–28*, 700.

30. Ibid., 701.

31. Ibid., 701–2.

32. Cranfield, *Gospel according to St. Mark*, 401–2.

33. Ibid.

34. While the events of the fall of Jerusalem were described in excruciating detail by Josephus and others, they simply are not the worst tribulation that men have brought or experienced on the earth. If this event was fulfilled in AD 70, Jesus must be speaking only about Jerusalem or Israel locally (the Jews as a people faced worse in the Holocaust, the Crusades, the Moslem occupation, and the Spanish Inquisition). In the context of predictive prophecy and prophetic perspective, the intent would be that the destruction of the temple and the tribulation brought on by the Roman army are a type of greater wrath experienced immediately before the return of Christ, perhaps connected with the loosing of Satan (Rev. 20:7ff.) and this on a global, not a local scale. This means that Jerusalem and the temple are, perhaps, a type of the apostate church in the last days.

35. Cranfield, *Gospel according to St. Mark*, 404. Others who support the possibility of double fulfillment are Ridderbos (*Matthew*, 445) and Hoekema (*Bible and the Future*, 151).

36. Hagner, *Matthew 14–28*, 704–5.

37. France, *Matthew*, 342.

38. Hagner, *Matthew 14–28*, 704.

39. Russell, *Parousia*, 76. Even the postmillenarian and preterist Kik must concede that this verse stands in contrast with the previous verses dealing with the events of AD 70. Since Kik contends that verses 4–35 deal with the historical events of AD 70, unlike verse 27, verse 28 marks a return to events of pre–AD 70. See Kik, *Eschatology of Victory*, 124.

40. Hagner, *Matthew 14–28*, 707.

41. Ridderbos, *Matthew*, 447.

42. Hagner, *Matthew 14–28*, 711–13.

43. Carson, *Matthew*, 495.

44. Kik's attempt to limit this event to God's judgment on Israel in AD 70, while plausible, unfortunately downplays the fact that the parousia is regularly connected to Christ's second advent throughout the Scriptures (Matt. 13:40–41; 16:27; 25:31; 1 Cor. 11:26; 15:52; 16:22; 1 Thess. 4:14–17; 2 Thess. 2:1–8; 2 Pet. 3:10–12; Rev. 1:7), even though in at least two other instances Christ's parousia has a different sense (Matt. 10:23; 16:28). Kik makes the exceptional cases the rule. See Kik, *Eschatology of Victory*, 127–35. Cf. Carson's response to this in *Matthew*, 492–94.

45. See Cranfield, *Gospel according to St. Mark*, 402; and Ridderbos, *Matthew*, 447ff.

46. Contra Kik, *Eschatology of Victory*, 136–43.

47. The term *elect* (*eklektos*) always refers to the people of God chosen by divine election. The *elect* is a synonym for the *church* (*ekklēsia*, the "called-out ones"). It is difficult to see this term merely applying to a group who accepted Christ during the second-chance salvation of the great tribulation. It should, therefore, be seen as a reference to the church, plainly on the earth during the period of tribulation. See Colin Brown, ed., *Dictionary of New Testament Theology*, vol. 1 (Grand Rapids: Zondervan, 1982), s.v. "elect."

48. These things refer to the tribulation of the interadvental period and specifically to events he has just been describing for Israel, i.e., the destruction of the city and the temple. Hagner, *Matthew 14–28*, 715.

49. Walvoord, *Matthew*, 193.

50. According to Hagner, "'This generation' is used consistently in the Gospel to refer to Jesus' contemporaries," specifically the sinful generation soon to come under God's judgment. See Hagner, *Matthew 14–28*, 715.

51. Kik, *Eschatology of Victory*, 151–57.

Chapter 15: Romans 11

1. Geerhardus Vos, *The Pauline Eschatology* (Grand Rapids: Baker, 1979), 90n16.

2. David E. Holwerda, *Jesus and Israel: One Covenant or Two?* (Grand Rapids: Eerdmans, 1995), 151.

3. Douglas Moo, *The Epistle to the Romans*, The New International Commentary on the New Testament (Grand Rapids: Eerdmans, 1996), 696.

4. Cf. Vos, *Pauline Eschatology*, 87–91; Holwerda, *Jesus and Israel*, 147–76; and Cornelis P. Venema, *The Promise of the Future* (Carlisle, PA: Banner of Truth, 2000), 127–39. Although Herman Ridderbos holds the opposite view, his reply to G. C. Berkouwer is also frequently cited in this debate: "It seems to me that Berkouwer, in *The Return of Christ*, takes altogether too little account of the future elements in Paul's pronouncements" in Romans 11. See Herman Ridderbos, *Paul: An Outline of His Theology* (Grand Rapids: Eerdmans, 1975), 359n71.

5. See William Hendriksen, *Israel in Prophecy* (Grand Rapids: Baker 1974); G. C. Berkouwer, *The Return of Christ* (Grand Rapids: Eerdmans, 1972), 323–58; Anthony Hoekema, *The Bible and the Future* (Grand Rapids: Eerdmans, 1982), 145–47; O. Palmer Robertson, "Is There a Distinctive Future for Ethnic Israel in Romans 11?" in *Perspectives on Evangelical Theology*, ed. Kenneth S. Kantzer and Stanley N. Gundry (Grand Rapids: Baker, 1979), 209–27; and Robert B.

Strimple, "Amillennialism," in *Three Views on the Millennium and Beyond*, ed. Darrell L. Bock (Grand Rapids: Zondervan, 1999), 112–18. This is the so-called Dutch school, even though all of those listed who defend the opposite view are also Dutch.

6. Strimple, "Amillennialism," 113.

7. See Holwerda, *Jesus and Israel*, 1–26.

8. Hoekema, *Bible and the Future*, 146–47; Strimple, "Amillennialism," 112–18; and Robertson, "Is There a Distinctive Future for Ethnic Israel?" 215. It should be noted that Robertson has since changed his views regarding the meaning of the phrase "all Israel" and now understands the phrase to mean the full number of the elect, Jew and Gentile. See O. Palmer Robertson, *The Israel of God* (Phillipsburg, NJ: Presbyterian & Reformed, 2000), 167–92.

9. J. Dwight Pentecost, *Things to Come* (Grand Rapids: Zondervan, 1978), 88–89.

10. Ibid., 247.

11. S. Lewis Johnson, "Evidence from Romans 9–11," in *A Case for Premillennialism: A New Consensus*, ed. Donald K. Campbell and Jeffrey L. Townsend (Chicago: Moody, 1992), 199–223.

12. John Calvin, *The Epistles of Paul the Apostle to the Romans and to the Thessalonians*, trans. Ross MacKenzie (Grand Rapids: Eerdmans, 1979), 255. Cf. Robertson, *Israel of God*, 188–89.

13. Hoekema, *Bible and the Future*, 145.

14. Johnson, "Evidence from Romans 9–11," 212.

15. Stanley Grenz, *The Millennial Maze* (Downers Grove, IL: InterVarsity, 1992), 171.

16. George Ladd, *A Theology of the New Testament*, rev. ed. (Grand Rapids: Eerdmans, 1993), 608.

17. Ibid. Cf. George Ladd, "Historic Premillennialism," in *The Meaning of the Millennium*, ed. Robert G. Clouse (Downers Grove, IL: InterVarsity, 1977), 27, where Ladd writes that there are "unavoidable indications that the Old Testament promises to Israel are fulfilled in the Christian church. The alert reader will say, 'This sounds like amillennialism.'"

18. Johnson, "Evidence from Romans 9–11," 206–7.

19. See Charles Hodge, *Commentary on the Epistle to the Romans* (Grand Rapids: Eerdmans, 1980), 353–82; and Robert Haldane, *Commentary on Romans* (Grand Rapids: Kregel, 1988), 530–60.

20. John Jefferson Davis, *The Victory of Christ's Kingdom* (Moscow, ID: Canon, 1996), 62. Davis also makes the point that there is no mention by Paul here of a restored Davidic kingdom, a telling weakness in the dispensational interpretation of the passage.

21. David Chilton, *Paradise Restored: A Biblical Theology of Dominion* (Fort Worth: Dominion, 1987), 129–31.

22. See, for example, the essays by E. Elizabeth Johnson and Douglas Moo in *Pauline Theology: Romans*, vol. 3, ed. David M. Hay and Elizabeth Johnson (Minneapolis: Fortress, 1995), 211–58.

23. Holwerda, *Jesus and Israel*, 150.

24. Strimple, "Amillennialism," 113.

25. Ibid., 114.

26. Moo, *Epistle to the Romans*, 572–76.

27. Holwerda, *Jesus and Israel*, 154–55.

28. Charles Cranfield points out that the key word in the passage is *mercy*, occurring seven times. See C. E. B. Cranfield, *The Epistle to the Romans*, vol. 2, The International Critical Commentary (Edinburgh: T & T Clark, 1979), 448.

29. Moo, *Epistle to the Romans*, 573–74.

30. Ibid., 574.

31. Contra Hoekema, *Bible and the Future*, 145; and N. T. Wright, *Climax of the Covenant* (Minneapolis: Fortress, 1993), 248–51.

32. Holwerda, *Jesus and Israel*, 155.

33. Moo, *Epistle to the Romans*, 671.

34. Robertson, "Is There a Distinctive Future for Ethnic Israel?" 213.

35. Strimple, "Amillennialism," 115.

36. That Paul is focusing on the present is a point made repeatedly by Robertson ("Is There a Distinctive Future for Ethnic Israel?").

37. Holwerda, *Jesus and Israel*, 164.

38. Ibid.

39. See, for example, Ridderbos, *Paul*, 354–61; cf. Moo, *Epistle to the Romans*, 684.

40. The meaning of Israel's fullness *(plērōma)* is a hotly debated point. Robertson's argument to the effect that Israel's fullness was a current condition when Paul wrote the epistle seems strained, especially in light of the context, which is the contrast with Israel's loss (i.e., Israel's numerical diminution). It seems to me that the context indicates that Paul is speaking of a time when Israel's present diminution gives way to great increase. I take this to be a reference to a future restoration of Israel's present loss. Cf. Robertson, "Is There a Distinctive Future for Ethnic Israel?" 214–16; and Moo, *Epistle to the Romans*, 688–90.

41. John Murray, *The Epistle to the Romans*, The New International Commentary on the New Testament (Grand Rapids: Eerdmans, 1979), 80–84. This is also the view of Hodge and Haldane. See note 19.

42. Chilton, *Paradise Restored*, 131.

43. Strimple, "Amillennialism," 118. Kenneth Gentry's reply to Strimple's argument is simply to reaffirm the postmillennial contention without exegetical support to the effect that there is a golden age entailing the salvation of the majority of the world's inhabitants yet to follow the fullness of Israel and the Gentiles. For Paul, the fullness of Israel is connected to the *eschaton*, not a millennial age. Cf. Kenneth L. Gentry, "A Postmillennial Response to Craig A. Blaising," in *Three Views on the Millennium and Beyond*, ed. Darrell L. Bock (Grand Rapids: Zondervan, 1999), 141.

44. See, for example, Moo, *Epistle to the Romans*, 692–96; Cranfield, *Epistle to the Romans*, 561–63; and Thomas R. Schreiner, *Romans*, Baker Exegetical Commentary on the New Testament (Grand Rapids: Baker, 1998), 597–99.

45. Moo, *Epistle to the Romans*, 696.

46. C. K. Barrett, *The Epistle to the Romans* (New York: Harper & Row, 1957), 215.

47. Vos, *Pauline Eschatology*, 87–88.

48. Holwerda, *Jesus and Israel*, 167.

49. Ibid.

50. Ibid., 167–68.

51. Moo, *Epistle to the Romans*, 712–13; and Holwerda, *Jesus and Israel*, 168.

52. Moo, *Epistle to the Romans*, 716.

53. Cranfield, *Epistle to the Romans*, 575; Moo, *Epistle to the Romans*, 717–18; and Schreiner, *Romans*, 617–18.

54. Robertson, "Is There a Distinctive Future for Ethnic Israel?" 220.

55. Hoekema, *Bible and the Future*, 144. Cf. Moo, *Epistle to the Romans*, 719; and Cranfield, *Epistle to the Romans*, 575.

56. This should not necessarily be taken to mean that once the fullness of the Gentiles comes in, no more Gentiles will be saved. As we will see, neither should we understand the phrase "all Israel" in an inclusive sense ("each and every"). It seems to me that Paul uses these terms with a bit less precision, i.e., when the age of Gentile salvation is over, *and the fullness of the elect has come in*, then the salvation of Israel begins and shortly culminates in the consummation.

57. Hoekema, *Bible and the Future*, 145. Cf. Robertson, "Is There a Distinctive Future for Ethnic Israel?" 220–25.

58. Moo, *Epistle to the Romans*, 720.

59. See Hoekema, *Bible and the Future*, 145, and the chart at the bottom of the page. See also Robertson, "Is There a Distinctive Future for Ethnic Israel?" 221.

60. See F. F. Bruce, *The Epistle of Paul to the Romans*, Tyndale New Testament Commentaries (Grand Rapids: Eerdmans, 1963), 222. Bruce's commentary on Romans is often cited by those seeking to give *houtōs* a temporal meaning, i.e., "then." (Cf. Gentry, "Postmillennial Response," 135). But Bruce cites no evidence for his conclusion. According to William Baur, William F. Arndt, F. Wilbur Gingrich, and Frederick W. Danker, *A Greek-English Lexicon of the New Testament and Other Early Christian Literature* (Chicago: University of Chicago Press, 1979), 597–98, *houtōs* is not given a temporal meaning.

61. Holwerda, *Jesus and Israel*, 170. Cf. Vos, *Pauline Eschatology*, 87–89.

62. Robertson, "Is There a Distinctive Future for Ethnic Israel?" 223.

63. Moo, *Epistle to the Romans*, 717–18.

64. Ibid., 722.

65. Hoekema, *Bible and the Future*, 146. Surely Hoekema's argument is framed with dispensationalists in mind.

66. Ibid.

67. Holwerda, *Jesus and Israel*, 170.

68. Pentecost, *Things to Come*, 267.

69. Holwerda, *Jesus and Israel*, 172–73.

70. Moo, *Epistle to the Romans*, 728.

71. Holwerda, *Jesus and Israel*, 173.

72. Ibid., 174.

Chapter 16: Revelation 20:1–10

1. See the helpful survey in G. K. Beale, *The Book of Revelation*, The New International Greek Testament Commentary (Grand Rapids: Eerdmans, 1999), 44ff.

2. John F. Walvoord, *The Revelation of Jesus Christ* (Chicago: Moody, 1978), 30.

3. See, for example, George E. Ladd, *A Commentary on the Revelation of John* (Grand Rapids: Eerdmans, 1987), 259–61.

4. Stanley Grenz, *The Millennial Maze* (Downers Grove, IL: InterVarsity, 1992), 65–89.

5. Cf. David Chilton, *The Days of Vengeance* (Fort Worth: Dominion, 1987), 485; and B. B. Warfield, "The Millennium and the Apocalypse," in *Biblical Doctrines* (Grand Rapids: Baker, 1981), 647.

6. Kenneth L. Gentry, *Before Jerusalem Fell: Dating the Book of Revelation* (Atlanta: American Vision, 1998).

7. Chilton, *Days of Vengeance*, 493ff.

8. Beale, *Book of Revelation*, 37; and D. A. Carson, Douglas J. Moo, and Leon Morris, *An Introduction to the New Testament* (Grand Rapids: Zondervan, 1992), 478–79.

9. Carson, Moo, and Morris, *Introduction to the New Testament*, 478.

10. Hal Lindsey, *There's a New World Coming* (Santa Ana: Vision House, 1973), 138.

11. Carson, Moo, and Morris, *Introduction to the New Testament*, 478.

12. R. Laird Harris, "Premillennialism," unpublished essay, 2002.

13. Charles Ryrie, *Dispensationalism Today* (Chicago: Moody, 1965), 86–87.

14. Vern S. Poythress, *Understanding Dispensationalists* (Grand Rapids: Zondervan, 1987), 79.

15. Walvoord, *Revelation of Jesus Christ*, 291.

16. Beale, *Book of Revelation*, 973–94.

17. Vern Sheridan Poythress, "Genre and Hermeneutics in Rev 20:1–6," *Journal of the Evangelical Theological Society* 36 (March 1993): 46.

18. Ibid. Cf. the dispensational response to this by Thomas D. Ice, "Dispensational Hermeneutics," in *Issues in Dispensationalism*, ed. Wesley R. Willis and John R. Master (Chicago: Moody, 1994), 29–49.

19. Beale, *Book of Revelation*, 973–74.

20. The camera angle analogy is found throughout Dennis E. Johnson's outstanding book, *Triumph of the Lamb* (Phillipsburg, NJ: Presbyterian & Reformed, 2001), 44–47.

21. R. Fowler White, "Reexamining the Evidence for Recapitulation in Rev. 20:1–10," *Westminster Theological Journal* 51 (Fall 1989): 319.

22. For a discussion of the structure of the book and the various ways in which the visions are related to one another, see William Hendriksen, *More Than Conquerors* (Grand Rapids: Baker, 1982), 16–23; Johnson, *Triumph of the Lamb*, 25–48; and Beale, *Book of Revelation*, 108–51.

23. Hendriksen, *More Than Conquerors*, 21.

24. Beale, *Book of Revelation*, 992.

25. Ibid.

26. Ladd, *Commentary on the Revelation of John*, 261.

27. Grenz, *Millennial Maze*, 170.

28. Craig A. Blaising, "Premillennialism," in *Three Views on the Millennium and Beyond*, ed. Darrell L. Bock (Grand Rapids: Zondervan, 1999), 215.

29. White, "Reexamining the Evidence for Recapitulation," 319–44. Cf. Beale, *Book of Revelation*, 974–83. White lists three main lines of argumentation and includes the motif of angelic descent as supporting evidence if not proof (see p. 336). Premillennial responses to White's essay can be found in Harold W. Hoehner, "Evidence from Revelation 20," in *A Case for Premillennialism: A New Consensus*, ed. Donald K. Campbell and Jeffrey L. Townsend (Chicago: Moody, 1992), 235–62; and Blaising, "Premillennialism," 212–21. White responds to criticism of his case for recapitulation in R. Fowler White, "Making Sense of Revelation 20:1–10? Harold Hoehner versus Recapitulation," *Journal of the Evangelical Theological Society* 37, no. 4 (December 1994): 539–51.

30. As Meredith Kline has argued, Armageddon should not be confused with the plains of Meggido but is instead a reference to the mount of gathering. The battle depicted in Revelation 16:16 occurs at the end of the present millennial age and describes the same event as Revelation 20:7–10. According to Kline, Revelation 16:16 is a picture of the Gog-Magog antichrist of Ezekiel 38–39, waging war on Christ's saints immediately before the end. See Meredith G. Kline, "Har Magedon: The End of the Millennium," *Journal of the Evangelical Theological Society* 39, no 2 (June 1996): 207–22.

31. George Ladd, for one, makes no mention of this problem whatsoever. See Ladd, *Commentary on the Revelation of John*, 255–56. Alan Johnson writes, "The scene here is the eschatological return of Christ and his judgment of the nations, not the whole intervening age." See Alan Johnson, *Revelation*, vol. 12, The Expositor's Bible Commentary, ed. Frank Gaebelein (Grand Rapids: Zondervan, 1981), 575.

32. White, "Reexamining the Evidence for Recapitulation," 321.

33. R. H. Mounce, *The Book of Revelation*, The New International Commentary on the New Testament (Grand Rapids: Eerdmans, 1977), 353.

34. Popular dispensationalist writers often see these chapters as predicting a Russian-Arab invasion of Israel during the tribulation period. For an effective history of the development of the dispensational view of Russia's role in end-times events, see Paul Boyer, *When Time Shall Be No More* (Cambridge, UK: Belknap, 1992), 152–80.

35. White, "Reexamining the Evidence for Recapitulation," 326–27; and Kline, "Har Magedon," 218–22.

36. Kline argues that this city is Har Magedon, effectively tying the prophecies of Revelation 16:14–16; 19:11–21; 20:7–10 to Gog and Magog of Ezekiel 38–39. See Kline, "Har Magedon," 220.

37. White, "Reexamining the Evidence for Recapitulation," 327.

38. The bowl judgments "complement and round out the portrayal of divine wrath in the seals and trumpets. It is in this fuller presentation of punishment in the bowls that it can be said God's wrath has been completely expressed." See Beale, *Book of Revelation*, 788.

39. According to John Walvoord, "The millennium as an aspect of God's theocratic program
. . . [is] a fulfillment of the promise given to David that his kingdom and throne would continue
forever over the house of Israel. . . . Advocates of this view hold that the millennium is a period
in which Christ will literally reign on earth as its supreme political leader and that many of the
promises of the Old Testament relating to a kingdom on earth in which Israel will be prominent
and Gentiles will be blessed will have complete and literal fulfillment." See Walvoord, *Revelation
of Jesus Christ*, 283–84.

40. Both Revelation 20:1–3 and verses 4–6 begin with the introductory formula, "I saw"
(*eidon*), which is used throughout the book to introduce symbolic visions. Cf. Beale, *Book of
Revelation*, 973.

41. Hendriksen, *More Than Conquerors*, 185.

42. Beale, *Book of Revelation*, 632. The texts supporting this include Pss. 73:13–14; 89:10;
Isa. 30:7; 51:9; Ezek. 29:3; 32:2–3; Hab. 3:8–15.

43. Chilton, *Days of Vengeance*, 499; and J. Marcellus Kik, *The Eschatology of Victory*
(Phillipsburg, NJ: Presbyterian & Reformed, 1971), 194.

44. Beale, *Book of Revelation*, 984.

45. Ibid.

46. Walvoord, *Revelation of Jesus Christ*, 282–95.

47. Ladd, *Commentary on the Revelation of John*, 262.

48. Kik, *Eschatology of Victory*, 205. Cf. Chilton, *Days of Vengeance*, 499 ff.

49. Beale, *Book of Revelation*, 58–64, 1017–21.

50. Ibid., 995.

51. There is a *hina* clause here, clearly indicating purpose "so that" he cannot deceive the
nations.

52. John F. Walvoord, *The Millennial Kingdom* (Grand Rapids: Zondervan, 1959), 51, 291–95.
See also Walvoord, "Is Satan Bound?" in *Vital Prophetic Issues*, ed. Roy B. Zuck (Grand Rapids:
Kregel, 1995), 83–95. Since Walvoord interprets the passage literally, any presence of evil in the
present age must indicate that this binding is yet future, i.e., during a future millennium. This
stems from a failure on Walvoord's part to give due credence to John's own explanation of the
binding of Satan, which does not eliminate all evil but prevents him from deceiving the nations.

53. Beale, *Book of Revelation*, 987–88.

54. Ibid., 985. Beale reminds us that the abyss does not have spatial connotations but "represents a spiritual dimension alongside and in the midst of the earthly, not above it or below" (p. 987).

55. Arthur Lewis, *The Dark Side of the Millennium* (Grand Rapids: Baker, 1980), 52.

56. Hendriksen, *More Than Conquerors*, 190.

57. Lewis, *Dark Side of the Millennium*, 52–53.

58. Beale, *Book of Revelation*, 991–93.

59. Richard Bauckham, *The Theology of the Book of Revelation* (New York: Cambridge
University Press, 1994), 107.

60. I remain convinced of the late dating of Revelation despite several recent attempts to argue
for pre–AD 70 authorship. Cf. Beale, *Book of Revelation*, 4–27; and Gentry, *Before Jerusalem Fell*.

61. Walvoord, *Revelation of Jesus Christ*, 296.

62. There is nothing in the text to indicate that those reigning with Christ are the twenty-four
elders of Revelation 5:10 associated with the new creation (cf. Beale, *Book of Revelation*, 360–64).

63. It is interesting to note that one who prides himself on a "literal interpretation" of Revelation is forced to do so much speculation. Those who reign for the thousand years are much
more likely to be those Christians who have died and are in heaven with Christ. Perhaps they
are the martyrs. If the rapture occurs seven years before the return of Christ, then there must
be a second unmentioned resurrection for those who died during the tribulation. This would
mean that we have the first resurrection at the rapture and another resurrection here, which may
include Old Testament saints. This would imply a qualitative difference between those who died

under the new covenant and those who died under the old (a feature unique to dispensational-ism) and another resurrection at the end of the millennium. This simply will not fit with the two-age model or the biblical use of "last day" (John 6:39, 40, 44, 54; 11:24, with John 12:48, which clearly places judgment and the resurrection together at the same time), "last trumpet" (1 Cor. 15:52, with Matt. 24:31), and "day of the Lord" (2 Pet. 3:10).

64. Beale, *Book of Revelation*, 995–96.

65. Ibid., 999.

66. Ibid., 997.

67. Hendriksen, *More Than Conquerors*, 191–92.

68. Ladd, *Commentary on the Revelation of John*, 265. Blaising calls this the *crux interpretum*, in "Premillennialism," 221–27.

69. Ladd, *Commentary on the Revelation of John*, 265–66. According to Ladd, "The phrase they 'came to life again' is a translation of the single Greek word *ezesan*. The crux of the entire exegetical problem is the meaning of this word. It is true that the word can mean entrance into spiritual life (John 5:25), but it is not used of any spiritual resurrection of the souls of the righteous at death. The word is, however, used of bodily resurrection in John 11:25; Rom. 14:9; Rev. 1:18; 2:8; 13:14; and most commentators admit that this is the meaning in v. 5." This was the argument that kept me premillennial for many years. However, if Ladd is right that these two resurrections must both refer to literal and bodily resurrections, then the two-age model, which is expressly clear about the return of Christ being directly connected with the judgment, must instead be spiritualized. Also, Ladd does not take into account the points raised by Carson and Morris to be discussed later to the effect that John 5:24–25 may indeed provide a pattern that indicates that John himself distinguishes between bodily and spiritual resurrections for each believer. Which will the interpreter choose to do, spiritualize the Gospel narrative or see one of these resurrections in Revelation (which is obviously a highly symbolic book) as referring to something that has already occurred? Amillenarians choose the latter, premillenarians the former.

70. Ibid., 267.

71. Grenz, *Millennial Maze*, 128. Arthur Lewis raises an interesting dilemma for premillenarians. Pointing out that the context is the reign of the saints in heaven, Lewis concludes, "Premillennialists, however, have gone far beyond the literal sense of the text in their identification of these reigning saints. They see both heavenly and earthly saints forming a 'new' Israel under a new Davidic king in fulfillment of all the political promises of the Old Testament. They believe that resurrected saints will mingle with unresurrected saints in that future kingdom, a view which the passage plainly denies. Whatever one makes of the phrase 'first resurrection' in Revelation 20:6, it has to be inclusive of all who reign with Christ. If, therefore, it is to be understood to be the bodily resurrection of believers, then it may not include the tribulation survivors who are yet unresurrected." See Lewis, *Dark Side of the Millennium*, 57–58.

72. See Oswald T. Allis, *Prophecy and the Church* (Phillipsburg, NJ: Presbyterian & Reformed, 1947), 2–5; and Beale, *Book of Revelation*, 1011–12.

73. Calvin writes regarding this point, "Our Lord Jesus Christ's saying [in John 5:24–25] means, then, that until we are renewed by the gospel and by the faith that proceeds from it, we are but as dead men. There is not one drop of life in us that deserves the name of life. And, to be brief, we are as if buried in the grave, and it is necessary for us to be drawn out of it again, by which we are given to understand that we are cut off from God's kingdom, and consequently that there is nothing but filth in us. And yet, in spite of all this, God vouchsafes to be linked with and united with such as put their trust in him and his goodness. That (I say) is, as it were, our rising again." See John Calvin, *Sermons on Ephesians* (Carlisle, PA: Banner of Truth, 1979), 129.

74. "The first resurrection is the translation of the soul from this sinful earth into heaven. It is followed at Christ's second coming by the second resurrection when the body, too, will be glorified." Hendriksen, *More Than Conquerors*, 192.

75. Beale, *Book of Revelation*, 1002–7.

76. B. B. Warfield, "Millennium and the Apocalypse," 653.

77. Beale, *Book of Revelation*, 1004.

78. Ibid.

79. Meredith G. Kline, "The First Resurrection," *Westminster Theological Journal* 37 (1975): 366. Cf. Beale, *Book of Revelation*, 1002–15.

80. Kline, "First Resurrection," 366–67.

81. Ibid.

82. Ibid.

83. Ibid., 367–68.

84. Ibid., 368–69.

85. Ibid.

86. Ibid., 370–71.

87. The verb *metabainō* is in the perfect tense.

88. Leon Morris, *The Gospel according to John*, The New International Commentary on the New Testament (Grand Rapids: Eerdmans, 1984), 316.

89. D. A. Carson, *The Gospel according to John* (Grand Rapids: Eerdmans, 1991), 256.

90. Beale, *Book of Revelation*, 1012.

91. Kline, "Har Magedon," 222.

92. Ibid., 221.

93. The first clause of verse 7a ("when the thousand years are over") is an indefinite future temporal clause further supporting the symbolic, not literal, interpretation of the "thousand years." See Beale, *Book of Revelation*, 1021.

94. Beale, *Book of Revelation*, 1022–23; and Kline, "Har Magedon," 218–22.

95. Beale, *Book of Revelation*, 1027.

96. Ladd is aware of the problem of evil in the millennium but nevertheless continues to argue that men and women in glorified bodies can still follow Satan while Christ is ruling in their midst. Ladd, *Commentary on the Revelation of John*, 269.

97. In his response to Arthur Lewis's book *The Dark Side of the Millennium*, Jeffrey Townsend tries to escape from the problem of evil in the millennial age by asserting that "all of the wicked survivors of the tribulation are put to death at the beginning of the millennial age so that only saved persons enter the thousand-year period. During the millennium the offspring of these saved entrants will be saved or lost according to their response to Jesus." This effectively answers Lewis's argument only if dispensational presuppositions are in place.

The problem is that the broader eschatology of the New Testament specifically tells us that "the age to come" commences with the second advent of Jesus Christ and that in the age to come "the dead will neither marry nor be given in marriage, and they can no longer die; for they are like the angels. They are God's children, since they are children of the resurrection" (Luke 20:35–36). See Jeffrey Townsend, "Is the Present Age the Millennium?" in *Vital Prophetic Issues*, ed. Roy B. Zuck (Grand Rapids: Kregel, 1995), 70.

98. According to Robert Saucy, "The millennium is only the final transition phase leading to the eternal state." But how can there be a transitional phase after the consummation? Especially one in which there are redeemed and unredeemed people and the possibility of a return to evil. Cf. Robert Saucy, *The Case for Progressive Dispensationalism* (Grand Rapids: Zondervan, 1993), 288.

99. Walvoord, *Revelation of Jesus Christ*, 301–2. Walvoord's comments make it clear that: (1) John says little about the conditions on the earth during this period of time. This is because the reign of Christ is in heaven during this period. The Old Testament passages cited fit better with the descriptions of the final state of man in Revelation 21–22 than with a period of time in which Christ is reigning in heaven and during which martyrs are produced. (2) Walvoord is comfortable with seeing Israel as the "bride of Christ." What about the church? The only way this imagery makes any sense is if the church is the Israel of the New Testament. (3) If the reign of Christ is in heaven, and martyrs come out of ongoing tribulation, then it cannot be

a period of peace on the earth. The whole book is written to comfort those who are at that minute being persecuted by the Roman Empire. Those who died would come to life and reign with Christ in heaven.

100. Walvoord, *Revelation of Jesus Christ*, 303–4. Walvoord's view of the millennium does not have the tremendous problem of evil of historic premillennialism. Because of the fact that there are—according to the dispensational view—nonresurrected men and women who go into the millennial age, then a satanic deception is not surprising. Those who follow Satan are those who are not resurrected and survive the tribulation and go into the millennium. The problem here is that the two-age model rules out the possibility of unglorified humanity after the return of Christ and the judgment.

Chapter 17: Signs of the End

1. Anthony Hoekema, *The Bible and the Future* (Grand Rapids: Eerdmans, 1982), 109.

2. D. A. Carson, *Matthew*, The Expositor's Bible Commentary, vol. 8, ed. Frank E. Gaebelein (Grand Rapids: Zondervan, 1984), 507.

3. According to Carson, "All that v. 34 demands is that the distress of vv. 4–28, including Jerusalem's fall, happens with the lifetime of the generation then living. This does *not* mean that the distress must end within that time but only that 'all these things' must happen within it" (ibid., 507).

4. Although Jesus's warning in verse 11 regarding false prophets restates the warning given in verses 4–5, this warning extends beyond the lifetimes of the apostles and falls into category 2—those signs of the end that characterize the entire interadvental age.

5. Flavius Josephus, "The Wars of the Jews," in *Josephus: Complete Works*, trans. William Whitson (Grand Rapids: Kregel, 1960), II.xiii.4; II.xvii.8–10; VI.v.2.

6. D. A. Carson, Douglas Moo, and Leon Morris, *An Introduction to the New Testament* (Grand Rapids: Zondervan, 1992), 472.

7. Josephus, "Wars of the Jews," IV–V.

8. I. Howard Marshall, *Commentary on Luke*, New International Greek Testament Commentary (Grand Rapids: Eerdmans, 1983), 773.

9. G. K. Beale and D. A. Carson, eds., *Commentary on the New Testament Use of the Old Testament* (Grand Rapids: Baker Academic, 2007), 377.

10. This matter is addressed in chapter 15.

11. See, for example, the discussions of this matter in Marshall, *Commentary on Luke*, 773–74; and John Nolland, *Luke 18:35–24:53*, Word Biblical Commentary, vol. 35c (Dallas: Words Books, 1993), 1002–3.

12. Carson, *Matthew*, 501.

13. Paul, L. Maier, *Eusebius—The Church History: A New Translation with Commentary* (Grand Rapids: Kregel, 1999), 3.7 (102).

14. R. T. France, *Matthew*, Tyndale New Testament Commentaries (Grand Rapids: Eerdmans, 1985), 331.

15. Ibid., 332.

16. H. N. Ridderbos, *Matthew: Bible Student's Commentary*, trans. Ray Togtman (Grand Rapids: Zondervan, 1987), 434.

17. Donald A. Hagner, *Matthew 14–28*, Word Biblical Commentary, vol. 33b (Dallas: Words Books, 1995), 692.

18. C. E. B. Cranfield, *The Gospel according to St. Mark*, The Cambridge Greek Testament Commentary (Cambridge: Cambridge University Press, 1959), 396.

19. Hagner, *Matthew 14–28*, 692.

20. Carson, *Matthew*, 498.

21. See, for example, Stephen S. Smalley, *1, 2, 3 John*, Word Biblical Commentary, vol. 51 (Waco: Word Books, 1984), 219.

22. See the discussion of the rise of a final Antichrist in chapter 11.

23. Geerhardus Vos, *The Pauline Eschatology* (Grand Rapids: Baker, 1982), 7–8.

24. Ibid..

25. Hoekema, *Bible and the Future*, 152.

26. Carson, *Matthew*, 498.

27. See, for example, the discussion in G. K. Beale, *The Book of Revelation*, New International Greek Testament Commentary (Grand Rapids: Eerdmans, 1999), 460–64.

28. Vos, *Pauline Eschatology*, 135.

29. John Calvin, *The Gospel according to St. John 11–21 and the First Epistle of John*, trans. T. H. L. Parker (Grand Rapids: Eerdmans, 1979), 104.

30. Beale, *Book of Revelation*, 433.

31. Ibid., 434–35.

32. See, for example, B. B. Warfield, *The Plan of Salvation* (Grand Rapids: Eerdmans, 1980), 99–103.

33. Geerhardus Vos, *Biblical Theology* (Grand Rapids: Eerdmans, 1948), 380.

34. Those signs of the end that herald the end of the age and are listed here are commonly enumerated in Reformed dogmatic texts. See, for example, Louis Berkhof, *Systematic Theology* (Grand Rapids: Eerdmans, 1986), 696–703; Charles Hodge, *Systematic Theology* (Grand Rapids: Eerdmans, 1979), III.792; and Francis Turretin, *Institutes of Elenctic Theology*, trans. George Musgrave Giger (Phillipsburg, NJ: Presbyterian & Reformed, 1997), III.585–90.

35. Cranfield, *Gospel according to St. Mark*, 399.

36. Douglas Moo, *The Epistle to the Romans*, New International Commentary on the New Testament (Grand Rapids: Eerdmans, 1996), 694–95.

37. G. K. Beale, *A New Testament Biblical Theology* (Grand Rapids: Baker Academic, 2011), 161.

38. Oscar Cullman, *Christ and Time: The Primitive Conception of Time and History*, trans. Floyd V. Filson (Philadelphia: Westminster, 1950), 87.

39. Hoekema, *Bible and the Future*, 136.

40. Vos, *Pauline Eschatology*, 133–35.

Chapter 18: Evaluating Millennial Options

1. Keith A. Mathison, ed., *Hyper-Preterism: A Reformed Critique* (Phillipsburg, NJ: Presbyterian & Reformed, 2004).

2. Louis Berkhof, *Systematic Theology* (Grand Rapids: Eerdmans, 1986), 698ff.; and Herman Bavinck, *The Last Things* (Grand Rapids: Baker, 1996), 107.

Scripture Index

Subject Index

abomination of desolation, 184, 187, 196–98, 202
Abrahamic covenant, 59–60, 85–87, 133, 286–87
  dispensationalists on, 33, 48, 208, 279
abyss, 235–36, 237, 241–42, 252
Adam, 61–62, 246
age of the Gentiles, 108–9
age of the Spirit, 74
age to come, 34, 76, 79–81, 95–99, 100, 103–5, 160, 246, 298n3(2), 315n97
  blessings of, 281
  visible reality as "not yet," 107
Alford, Henry, 37, 243
Allison, Dale, 306n10
Allis, Oswald T., 109
"all Israel," 17, 208, 210, 217–21, 286, 309n8, 310n56
already/not yet, 23, 75–76, 81, 96, 99–100, 102, 107, 112, 143, 202, 270, 288
  absent in preterism, 225
  in Daniel's prophecy, 184
  in dispensationalism, 284
  interadvental age as, 266
  of kingdom of God, 12, 116, 126–27
  in partial preterism, 283–84
  in postmillennialism, 110–12

amillennialism, 29, 39–41
  chart of, 45
  as "demonic and heretical," 41, 49
  grounded in redemptive history, 22
  no less literal than New Testament, 87
  on prophetic passages, 288
  on second coming, 274
analogy of faith, 48, 51, 234–35
Ancient of Days, 147, 242
angels, 236
Anna, 75
Anointed One, cutting off of, 182
Antichrist, 28, 34, 38, 145–57, 268–69, 273
antichrists, 149, 152, 154, 192, 260–62, 269
Antiochus Epiphanes, 148, 196–98
anti-Semitism, 41, 49, 208, 210, 274
apocalyptic literature, 32, 225–28, 234, 277
apokalypsis, return of Christ as, 171–72
apostasy, 78, 102, 110, 140–41, 149–50, 155, 249, 268, 271, 276
appearance, return of Christ as, 171

Aquinas, 41
Armageddon, 231, 312n30
Augustine, 38, 40–41, 243

Babel, 147
Babylon, 147, 154, 156
  as apostate Israel, 224–25
  as Rome, 31–32
Babylonian captivity, 19
Babylonian empire, 121
Bahnsen, Greg, 39, 300n28
Barrett, C. K., 215
Bavinck, Herman, 16–17, 286
Beale, G. K., 32, 78, 237, 243, 244, 249, 265, 270, 313n54
beast, 146–48, 151–56, 250, 256
Berkhof, Louis, 16–17, 40, 151, 286
Berkouwer, G. C., 308n4
Bible. *See* Scripture
birth pains, 169, 191, 193, 260–61, 271
Blaising, Craig, 230, 299n14
blessed hope, 81, 159–65, 289
blessings
  on last day, 72–73, 80–81, 106–7
  secured by Christ, 183
bodily resurrection, 130, 234
Boice, James, 37
bowl judgments, 233, 312n38

325

Kim Riddlebarger is senior pastor of Christ Reformed Church (URCNA) in Anaheim, California, and a cohost of the popular *White Horse Inn* radio/internet broadcast. He has also served as visiting professor of systematic theology at Westminster Seminary California. He is a graduate of Westminster Seminary California (MAR) and has a PhD from Fuller Seminary.

Also Available from
KIM
RIDDLEBARGER

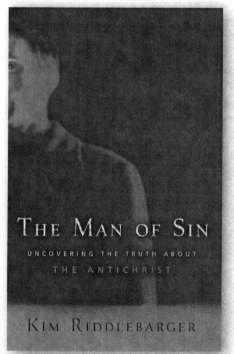

Connect with

Relevant. Intelligent. Engaging.

Sign up for announcements about
new and upcoming titles at

www.bakerbooks.com/signup

 ReadBakerBooks

 ReadBakerBooks

Sample Our Newest Releases!

Videos

Book
Samples

CPSIA information can be obtained
at www.ICGtesting.com
Printed in the USA
LVOW10s1628170517
534870LV00004B/817/P

9 780801 015502